RACE, NATION, AND REFUGE

RACE, NATION, AND REFUGE

THE RHETORIC OF RACE IN ASIAN AMERICAN CITIZENSHIP CASES

Doug Coulson

Cover Image: "They shall not perish . . . American Committee for Relief in the Near East" poster created by Douglas Volk, 1918.

Published by State University of New York Press, Albany

For information, contact State University of New York Press, Albany, NY
www.sunypress.edu

Production, Ryan Morris
Marketing, Anne M. Valentine

Library of Congress Cataloging-in-Publication Data

Names: Coulson, Doug, [date]- author.
Title: Race, nation, and refuge : the rhetoric of race in Asian American citizenship cases / Doug Coulson, State University of New York.
Description: Albany : State University of New York Press, 2017. | Based on author's thesis (doctoral - University of Texas at Austin, 2013) issued under title: The rhetoric of common enemies in the racial prerequisites to naturalized citizenship before 1952. | Includes bibliographical references and index.
Identifiers: LCCN 2016048647 (print) | LCCN 2016050701 (ebook) | ISBN 9781438466613 (hardcover : alk. paper) | ISBN 9781438466620 (e-book)
Subjects: LCSH: Emigration and immigration law--United States--History. | Citizenship--United States--History. | Race discrimination--Law and legislation --United States--History. | Asians--Legal status, laws, etc.--United States--History.
Classification: LCC KF4835 .C68 2017 (print) | LCC KF4835 (ebook) | DDC 342.7308/308995--dc23 LC record available at https://lccn.loc.gov/2016048647

10 9 8 7 6 5 4 3 2 1

CONTENTS

ACKNOWLEDGMENTS

No book exists without a social life of its own. I am extremely grateful to many individuals and institutions who offered valuable support as I worked on this project. My study of the racial eligibility requirements of naturalized citizenship law in the United States began during my doctoral studies at The University of Texas at Austin, and I first want to thank my advisors Patricia Roberts-Miller and Susan Heinzelman, along with Davida Charney, Sanford Levinson, Gretchen Murphy, and Jeffrey Walker, who served on my committee. They all offered immensely helpful guidance during the early stages of my research. I have also benefited from the comments, support, and encouragement of many others throughout the life of this project, including Marian Aguiar, Marilyn Altamira, Randall Auxier, Todd Battistelli, Erin Boade, Jack Chin, Marilyn Coulson, Richard Coulson, Kathleen Cleaver, Angela Daniels, Megan Eatman, Nikki Gray, Tekla Hawkins, Paul Hopper, David Kaufer, Nathan Kreuter, Amanda Moulder, Erin Mulhern, Stephanie Muller, Stephanie Odom, John O'Shea, Terry Phelps, Andreea Ritivoi, Bryan Russell, Christian Shippee, Connie Steel, David Thind, and Nyssa Wilton.

In addition, I am grateful for the considerable institutional support that this project has received. Carnegie Mellon University and The University of Texas at Austin both provided generous support. The librarians at the Hunt Library at Carnegie Mellon University, The University of Texas at Austin Libraries, and the Tarlton Law Library at The University of Texas School of Law all provided excellent research support, and the archivists at the National Archives at San Francisco, Seattle, Laguna Niguel, and Washington, D.C., provided me with invaluable assistance identifying and obtaining copies of archival documents. In particular, I am grateful to Charles Miller at the National Archives in San Francisco and Kathleen Crosman at the National Archives in Seattle for their kind and insightful assistance as I navigated the archives. I delivered talks regarding the project at the Oklahoma City University School of Law and at Carnegie Mellon University in April 2011 and January 2013, respectively, and I presented a paper regarding the project to the 2015 Conference of Harvard Law School's Institute for Global Law and Policy (IGLP). I also presented portions of the Introduction and chapter 2 to the IGLP workshop in Doha, Qatar, in 2013 and papers regarding chapter 3 at the 2011 Federation Rhetoric Symposium and the 2012 Conference of the Association for the Study of Law, Culture, and the Humanities. The discussions that followed these presentations all greatly benefited me.

Because parts of this book were previously published in article form, I would also like to thank the publishers for the permission to include the previously published material here. Specifically, chapter 2 includes portions of "British Imperialism, the Indian Independence Movement, and the Racial Eligibility Requirements in the Naturalization Act: *United States v. Thind* Revisited," *Georgetown Journal of Law & Modern Critical Race Perspectives* 7 (2015): 1–42, and chapter 3 includes portions of "Persecutory Agency in the Racial Prerequisite Cases: Islam, Christianity, and Martyrdom in *United States v. Cartozian*," *University of Miami Race and Social Justice Law Review* 2 (2012): 117–88.

Finally, I am extremely grateful to SUNY Press for its interest in this project and its decision to publish the book, as well as to the two anonymous peer reviewers who commented on the manuscript.

INTRODUCTION

Forgetting, I would even say historical error, is an essential factor in the creation of a nation and it is for this reason that the progress of historical studies often poses a threat to nationality. Historical inquiry, in effect, throws light on the violent acts that have taken place at the origin of every political formation, even those that have been the most benevolent in their consequences.

—ERNEST RENAN, "What Is a Nation?"

There is a cement to the whole people, subtler, more underlying, than anything in written constitution, or courts or armies—namely, the cement of a death identified thoroughly with that people, at its head, and for its sake. Strange, (is it not?) that battles, martyrs, agonies, blood, even assassination, should so condense—perhaps only really, lastingly condense—a Nationality.

—WALT WHITMAN, "Death of Abraham Lincoln"

Necessity has no law.

—LEGAL MAXIM

On May 8 and 9, 1924, an evidentiary trial was held in the United States District Court for the District of Oregon to determine whether Armenian immigrant Tatos Cartozian was racially eligible to become a United States citizen by naturalization. The United States Bureau of Naturalization, then under the direction of the Department of Labor and represented by lawyers from the Department of Justice, opposed Cartozian's naturalization based on the assertion that Armenians were Asian and therefore neither "free white persons" nor "aliens of African nativity" or "persons of African descent" as required to be eligible for naturalization at the time. The Armenian community raised $50,000 in donations (equivalent to about $700,000 today) and hired the prestigious Portland law firm McCamant and Thompson to defend Cartozian. The defense claimed that Armenians were "free white persons" and therefore eligible for naturalization because they had descended from European ancestors and remained socially, culturally, and politically European as a result of a strict segregation in Asia despite residing there for centuries. The defense supported this claim with the testimony of twenty-three witnesses, including Columbia University anthropologist Franz Boas, Harvard ethnologist Roland Dixon, German geographer and political economist Paul Rohrbach, and James Barton, executive of the American Board of Commissioners for Foreign Missions, who headed the relief expedition in Turkey following the Armenian Genocide of World War I. The defense also introduced twenty-two exhibits into evidence, including a comparative list of English and Armenian words and a tabulation of 339 answers to a questionnaire sent to Armenian men in the United States regarding their residence, citizenship, occupation, and membership in Christian churches and in professional, civic, and fraternal organizations.[1]

The National Archives has preserved a complete copy of the trial transcript in *Cartozian*, and what I find most interesting about the trial is not the evidence presented regarding ethnological racial classifications, which certainly formed part of the defense's case, but the ways in which the defense foregrounded appeals to the experience of being threatened or harmed by an external adversary of the United States. A lawyer for Cartozian asked one witness, for example, "What was the attitude of the Armenian race in so far as you came in contact with them during the World War?," to which the witness replied:

> It was one of the most inspiring experiences in my life. They were willing to serve, not only as enemies of Turkey, not only to defend their own native country, but they felt a deep loyalty to this country. All of them were willing to enter the army; and I know a great many cases of Armenians who came a great distance, paid their own expenses and entered the United States army and never were sent across to fight the Turks.[2]

Throughout the trial, the defense also framed Armenian history as a story of suffering religious persecution by Turks, Kurds, and Syrian Muslims in Asia Minor due to Armenian Christianity and sympathy for Europeans, drawing explicitly on cultural memories of the Crusades and popular epithets of the Armenians as "guides to the Crusaders" by repeatedly emphasizing Armenian Christianity and asking witnesses about the effect that the Crusades had on Armenians. By framing Armenian suffering as a sacrifice made on behalf of European civilization, the defense appealed to fears of Turkish aggression and to Islamophobia shared by Armenians and Americans.[3] In the end, the court ruled that Armenians were "free white persons" and therefore racially eligible for naturalization.

The Armenians were but one of many groups whose racial eligibility for naturalization in the United States was contested in the late nineteenth and early twentieth centuries based on the assertion that they were Asian and therefore neither "free white persons" nor "aliens of African nativity" or "persons of African descent," including groups from the Far East and Central Asia as well as many from the Middle East such as Afghans, Arabs, Iraqis, Palestinians, and Syrians, whose applications for citizenship raised tensions between race, religion, and national identity similar to those in *Cartozian*. The United States Constitution grants Congress the power to "establish a uniform Rule of Naturalization,"[4] and in 1790 the First Congress passed a naturalization act that limited eligibility for naturalization to "free white persons." Shortly after the Civil War, Congress also extended racial eligibility for naturalization to "aliens of African nativity and persons of African descent," and as a result racial eligibility for naturalization was limited to these racial categories until 1940. Many interpreted the provisions to exclude Asians, but because the distinction between "white" and Asian was considerably unstable controversies proliferated regarding racial classifications under the law.[5] After 1940, eligibility for naturalization was also extended to "descendants of races indigenous to the Western Hemisphere," "Filipino persons or persons of Filipino descent," "Chinese persons or persons of Chinese descent," and "persons of races indigenous to India," but the racial eligibility provisions were not removed from the naturalization act until 1952.[6] Between 1878 and 1954, many federal and state courts as well as the United States Board of Immigration Appeals issued written opinions interpreting the racial eligibility provisions of the act in response to the contested naturalization applications of immigrants from the East who claimed to be "free white persons," and similar cases were decided without resulting in written or published opinions.[7] These cases reveal contested views regarding the racial classification of Afghan, Arab, Armenian, Burmese, Chinese, Filipino, Hawaiian, Hindu, Iraqi, Japanese, Kalmyk, Korean, Mexican, Palestinian, Parsi, Syrian, Tatar, Turkish, Thai, and Vietnamese immigrants, as well as American Indians.[8] I refer to these cases as the "racial eligibility cases" and to all of the discourse regarding the racial eligibility provisions of the naturalization act as "racial eligibility discourse."

The exclusion of Asians from racial eligibility for naturalization in the United States formed part of a broader policy of Asian exclusion reflected in many federal and state laws that arose in the context of intense racial discrimination against Asian immigrants. The first federal anti-Chinese legislation was passed in 1875, restricting women from China, Japan, or "any Oriental country" from immigrating to the United States for "immoral purposes," and seven years later Congress passed the Chinese Exclusion Act, which prohibited the immigration of Chinese laborers into the United States. The Immigration Act of 1917 further prohibited all immigration from a vast section of Asia and the Middle East referred to as the "Asiatic Barred Zone," and the Immigration Act of 1924 established immigration quotas that privileged European immigrants and excluded those "ineligible to citizenship" from immigration altogether, effectively prohibiting Japanese immigration.[9] In addition, Asians were excluded from labor unions and denied employment, refused leases, and prohibited from owning or leasing land through alien land laws and restrictive land covenants, they were segregated in public schools, theaters, and other spaces, refused service in restaurants and access to public recreational facilities, and they were prohibited from marrying any "white" person.[10] They were also victimized by mob violence, from being pelted with rocks to being forcibly expelled from towns. In 1907, for example, American laborers drove seven hundred Asian Indians from Bellingham, Washington, into Canada and also expelled Asian Indians from Everett, Washington. Ultimately, Japanese Americans were rounded up and forcibly incarcerated in internment camps during World War II.[11] The racial eligibility provisions of the naturalization act played a crucial role in this pattern of discrimination and exclusion. Because citizenship was required to vote, to obtain a passport, and was sometimes required to own land, incorporate a business, obtain professional licenses, obtain civil service or public works jobs, and possess firearms, the racial ineligibility of Asian immigrants for naturalization had a substantial impact not only on their sense of belonging but on their ability to exercise important rights.[12]

My interest in the racial eligibility cases arose out of my interest in legal rhetoric, particularly advocacy in judicial and other adjudicative proceedings. Despite the deeply intertwined histories of rhetoric and law and the fact that the success of legal advocates rises or falls with their ability to engage in argument,[13] modern legal theory promotes the view that legal discourse belongs to a technical domain of language in which rhetorical considerations are irrelevant or even dangerous.[14] I contest this view and believe legal discourse can only be adequately understood by considering its rhetorical dimension. Modern legal theory's denial of rhetoric has been variously attributed to the professionalization of law that accompanied the rise of law schools in the late Middle Ages and early Renaissance, the fact that the rules of evidence and procedure in Western democratic legal systems have already incorporated classical rhetorical theory, the fact that lawyers increasingly receive rhetorical training through apprenticeship and imitation in practice rather than formal education, and the effect of the Scientific Revolution and Enlightenment view that invention should be exclusively governed by philosophical deduction and the scientific method.[15] I would add to this list Aristotle's original separation of the forensic, or judicial, speech genre from epideictic speech, in which the Greeks included ceremonial and ritual discourse, eulogy, epic and lyric poetry, philosophy, and history.[16] Well before the advent of modernism, this division arbitrarily excluded from consideration the ways in which a wide range of speech in judicial settings shapes individual and group identity. As James Stratman notes, the collective result of these historical developments has been that "rhetorical theory has been forced to maintain an apologetic stance toward law and lawyers, needing to demonstrate its relevance and value in the face of great skepticism,"[17] and legal historian David Cairns notes another result in his conclusion that no one has even tried to explain modern legal advocacy to the extent that Aristotle or Quintilian did that of the classical era.[18]

In contrast to the modern denial of law's rhetorical dimension, James Boyd White writes that we should understand law as a branch of rhetoric, that "particular set of resources made available by a culture for speech and argument on those occasions, and by those speakers, we think of as legal." In support of this conclusion, White argues that the best way to understand a legal rule is as "a topic of thought and argument—as one of many resources brought to bear by the lawyer and others both to define a question and to establish a way to approach it."[19] Legal rules, in other words, constitute but one of many discursive resources available to legal advocates. As Marouf Hasian argues, there are many social actors involved in the creation, maintenance, and recirculation of jurisprudential ideas. Studies of legal discourse must accordingly appreciate the ways in which reasoning in legal contexts interacts with a broader rhetorical culture.[20] Hasian draws on Celeste Condit and John Lucaites's work in which they explain how a rhetorical culture draws attention to the

> linguistic usages available to those who would address a historically particular audience as a public . . . In this rhetorical culture we will find the full complement of commonly used allusions,

aphorisms, characterizations, ideographs, images, metaphors, myths, narratives, and *topoi* or common argumentative forms that demonstrate the symbolic boundaries within which public advocates find themselves constrained to operate.[21]

Considered alongside White's claim about the function of legal rules as topics of thought and argument, a rhetorical approach to law considers rules but one of the full complement of discursive forms that Condit and Lucaites describe. As Lucaites writes elsewhere, in this view legal discourse "functions to produce and reproduce power and legitimacy in the context of an active rhetorical culture."[22]

James Boyd White similarly argues that law's rhetorical culture involves "forms of meaning that are inherently performative, not reducible to a message," requiring that we think "in the context of a particular case."[23] In this respect, a rhetorical approach to law shares some commonalities with that of modern movements for legal reform such as American legal realism and Critical Legal Studies.[24] Critiquing the claim that courts both can and should apply laws passed by a legislature independent of cultural and political forces, American legal realists of the early twentieth century claimed that what the law is "in fact" cannot be found in legal rules but only in how legal institutions apply the law in particular cases. One leading proponent of realism, Judge Jerome Frank, wrote a two-part article series expanding on United States Supreme Court Justice Oliver Wendell Holmes's statement that "the prophecies of what the courts will do in fact, and nothing more pretentious, are what I mean by the law."[25] Like White's claim that the best way to understand a legal rule is as a topic of thought and argument, Frank writes that the "so-called rules and principles" of law are only one among many of the factors that influence judges to reach specific decisions and have a far smaller influence on decisions than legal formalists suppose.[26] Instead, Frank argues, judges decide cases "by a 'hunch' as to what is fair and just or wise or expedient."[27] The lawyer's task is simply to determine what produces these "hunches," including by studying the emotional attitudes and predilections of judges.[28] Judicial opinions are not reliable guides to judicial decision making, Frank writes, but "*censored expositions*" constructed after the fact to justify decisions, revealing "little of how judges come to their conclusions."[29]

Based in part on the work of American legal realists, Critical Legal Studies applies Critical Theory to critique the liberal ideal of law as objective, determinate, and independent of cultural and political forces. According to Critical Legal Studies, this ideal is a fiction that lends existing social structures a false appearance of legitimacy and inevitability rather than liberating people from existing structures of power. Seeking to demystify the symbolic authority of the law,[30] Critical Legal Studies proposes an ideological critique of legal doctrine as a transformative practice to combat existing power structures.[31] Many in rhetorical studies have noted the rhetorical dimension of this approach to law,[32] but some have expressed concern that the ideological approach of Critical Legal Studies is too abstract to account for the situated interaction of speakers and audiences.[33] Critical Legal Studies has also inspired more specific movements for legal reform such as Critical Race Theory, however, which more clearly accounts for law's rhetorical dimension. In response to the slow progress of the civil rights reforms of the Cold War, Critical Race Theory began to study the relationship of race and power by offering analyses of the ways in which race is culturally constructed and informs legal practices.[34] Among its central tenets, Critical Race Theory rejects the idea that racism is aberrant rather than normal, that racism is a matter of individuals rather than systems, that "color-blindness" will eliminate racism, and that one can fight racism in isolation from other forms of oppression.[35] In addition, Critical Race Theory adopts a distinctive rhetorical strategy by investigating issues of audience, genre, voice, and canonization in what Catherine Prendergast calls a "deliberately dissonant rhetorical stance" that emphasizes narrative as a means of exploring the legal construction of identity in contrast to the abstraction of legal doctrine. As Prendergast explains, this rhetorical strategy is "itself part of the message and itself a response to the racialized atmosphere" in which such scholars work and write.[36]

I adopt a critical rhetorical approach to legal discourse as a locus for the construction of identity, power, and legitimacy, or what one might call sovereignty, through situated performances. According to Raymie McKerrow, a critical rhetoric "examines the dimensions of domination and freedom as these are exercised in a relativized world," recognizing that "power is not only repressive but potentially productive."[37] A critical rhetorical approach recognizes the materiality of discourse, viewing it as mediated and fragmented, "unconnected, even contradictory or momentarily oppositional" in its mode of presentation, and disputes the distinction between knowledge and power. Rather than focus on questions of truth and falsity, a critical rhetorical approach shifts the focus to how "symbols come to possess power—what they 'do' in society as contrasted to what they 'are.'" This practice adopts a nominalist perspective, which approaches symbols as contingent, "the reasons for their emergence . . . not premised on fixed, determinate models of inquiry," and recognizes the importance of absences as well as presences in discursive practices.[38] Michael Lacy and Kent Ono describe a critical rhetoric as one premised on "a non-essentialist, perhaps anti-essentialist, performative rhetoric" that "examines and reconstructs discourse and diffuse discourse fragments from mundane discursive sites," and they claim that a critical rhetorical approach is particularly suited to examining racial discourse because it allows for the identification and analysis of both overt and inferential forms of racism and helps to explain "how it is that, in a society that often memorializes abolitionists and African American civil rights protesters, the production of representations equating African Americans with apes is still possible, indeed commonplace."[39]

I began my study of racial eligibility discourse by reading the written judicial opinions that were designated for publication in official reporter series. For the most part, courts are neither required to issue written opinions explaining their decisions nor required to publish any opinions they write. Instead, both the decision to write an opinion and the decision to publish one are motivated by rhetorical considerations. Judges write and publish opinions not because they are required to but because it is customary and they must remain sensitive to the need for public acceptance of judicial decisions given the limited power of the judiciary.[40] Thus, opinions may be not only "*censored expositions*" constructed after the fact to justify decisions based on hunches, as Judge Frank claims, but reflect a variety of unreliable performances designed to gain the adherence of audiences.[41] When I began reading the published opinions in racial eligibility cases, I expected to find efforts to naturalize racial categories rather than a recognition of the fact that race is produced through a political process. I was surprised to discover, however, that the opinions often advanced self-consciously political criteria for racial classifications. In Rogers Smith's review of Ian Haney López's book *White by Law: The Legal Construction of Race*, the first book-length study of the racial eligibility cases, Smith writes that the core difficulty with *White by Law* is that it explains the incoherence of the racial classifications in racial eligibility cases by the tendency of "whites" to be blind to race and not see themselves in racial terms. As Smith notes, the phenomenon López describes is far more a product of the post–World War II era when the United States officially repudiated racial ideologies than of earlier periods when American intellectuals and officials "elaborated highly visible, self-conscious, and excruciatingly articulate doctrines of 'whiteness.'"[42] As I explain in chapter 1, the openly political criteria for racial classification advanced in the racial eligibility cases were also influenced by the role of the United States Bureau of Naturalization after it was granted the power and responsibility to intervene in racial eligibility cases during the first decade of the twentieth century.

Many of the judicial opinions in racial eligibility cases included lengthy geographical, political, religious, and cultural histories of racial groups rather than biological criteria to justify their racial classifications, in some cases referencing sources as old as the Hebrew and Christian scriptures, the ancient Greek historian Herodotus and ancient Greek geographer Strabo, and travel writers from the Middle Ages and the Renaissance, among other sources, encompassing hundreds or thousands of years of history in the space of a single opinion.[43] One judge concluded that although the conflict between the American colonists and the French during the French and Indian Wars initially rendered it unlikely that the French would have been included within the phrase *free white person*, the phrase "automatically expanded" to include them following France's alliance with the United States during the Revolutionary War because their alliance demonstrated a common heritage. He added that the phrase *free white person* was so unrelated to biological ancestry that Martians might even be included within its scope:

> When the long looked for Martian immigrants reach this part of the earth, and in due course "a man from Mars" applies to be naturalized, he may be recognized as white within the meaning of the act of Congress, and admitted to citizenship; but he may not be a Caucasian.[44]

Another judge concluded that although ethnologists had classified Parsis, Afghans, Hindus, Arabs, and Berbers as Caucasian, they might not have been intended by the phrase *free white person* because they were not among those immigrants who "contributed to the building up on this continent of the community of people which declared itself a new nation."[45] By contrast, a later judge held that Arabs were racially eligible for naturalization in part because European and Arabic cultures were historically intertwined, noting that Arabs were "one of the chief channels by which the traditions of white Europe, especially the ancient Greek traditions, have been carried into the present."[46] In these and other opinions in racial eligibility cases, judges openly reflected on the contingency of race.

If the judges in racial eligibility cases were offering such criteria to justify their racial classifications, I wondered, what criteria had the parties and witnesses offered? What conflict of opinions, interpretations, interests, and values were expressed in the competing arguments in the cases? How did the wider range of participants in racial eligibility discourse use rhetorical resources to advance racial classifications? What discursive practices do their arguments reveal, and what can they tell us about racial formation?[47] Michael Omi and Howard Winant define race as "an unstable and 'decentered' complex of social meanings constantly being transformed by political struggle," which is "at best imprecise, and at worst completely arbitrary."[48] Writing separately, Winant describes race as "slippery and contradictory" because it is simultaneously "evanescent and formidable, ephemeral yet intense, . . . conspicuous and unspecifiable."[49] Similarly, rhetorical scholars have described the "fluid, multivalent, contingent, and ever-changing nature" of race,[50] and some have noted that whiteness in particular is not only contradictory but "conceals and obfuscates power relationships,"[51] in part by assuming the position of an "uninterrogated space."[52] As Ian Haney López writes, whether one is classified as "white" may depend on

> where one is, Watts or Westchester, Stanford University or San Jose State; on when one is there, two in the afternoon or three in the morning, 1878 or 1995; on the immediate context, applying to rent an apartment, seeking entrance into an executive club, or talking with a police officer.[53]

Others have similarly noted the role of geographical spaces in constructing racial and other group identities, a particularly important consideration for the construction of migrant identities.[54] Matthew Frye Jacobson describes race as a palimpsest, "a tablet whose most recent inscriptions only imperfectly cover those that had come before, and whose inscriptions can never be regarded as final."[55] Race is a history of representations, or a rhetorical history.

It is important to note, however, that this book is not a study of race or racism in all of its instantiations but a rhetorical study of racial formation, which Omi and Winant define as "the sociohistorical process by which racial categories are created, inhabited, transformed, and destroyed" through historically situated projects that connect what race means "in a particular discursive practice" with "the ways in which both social structures and everyday experiences are racially *organized*."[56] Because the records of racial eligibility discourse present the arguments and evidence regarding who was or was not "white" in particular cases and social contexts, they uniquely reveal such racial projects during a critical period of American history. As López notes of the cases:

> The courts had to establish by law whether, for example, a petitioner's race was to be measured by skin color, facial features, national origin, language, culture, ancestry, the speculations of scientists, popular opinion, or some combination of these factors. Moreover, the courts also had to decide which of these or other factors would govern in the inevitable cases where the various indices of race contradicted one another. In short, the courts were responsible for deciding not only who was White, but *why* someone was White.[57]

In addition, the judicial venues of the cases provided opposing parties with the opportunity to speak, respond to opposing arguments, and introduce witnesses and documentary evidence regarding racial classifications, much of which was inscribed into public records.

Previous studies of racial eligibility discourse have been almost entirely limited to the published judicial opinions in racial eligibility cases. As a result, they have not only neglected unpublished judicial opinions and oral remarks that judges made during hearings but have also neglected the discursive practices of other legal actors that appear in pleadings, briefs, trial and hearing transcripts, correspondence and memoranda, and congressional hearings and debates regarding the racial eligibility provisions of the naturalization act. In *White by Law*, López acknowledges that further social and historical contextualization of the cases is warranted but does not specifically reference the need for closer examination of the arguments advanced by these other actors.[58] In order to study a wider range of the discursive practices in racial eligibility discourse, I conducted an extensive review of National Archives records from judicial case files, United States Attorneys' files, and files from the Department of Commerce and Labor, which oversaw the Bureau of Naturalization at the time. In addition, I searched newspaper databases for evidence of unpublished oral and written judicial opinions as well as databases containing opinions of the United States Board of Immigration

Appeals that were issued after the Immigration Act of 1924 incorporated the racial eligibility provisions of the naturalization act into immigration law. I also searched legislative hearings and debates regarding the racial eligibility provisions of the naturalization act from 1790 to 1952 in the *Congressional Globe* and *Congressional Record* and interpretations of the legislation in United States Attorney Generals' opinions and other executive documents. From these sources, I gathered a substantial corpus of racial eligibility discourse that includes pleadings, briefs, trial and hearing transcripts, trial exhibits, published and unpublished judicial opinions, congressional hearings and debates, legislation, correspondence and memoranda from the United States Bureau of Naturalization, and other executive documents.

While this corpus is far more extensive than that of any previous study of racial eligibility discourse, I do not claim to have exhausted the potential sources of the discourse. It is difficult to even imagine that one could exhaustively review all of the sources of racial eligibility discourse given the vast number of locations they have resided. The discoverable records must also be interrogated for their own rhetorical character, for, as Barbara Biesecker notes, the archive "always already is the provisionally settled scene of our collective invention."[59] Although the archive has long been a locus of rhetorical analysis and criticism, Charles Morris argues that the archive should not be understood as "a passive receptacle for historical documents and their 'truths,' or a benign research space, but rather as a dynamic site of rhetorical power," including those "'silences' that thwart the recognition, retrieval, interrogation, and articulation" of marginalized historical voices.[60] Similarly, Ann Stoler writes that colonial archives were "both sites of the imaginary *and* institutions that fashioned histories as they concealed, revealed, and reproduced the power of the state." As a result, it is important when doing archival work to critically reflect on "the making of documents and how we choose to use them, on archives not as sites of knowledge retrieval but of knowledge production, as monuments of states as well as sites of state ethnography."[61]

With regard to racial eligibility discourse, there is more to consider than the decisions of courts to write or publish judicial opinions. Because the production of transcripts of judicial proceedings typically only occurs if litigants or third parties request and pay for them, often at significant or even prohibitive cost, transcripts are not produced in most judicial proceedings. In addition, countless decisions were made by court personnel regarding whether any records of racial eligibility discourse that were produced were preserved or destroyed. The National Archives was first established in 1934, well after the majority of the racial eligibility discourse considered in the current study and at a time when racial eligibility cases had already begun to decline in number. Previously, federal court records had been kept in basements, attics, abandoned buildings, and other storage places with "little security or concern for storage conditions."[62] The decisions regarding the preservation and storage of records of racial eligibility cases were likely informed by judgments about the importance of the records, and the manner in which any records collected by the archives were filed and labeled also impacts their discoverability.

In the corpus of racial eligibility discourse that I compiled, however, it is observable that from the mid-nineteenth through the mid-twentieth century the racial eligibility discourse of the legislative, executive, and judicial branches of government all included frequent appeals to unify against a shared external threat as a basis for either including or excluding particular groups from racial eligibility for naturalization and emphasized such appeals in a manner that suggests they were considered particularly persuasive of racial identity. In 1870, for example, during legislative debates regarding a proposed amendment to remove the phrase *free white person* from the naturalization act, United States senators repeatedly described the Chinese as a dangerous Mongolian horde that threatened the national security of the United States.[63] As Missouri senator Carl Schurz imagined the prospect of admitting Chinese immigrants to citizenship:

> A heated fancy—I cannot use any other expression—is drawing the picture before our eyes of thirty, forty, fifty, or one hundred million Chinamen suddenly flowing from their native homes across the Pacific ocean, sweeping over this country, and fairly submerging, as under a deluge of barbarism, our whole civilization and all that is dear to us.[64]

In an amicus curiae brief submitted in a later racial eligibility case involving a Mexican applicant, former Texas judge and United States Representative Thomas Paschal distinguished the racial eligibility of Mexicans, whom he described as having been "subjugated" by Spanish conquerors, from those contemplated during the 1870 debates who "stood hovering on the shores of the Chinese waters, ready and anxious to swarm upon us, like the Goths and Huns upon ancient Rome."[65]

Decades later, when Congress extended racial eligibility for naturalization to the Chinese in order to reward and secure their alliance during World War II, the Japanese were described as "our most contemptible enemy" and as "vicious" and "treacherous,"[66] while the Chinese were described as "a very gallant and heroic nation . . . fighting . . . one of the strongest and mightiest armies in the world."[67] During these debates, one legislator described the Chinese as "a people which have shared with us the common danger,"[68] and another warned against their continued exclusion given the existential crisis presented by the war, stating that

> no one will dispute that this Nation is in the most critical hour in its whole history. The feeling of self-sufficiency and self-confidence with which we have always approached our problems is not wholly justified under the present circumstances.[69]

These and other legislators amplified the threat that the Japanese posed during World War II and openly appealed to the power of the existential threat of war to transcend the desire for Chinese exclusion that had prevailed in the nation for a century.

In a case before the United States Board of Immigration Appeals during the early Cold War, the board also appealed to the propensity to unify against a shared external threat when affirming the racial eligibility for naturalization of Kalmyk refugees from the Soviet Union who sought admission to the United States. Based on the 1924 Immigration Act, which prohibited entry into the United States by those "ineligible to citizenship," immigration officials denied entry to the refugees based on the conclusion that they were not "free white persons" and were therefore ineligible to citizenship and entry into the United States. The board reversed the decision of the immigration officers, holding that Kalmyks were "free white persons" despite their history of classification as Mongolian and their Asian origin. In the board's written opinion, it highlighted the Kalmyk history in southern Russia including their systematic displacement and deportation by the Soviet Union:

> On February 11, 1943, the Soviet Politbureau and the State Committee of Defense . . . determined that the Kalmuks should be displaced and deported . . . This order was actually executed on . . . (Red Army Day), when without warning and at gun-point, the Kalmuk population was herded into unheated railroad cars.

> Since they were sent on their journey in locked cars, without benefit of food or water, many died en route, while the rest were scattered in various spots of the Soviet Union.[70]

In this passage, the board foregrounded the Soviet persecution of Kalmyks in order to justify classifying the refugees as "free white persons" for purposes of naturalization.

Many exemptions from the racial eligibility provisions of the naturalization act were also introduced for military veterans who served in the United States military during World War I and World War II. Such exemptions were made for Filipino and Puerto Rican veterans in 1918, American Indian veterans in 1919, World War I veterans in 1935, and World War II veterans in 1942.[71] As Immigration and Naturalization Service lawyer Charles Gordon wrote of the impact of war on racial eligibility for naturalization during World War II, "under the stress of a great common adventure, we are able to shed some of our misconceptions and to recognize some of our mistakes."[72] Many lower federal courts also granted naturalizations to Asian veterans without legislative exemptions in defiance of the racial eligibility provisions of the naturalization act,[73] and in some instances the United States Bureau of Naturalization exercised its discretion to decline to object to the naturalization of Asian soldiers who had served in the United States military during wartime.[74] The bond of "comrades-in-arms," who "shared with us the common danger,"[75] it seems, often transcended perceived racial differences for purposes of eligibility for naturalization.

Since Ian Haney López sparked renewed interest in the racial eligibility cases with *White by Law*, many scholars in the humanities and social sciences have argued that the performative efforts of naturalization applicants to establish assimilability with Western Europeans were crucial to how racial classifications were determined in the cases. For example, Ariela Gross argues that the racial classifications in racial eligibility cases were determined according to whether a particular group was capable of "performing whiteness" by doing the sorts of things "white" people did, such as attending "white" churches or dances, sitting on juries and voting, or exhibiting female sexual purity.[76] Similarly, John Tehranian writes that the performative criteria used to determine racial classifications under the naturalization act gave rise to a "dramaturgy of whiteness" as successful applicants demonstrated their racial identity in their "character, religious practices and beliefs, class orientation, language, ability to intermarry, and a lot of other traits that had nothing to do with intrinsic racial grouping."[77] López argues that the applicants' complicity in the construction of whiteness by asserting their assimilability with the "white" community had debilitating effects on the applicants,[78] and Janice Okoomian concludes that the cases carried bodily consequences for Armenians because whiteness "as a disciplinary regime configures bodies as they are assimilated, excluding some behaviors and signs while producing others."[79]

In contrast to the focus of such studies on imitative racial performances in racial eligibility cases, I examine the appeals to unify against shared external threats as they appear both in racial eligibility cases and in the broader corpus of racial eligibility discourse. The focus on imitative performance fails to account for cases in which applicants were held to be racially ineligible for naturalization despite having offered impressive evidence of assimilability as well as for cases in which applicants were held racially eligible for naturalization despite offering little evidence of assimilability. When considered as a rhetorical strategy, in other words, efforts to imitatively perform whiteness often failed to persuade audiences that the applicants in the cases were "free white persons." In the first racial eligibility case to reach the United States Supreme Court, for example, the Court itself noted that the Japanese applicant in the case had lived in the United States for twenty years, attended American schools and churches, and maintained the use of English in his home, but because he was Japanese he was nonetheless held to be non-"white" and therefore racially ineligible for naturalization.[80] Similarly, a federal district judge in South Carolina repeatedly held that Syrian applicants were not "free white persons" and were therefore racially ineligible for naturalization despite ample evidence that they had long belonged to the Judeo-Christian religious tradition by both faith and geography.[81] On the other hand, various Turkish, Arab, Parsi, Asian Indian, Kalmyk, and Tatar applicants were held to be "free white persons" and therefore racially eligible for naturalization despite their geographical origins and acculturation in Asia and their Islamic, Zoroastrian, Hindu, Sikh, and Buddhist religious backgrounds.[82] Accordingly, the racial eligibility cases cannot be adequately understood by reference to the "performance of whiteness and perceived assimilatory capacity" of the applicants alone.[83]

By focusing on the role of shared external threats in racial eligibility discourse, I also examine the function of enemies in the discursive practices of political group formation and how such appeals may prove more determinative than legal doctrine and even foreshadow it. The discursive construction of enemies is a form of rhetorical transcendence, by which divisions are overcome by shifting perspective.[84] Since Kenneth Burke proposed that persuasion operates through the process of identification between one individual or group and another, or the struggle between "us" and "them," the term *identification* has become familiar in rhetorical theory and analysis.[85] Among the more powerful forms of identification, Burke describes "the workings of antithesis, as when allies who would otherwise dispute among themselves join forces against a common enemy."[86] In even stronger terms, Ioannis Evrigenis writes that the bond of common difference from an antagonistic outside entity is an essential part of group identity formation and "always an element of the process by which individuals form their political identities and identify with political groups,"[87] and Murray Edelman writes that enemies are an inherent part of the political scene due to their power to generate defensive alliances:

> Because the evocation of a threatening enemy may win political support for its prospective targets, people construct enemies who renew their own commitment and mobilize allies: witches in seventeenth-century Salem, communists in the army in the 1950s, Jews in Nazi Germany, homosexuals, a foreign regime associated with an unpopular ideology, dissident peasants in Vietnam or El Salvador.[88]

Jeremy Engels describes the rhetorical construction of enemies as a "solidarity of fear" and "kinship in arms," noting that during the American Revolution "unity was premised as much on the danger of an external enemy as it was on shared ideals such as life, liberty, and the pursuit of happiness," as frequently reflected in writings of the period.[89] To achieve this solidarity, Engels writes, speakers and writers use "discourses of fear, paranoia, and anxiety to focus their audience's thoughts on how best to defend themselves and their families from the enemy."[90]

In racial eligibility discourse, the threatening or harmful quality of external threats was often amplified by attributing a relatively high degree of grammatical transitivity to the actions of such threats and a correspondingly low degree of transitivity to those groups found racially eligible for naturalization. Although transitivity is most commonly used to refer to the classification of transitive and intransitive verbs depending on whether they allow or take an object, linguists have identified transitivity as a property of all languages that describes situations in which one participant in a clause transfers action or "'does something to' another" in a relative and contextual manner that is gradable rather than absolute. In other words, an action is not either transitive or intransitive but can only be described as relatively high or low in transitivity depending on factors such as the distinctness of the participants in the action, the deliberateness, suddenness, and completeness of the action, and the relative affectedness of both participants. An action that has little or no effect on the actor who does something to the other, but a substantial effect on the target of the action, reflects a greater transfer of action and is therefore higher in transitivity than an action that has more effect on the actor or less effect on the target.[91]

Based on my study of racial eligibility discourse, I propose that the degree of transitivity attributed to an external threat relative to the groups bound together by the threat in a "solidarity of fear" or a "kinship in arms" is a significant factor in the intensity of rhetorical transcendence. Successful advocates for political group inclusion will accordingly tend to attribute high transitivity to the actions of an external actor while attributing little or no transitivity to their own actions. Some studies of linguistic agency suggest as much, such as those finding that the assignment of agency for viral transmission to a virus (e.g., "H1N1 may infect thousands") rather than to people (e.g., "thousands may contract H1N1") heightens the perceived severity of the virus and personal susceptibility to it, increases the perception that vaccinations are effective, and increases support for mandatory vaccinations.[92] In addition, rhetorical studies of transitivity have demonstrated that it can serve an important function in identity formation by, for example, constructing responsibility for mistakes made during a law enforcement raid through the assignment of agency in a report regarding the raid and by creating political legitimacy for former political elites in exile during the Cold War.[93] By assessing the relative transitivity attributed to external threats and to naturalization applicants, I demonstrate that transitivity served a powerful rhetorical function in identity formation in racial eligibility discourse, which I believe opens new avenues for studying the rhetorical function of enemies.

Political theorists have also noted the close association between the transcendent bond of unity against shared external threats and the concept of sovereignty. Ioannis Evrigenis writes that although fear may vary in how much it is foregrounded as a cause of political group identification, it is always present and is particularly apparent during crucial moments in the life of a group, such as at its founding and "during crises that threaten the unity and continued existence of the group."[94] According to Evrigenis, fear is particularly important in the process of political group formation because security is a foundational requirement of a group's existence and flourishing. The primacy of self-preservation

> provides a way of overcoming barriers to group formation and collective action that are insurmountable by positive means alone. The emergence of a threat calls for the reclassification of existing threats and consequently for the rearrangement of one's priorities.[95]

This rearrangement of priorities, Evrigenis writes, constitutes the origin and justification of the modern state,[96] and Neal Wood similarly argues that sovereignty is the domestication of the idea that fear of an external enemy promotes internal unity.[97]

The prominence of appeals to external threats in racial eligibility discourse even suggests that when sovereignty is defined pluralistically it constitutes the central meaning of racial formation. In his critique of the monistic concept of sovereignty, political theorist Harold Laski argues that the true meaning of sovereignty lies not in a state's monopoly on coercive power but in its ability to secure assent, reflected in "the fused good-will for which it stands." There is nothing absolute and unqualified about sovereignty, but it is a matter of degrees and is dispersed among all of the groups that exist in the state and compete for influence. The state gains more strength by seeking "common ground" with the interests of groups concerned in any given conflict than by passing coercive legislation with which they have no sympathy.[98] Legal scholar Robert Cover adopts a similarly pluralistic view of sovereignty in his description of the problem that courts confront not as the difficulty of interpreting ambiguities in a unified system of norms promulgated by the state but as a conflict between a multiplicity of coexisting normative systems in society,[99] and Scott Lyons notes that sovereignty is a rhetorical process not exclusively constituted by self-government but focused as well on perpetuation of community and cultural practices.[100] Several studies of race and law have also specifically identified a link between race and sovereignty. Sumi Cho and Gil Gott have argued that sovereignty is "utterly racial in origin and development," for example, having "developed homologously with the structures of societal racial formation,"[101] and

Falguni Sheth claims that race is instantiated through sovereign power that confronts a threat to the coherence of a polity which must be domesticated or managed in order for the state to maintain control of its population.[102] Similarly, Michael Omi and Howard Winant argue that the state itself is inherently racial.[103]

In contrast to previous studies of the racial eligibility cases, which have mostly examined the period culminating in the United States Supreme Court's opinion in *United States v. Thind* (1923)—the final statement of the Court on the racial eligibility provisions of the naturalization act in which the Court held that a "high-caste Hindu, of full Indian blood" was not a "free white person" within the meaning of the naturalization act—I mostly examine *Thind* and the post-*Thind* period. In addition to *Thind*, I examine cases that immediately followed *Thind* seeking to cancel the naturalization certificates of Asian Indians who had been naturalized before *Thind*. I also examine the *Cartozian* trial and a handful of cases from World War II and the early Cold War period regarding the significance of the Chinese Exclusion Repeal Act and the racial eligibility for naturalization of Kalmyk and Tatar refugees from the Soviet Union. In a series of cases during this period, the appeals to unify against a shared external threat took the particular form of depicting naturalization applicants as political or religious refugees at risk of becoming stateless if they were held racially ineligible for naturalization in the United States. I argue that by drawing on the category of stateless persons that emerged in response to the often tense relationship between race and nationality during this period, the participants in these cases anticipated the "well-founded fear of persecution" standard of later political asylum law. As Hannah Arendt writes, although the right of asylum did not become law during the early twentieth century it "led a somewhat shadowy existence as an appeal in individual exceptional cases for which normal legal institutions did not suffice,"[104] and I argue that the discursive practices of the participants in racial eligibility cases during this period reflect this shadowy existence.

In chapter 1, I examine the history of race and citizenship in the United States from the mid-nineteenth century through the United States Supreme Court's first opinion regarding racial eligibility for naturalization in *Ozawa v. United States* (1922). I begin by discussing the many annexation treaties that naturalized the inhabitants of western territories without regard to race during the nation's territorial expansion and the role played by the perceived threat of Asian immigrants imagined as dangerous Mongolian invaders in the first interpretations of the naturalization act that emerged in the late nineteenth century. I then turn to the creation of the Bureau of Naturalization in the early twentieth century and its rejection of the Aryan and Caucasian racial classifications as indices of whiteness in favor of an interpretation that relied on ordinary usage of the word *white,* leading the bureau to adopt an openly political interpretation of race for purposes of naturalization. The bureau claimed that the phrase *free white person* in the naturalization act referred to the people of Western civilization and could only be determined in the light of history, and this interpretation exerted significant influence on judicial interpretations of the act. I conclude with an analysis of the arguments and opinion in *Ozawa,* the first of two test cases regarding the racial eligibility provisions of the naturalization act to be decided by the United States Supreme Court. My analysis focuses on how the applicant in the case, Takao Ozawa, cited the historical reputation of the Japanese as "dangerous enemies" in support of his claim that they were "free white persons," and I argue that this strategy is likely to have undermined his case by reinforcing perceptions of the Japanese as threatening. Accordingly, I argue that *Ozawa* reflects an unsuccessful strategy of foregrounding the agentive potency of an applicant's own group rather than a shared external threat in racial eligibility discourse. I conclude by considering the function of appeals to unify against a shared external threat in racial formation and the relationship between race and territoriality.

In chapter 2, I consider the role of Indian nationalism and the Indian caste system in *United States v. Thind* (1923) and *United States v. Pandit* (1925), a post-*Thind* proceeding to cancel the naturalization certificate of an Indian American based on the claim that he had been racially ineligible for naturalization at the time it was granted almost a decade before. I first critique previous commentaries regarding *Thind* that have neglected the Supreme Court's express approval of two cases holding that high caste Hindus were "free white persons" for purposes of naturalization only three months earlier in *Ozawa,* and I consider the applicant Bhagat Singh Thind's political activities as a founding member of a violent Indian independence movement known as the Ghadr Party as an explanation of the Court's reversal regarding Hindu racial eligibility for naturalization. I analyze Thind's Supreme Court briefs, in which he repeated a longstanding Indian nationalist argument that claimed that the Aryan ancestry of high caste Hindus and the caste restrictions on intermarriage under Hindu law rendered high caste Hindus "more 'white' than the 'whites,'" and I argue that this strategy likely undermined Thind's case. I find further support for this conclusion in the government's brief, which cited British imperialist sources reflecting negative associations of the Indian caste system, and in the contrast presented by the rhetorical strategy of the Asian Indian lawyer Sakharam Pandit during a proceeding that the government filed to cancel his naturalization certificate after *Thind*, in which Pandit reversed his relationship to the Indian caste system by claiming that if he returned to India after having become an American citizen he would be an outcast, one of India's "untouchables," and a stateless person. I argue that this strategy framed Pandit in a relationship of shared suffering with Europeans against the perceived dangers of the Indian caste system, and I conclude by arguing that Pandit's strategy forms part of a frequent appearance of appeals to unify against a shared external threat in racial eligibility discourse by drawing upon the new category of stateless persons that emerged after World War I, a strategy that reflects an incipient form of the "well-founded fear of persecution" standard of later political asylum law.

In chapter 3, I examine the *Cartozian* trial in the context of the existential crisis for Armenian refugees after the Armenian Genocide of World War I left many Armenians stateless. I first analyze the trial transcript, focusing on the arguments of Cartozian's lawyers that depicted Armenian history as a narrative of Turkish, Kurdish, and Syrian Muslim persecution of Armenians in Asia Minor and frequently referred to the Armenian Genocide and statelessness as a basis for concluding that Armenians were not truly Asian despite residing in Asia for centuries. I then compare the arguments contained in the trial transcript with Judge Charles Wolverton's judicial opinion in the case, particularly language at the heart of the opinion that suggests Judge Wolverton adopted the defense's historical claim regarding the conflict between the Armenians and their Islamic neighbors as a central justification for his conclusion that Armenians were "free white persons." I conclude by discussing martyrdom as a common form of appeal to unify against a shared external threat in which a victim's death is framed in a broader context of intergroup relations and how the defense advanced this form of appeal through its narrative of religious persecution of Armenians.

In chapter 4, I examine the legislative debates regarding the extension of racial eligibility for naturalization to the Chinese, Asian Indians, and Filipinos during World War II and the early Cold War as well as judicial interpretations of the racial eligibility provisions of the nationality act that followed those legislative changes, along with two opinions of the United States Board of Immigration Appeals that held Tatar and Kalmyk refugees from the Soviet Union to be "free white persons" for purposes of naturalization. I demonstrate that the legislative debates during this period explicitly appealed to the need to strengthen alliances in Asia against Japanese aggression in the Pacific during the war and against the spread of Soviet communism after the war as a basis for repealing the nation's Asian exclusion policy, as well as how these legislative changes led courts to question the Supreme Court's opinion in *Thind* and adopt a more inclusive interpretation of racial eligibility for naturalization to suit foreign policy goals. I conclude by arguing that a growing idealism that emerged during World War II regarding American race relations, often expressed by citing the Declaration of Independence's proclamation that "all men are created equal," reflects the influence that the appeal to unify against shared external threats can have on memory during times of crisis. I also analyze how a shared external threat is amplified in the Declaration of Independence's own list of grievances against King George, making recitation of the Declaration a particularly powerful expression of unity during times of crisis.

In conclusion, I discuss the implications of the racial eligibility discourse in this study for understanding racial and national identity formation, the relationship between the ubiquity and emphasis given to appeals to unify against a shared external threat in racial eligibility discourse and the concepts of refuge, sanctuary, and asylum, and how racial eligibility discourse illustrates the rhetorical dimension of Derrick Bell's interest convergence thesis. I consider the work of Bell and a growing body of scholars regarding the influence of the Cold War on race relations and civil rights in the United States alongside scholarship regarding the rhetorical construction of enemies and the challenges that emergencies pose to legality as a way of understanding the prominence of appeals to transcend divisions by unifying in common defense of the nation. I argue that this premise explains both the prominence of appeals to shared external threats in racial eligibility discourse and the fraught relationship between race and law.

1

MONGOLIAN INVADERS, THE BUREAU OF
NATURALIZATION, AND *OZAWA*

Although eligibility for naturalized citizenship was limited to "free white persons" from the time the nation's first naturalization act was passed in 1790, the earliest published judicial opinion to address the racial eligibility provision of the act was issued in *In re Yup* in 1878. In *Yup*, Judge Lorenzo Sawyer of the United States Circuit Court for the District of California decided whether a "native and citizen of the empire of China, of the Mongolian race," was a "free white person" for purposes of naturalization. Sawyer held that the applicant was not "white," writing in his published opinion that the words "white person,"

> in this country, at least, have undoubtedly acquired a well settled meaning in common popular speech, and they are constantly used in the sense so acquired in the literature of the country, as well as in common parlance. As ordinarily used everywhere in the United States, one would scarcely fail to understand that the party employing the words "white person" would intend a person of the Caucasian race.

After referring to the leading ethnological authorities of the nineteenth century, Sawyer claimed that

> neither in popular language, in literature, nor in scientific nomenclature, do we ordinarily, if ever, find the words "white person"

1

used in a sense so comprehensive as to include an individual
of the Mongolian race.[1]

Based on popular perceptions of the Caucasian and Mongolian racial division, which classified the Chinese as Mongolian, Sawyer concluded that
it was beyond dispute that because the Chinese were not Caucasian they
were not "white."

The certainty with which Judge Sawyer regarded the racial classification
of the Chinese was echoed in other cases. In a 1909 case regarding the racial
eligibility of Armenians for naturalization, for example, the United States
attorney argued that

> without being able to define a white person, the average man
> in the street understands distinctly what it means, and would
> find no difficulty in assigning to the yellow race a Turk or Syrian
> with as much ease as he would bestow that designation on a
> Chinaman or a Korean.[2]

Despite this argument, there are no reported cases in which the Bureau
of Naturalization opposed the racial eligibility for naturalization of a Turk,
and there is evidence that the bureau mostly deferred to early judicial precedent holding Syrians to be "free white persons" for purposes of naturalization.
In a case involving a Parsi applicant the following year, a federal appeals court
similarly wrote that "for practical purposes there is no difficulty in saying
that the Chinese, Japanese, and Malays and the American Indians do not
belong to the white race."[3] In these and other early cases interpreting the
racial eligibility provisions of the naturalization act, the racial classifications
made were depicted as so obvious that they required little explanation beyond
brief citation of ethnological authorities or previous judicial precedent.

The certainty of such statements is belied by a considerably more fraught
history of racial classification in the United States, however, dating from
the time of the nation's founding. As Michael Keevak describes, in initial
encounters Europeans "almost uniformly" described natives of the Far East as
"white" and even described their whiteness in particularly superlative terms,
such as "rather white" (*zimblich weiß*), "truly white" (*véritablement blanc*),
"completely white" (*fulkomligen hvita*), "white like us" (*bianchi, si come siamo
noi*), and "as white as we are" (*aussi blancs que nous*). In correspondence with
his former aide Tinch Tilghman, George Washington expressed surprise

that Tilghman had compared the physical appearance of Chinese sailors to American Indians because Washington thought that the Chinese, "tho' droll in shape and appearance, were yet white."[4] In 1860, the United States census included 33,149 male and 1,784 female Asians in the "white" population,[5] and Chinese immigrants arriving in the United States in the nineteenth century were granted naturalization certificates in Eastern states for decades before the Chinese Exclusion Act prohibited Chinese naturalizations. As early as the 1830s, Chinese naturalizations were recorded in New York and North Carolina,[6] and in 1870 a Boston newspaper article recounted the longstanding practice in Massachusetts of naturalizing "Chinese as well as other Asiatics" since at least 1843.[7] The United States Circuit Court for the District of Massachusetts also found as late as the turn of the twentieth century that it had long been its practice to naturalize Asian immigrants.[8] In 1879, a San Francisco newspaper article remarked that although Judge Sawyer had ruled against Chinese naturalizations in California "one Judge Larrimore in New York is making American citizens out of Chinamen as fast as he can."[9]

As late as World War I, the classification of the Japanese as "white" was even explicitly defended by ethnologists and other scholarly commentators. In an 1894 article in the *American Law Review*, legal scholar John Wigmore argued that "in the scientific use of language and in the light of modern anthropology, the term 'white' may properly be applied to the ethnical composition of the Japanese,"[10] and in a 1913 article in the *North American Review* William Griffis wrote that "to class the Japanese as 'Mongolians' is absurd."[11] In 1909, Judge Francis Lowell of the United States District Court for the District of Massachusetts wrote that "at one time Chinese and Japanese were deemed to be white, but are not usually so reckoned today" because "the change of sentiment and usage . . . produced a change in the construction" of the naturalization act, and as a result "its meaning has been narrowed so as to exclude Chinese and Japanese in some instances."[12] Drawing on previous ethnological accounts, H. G. Wells claimed in his 1920 bestseller *Outline of History* that the Japanese and others in the Indian Ocean and Pacific Rim descended from the Mediterranean people of Europe who migrated to Central Asia and the Pacific,[13] and the United States census of 1910 reflected hundreds of Japanese who had been granted naturalizations.[14] Like the Chinese, the racial classification of the Japanese was considerably unstable, and the Chinese were often classified as "white" before the United States Supreme Court held them racially ineligible for naturalization in 1922.[15] Notwithstanding the naive realism reflected in some early judicial opinions interpreting the racial eligibility provisions of the naturalization act, racial formation is always highly unstable.

In order to provide the historical context needed to understand the racial eligibility cases, this chapter examines the relationship between race and citizenship in the United States from the nineteenth century through the early 1920s when the United States Supreme Court issued its only two opinions interpreting the racial eligibility provisions of the naturalization act in *Ozawa* and *Thind*. I begin by examining the period of territorial expansion during the nineteenth century when countless American Indians, Mexicans, Asians, and Pacific islanders—groups later held to be racially ineligible for naturalization—were collectively naturalized under the provisions of various treaties. Despite these collective naturalizations of Asians and other non-European residents in territorial expansion treaties, as anti-Chinese sentiment developed in the late nineteenth century an Asian exclusion policy emerged in interpretations of the racial eligibility provisions of the naturalization act. I examine the emergence of this policy and the interpretive approach adopted by the United States Bureau of Naturalization after its creation in the early twentieth century, then analyze the rhetorical significance of naturalization applicant Takao Ozawa's expression of Japanese nationalism in *Ozawa*.

RACIAL INCLUSIVENESS DURING TERRITORIAL EXPANSION

Throughout the nineteenth century, the various treaties and legislative acts that annexed new territories to the United States reflect the contradictions in the nation's policy regarding racial eligibility for citizenship as the nation made citizens of American Indians, Mexicans, Asians, and Pacific islanders by collectively naturalizing the inhabitants of most newly annexed territories without regard to race. The Louisiana Purchase of 1803 granted American citizenship to all inhabitants of the Louisiana territory, including those of French, Spanish, and Mexican descent as well as a substantial number of free blacks and mulattoes.[16] Similarly, the annexations of Florida, Texas, and southern portions of Arizona and New Mexico in 1819, 1845, 1848, and 1853 provided American citizenship to all of the citizens of the annexed territories and in most cases to all of the inhabitants without regard to race.[17] As United States Supreme Court Justice John McLean noted in his dissenting opinion in *Dred Scott*, on the question of citizenship the nation had "not been very fastidious" because it "made citizens of all grades, combinations, and colors" during its many territorial expansions.[18] The territorial expansions reflect the fact that the need to clearly define the nation's borders transcended any racial difference that may have been perceived.

The collective naturalization provisions of the annexations were occasionally observed to conflict with the racial eligibility provisions of the naturalization act, but the conflicts were mostly ignored. With regard to Mexicans, the judiciary even relied on their collective naturalization in various annexation treaties to hold them racially eligible for naturalization under the naturalization act. In an 1897 opinion in *In re Rodriguez*, Judge Thomas Maxey of the United States District Court for the Western District of Texas justified his decision that a "pure-blooded Mexican" with no Spanish descent was racially eligible for naturalization based largely on the fact that the Adams-Onís Treaty, the Treaty of Guadalupe Hidalgo, and the Gadsden Treaty had collectively naturalized numerous Mexican inhabitants:

> A reference to the constitution of the republic of Texas and the constitution, laws, and treaties of the United States will disclose that both that republic and the United States have freely, during the past 60 years, conferred upon Mexicans the rights and privileges of American citizenship . . . by various collective acts of naturalization.

Because *Rodriguez* was the only published judicial opinion regarding Mexican racial eligibility for naturalization, it mostly settled the question of Mexican racial eligibility for naturalization under the naturalization act by serving as precedent for later cases. Although some have questioned whether Maxey actually found Mexicans to be "free white persons" in *Rodriquez* because the opinion does not explicitly state the finding, in 1944 the Board of Immigration Appeals explicitly found that a native and citizen of Mexico was "a person of the white race" for purposes of their eligibility for citizenship.[19]

After the Civil War, the United States also reaffirmed the English common law rule of birthright citizenship by which a person's citizenship is determined by their place of birth rather than their parents' nationality.[20] In 1868, the Fourteenth Amendment to the United States Constitution granted citizenship to "all persons born or naturalized in the United States, and subject to the jurisdiction thereof."[21] Although the reaffirmation of birthright citizenship in the Fourteenth Amendment was specifically designed to reverse the United States Supreme Court's decision in *Dred Scott*, which had held that African Americans were constitutionally incapable of becoming citizens, the principle more broadly repudiated racial eligibility criteria for citizenship with regard to anyone born in the United States. In 1884, the United States Supreme Court held that American Indians who maintained their tribal relations could not become citizens by birth under the Fourteenth Amendment because they were not "subject to the jurisdiction" of the United States,[22] but in 1897 the Supreme Court held that a child born in San Francisco of Chinese parents became a United States citizen under the Fourteenth Amendment because "every citizen or subject of another country, while domiciled here, is within the allegiance and protection, and consequently subject to the jurisdiction, of the United States."[23] As in the nation's territorial expansions, one consequence of the Civil War was to reaffirm birthplace citizenship as part of an effort to establish national unity. Although racial discrimination in the form of racial segregation laws, poll taxes, literacy tests, and other measures continued to undermine the full exercise of citizenship rights by racial minorities, the Fourteenth Amendment afforded formal legal protection to every person born in the United States without regard to race.

The history of American Indian citizenship during the nineteenth and early twentieth centuries also reflected the contingency of racial eligibility for citizenship on threats to the nation, culminating in the unilateral naturalization of all noncitizen Indians as a reward for their support of the nation during World War I. Although courts found that American Indians were racially ineligible for naturalization under the naturalization act because they were not "free white persons,"[24] all American Indians living in the United States were naturalized by various treaties and statutes long before the racial eligibility provisions of the naturalization act were removed. In a particularly notable example of the contingency of American Indian citizenship on threats to the nation, United States Supreme Court Justice Roger Taney wrote in his majority opinion in *Dred Scott* that American Indians, unlike African Americans, were capable of becoming citizens based in part on his conclusion that while African Americans were prohibited from serving in state militias, American Indians were treated with the respect given to foreign governments and "their alliance sought for in war." In other words, the ability and desirability of American Indians to defend the nation in times of crisis distinguished their eligibility for citizenship from that of African Americans. According to Taney, however, in their "untutored and savage state" no one would have thought of admitting American Indians to citizenship in a "civilized" community because

> the atrocities they had but recently committed, when they were the allies of Great Britain in the Revolutionary war, were yet fresh in the recollection of the people of the United States, and they were even then guarding themselves against the threatened renewal of Indian hostilities.

As these comments reflect, Taney imagined the history of American Indian citizenship in the United States to be contingent on their potential for military enmities and alliances.

The contingency of citizenship on such threat assessments not only explains broad policy decisions such as those collectively naturalizing all of the inhabitants of new territories without regard to race, but is also reflected in the language of individual arguments and opinions in judicial cases. Justice Taney also wrote in *Dred Scott*, for example, that the First Congress only considered those eligible for naturalization "whose rights and liberties had been outraged by the English government; and who . . . assumed the powers of Government to defend their rights by force of arms."[25] The transitive verb *outrage* indicated an excessive wrong, violation, or assault, and it was specifically associated with literal or metaphorical rape.[26] Similarly, as Sumi Cho and Gil Gott note of United States Supreme Court Justice John Marshall's series of opinions in the early nineteenth century regarding American Indian sovereignty, the Court granted Indians a sort of "quasi-sovereignty" in which they were denied full sovereignty as independent nations but granted a measure of autonomy from the states based on the imaginary of Indian savagery. For Marshall, the "fierce and warlike" character of Indians rendered them racially incommensurable with Europeans. Cho and Gott write that Marshall's analysis of the perceived savagery of Indians "necessitated the degree of sovereignty afforded" by the Court, and the sovereignty granted them was inversely proportionate to the threat they were perceived to pose.[27] The same is true of Justice Taney's remarks regarding the eligibility of Indians for American citizenship in *Dred Scott*.

The eligibility of Indians for citizenship in the United States was contingent on the threat particular Indian tribes were perceived to pose, however, rather than on a general imaginary of Indian savagery. Despite Justice Taney's conclusion that it was unlikely that Indians would be desired as citizens given the threat they were perceived to pose to the European colonists of North America, hundreds of thousands of Indians were collectively naturalized during the nineteenth and early twentieth centuries through various treaties as individual tribes were incorporated into the nation.[28] In support of Indian removal efforts, between 1817 and 1868 citizenship was formally granted to the Cherokees, the Choctaws, the Brothertown Indians, the Stockbridge Indians, the Wyandotts, the Ottawas, the Kickapoos, the Delawares, the Pottawatomies, various Kansas tribes, and the Sioux.[29] Similarly, the Oklahoma Organic Act of 1890 provided for the naturalization of 101,506 Indians in Indian Territory.[30] Although efforts to naturalize Indian tribes were both fraught with congressional exceptions and resisted by Indians,[31] what is important for purposes of the present study is that the formal incorporation of Indian tribes into the nation often proceeded according to the distinction between civilized and savage much like Marshall's and Taney's analyses of Indian sovereignty and their capacity for citizenship. The Dawes Act of 1887 divided tribal land into allotments for individual Indians and granted citizenship to every Indian born in the United States "who has voluntarily taken up . . . his residence separate and apart from any tribe of Indians therein, and has adopted the habits of civilized life," resulting in the citizenship of 53,168 Indians by 1900.[32] The willingness of Indians to volunteer for military service during World War I was also rewarded with the eligibility for naturalization of roughly ten thousand American Indian veterans in 1919 and with the unilateral naturalization of all remaining noncitizen Indians in 1924.[33] Despite decades of continued opposition to the right of Indians to vote and exercise other rights of citizenship, the formal grant of citizenship to Indians reflected in this series of acts largely prevailed to alter their legal status.[34]

The concepts of civilized and savage as criteria for the eligibility of American Indians for citizenship is also evident in the nation's 1867 treaty with Russia for the purchase of Alaska. In the Alaska treaty, numerous aboriginal and creole residents of Alaska were naturalized depending on whether they were designated as belonging to "civilized" or "uncivilized" tribes. In 1904, a court in Fairbanks, Alaska, published an opinion in *In re Minook* involving an application for naturalization by a man born of a Russian father and an Eskimo mother who believed himself to be a subject of Russia. The applicant John Minook was born at St. Michael in the Russian possessions in North America and his parents resided in Alaska when it was ceded to the United States. Contrary to Minook's belief that he was a subject of Russia who had to apply for naturalization, it was suggested on his behalf that he was already an American citizen under the naturalization clause of the Alaska treaty. The naturalization clause of the treaty provided that the inhabitants of Alaska could return to Russia within three years or they would automatically become American citizens if they elected to remain in Alaska. An exception to the treaty's grant of naturalized citizenship to the inhabitants was made for "*uncivilized* native tribes," however, who did not become American citizens but became subject to "such laws and regulations as the United States may from time to time adopt in regard to aboriginal tribes of that country."[35]

The court in *Minook* concluded that the Russian Empire recognized a difference between "the settled tribes who lived in permanent villages in fixed habitations, and who were wholly or in greater part, members of the established Russian Church," on the one hand, and "the uncivilized native tribes—the pagan tribes," on the other. As a result, the court concluded that at the time of the treaty Russian law recognized the Russian colonists, their creole children, and "those settled tribes who embraced the Christian faith" as Russian subjects, but not the "uncivilized native tribes," or "those tribes not wholly dependent—the independent tribes of pagan faith who acknowledged no restraint from the Russians, and practised their ancient customs." As a result, the court found that the uncivilized tribes excluded from the benefits of the naturalization clause in the Alaska treaty were "pagan" tribes who "acknowledged no allegiance to Russia, and lived the wild life of their savage ancestors."[36] The court compared the Alaska treaty and its distinction between civilized and uncivilized tribes to the Dawes Act and held that Minook was already an American citizen either as an inhabitant entitled to the automatic grant of naturalization under the Alaska treaty or as a member of an uncivilized native tribe who had voluntarily taken up his residence "separate and apart from any tribe of Indians therein, and . . . adopted the habits of civilized life" under the Dawes Act.[37] Like the Louisiana Purchase, the Treaty of Guadalupe-Hidalgo, the Treaty with Spain, and the Gadsden Treaty, the Alaska treaty collectively naturalized numerous aboriginal people and creole descendants of mixed aboriginal and Russian lineage in order to clearly delineate the nation's borders as it expanded its territory. The naturalization provision of the Alaska treaty, however, conditioned aboriginal eligibility for citizenship on an assessment of whether their social and political history was "civilized" or "uncivilized" with regard to Russians.

In 1898, the annexation of Hawaii also collectively naturalized numerous inhabitants who were found racially ineligible for naturalization under the naturalization act. Although in 1889 the Supreme Court of Utah held that a "native of the Hawaiian islands," appearing "of Malayan or Mongolian complexion, a shade lighter than the average of his race," whose "ancestors were Kanakas," was racially ineligible for naturalization because he was not a "free white person,"[38] the Hawaiian Organic Act of 1900 collectively naturalized all of the inhabitants of the Hawaiian islands who were citizens of the Kingdom of Hawaii, including all of those born or naturalized in Hawaii during the Hawaiian monarchy and later governments. This included many Chinese, Japanese, and native Hawaiian inhabitants.[39] Not only did Hawaii follow the principle of birthright citizenship, but it imposed no racial limits on naturalization. The naturalization records of the Hawaiian Islands from 1844 to 1894 reflect 763 Chinese, 136 Pacific islanders, and 3 Japanese among naturalized citizens, and the Hawaiian census of 1900 included among the inhabitants of Hawaii 61,111 Japanese, 29,799 Hawaiians, 25,767 Chinese, and 8,272 others who were classified as non-Caucasian. Many of these inhabitants would have been naturalized by the Hawaiian Organic Act.[40] Similarly, Congress collectively naturalized all of the inhabitants of Puerto Rico in 1917 and all of the inhabitants of the Virgin Islands in 1927, including many who had been racially classified as non-"white" under the racial eligibility provisions of the naturalization act.[41]

The collective naturalizations of inhabitants of new territories during the nation's territorial expansion illustrate either that no racial differences were perceived between the inhabitants or that the need to clearly delineate the nation's territorial sovereignty transcended any racial differences that were perceived,[42] and the racial eligibility provisions of the naturalization act were similarly contingent on perceived threats to the nation's borders and the enmities and alliances they prompted. Judge Oliver Dickinson of the United States District Court for the Eastern District of Pennsylvania explicitly appealed to this principle in the 1917 case of *In re Singh*, writing in his published opinion in the case that the meaning of the phrase *free white person* in the naturalization act was considerably broadened as an effect of the Revolutionary War. According to Dickinson,

> As the inhabitants of what was then the United States were
> a more or less homogeneous people who or whose immedi-
> ate forbears had come from what has been termed "Northern

Europe," and as the vast territories then known as Florida and as Louisiana formed no part of our national domain, and as our people had been in almost continuous conflict with the French and Spaniards, it is doubtful whether the words "white persons," as used in common speech, originally included any of the so-called Latin races.

In other words, the conflict between the British colonies in North America and the French and Spanish during the French and Indian Wars initially rendered it unlikely to Dickinson that the French and Spanish would be encompassed by the phrase *free white persons,* but

> the events of the Revolution . . . and the gratitude which our people felt toward France, and more especially the large number of French Huguenots who had come to make their homes here, caused instant recognition of the French as having a common heritage with us, and the phrase automatically expanded to include them. The desire to be consistent forced us to include the Spaniards and Portuguese, and later the Italian peoples, and broadly the Latin race.[43]

In this and other instances of racial eligibility discourse, national enmities and alliances assumed a more prominent position in explanations of racial classifications than biological descent.

The relationship of territorial expansion to the racial eligibility provisions of the naturalization act has been largely ignored in previous studies of the racial eligibility cases. In one noteworthy exception, however, Matthew Frye Jacobson argues that the racial eligibility cases played a crucial role in confirming the whiteness of Southern and Eastern Europeans whose whiteness Anglo-Saxons deemed inferior as expansion into the Pacific and the depiction of Pacific natives as dangerous "savages" dissolved the boundary between "superior" and "inferior" whites from Europe.[44] Jacobson claims that the efforts of a variety of Asian applicants to secure naturalization "were part of what kept the probationary white races of Europe white" because

> like the nation's frontier warfare and its perpetual narrations, . . . these legal skirmishes along the borders of naturalized citizenship staked out a brand of monolithic whiteness which corroborated

the reasoning of 1790 precisely in a period when that reasoning was undergoing massive revision.[45]

Jacobson writes that the phrase *free white person* in the naturalization act signified "a powerful crucible whose exclusions based upon distinctions of color blurred other potentially divisive physical distinctions," forming a true "melting pot" in which the whiteness of Southern and Eastern Europeans was confirmed.[46] The "crucible of empire" that Jacobson describes, however, neglects the more pervasive role that enmities and alliances played in a wider variety of cases and periods in racial eligibility discourse. While the image of the crucible aptly captures the powerful transcendent effect of shared external threats on perceived racial difference, persuasive appeals to such threats were not limited to the whiteness of Southern and Eastern Europeans or to Pacific expansion alone but appear throughout the discourse surrounding the racial eligibility provisions of the naturalization act.

FEARS OF MONGOLIAN INVASION

The relationship between racial formation and the desire to control and manage the nation's borders is also evident in the fact that the objection to the racial eligibility of Asians for naturalization was often premised on the Mongolian racial classification. The controversy regarding Asian racial eligibility for naturalization first appears in a heated debate in the United States Senate on July 4, 1870, regarding an amendment to remove the racial eligibility provision from the naturalization act as part of Civil War Reconstruction. During the 1870 debates, West Coast senators objected that removing the racial eligibility provision would permit the Chinese to become American citizens. This conclusion was premised on the claim that the Chinese were not "free white persons," and as evidence for this claim many of those who objected to Chinese eligibility for naturalization asserted that the Chinese belonged to the Mongolian race. Oregon Senator George Williams remarked, for example, that "Mongolians, no matter how long they may stay in the United States, will never lose their identity as a peculiar and separate people."[47] As noted above, Judge Sawyer also referred to the classification of the Chinese as Mongolian in *Yup*,[48] and the Mongolian racial classification is found throughout the history of racial eligibility discourse as presumptive evidence of a non-"white" status. In 1908, one United States attorney even claimed that Finnish immigrants were not racially eligible for naturalization because they were believed to have Mongolian ancestry.[49]

In Michael Keevak's study of Western racial depictions of Asians, he writes that although the Mongolian racial classification initially arose when Johann Friedrich Blumenbach created his five-part division of humanity into the Caucasian, Mongolian, Malayan, Ethiopian, and American races at the end of the eighteenth century, it was mostly the creation of mid-nineteenth-century racialist science. The word *Mongol* had appeared before, but the people of northeastern Asia had most often been racially classified as "Tartars" from the time of the travel narratives of Marco Polo, John of Plano Carpini, and William of Rubrick. The Tartar racial classification included the Mongols, Manchus, Kalmyks, Buryats, and Tibetans, among others, and China was simply called Tartary or Tartaria. The Tartar racial classification was rejected, however, when Catherine the Great sought to define and control the eastern borders of the Russian Empire in the late eighteenth century. In connection with the effort to define and control Russia's border with Asia, scholars in cooperation with the Imperial Academy of Sciences in St. Petersburg rejected the Tartar racial classification and introduced new classifications that included the Mongolian. Under the Mongolian racial classification produced from this effort, the Tartar racial classification was broadened to include both the Chinese and Japanese along with all other natives of the Far East.[50]

This new classification associated all natives of Asia with, in Keevak's words, "the idea of barbaric hordes and merciless slaughter, centering on Attila the Hun, Genghis Khan, and Tamerlane, that familiar triad who were now regularly called 'Mongols.'"[51] The introduction of the Mongolian racial classification became the basis of a revision of European history as well as new fears of Mongolian invasions. In S. Wells Williams's mid-nineteenth-century study of China, he described "vast swarms" of Mongol tribes who had "overrun, in different ages, the plains of India, China, Syria, Egypt, and Eastern Europe," exterminating rather than subjugating those they conquered,[52] and in the early twentieth century Lothrop Stoddard described the Mongols as part of "a millennium of Asiatic aggression" against Europe that began with "the Huns in the last days of Rome."[53] The Mongolian racial classification reflected a renewed fear of Asian aggression, as Keevak explains:

> the Mongolian was . . . considered a wandering and dangerous
> human type that perhaps threatened to overrun the world once

again, a fear of the populous East that would be invoked by such
thinkers as [Thomas] Malthus, whose contemporaneous theory
of overpopulation and limited food supply ignited the specter
of a new "Northern Immigration," reminiscent of the invasions
of Attila and Genghis Khan.

According to Keevak, it was only at the end of the nineteenth century that
"the idea of a yellow East Asia would fully take hold in the Western imagination, crystallizing in the phrase 'the yellow peril' to characterize the perceived
threat that the people of the Far East were now said to embody." The association of yellow skin with Asian races during the nineteenth century brought
together what had been closely allied for centuries, "yellow skin, numerous
'Mongolian' invasions, and the specter of large numbers of people from the
region migrating to the West."[54]

The image of dangerous Mongolian invaders appeared frequently in
American public discourse in the late nineteenth and early twentieth centuries. In 1854, the California Supreme Court held that a law prohibiting
any "Black, or Mulatto person, or Indian" from testifying for or against a
"white" person also prohibited the testimony of Chinese witnesses based
on the conclusion that the word *Indian* referred not only to American
Indians but to "the whole of the Mongolian race,"[55] and in 1863 the
California legislature amended the law to explicitly exclude the testimony
of "Mongolian" witnesses.[56] By 1880, the California legislature had prohibited the admission of "Mongolian" children to public schools[57] and the
marriage of a "Mongolian" to any "white" person.[58] During an 1882 town
hall in San Francisco demanding a federal ban on Chinese immigration,
one speaker warned of an impending "Mongolian flood" that would be
"more fatal to the life of this public than was the invasion of the Goths,
Vandals and Huns to the Roman Empire,"[59] and in 1886 former United
States senator William Steward published a pamphlet opposing Chinese
immigration in which he cited "the great Mongolian invasions of Western
Asia and Eastern Europe, and the supplanting of the native populations
by the invaders."[60] The threat Mongolians were imagined to pose was eventually simply expressed by the transitive verb *Mongolianize*. In 1884, for
example, Edward Gilliam wrote in the *North American Review* that Asian
immigrants "threaten . . . to Mongolianize the Pacific slope,"[61] and in 1910
the Asiatic Exclusion League warned that California agricultural labor was
being "Mongolianized."[62]

The Mongolian racial classification also figures prominently in Chinese invasion fiction that proliferated in the late nineteenth and early twentieth centuries, beginning with Abwell Whitney's *Almond-Eyed*, Pierton Dooner's *Last Days of the Republic*, and Robert Woltor's *A Short and Truthful History of the Taking of Oregon and California in the Year A.D. 1899*, all published between 1878 and 1882.[63] In Dooner's *Last Days of the Republic*, the Chinese Empire conquers the United States following a "Mongolian invasion" facilitated by the country's generous immigration and naturalization laws. The novel includes a fictional federal court case that holds the racial eligibility provisions of the naturalization act to be unconstitutional because they "discriminated against the Mongolian," and once this barrier is removed "the great empire of the East was now in position to turn loose, without the shadow of reserve, the flood-gates of her pent-up human torrent." By the end of the story, "Mongolian Governors" in numerous states have declared martial law and branded "white" militias unlawful and riotous assemblies.[64] Similarly, in "The Battle of Wabash," an epistolary story published under the pseudonym Lorelle in the October 1880 issue of the *Californian*, a future author describes how a "Mongolian" army spread "a reign of horror, unknown even under the rage of the Huns, Vandals, and Goths . . . all over the land" until the American army was ultimately "exterminated."[65] In Woltor's *A Short and Truthful History*, the fictional "survivor" of an invasion by Chinese military and an uprising of a fifth column of Chinese immigrants compares the fate awaiting "the Caucasian race in America at the hands of the alien Mongolian, now irremediably engrafted on her shore," to the removal and genocide of American Indians by Europeans.[66] These fictional fantasies continued well into the twentieth century, as reflected in Philip Nowlan's *Armageddon 2419 A.D.* (1928) and *The Airlords of Han* (1929), in which Buck Rogers wakes up in the twenty-fifth century to discover that the Mongolian Han, a race originating "somewhere in the dark fastnesses of interior Asia," has "spread itself like an inhuman yellow blight over the face of the globe."[67]

During the 1870 legislative debates regarding the proposed amendment to remove the racial eligibility provision of the naturalization act, West Coast senators not only drew explicitly on the Mongolian racial classification to argue that Asians were not "free white persons" but also used the language of "hordes" and "barbarism" that emerged with the Mongolian racial classification in the mid-nineteenth century. During the debates, senators described Asian immigrants as a "countless horde of aliens," an "influx of paganism and despotism," "hostile to free institutions," inhabiting a civilization "at war with ours."[68] As a compromise to defeat the proposed amendment to remove the word *white* from the act so that the argument that Asians were racially excluded from naturalization could be maintained, senators succeeded in substituting an amendment that did not remove the racial eligibility provision from the act but instead simply extended eligibility for naturalization to both "free white persons" and "aliens of African nativity and persons of African descent."[69] Recognizing the power of national crisis in racial eligibility discourse, a New York state court judge would later describe the extension of racial eligibility for naturalization to Africans as occurring "under the stress of the feeling generated by the late war."[70] The 1870 debates profoundly influenced later interpretations of the racial eligibility provisions of the naturalization act, often cited as evidence of a congressional intent that the Chinese and other natives of Asia were racially ineligible for naturalization because they were neither "white" nor "African."[71] As a result of this congressional history, many immigrants from Asia sought to establish their racial eligibility for naturalization by claiming that they were "free white persons" under the act.

The imaginary of dangerous Mongolian invaders also appeared in the United States Supreme Court's 1889 opinion in *Chae Chan Ping v. United States*, in which the Court held that the government had the absolute and unlimited power to unilaterally revoke certificates that had previously granted Chinese persons who had left the United States permission to return. Writing for the Court, Justice Stephen Field wrote that whatever license such certificates provided was revocable by the government "at its pleasure" because the power to exclude foreigners is an "incident of sovereignty." Field described the "great danger" that the West Coast perceived in the prospect that it would be "overrun" by "crowded millions of China" in "an Oriental invasion," and he defended the nation's duty to "preserve its independence, and give security against foreign aggression and encroachment," including that from "hordes of its people crowding in upon us," who, unwilling to assimilate, were "dangerous to its peace and security."[72] In many respects, *Chae Chan Ping* created the concept of plenary power, in this context Congress's full and complete authority to regulate the nation's borders without judicial review, which, as Sumi Cho and Gil Gott note, "embeds a racialized history in which race and law were mutually constituted."[73] The word *horde* in the 1870 debates and in *Chae Chan Ping* particularly invokes the image of dangerous Mongolian invaders and threats to the territorial integrity of the nation, from which national sovereignty and related concepts were constructed.[74]

Although the 1870 debates regarding the racial eligibility provision of the naturalization act were often cited as congressional intent to exclude Asians from naturalization, because many courts continued to find that Chinese immigrants were "free white persons" and racially eligible for naturalization under the naturalization act, Congress also expressly provided in the Chinese Exclusion Act of 1882 that "no State court or court of the United States shall admit Chinese to citizenship."[75] This provision further complicated interpretations of the racial eligibility provisions of the naturalization act, as courts questioned why the express prohibition was necessary if, as one court put it, it was "simply declaratory of the existing conditions, unless it was feared that some one might figure out that the Chinese were free white persons or of African nativity or descent."[76] In *Rodriguez*, Judge Maxey wrote that Judge Sawyer's opinion in *Yup* appeared to indicate that the 1870 amendment of the naturalization act was intended "solely as a prohibition against the naturalization of members of the Mongolian race," leading Maxey to ask why Congress would expressly prohibit Chinese naturalizations in the Chinese Exclusion Act if they were not previously eligible.[77] Despite this apparent contradiction, however, many interpreted the congressional actions regarding racial eligibility for naturalization in the nineteenth century to reflect a policy of Asian exclusion. This interpretation of congressional intent exerted a powerful influence on later interpretations of the racial eligibility provisions of the naturalization act.

THE BUREAU OF NATURALIZATION'S HISTORICAL INTERPRETATION OF RACE

Because the vast majority of the published judicial opinions in racial eligibility cases occurred after the United States Bureau of Naturalization was formed in 1906, the bureau's role in racial eligibility cases is crucial for understanding racial eligibility discourse. From 1790 to 1906, the naturalization act provided that any common law court of record in a state in which an applicant resided could grant a naturalization certificate.[78] This empowered many small municipal courts and justices of the peace to grant naturalizations, a practice that eventually led to inconsistent naturalization decisions and fraud as immigration increased in the late nineteenth century. In response to these problems, President Theodore Roosevelt commissioned a study of the naturalization laws by the State Department, the Department of Justice, and the Department of Commerce and Labor, to be accompanied by a proposed draft of a new naturalization act.[79] Based on the recommendations of Roosevelt's commission, the Naturalization Act of 1906 limited jurisdiction over naturalizations to federal courts and state courts of record having a seal and a clerk with no monetary limit on their jurisdiction. These changes effectively removed jurisdiction over naturalizations from many smaller courts.

The new act also expanded the Bureau of Immigration into a new Bureau of Immigration and Naturalization and moved it from the Treasury Department to the Department of Commerce and Labor.[80] In addition to imposing an open hearing and recordkeeping requirement and criminal penalties for issuing false and counterfeit naturalization certificates, the 1906 act provided the federal government with the right to intervene in any naturalization proceeding, cross-examine the applicant and any witnesses, produce evidence, and oppose the application.[81] The act also separately charged United States district attorneys with the duty of instituting proceedings

> in any court having jurisdiction to naturalize aliens in the judicial district in which the naturalized citizen may reside at the time of bringing the suit, for the purpose of setting aside and canceling the certificate of citizenship on the ground of fraud or on the ground that such certificate of citizenship was illegally procured.[82]

These provisions essentially empowered the government to intervene in naturalization proceedings at its discretion and specifically enjoined United States district attorneys to institute proceedings to cancel naturalization certificates found to have been fraudulently or illegally procured.

The relationship between the government's right to intervene in original naturalization proceedings and its duty to institute cancellation proceedings led some lower courts to disagree regarding the scope of jurisdiction in cancellation proceedings, particularly where the government sought to cancel naturalization certificates as "illegally procured" based solely on its disagreement with a court's interpretation of the law. Some courts held that an appeal from a judgment granting a naturalization certificate was the only recourse for such errors of law, while other courts found that a naturalization certificate could be canceled at any time regardless of whether the action was based on factual or legal error as long as the applicant had been ineligible for naturalization when the certificate was granted.[83] Although the United States Supreme Court never considered whether a naturalization certificate based on an erroneous racial classification was "illegally procured" under the act, after the Court held that high caste Hindus were racially ineligible for naturalization in 1923 some federal courts granted government requests to cancel naturalization certificates that had been previously granted to applicants from the Indian subcontinent.[84] These cancellation proceedings are discussed in chapter 2.

As a result of the rights and duties given to the new Bureau of Naturalization, the bureau and its lawyers in the Department of Justice assumed a leading role in interpreting the racial eligibility provisions of the naturalization act. In fact, the government's role became so important after the Bureau of Naturalization was created that if the government did not oppose a naturalization on racial grounds its silence became a basis for holding that the applicant was racially eligible for naturalization by default. In a 1910 judicial opinion, for example, Judge Francis Lowell of the United States District Court for the District of Massachusetts wrote that the court routinely granted applications that were not opposed by the government:

> Where the attorney attends at the hearing, and in behalf of the United States examines the petitioner and his witnesses with the freedom permitted in cross-examination; where the right to offer additional evidence is fully recognized, being often exercised in like case—the court is ordinarily justified in restricting its function to a decision as between litigants . . . After a hearing conducted as above described, the court will ordinarily admit [the applicant] to citizenship in the absence of declared opposition by the United States.[85]

As Lowell's comment reflects, the bureau's role fundamentally changed the institutional practices of the courts surrounding the racial eligibility provisions of the naturalization act.

The bureau's influence on the interpretation of the racial eligibility provisions of the naturalization act was consistent with the political branch of government to which it belonged. Soon after the bureau was formed, Chief of Naturalization Richard Campbell became the target of criticism from the secretary of commerce and labor, other government agencies within the political branch, and the public when he questioned whether "Turks, peoples of the Barbary states and Egypt, Persians, Syrians, and 'other Asiatics'" were racially eligible for naturalization. His comments regarding Turks, Syrians, and other groups within the Ottoman Empire raised particular concerns. Almost immediately, the Ottoman chargé d'affaires published an open letter in the *Washington Post* objecting to Campbell's interpretation,[86] the State Department objected to the interpretation,[87] and the Department of Justice instructed its attorneys to "take no further proceedings with respect to naturalization until the department has had an opportunity to give the subject proper study."[88] The State Department's influence on racial eligibility discourse can be seen in other instances as well. During legislative debates regarding the Asiatic Barred Zone restriction in the Immigration Act of 1917, for example, United States Senator Henry Cabot Lodge noted in reference to the racial eligibility provisions of the naturalization act that the State Department had asked, "in the interest of foreign relations," that Congress avoid naming specific racial groups for exclusion.[89]

When Secretary of Commerce and Labor Charles Nagel learned of Campbell's statement, he immediately admonished Campbell for misstating the bureau's position. In a November 11, 1909, letter, Nagel reminded Campbell of the bureau's policy of leaving the interpretation of the racial eligibility provisions of the naturalization act to the courts and that the bureau "may be considered to have complied with its duty when it has placed the court in possession of facts."[90] This policy was later confirmed in a memorandum from Campbell to the naturalization examiners throughout the country in which he advised them with regard to "the doubt heretofore expressed by this office in regard to whether Asiatics, so-called, may be naturalized," that they should limit themselves to seeing that

> the race or nationality of the petitioner is made known to the court, either on the record or at the hearing, and to advise the court of the existence of any prior judicial decisions in the premises. The proper interpretation of the statute . . . is a matter which rests with the courts, and it is no part of the business of this Department to endeavor to secure any particular interpretation. It is desired, therefore, that, having apprised the court of the facts in any particular case, you should refrain from urging the adoption of one construction or the other.[91]

References to the government's arguments in the published judicial opinions in racial eligibility cases often reflected this policy.[92]

Despite this policy, however, the bureau also exploited the racial eligibility provisions of the naturalization act as a discretionary basis on which to achieve its political objectives. In a November 9, 1909, letter to Chief Campbell, for example, Secretary Nagel remarked that

> we want to avoid unnecessary agitation and embarrassment to any people who have been admitted to this country, and especially ought we to be concerned more with the present reputation than with the original nativity of the applicant.[93]

While this remark could have referred to the perceived assimilability of an applicant's race, Nagel made a similar remark in his reply to a complaint from a member of the public regarding Campbell's interpretation of the racial eligibility provisions of the naturalization act by assuring the complainant that "I took steps some weeks ago looking to a discontinuance of any aggressive measures on [Campbell's] part" and "plainly speaking, we are more concerned with the general character of the immediate applicant than we are with his nativity."[94] The latter remark appears to have referred to assessing the character of individual applicants when determining whether to oppose their racial eligibility for naturalization. This practice is apparent, for example, in the bureau's decision to oppose the racial eligibility for naturalization of Indian independence activists whose political activities concerned the British government, which is discussed in chapter 2.

In order to understand the bureau's influence on racial eligibility discourse, it is important to first understand how early courts interpreted the phrase *free white person* in the naturalization act. The most foundational issue that faced early courts was whether the phrase *free white person* was intended as an inclusive or exclusive phrase. Many courts concluded that the phrase *free white person* was simply intended as a "catch-all" for all but those designated for exclusion, such as Africans and American Indians. In 1909, for example, Judge Francis Lowell wrote in an opinion explaining the naturalization of four Armenian applicants that the usage of the American colonies and of the United States in early census classifications and laws requiring segregation in public schools and transportation indicated that the word *white* was only used "to designate persons not otherwise classified," including Africans and American Indians as well as "French neutrals" who were classified separately from "whites" in the 1768 provincial census of Massachusetts. Because in the 1790 census "everybody but a Negro or an Indian was classed as a white person," and this had also been the practice in federal courts, Lowell concluded that Asians were "white" by virtue of the fact that they were not African or American Indian.[95] Other courts and litigants reached the same conclusion until it was rejected by the United States Supreme Court in 1922, when the Court wrote that to say that the phrase *free white person* was intended to exclude only Africans and American Indians ignored the affirmative form of the act: "The provision is not that Negroes and Indians shall be excluded but it is, in effect, that only free white persons shall be included."[96]

In addition to determining whether the phrase *free white person* was an inclusive or exclusive phrase, courts struggled to identify specific criteria by which to racially classify applicants. Because the naturalization act used the color terminology of *white* rather than geographical terms such as *European*, ethnological terms such as *Caucasian*, or philological terms such as *Aryan*, many courts and litigants debated the use of appearance, complexion, or skin color as criteria of racial classification. Some also referred to appearance, complexion, or skin color without explicitly addressing its relevance to racial classification. In a case involving a Hawaiian native's application for naturalization, for example, the Utah Supreme Court described him as "in appearance . . . of Malayan or Mongolian complexion, a shade lighter than the average of his race," but the court then relied on ethnological authorities to conclude that the applicant was not "white" because he was not classified as Caucasian by ethnologists.[97] In a naturalization proceeding in the United States District Court for the Southern District of Georgia involving an Afghan man born in Calcutta, India, the judge not only referenced skin color but even compelled the applicant to submit to a physical inspection during the proceedings:

> The applicant's complexion is dark, [but] on being called to pull up the sleeves of his coat and shirt, the skin of his arm where it had been protected from the sun and weather by his clothing was found to be several shades lighter than that of his face and hands, and was sufficiently transparent for the blue color of the veins to show very clearly.[98]

In his United States Supreme Court brief in *Ozawa*, Takao Ozawa argued that "it is a common observation that the women of the Kyoto region in Japan, particularly the higher class, are white, not darker than many of the women of this country,"[99] and even in one of the latest cases to consider racial eligibility for naturalization the Immigration and Naturalization Service attempted to introduce comparative photographs of Tatar and Kalmyk immigrants from the Soviet Union to prove that Kalmyks were "more oriental than European" and therefore not "white" for purposes of naturalization.[100]

Despite such appeals to appearance, complexion, or skin color in many of the cases, however, nearly all courts rejected the "utter impracticability" of such criteria for racial classification.[101] In 1914, one federal judge noted that the idea that a court could determine an applicant's race by ocular inspection had been rejected by most courts, which had concluded that an applicant's racial classification was "not to be determined by the question whether or not upon ocular inspection he may in the opinion of the judge be actually white in color."[102] The United States Supreme Court similarly rejected the criterion of skin color due to its impracticability in *Ozawa* because it

> differs greatly among persons of the same race, even among Anglo-Saxons, ranging by imperceptible gradations from the fair blond to the swarthy brunette, the latter being darker than many of the lighter hued persons of the brown or yellow races. Hence to adopt the color test alone would result in a confused overlapping of races and a gradual merging of one into the other, without any practical line of separation.[103]

In 1951, the United States Board of Immigration Appeals wrote that "the test of eligibility for naturalization . . . has *never* been whether a particular person looks like a white person,"[104] and despite the presence of such criteria in the arguments of some racial eligibility cases, none of the published judicial opinions relied on appearance as a substantial basis for any racial classification.

Some courts cited the racial classifications of ethnologists and philologists, including Johann Friedrich Blumenbach, Franz Bopp, Daniel Brinton, George Buffon, Georges Cuvier, Thomas Huxley, Augustus Keane, Carl Linnaeus, and Max Müller, particularly the division between the Caucasian and Mongolian racial classifications and the earlier theory of an Aryan or Indo-European race that later became merged with the Caucasian racial classification.[105] Other courts made no reference to ethnology or philology, however, or rejected such authorities because they offered conflicting definitions of the Caucasian racial classification, because the First Congress was unlikely to have known of the classification, or because the "ordinary usage" rule of statutory interpretation requires that the words of a statute be interpreted according to their ordinary usage unless a technical definition is clearly indicated.[106] As the government argued before the court of appeals in *Thind*, "no more technical definition of the words 'white persons' could well be imagined than to adopt the terms of the ethnologists."[107] Although both of the applicants who argued their cases before the United States Supreme Court cited ethnological and philological authorities, the Court rejected them.[108] In *Ozawa*, the Court wrote that "it does not seem to us necessary . . . to follow counsel in their extensive researches" in the science of ethnology, and the Court interpreted the phrase *free white person* to include only those "popularly" known as Caucasian, a conclusion it reiterated in *Thind*, noting that the act did not contain the word *Caucasian* but the phrase *white person,* words "of common speech and not of scientific origin."[109] Accordingly, ethnological and philological racial classifications were at best controversial in early racial eligibility cases and rejected by the United States Supreme Court in the early 1920s.

In contrast to these criteria, the Bureau of Naturalization advanced a historical and geographical interpretation of the racial eligibility provisions of the naturalization act that flexibly supported the objectives of the political branch. In its briefs and arguments in the cases in which it intervened, the government claimed that the phrase *free white person* in the naturalization act referred neither to appearance nor to the racial classifications of ethnologists or philologists but to "Europeans and persons of European descent," a determination that the government claimed "cannot be wholly determined upon either geographical, philological, or ethnological lines," but "can only be determined in the light of history." The phrase included only those people who "from tradition, teaching, and environment, would be predisposed toward our form of government, and thus readily assimilate with the people of the United States."[110] According to the government, the phrase *free white person* simply constituted "a brief and convenient designation descriptive of the prevailing ideals, standards, and aspirations of the people of Europe."[111] This interpretation presented a particularly confusing relationship between historical and geographical dimensions of race. While the government denied that an applicant's birthplace was sufficient to define race, Department of Commerce and Labor documents reveal the government's conclusion that "any attempted distinction between the native races of India [e.g., between Hindus, Parsis, and Afghans] would be fanciful and unsound and lead to confusion,"[112] and more than once the government emphasized the birthplace of Syrian and Armenian applicants in the Ottoman Empire as proof that they were Asian and not "white." In some cases, courts even carefully reviewed the latitude and longitude of an applicant's birthplace to determine its geographical proximity to Europe.[113]

The government also placed particular emphasis on the fact that the word *free* in the phrase *free white person* limited the meaning of the phrase, indicating that the phrase was not designed simply to exclude slaves but referred to a type of civilization that included both Europe and its colonies:

> Western civilization, which now includes the Americas, is something more than European civilization; although the largest field of its operations was Europe. It is something more than the Aryan family; for the Semitic races—including the Phoenecian, Assyrian, Arabian, Chaldean, Aramaic and Hebrew—which are not Indo-European or Aryan, are not excluded from it. Indeed, our Western civilization began with the Semitic races in Egypt, extended to Assyria and Chaldea, passed thence into Crete and Greece, and finally found its dominating expression in the great Roman Empire, which was essentially a Mediterranean civilization. Thence it proceeded northward, into the forests of Gaul, and crossed the Channel into England.
>
> Western civilization may, therefore, include so much of the Near East as contributed to, and was assimilable, with the development of Western civilization of Greece and Rome. Language, literature, religion, government and races, both of the Aryan and of the Semitic roots, became blended into the European civilization of Rome, and were extended by the genius of Columbus to the Americas.[114]

Focusing as it does on historical enmities and alliances, this interpretation of the racial eligibility provisions of the naturalization act explicitly recognized race as the sort of "unstable and 'decentered' complex of social meanings constantly being transformed by political struggle" which Michael Omi and Howard Winant describe in their study of racial formation.[115]

By emphasizing the word *free* as a limitation on the phrase *white person,* the government claimed that the phrase *free white person* did not include all of those people included in the "white race," or all Aryans, Indo-Europeans, or Caucasians, but "only those peoples of the white race who, at the time of the formation of the government, lived in Europe and were inured to European governmental institutions."[116] In certain respects, this emphasis on the word *free* was consonant with colloquial uses of "white" to indicate autonomy or its dispensation in expressions such as *free, white, and twenty-one, you have behaved to me like a white man,* or, *I meant to act white by you,* which emerged in the United States during the latter half of the nineteenth and the early twentieth century.[117] Such expressions suggested the qualities that Orlando Patterson describes as "sovereignal freedom," or "the power to act as one pleases, regardless of the wishes of others . . . the power to restrict the freedom of others or to empower others with the capacity to do as they please with others beneath them."[118] Relying on this interpretation of the racial eligibility provisions of the naturalization act, for example, in one case United States attorneys argued that although a Syrian naturalization applicant was a "member of what is known as the white or Caucasian race" he was not a *free white person.*[119] The phrase *free white person* was both broader and narrower than the Aryan, Indo-European, or Caucasian racial classifications and could be determined only by examining the historical relationship of particular groups to Western civilization.

The extent to which this interpretation of the racial eligibility provisions of the naturalization act depended on a history of enmities and alliances is particularly reflected in the government's brief in the 1909 case of *United States v. Balsara* regarding whether a Parsi from Bombay, India, should be classified as a "free white person" for purposes of naturalization. To support its argument that Congress did not intend all Caucasians to be included within the phrase *free white persons,* the government cited the conflict between American merchants and pirates from the Barbary states whose inhabitants Johann Friedrich Blumenbach had classified as Caucasian. Noting that "it is a well known historical fact that pirates from the Barbary states had plundered for years prior to the nineteenth century, almost without hindrance, the shipping of the world," the government argued that if Congress had intended to make all Caucasians eligible for naturalization they must have included the "swarthy Algerian who had plundered our merchant vessels for years and with whom they were about to engage in a maritime war," a conclusion the government apparently found self-evidently unreasonable.[120] This argument echoed Justice Taney's references to the "threatened renewal of Indian hostilities" and the American colonists being "outraged by the English government" in *Dred Scott* and Judge Dickinson's reference to the alliance of the American colonists with French Huguenots during the Revolutionary War in *Singh*.[121] In all of these instances, it was the history of enmities and alliances between Europeans and certain racial groups that was advanced to determine whether they should be classified as "free white persons."

The government's interpretation of the racial eligibility provisions of the act is also reflected in its selection of cases in which to intervene and oppose applications on racial grounds. The government did not oppose Jewish, Arab, or Turkish naturalizations in any reported cases.[122] The reported cases indicate that the government primarily limited its opposition to the naturalizations of Asian Indian, Parsi, and Afghan applicants from the Indian subcontinent, Syrians and Armenians from the Ottoman Empire, and Chinese, Japanese, Koreans, Filipinos, and Pacific islanders from Asia and the Pacific Rim, but even in the cases in which the government chose to intervene, its motive was often unclear. In a November 18, 1909, response to a law firm's inquiry regarding Syrian racial eligibility for naturalization, for example, Secretary Nagel reported that he was aware of only three cases in which Syrians were denied naturalization and only two cases in which Turks were denied naturalization, and internal Department of Commerce and Labor documents reveal that the bureau chose not to pursue appeals in the cases.[123] In other words, while United States attorneys opposed Syrian naturalizations in a few cases, it is not clear that the Bureau of Naturalization ever sanctioned this position and there is evidence that the bureau accepted judicial decisions that favored Syrian naturalizations. The archival evidence suggests that the government often selected test cases in order to clarify the law in response to regionally conflicting judicial decisions, sometimes using "friendly" test cases designed to secure the racial eligibility of particular groups rather than their ineligibility. One example of this practice can be seen in the *Cartozian* case discussed in chapter 3.

In addition, the bureau frequently declined to object to the racial eligibility for naturalization of Asian soldiers who served in the United States military. After a 1918 act that granted an expedited path to citizenship for alien soldiers generated some controversy among the lower federal courts regarding whether Asian soldiers remained ineligible for naturalization under the racial eligibility provisions of the naturalization act, the bureau was initially conflicted on the question, but changed its position after Deputy Commissioner Raymond Crist wrote a memorandum arguing that the 1918 act was intended to include "any alien who could be prevailed upon during its greatest national crisis to enter the military or naval service of the United States" and that any other interpretation would "repudiate those upon whom the Nation has leaned and depended to sustain the fundamentals upon which its national life exists."[124] Following Crist's memorandum, the bureau continued to oppose Asian soldier naturalizations but largely deferred to the courts and stopped filing cancellation proceedings when courts granted naturalization certificates to Asian soldiers.[125] In a June 4, 1924, memorandum from Chief Naturalization Examiner Henry Hazard to Commissioner of Naturalization Raymond Crist, Hazard noted the bureau's continued practice of using its discretion "in reaching the conclusion that cancellation proceedings are not to be instituted in the cases of World War veterans on account of race."[126] Similarly, Hazard remarked in a May 24, 1924, memorandum to Crist that "this is peculiarly a time when the United States should be careful in maintaining friendly international relations."[127] The bureau's use of its discretion in this manner is also reflected in a list of Hindu veterans against whom the bureau chose not to file cancellation proceedings after *Thind*.[128] Under pressure from nativist groups, however, the bureau ultimately brought a test case to the United States Supreme Court regarding the scope of the 1918 act, and in *Toyota v. United States* (1925) the Court held that the act exempted only Filipino and Puerto Rican veterans from the racial eligibility provisions of the naturalization act, repudiating the Bureau of Naturalization's position.[129]

In Ian Haney López's study of the racial eligibility cases in *White by Law*, he attributes the emergence of what he calls the "common knowledge" interpretation of race in the racial eligibility cases of the early twentieth century to changes in immigrant demographics and anthropological thinking that emerged around the turn of the twentieth century. According to López, courts interpreting the racial eligibility provisions of the naturalization act only questioned racialist science when it contradicted popular beliefs about race.[130] It is important to recognize, however, not only that the ordinary usage rule of statutory interpretation cited by many of the courts in racial eligibility cases required that they reject scientific definitions of statutory terms unless such definitions were clearly indicated, but that the creation of the Bureau of Naturalization and its historical interpretation of race had a substantial impact on interpretations of the racial eligibility provisions of the naturalization act after 1906.

JAPANESE NATIONALISM IN *OZAWA*

The prominence of appeals to shared suffering, common enemies, and service in the United States military during wartime in racial eligibility discourse parallels other instances in American legal history in which race has signified relative sovereignty that is contingent on the position of minorities with regard to external threats and the alliances they inspire. Sumi Cho and Gil Gott argue that the inextricability of racial and legal history in the United States—particularly with regard to such foundational legal principles as plenary power, federalism, and separation of powers—indicates that race and sovereignty are mutually constitutive, that sovereignty "developed homologously with the structures of societal racial formation," and is therefore "utterly racial in origin and development."[131] Similarly, Falguni Sheth claims that race is instantiated through sovereign power and that the target of race is what she calls the "unruly," a "threat to the coherence of a polity" that "needs to be domesticated or at least managed in order for the state to maintain control of its population."[132] Indeed, the relationship between race and the construction of an enemy or "other" has been discussed by numerous theorists. The racial classifications made under the racial eligibility provisions of the naturalization act reflect the relationship between these elements. As discussed earlier in this chapter, the contingency of racial classifications on external threats can be seen not only on a policy level but in the construction and amplification of threats in the arguments of specific cases.

The construction and amplification of threats in racial eligibility discourse is particularly reflected in the relative grammatical transitivity attributed to the actions of the racial groups seeking naturalization and to those of external adversaries. Although such linguistic features are sometimes reflected in the written judicial opinions in the cases, a review of the opinions alone often elides the presence of these features in the briefs and trial transcripts as well as other important contextual information required to interpret the opinions. The most familiar definition of transitivity in a grammatical sense is the classification of transitive and intransitive verbs depending on whether verbs allow or take an object. In the clauses *pirates from the Barbary states had plundered . . . the shipping of the world* and *the swarthy Algerian . . . had plundered our merchant vessels* from the government's brief in *Balsara*, for example, the verb *plundered* is transitive because it allows or takes the object *shipping* in the first clause and *vessels* in the second.[133]

According to linguists, however, transitivity is a considerably more complex cross-linguistic property of language, and the presence of an object of the verb is only one component. More broadly, transitivity is a global property of an entire clause, such that "an activity is 'carried-over' or 'transferred'" from an agent to a target of the action. Thus, transitivity has traditionally required at least two participants and some element of effective action, but it is a relative and contextual quality of an action that is gradable on a scale of intensity rather than being either transitive or intransitive.

In one of the most widely cited studies of transitivity, Paul Hopper and Sandra Thompson propose ten components of transitivity that allow clauses to be gradable on a scale according to the intensity of the transfer of action from one participant to another. The first component is whether there are one or two participants involved, because transitivity is created by the transfer of action from one participant to another. Second, actions rather than states of being create greater transitivity because actions can be transferred from one participant to another but states cannot be. Third, completed actions are more transitive than those that are only in progress. Fourth, sudden or punctual actions are more transitive than those completed gradually or slowly. Fifth, deliberate actions are more transitive than accidental ones. Sixth, actions that are stated affirmatively create greater transitivity than those stated negatively. Seventh, actions stated as actually having occurred and corresponding with a real event, as opposed to merely threatened or hypothetical actions, are more transitive. Eighth, actions that are not only deliberate but also causally attributed to the agency of the actor are more transitive. Ninth, actions that have a greater effect on their target are more transitive. Finally, transitivity is proportionate to the distinctness of the target from the actor and from the target's background—when the participants are more individual or specific the transfer of action between them is more transitive.[134] In addition to the components proposed by Hopper and Thompson, several linguists have proposed that the relative affectedness of the actor and the target of an action creates transitivity rather than the effect on the target alone, so that the unaffectedness of the actor is also a component of transitivity.[135]

By way of example, despite the similarity of the clauses *pirates from the Barbary states had plundered . . . the shipping of the world* and *the swarthy Algerian . . . had plundered our merchant vessels*,[136] the latter clause is more transitive because the target, "our merchant vessels," is more distinct from the actor, "the swarthy Algerian," and from the target's background. "The swarthy Algerian" is more distinct than the actor of the first clause, "pirates from the Barbary states," because the former is individual, even if it is a personification of the same group, just as "our merchant vessels" is more distinct than the target of the first clause, "the shipping of the world," and the second clause thereby places the action of plundering into sharper relief and makes it more transitive. Perhaps, coming second, it served as an amplification both by repetition and increased transitivity of a point that had already been made. The transitivity of the action could also be diminished by stating it as incomplete or attenuated, perhaps by altering the verbal clause to *were plundering* or *were attempting to plunder* rather than *had plundered*, or by rendering the action less clearly deliberate and caused by the actor's agency, as in the clauses *hindered our shipping* or *interrupted our vessels*, or by reducing the effect of the action on the target, as in the clauses *sometimes plundered our merchant vessels* or *plundered some of our merchant vessels*. It is also important to note that the clause could be stated in the passive voice but still be highly transitive, so that the clause *our merchant vessels were plundered by the swarthy Algerian* would not diminish the transitivity of the action. It is not the active or passive voice that is most important, but the relationship between the actor, target, and transitive verb in a clause. In Justice Taney's description of those "outraged by the English government" in *Dred Scott*,[137] the clause is stated in the passive voice but describes a highly transitive act of the English government toward the American colonists.

In later chapters, I examine the transcendent effect created by foregrounding external threats on perceived racial difference in racial eligibility discourse. At crucial moments in which perceived racial differences were transcended in this discourse, individual speakers or writers attributed relatively high transitivity to the actions of external actors toward the United States and toward particular groups seeking racial eligibility for naturalization. These actors included the Japanese Empire, the Indian caste system, the Turks and other Muslim groups from the Ottoman Empire, and the Soviet Union. By attributing high transitivity to their actions, the threat they were perceived to pose to the United States and those seeking racial eligibility for naturalization was amplified, creating a powerful appeal to unify against a shared external threat. Before considering this strategy, however, it will be useful to examine negative examples of cases in which applicants attributed relatively high transitivity to the actions of their own racial group rather than to an external actor, beginning with *Ozawa*. I argue that when applicants attributed high transitivity to their own racial groups rather than to an external actor, they not only failed to invoke the unifying power of a shared external threat to transcend racial differences but amplified any threat they may have been perceived to pose.

A Japanese man who was born in Japan but had resided in the United States for twenty years at the time of his application for naturalization, Takao Ozawa presented the United States Supreme Court with its first occasion to interpret the racial eligibility provisions of the naturalization act in more than forty years of lower court opinions interpreting the provisions.[138] In 1914, Ozawa filed his application for naturalization in the United States District Court for the Territory of Hawaii. The government initially opposed Ozawa's application based on the claim that as a Japanese man he was racially ineligible for naturalization because the Japanese were not "free white persons." In Ozawa's district court brief, he explained that he had been "living like an American" during the past twenty years in the United States. He was a graduate of a Berkeley, California, high school and had been a student of the University of California at Berkeley before he moved to Honolulu after the San Francisco earthquake of 1906, he educated his children in American schools, he attended American churches, and he spoke English rather than Japanese in his home. He also claimed to have never reported his name, address, occupation, or other information to the Japanese consulate as required of Japanese subjects living abroad. His loyalty was to the United States, not to Japan, he claimed. Like the Bureau of Naturalization, Ozawa emphasized the importance of the limiting word *free* in the phrase *free white person* in the naturalization act. In contrast to the government, however, Ozawa claimed that the phrase *free white person* simply referred to the qualities of loyalty and industriousness that characterize good citizens rather than to any racial classification. Accordingly, he claimed that all civilized people, including the Japanese, were as eligible as Europeans for naturalized citizenship in the United States.[139]

Judge Sanford Dole rejected Ozawa's interpretation of the act and denied his application for naturalization, citing previous judicial precedent that had denied Japanese naturalizations and the ordinary usage rule of statutory interpretation, which suggested to Dole that the phrase *free white person* referred exclusively to the European colonists who had founded the United States. In his written opinion, Dole wrote that when the original naturalization act was passed there would have been less danger involved in incorporating into the body politic "those for which the colonists had made such sacrifices, and had incurred such risks" than there would be in incorporating "people who were more remote, not simply in their origin or in the tinting of their complexion, but in their ideals and standards."[140] After Ozawa appealed Dole's decision to the United States Court of Appeals for the Ninth Circuit, the Ninth Circuit certified the question of Japanese racial eligibility for naturalization to the United States Supreme Court through an infrequently used procedure by which appellate courts can request guidance from the Supreme Court on a legal question before deciding a case.[141] Although Ozawa filed his Supreme Court brief less than a month after World War I ended, the government did not file its brief until nearly four years later after the solicitor general requested a continuance for diplomatic reasons while the Paris Peace Conference was pending. As a result, Ozawa's appeal to the Supreme Court was not heard until after the Paris Peace Conference and other postwar negotiations regarding the League of Nations and territorial borders had been concluded.[142]

It is not surprising that the government's brief was delayed, because the case raised sensitive diplomatic issues that were at stake in the Paris Peace Conference. Shortly after the turn of the century, Japan's victory over Russia in the Russo-Japanese War had inspired an aggressive Japanese nationalism that many viewed as "the first real challenge to white world supremacy."[143] To capitalize on its victory, Japan sought to mobilize an alliance of Asian countries against the Western powers, sometimes referred to as "Pan-Mongolism," prompting a fear of Japan in the United States that particularly coalesced around the racial exclusion issue.[144] At the Paris Peace Conference, Japan undermined negotiations for the League of Nations by demanding that racial equality be recognized in the League Covenant. Throughout the negotiations, Japan maintained that the removal of racial discrimination was the single most important factor in securing world peace and that without it the League of Nations would be a "miserable contradiction." Japan submitted a draft proposal prohibiting the contracting parties from making any discrimination on account of race or nationality, which Japan insisted must be included in the preamble to the League Covenant.[145] A member of the Japanese Imperial Diet even warned the American and British delegations that there could be no League of Nations until racial discrimination was eliminated.[146]

Japan's racial equality proposal would have prohibited the Asian exclusion policies of immigration and naturalization laws in Great Britain and its former colonies in Australia, New Zealand, Canada, and the United States.[147] One

American delegate at the Paris Peace Conference wrote in his diary of his concern that the proposal would "allow Asiatics to repeal the Asiatic Exclusion Law of the United States," and Australians feared the same fate for their exclusionary administrative practices known as the White Australia Policy.[148] Initially, a majority of the League delegates voted in favor of Japan's proposal and none voted against it, but the British delegation lodged such strong opposition to it on behalf of Australia that President Woodrow Wilson took the unprecedented step as chair of the commission to unilaterally declare that a unanimous vote would be required to adopt the proposal.[149] The use of this unprecedented procedural move to defeat the proposal met with hostility in Japan, where the Osaka *Mainichi* warned of Wilson's "dangerous justice,"[150] and the defeat of the proposal left Japan bitter and hostile toward the Western powers, particularly the United States, throughout the interwar period.[151] The racial equality proposal and a domestic jurisdiction clause that raised the prospect that the council might declare immigration to be subject to the League's jurisdiction became critical in the decision of the United States not to join the League,[152] which some say inevitably led to the failure of interwar diplomacy and eventually to World War II.[153] The importance of the Asian exclusion policy in American immigration and naturalization law to the conflict in the Pacific theater during World War II is further discussed in chapter 5.

In many ways, Ozawa's stance in his naturalization case paralleled that of Japan toward the Western powers during the Paris Peace Conference and the interwar period. In his district court brief, Ozawa presciently argued that if the court held the Japanese to be racially ineligible for citizenship it would "only create bitter feeling in the minds of [the] Japanese against the United States," transforming a good friend into an "enemy." The final result, Ozawa claimed, would be "the greatest war between the European and Asiatic people." The final line of his brief was as much a warning as a plea: "For the safety and honor of the United States, I sincerely hope that the United States will treat [the] Japanese fairly."[154] The United States attorney found Ozawa's brief so threatening that he added a moral character objection to Ozawa's application for citizenship, stating that although Ozawa's character witnesses would have ordinarily been enough to establish his good character, "unfortunately for himself he filed a brief." Ozawa's brief, the United States attorney wrote,

> disclosed the fact that the petitioner is not morally a fit subject
> for naturalization for in that brief he threatens the United States

with the government of his own country Japan if he is not allowed to become a citizen of the United States . . . Under his own statement filed in this court, I challenge his right to be admitted as a citizen upon this question alone.[155]

Like the Osaka *Mainichi*'s warning of Wilson's "dangerous justice" at the Paris Peace Conference, Ozawa's response to the government's objection to his racial eligibility for naturalization expressed an aggressive Japanese nationalism.

The central theme of Ozawa's district and appellate court briefs was that the superiority of the Japanese people made them fit for citizenship and that they were therefore "free white persons" who were eligible for naturalization. In the briefs he filed in the United States Court of Appeals for the Ninth Circuit and in the the United States Supreme Court, Ozawa continued to maintain that the phrase *free white person* simply referred to the qualities that characterized good citizens rather than to any racial classification and that the Japanese were eligible because they were "a superior people, fit for citizenship."[156] He argued that the Japanese adhered to Western ideals of honor, duty, patriotism, family life, and religion better than Europeans, and that the Japanese in Hawaii owned more businesses and had lower crime rates than the European residents. "In art and literature," Ozawa's appellate briefs claimed, "the criticism of the Japanese today is of the abandonment of their ideals, and too easy adaptation of western methods."[157]

Although Ozawa claimed that the phrase *free white person* did not refer to a racial classification, he alternatively argued that ethnologically the Japanese also belonged to the "white" racial division, "speaking an Aryan tongue and having Caucasian root stocks." According to Ozawa's briefs, the Japanese descended from Caucasian ancestors who originated in the Mediterranean and migrated east through the Indian Ocean and the Pacific to Polynesia and Japan. They were related to the Polynesians, Hawaiians, and Ainu, an indigenous group of Japan and Russia whom ethnologists almost unanimously classified as Caucasian. Ozawa supported these claims regarding Japanese racial origins with a substantial list of citations to the *Encyclopedia Britannica*, ethnological, linguistic, and travel authorities, archaeological evidence of commonalities between dolmen mounds in Japan and Europe, and evidence that the ancient Japanese *mitsudomoe* symbol—a sort of three-sided "yin yang" symbol commonly found in Japan—originated in the Mediterranean, where it was found "on the spindle weights of Troy."[158]

In addition, Ozawa introduced a peculiar maritime race theory to support his claim of Japanese superiority, claiming that "the dominant races of man are maritime" and that "to make a great maritime people requires a high proportion of broken coast line to the area of the country, and preferably islands running north and south with a variety of climate," like Japan. He noted that the Japanese were commonly called "The Yankees of the Orient" and he heralded their "mental alertness," which he claimed was more European than Asian. Quoting at length from travel writer George Kennan, he described how beginning in the seventeenth century the Japanese were "the most daring and adventurous navigators in all the Far East, "hardy and expert sailors" with "a natural intrepidity," whose ships sailed to Siberia as early as the sixth century to invade Manchuria. Premised on the conclusion that the phrase *free white person* in the naturalization act signified a racial superiority evidenced by military prowess and colonial domination, these and related arguments foregrounded the imperial power of the Japanese.[159]

In connection with this appeal to Japanese imperial power, Ozawa's briefs also claimed that the colonial power of Japanese mariners was superior to that of Europeans. He claimed, for example, that in 1594, "twenty-six years before our Pilgrim Fathers landed on the coast of Massachusetts, the Japanese had a regular line of merchant ships running to Luzon, Macao, Annam, Tonquin, Cambodia, Malacca, and India," and that

> long before the Mayflower sailed from Plymouth [the Japanese] had settlements, or colonies, in countries that are farther away from Japan than Massachusetts is from England. They took possession of the Luchu Islands, overran Formosa, helped the Spanish Governor of the Philippines to put down a revolt of the Chinese in Luzon, gained a strong foothold in Siam, and, fighting there in defense of the King, defeated invading forces of both Spaniards and Portuguese. Everywhere they were regarded as dangerous enemies, and in the library of Manila there is still in existence a copy of a letter written by a Spanish friar to his home government in 1592, warning the authorities of Spain that the Japanese were "a very formidable people."

Ozawa's Supreme Court brief added that in the Middle Ages the Japanese "would have regarded our invasion of Cuba with a force of 16,000 men as a very trivial affair," having transported 200,000 men to Korea.[160] As these passages reflect, Ozawa not only promoted Japanese maritime competence but their reputation as "dangerous enemies" to prove that they were racially eligible for naturalization in the United States. In addition, Ozawa often attributed relatively high transitivity to Japanese actions, such as his claim that the Japanese "took possession of the Luchu Islands," "overran Formosa," "gained a strong foothold in Siam," and "defeated invading forces." Given the widespread fear of Japanese imperialism and invasion that circulated among exclusionists at the time,[161] Ozawa's emphasis on Japan's imperial conquests was more likely to have amplified than diminished such fear.

One of the objections to Japanese immigration at the time was that that they were not "assimilable" with Western civilization, sometimes including the claim that they did not even want to assimilate. During testimony regarding the Immigration Act of 1924, one exclusionist claimed that "of all races ineligible to citizenship, the Japanese are the least assimilable and the most dangerous to this country."[162] In Ozawa's Supreme Court brief, he responded to the objection to Japanese assimilability by using the transitive verb *assimilate* with regard to the Japanese in the actor's role, arguing that "we could hardly require the Japanese to *assimilate* our manners, for their manners, particularly of the women, are far superior to our own." Citing an educator familiar with Japanese history and culture, Ozawa also claimed that "since the Japanese have become a settled people, . . . they have been *assimilating* everything they were shown from other nations," having "borrowed from China and Korea letters, literature and the art of porcelain making" and "improved by their peculiar genius on everything they borrowed." Japanese contact with Western people had similarly enabled them "to *assimilate* science, industries, commerce, and politics with a rapidity that no other nation has ever shown."[163] The word *assimilate* in these examples is relatively transitive, describing volitional actions that involved two reasonably distinct participants, and transitivity is further attributed to the action by the similarly transitive verbs *borrowed* and *improved*. The use of "assimilate" in these passages is substantially different from the relatively intransitive description of immigrants as *assimilable,* which refers to the capacity of a person to be transformed by a culture rather than to absorb or transform it.[164] Although Ozawa's use of the verb *assimilate* had an indefinite conclusion and affected the actor in a manner similar to consumption verbs such as *eat,*[165] it was significantly more transitive than the adjective *assimilable* and followed the pattern in Ozawa's briefs of attributing relatively high transitivity to Japanese actions.

In response to Ozawa's brief, the government claimed that the provision extending racial eligibility for naturalization to "free white persons" was intended to include only the European colonists "who fought the Revolutionary War" and their descendants. In this argument, the government echoed Justice Taney's reference to the American colonists being "outraged by the English government" in *Dred Scott* and Judge Dickinson's reference to the alliance of American colonists with French Huguenots during the Revolutionary War in *Singh*.[166] It was unlikely that the First Congress had ever seen people of the Far East, the government claimed, because the region was remote and inaccessible, Asians "having manners, customs and language which seemed strange, unwilling to mingle with western people," and Japan itself having a "policy of isolation." The government also rejected the contention that the Japanese had ever been classified as "white persons" and cited ethnological authorities that classified them as Mongolian.[167] At the same time, however, the government claimed that it was "not important to the present purpose to settle accurately all these interesting questions" of ethnology, but it was "enough that there remains undisturbed the legal and popular conception that the Japanese are not white persons within the meaning of the naturalization laws."[168]

Although the government's brief did not explicitly invoke the imaginary of dangerous Mongolian invaders beyond citing ethnological authorities that had classified the Japanese as Mongolian, the California attorney general filed a brief on behalf of the State of California as amicus curiae that did explicitly invoke fears of Mongolian invasion. The State of California's brief described the agricultural development of the Western states as a "clashing of races . . . competing with each other for their very existence," in which "the racial type is of supreme moment," warning that "the American farm home life as America has known it" would cease to exist if it were placed in competition with "Oriental farmers." The State of California also cited the "earth hunger" of the Japanese and their "craving for expansion and desire to leave the shores of their own overcrowded land, and come to the hospitable lands and climate of our western states."[169] In addition to the invasion fiction discussed earlier in this chapter, American propaganda during World War I had reinforced the imaginary of dangerous Mongolian invaders by framing the Germans as Huns based on their perceived military expansionism,[170] and shortly after the war Lothrop Stoddard had written in *The Rising Tide of Color Against White World Supremacy* that the Mongolian "beats restlessly against the white world's race-frontiers" and that racial expansion was "the key-note of Japanese foreign policy."[171] The State of California drew upon such fears by referring to the "earth hunger" of the Japanese and depicting agricultural competition between Japanese immigrants and European Americans in California as an existential "clashing of races."

In the Supreme Court's opinion in *Ozawa*, Justice George Sutherland wrote on behalf of a unanimous Court that the parties had discussed the meaning of the words *white person* in the naturalization act "with ability and at length, both from the standpoint of judicial decision and from that of the science of ethnology," but that the Court did not find it necessary "to follow counsel in their extensive researches in these fields." Instead, Sutherland wrote, it was enough to note that the words indicated a racial rather than an individual test and that the federal and state courts had almost uniformly held that they "were meant to indicate only a person of what is *popularly* known as the Caucasian race." The Court's opinion expressly approved of a series of lower court opinions involving Japanese, high caste Hindu, and Syrian applicants in which the courts had interpreted the racial eligibility provisions of the naturalization act in accordance with the ordinary usage rule of statutory interpretation rather than by reference to ethnological definitions of race, and the opinion noted that "we see no reason to differ" with "the conclusion reached in these several decisions." According to Sutherland, the conclusion of the lower courts that the Japanese were not "free white persons" for purposes of naturalization had "become so well established by judicial and executive concurrence and legislative acquiescence that we should not at this late day feel at liberty to disturb it in the absence of reasons far more cogent than any that have been suggested."[172] Because the majority of published judicial opinions involving the question had decided that the Japanese were not "free white persons" and the Court found "no reported case definitely to the contrary," it simply upheld existing lower court precedent. The Court specifically declined to review the ethnological authorities that the lower courts had relied on to racially classify the Japanese or the ethnological authorities that Ozawa and the government had cited in their briefs.[173] By declining to even consider ethnological evidence of racial classifications, the Court effectively repudiated it as a basis for interpreting the racial eligibility provisions of the naturalization act.

THE CONSTRUCTION OF ENEMIES AND RACIAL TERRITORIALITY

The relationship between out-group threats and in-group cooperation has been the subject of numerous studies of intergroup conflict by social and evolutionary psychologists, sociologists, anthropologists, and others. When William Sumner coined the terms *in-group* and *out-group* in the early twentieth century, he observed that "the relation of comradeship and peace in the we-group and that of hostility and war towards others-groups correspond to each other," because "the exigencies of war with outsiders are what makes peace inside, lest internal discord should weaken the we-group for war."[174] The impulse to transcend internal differences is intensified in times of crisis, particularly when confronted with threats from an external group. Based on Sumner's conclusions, social scientists later developed a model of intergroup conflict known as "realistic" group conflict theory, which claims that conflict is caused by the actual or perceived existence of conflicting goals or competition over limited resources or power and is reduced by the existence of superordinate goals, defined as "goals which are compelling for members of two or more groups and cannot be ignored but which cannot be achieved by the efforts and resources of one group alone."[175]

According to realistic group conflict theory, superordinate goals are necessary to induce members of an in-group to reformulate their views of the out-group so that "information about the out-group—ignored, rejected, or distorted before—will be viewed in a new, more positive light."[176] This has important implications for group identity formation. As Muzafer Sherif and Carolyn Sherif write, until a superordinate goal is introduced,

> attempts to disseminate correct information, conferences of leaders, exhortations to take every man for what he is rather than seeing him through the darkening influence of negative images or stereotypes, and intergroup contacts on pleasant occasions prove to be rather futile.[177]

One particularly compelling superordinate goal is the shared threat posed by an external enemy.

Similarly, those who write about their experiences on the front lines of wars often reflect on the powerful solidarity that arises between individuals who have been under fire together in war.[178] As veteran war correspondent Chris Hedges writes, "The communal march against an enemy generates a warm, unfamiliar bond with our neighbors, our community, our nation, wiping out unsettling undercurrents of alienation and dislocation," and "reduces and at times erases the anxieties of individual consciousness."[179] As Hedges explains the close bond felt by fellow soldiers in war,

> The closeness of a unit, and even as a reporter one enters into
> that fraternity once you have been together under fire, is possible
> only with the wolf of death banging at the door. The feeling
> is genuine, but without the threat of violence and death it cannot
> be sustained.[180]

The feelings of those who share fear and suffering in war are frequently
expressed in the strongest terms, noting that the solidarity they experienced
in war "allowed them to love men and women they hardly knew, indeed,
whom they may not have liked before the war,"[181] and led them to believe
they had a more complete communion with their comrades in arms than with
their lovers. This transcendent experience can also be the subject of an idyllic
longing when war ends,[182] as reflected in the title of British journalist Anthony
Lloyd's memoir about the Bosnian war, *My War Gone By, I Miss It So.*[183]

Other commentators on intergroup conflict have noted the important
stakes of establishing who initiates a conflict. As Robert Ivie writes, for
example, American justifications for war typically depict an enemy's behavior
as "voluntary" and "initial" while depicting America's response as "involuntary" and "defensive."[184] According to psychologist Lawrence LeShan, both
sides in a war tend to view the conflict as having been started by the other,
who acts as the aggressor, and to view themselves by contrast as acting out
of self-defense,[185] and Elias Canetti writes that

> it is the first death which infects everyone with the feeling
> of being threatened. It is impossible to overrate the part played
> by the first dead man in the kindling of wars . . . It need not
> be anyone of particular importance, and can even be someone
> quite unknown. Nothing matters except his death; and it must
> be believed that the enemy is responsible for this. Every possi-
> ble cause of his death is suppressed except one: his membership
> of the group to which one belongs oneself.[186]

To reformulate these observations from a linguistic standpoint, one may
say that those involved in a conflict will typically attempt to attribute relatively high transitivity to the actions of an external adversary and relatively
low transitivity to their own actions.

In Lucy Salyer's study of the racial eligibility cases involving Asian veterans of the United States military following World War I, she argues that the

martial citizenship ideal promoted by the government as an Americanizing effort during World War I outlasted the war and undermined the assumptions of racial nativism.[187] As a result, the story of Asian veterans and the dilemma they posed for courts interpreting the racial eligibility provisions of the naturalization act reveals that "racialist definitions of citizenship . . . could be dislodged when other ideals of citizenship—in particular, the warrior ideal—better served strategic and ideological needs."[188] Similarly, Rogers Smith notes that the major transformations in American citizenship toward liberal democratic ideals of inclusiveness have come during periods when the nation fought wars against adversaries hostile to such ideals, and only when such wars made egalitarian principles advantageous did Americans extend citizenship rights to minorities and women. Many historians have also noted the capacity of military service to transform suspect racial and ethnic groups into loyal Americans,[189] much as Matthew Frye Jacobson claims that Pacific expansion and the depiction of Pacific natives as dangerous "savages" dissolved the racial divisions among European immigrants.[190]

Consistent with the observation that inclusive ideals of citizenship have mostly succeeded during periods of war, Derrick Bell's interest convergence thesis predicts that "the interest of blacks in achieving racial equality will be accommodated only when it converges with the interest of whites." According to Bell, constitutional protection cannot be determined in race cases by "the character of harm suffered by blacks or the quantum of liability proved against whites," but instead such protection reflects "the outward manifestations of unspoken and perhaps subconscious judicial conclusions that the remedies, if granted, will secure, advance, or at least not harm societal interests deemed important by middle and upper class whites." The argument that racially segregated schools were inferior only succeeded in the Court's decision in *Brown v. Board of Education* (1954), for example, because the decision provided "immediate credibility to America's struggle with Communist countries to win the hearts and minds of emerging third world peoples" and offered assurance to American blacks that "the precepts of equality and freedom so heralded during World War II might yet be given meaning at home."[191] Others have expanded on Bell's thesis in studies of how civil rights reforms were influenced by Cold War foreign policy goals.[192] There is also a rhetorical dimension to Bell's interest convergence thesis, however, in that whether and how someone is racially classified frequently depends on how interests are framed. Interest convergence is not simply a fact that can be determined by empirical observation, but is a function of discursive practices.

The role of shared external threats in the relationship between race and citizenship in the United States during the nineteenth century particularly emphasizes a concern for territorial sovereignty with considerable importance for the construction of migrant identities. This concern for territorial sovereignty can be seen in the relationship between the Asian exclusion policy of the United States and the Mongolian racial division which emerged out of a desire to control and manage Russia's border with China based on an imaginary of dangerous Mongol invaders overwhelming Western territories with historical analogues in the Sack of Rome by Goth and Hun invaders. This imaginary functioned to construct the border of Western civilization that the Bureau of Naturalization adopted as a criterion for interpreting the meaning of the phrase *free white person* in the naturalization act alongside evidence of the geographical nativity of various goups. In addition to American Indians and Pacific islanders, Mongolians formed the chief threat amplified in racial eligibility discourse during the nineteenth century. All of these groups represented threats to the territorial sovereignty of the United States in the American imagination of the time.

Drawing on Henri Lefebvre's conclusion that space is both socially and materially produced, Elise Boddie argues that race is not only a characteristic of individuals but "places can also have a racial identity and meaning based on socially ingrained racial biases regarding the people who inhabit, frequent, or are associated with particular places and racialized cultural norms of spatial belonging and exclusion." One consequence of this conclusion, Boddie claims, is a distinctive form of discrimination she calls "racial territoriality," which occurs "when the state excludes people of color from—or marginalizes them within—racialized white spaces that have a racially exclusive history, practice, and/or reputation."[193] Similarly, in Cheryl Harris's description of how whiteness evolved into a form of property protected by American law she argues that whiteness and property "share a common premise—a conceptual nucleus—of a right to exclude." According to Harris, whiteness "increased the possibility of controlling critical aspects of one's life rather than being the object of others' domination."[194] Neither Boddie's nor Harris's formulation examines the contingencies of racial formation, however, nor the role of territoriality in the process. The relationship between race and territoriality is also suggested by Sumi Cho and Gil Gott's claim that sovereignty "developed homologously with the structures of societal racial formation"[195] and by Falguni Sheth's claim that race is instantiated through sovereign power and the management of those perceived as "unruly" or threatening to the coherence of a polity.[196] Similarly, Lefebvre defines sovereignty as a space produced by violence, in that "sovereignty implies 'space,' and what is more it implies a space against which violence, whether latent or overt, is directed—a space established and constituted by violence."[197]

The rhetorical strategy of transcending perceived racial differences in the face of a shared external threat appears frequently in racial eligibility discourse, rendering the racial classifications in racial eligibility cases inseparable from the geopolitical position of the nation in the nineteenth and early twentieth century. Whether an applicant was determined to be "inured to European governmental institutions," "predisposed toward our form of government," or to share "the prevailing ideals, standards, and aspirations" of Western civilization in the Bureau of Naturalization's historical interpretation of the racial eligibility provisions of the naturalization act often depended on whether they were framed as a target of the nation's enemies.[198] Like applicants for political asylum required to demonstrate a "well-founded fear of persecution," the applicants in racial eligibility cases were most successful when the agentive potency of the nation's enemies was foregrounded rather than their own.[199] As the chapters that follow will show, in a series of racial eligibility cases after World War I this rhetorical strategy even foreshadowed the development of political asylum law.

2

THE GHADR PARTY AND
THE INDIAN CASTE SYSTEM IN *THIND*

On November 11, 1937, the sixth grade class of Herman Klix Elementary School of Mt. Clemens, Michigan, sent the following letter to United States Secretary of State Cordell Hull:

> Dear Sir,
>
> We have been studying about India, and we would like to know if a native of India could become a citizen of the United States. We would especially like to know about untouchables.
>
> Sincerely yours,
>
> The Sixth Grade[1]

More than a decade before the children sent this letter, the United States Supreme Court issued its second opinion regarding the racial eligibility provisions of the naturalization act, addressing whether a "high-caste Hindu, of full Indian blood, born at Amrit Sar, Punjab, India," was a "free white person" within the meaning of the act. The children's letter received a typical bureaucratic response. The secretary of state forwarded it to the Department of Labor which oversaw the Bureau of Naturalization, and the chief naturalization examiner sent a reply addressed not to the children but to the principal of Herman Klix Elementary.[2] With regard to the racial eligibility of natives of India for citizenship, the examiner stated:

45

The principal law governing racial limitation of naturalization in this country is found in Section 2169 of the Revised Statutes of the United States which reads: "The provisions of this title (Naturalization) shall apply to aliens being free white persons, and to persons of African descent."

The Supreme Court of the United States decided in the case of the United States of America, appellant, v. Bhagat Singh Thind, that a high caste Hindu of full Indian blood, born in India, was not a white person within the meaning of Section 2169 of the Revised Statutes of the United States, and therefore, was not eligible to naturalization. A copy of the Court's decision in that case is attached.

The examiner declined to address the racial eligibility for naturalization of India's Dalits or untouchables—the casteless population of India traditionally associated with occupations considered ritually impure—stating only that their eligibility was outside "the province of the duties of this Service."[3]

From the copy of *Thind* that was attached to the examiner's letter, the children of Herman Klix Elementary could have learned that the Supreme Court reversed an order issued by Judge Charles Wolverton of the United States District Court for the District of Oregon granting Thind's naturalization consistent with other lower court decisions that had found Hindus to be "free white persons" for purposes of naturalization. While Justice George Sutherland, writing for the Supreme Court, found that high caste Hindus might have descended from Aryan ancestors who migrated from Central Asia to India in antiquity before moving west to Europe, he concluded that "it is not impossible, if that common ancestor could be materialized in the flesh, we should discover that he was himself sufficiently differentiated from both of his [Indian and European] descendants to preclude his racial classification with either."[4] The question of whether a high caste Hindu could become a citizen of the United States under the naturalization act was not, Sutherland wrote,

whether by the speculative processes of ethnological reasoning we may present a probability to the scientific mind that [Indians] have the same origin [as Europeans], but whether we can satisfy the common understanding that they are now the same or sufficiently the same to justify the interpreters of a statute—written in the words of common speech, for common understanding, by unscientific men—in classifying them together in the statutory category of white persons.[5]

Sutherland argued that the Aryans who invaded India in antiquity had intermarried with dark-skinned Dravidians, "destroying to a greater or less degree the purity of the 'Aryan' blood" to such an extent that contemporary Indians were "readily distinguishable from the various groups of persons in this country commonly recognized as white."[6] In reaching this conclusion, he largely relied on and reiterated the ordinary usage rule of statutory interpretation that he had applied to the racial eligibility provisions of the naturalization act in *Ozawa*.[7]

From Sutherland's opinion in *Thind*, the children of Herman Klix Elementary could also have learned the basic principle of racial segregation and exclusion that prevailed in the United States at the time. Sutherland invoked the "separate but equal" doctrine that was used to support racial segregation from *Plessy v. Ferguson* (1896) until the doctrine was rejected by a series of cases culminating in *Brown v. Board of Education* (1954), declaring at the conclusion of his opinion that "it is very far from our thought to suggest the slightest question of racial superiority or inferiority," but instead, "what we suggest is merely racial difference, and it is of such character and extent that the great body of our people instinctively recognize it and reject the thought of assimilation."[8] What cannot be discovered from Sutherland's opinion in *Thind*, however, is that the United States government opposed Thind's petition for naturalization under pressure from the British government based on Thind's membership in the Ghadr Party, an Indian independence movement based in San Francisco that promulgated the goal of inciting an armed rebellion against the British government in India.[9] During a speech Thind gave a decade after the Supreme Court issued its opinion in *Thind*, he directed his bitterness regarding the Court's decision in *Thind* as much at the British as at the American government, claiming that the United States "sided with perfidious Albion to insult India in the matter of citizenship."[10] Other Indians similarly viewed *Thind* as a political decision motivated by a desire to appease British fears of Indian independence activists,[11] and the parties' Supreme Court briefs cited competing British sources to support their positions regarding the racial classification of Indians. In addition, Sutherland's opinion evaded the fact that *Thind* effectively reversed the Court's own approval only three months earlier in *Ozawa* of lower court opinions holding that Hindus were racially eligible for naturalization.

As the Supreme Court's last statement on the racial eligibility provisions of the naturalization act, *Thind* has been the subject of substantial commentary and heralded as an important Asian American civil rights case, reflected in recent dramatic reenactments by the North American South Asian Bar Association in 2010, the Asian American Bar Association of New York in 2012, and the Los Angeles–based Asian American theater group and its Youth Arts Education program in 2016. This chapter considers previously neglected aspects of Thind's case through a rhetorical analysis of briefs, judicial opinions, National Archives documents, and British intelligence documents. I begin by demonstrating how *Thind* overruled a majority of lower courts which had held Indians to be racially eligible for naturalization, two of which the Court itself had approved in *Ozawa*, a reversal of the Court's own precedent unaddressed either by Sutherland's opinion or by previous studies of *Thind*. In an effort to account for this curious and sudden reversal, I consider Thind's political activities in furtherance of Indian independence and the efforts of British and American intelligence officials to oppose his naturalization on the basis of those activities, Thind's assertion of his high caste status as proof of whiteness and the government's citation of British authorities reflecting the negative associations of caste, and Sutherland's distortions of the arguments presented by the parties in a manner that suggests a political decision. I also contrast *Thind* with a proceeding filed to cancel the naturalization certificate of Sakharam Pandit immediately after *Thind*, in which Pandit reversed his relationship to the Indian caste system by framing himself as its victim, claiming that if he returned to India after having become an American citizen he would be an outcast, one of India's "untouchables," and a stateless person. I conclude by arguing that Pandit's rhetorical strategy formed part of a frequent appearance of appeals to unify against a shared external threat in racial eligibility discourse after World War I that drew on the newly emerging category of stateless persons, an incipient form of the "well-founded fear of persecution" standard of later political asylum law.

CONFLICTING INTERPRETATIONS OF OZAWA AND THIND

Although many naturalizations were granted to Japanese immigrants in the late nineteenth and early twentieth centuries without producing a written or published judicial opinion, before *Ozawa* federal and state courts had published seven opinions regarding Japanese racial eligibility for naturalization unanimously holding that the Japanese were not "free white persons" and were therefore racially ineligible for naturalization.[12] Judge Dole had therefore reached a decision in *Ozawa* that was consistent with the published judicial precedent at the time, and the case did not present the Supreme Court with a conflict among lower courts. In *Thind*, too, Judge Wolverton had followed the majority of published judicial opinions regarding the racial eligibility of Asian Indians for naturalization, but the lower courts were split on the question 2-to-1, with two courts holding them racially eligible for naturalization and one holding them ineligible.[13] As with the Japanese, however, many naturalizations were granted to Indian immigrants without producing a written or published judicial opinion. Following the same procedural course as *Ozawa*, after Judge Wolverton's decision in *Thind* was appealed to the United States Court of Appeals for the Ninth Circuit it certified the question to the Supreme Court of whether "a high-caste Hindu, of full Indian blood, born at Amritsar, Punjab, India," was a "free white person" within the meaning of the naturalization act. Like *Ozawa*, the Supreme Court's opinion in *Thind* was a unanimous opinion of the Court written by Justice Sutherland and was issued during the same term as *Ozawa*. The same justices did not hear both cases, however, because Justice William Day retired on November 12, 1922, the day the Court issued its opinion in *Ozawa*, and Justice Pierce Butler took his judicial oath on January 2, 1923, approximately a week before the Court heard oral arguments in *Thind*. Nonetheless, the cases were decided by a nearly identical Court during the same term.

In *Thind*, Sutherland reiterated *Ozawa*'s holding that the racial eligibility provisions of the naturalization act were governed by the ordinary usage rule of statutory interpretation, which dictates that the words of a statute are to be interpreted according to their ordinary usage—i.e., their "common" or "popular" meaning—unless a technical meaning is clearly indicated.[14] In response to *Thind*'s claim that he was a "free white person" because as a "high-caste Hindu, of full India blood" he shared a common Aryan ancestor with Europeans,[15] Sutherland explained that the words *free white person* in the naturalization act were "synonymous with the word 'Caucasian' only as that word is popularly understood." He stated that the statutory language was to be interpreted as "words of common speech and not of scientific origin . . . written in the common speech, for common understanding, by unscientific men,"[16] and he emphasized the fact that the act used the phrase *white person* rather than the word *Caucasian,* a word he concluded was probably unknown to the First Congress in 1790:

> When we employ [the word *Caucasian*] we do so as an aid to the ascertainment of the legislative intent and not as an invariable substitute for the statutory words. Indeed, as used in the science of ethnology, the connotation of the word is by no means clear and the use of it in its scientific sense as an equivalent for the words of the statute, other considerations aside, would simply mean the substitution of one perplexity for another. But in this country, during the last half century especially, the word by common usage has acquired a popular meaning, not clearly defined to be sure, but sufficiently so to enable us to say that its popular as distinguished from its scientific application is of appreciably narrower scope. It is in the popular sense of the word, therefore, that we employ it as an aid to the construction of the statute, for it would be obviously illogical to convert words of common speech used in a statute into words of scientific terminology when neither the latter nor the science for whose purposes they were coined was within the contemplation of the framers of the statute or of the people for whom it was framed.[17]

In support of this conclusion, Sutherland cited *Maillard v. Lawrence* (1853), which provided the following explanation of the ordinary usage rule of statutory interpretation:

> If language which is familiar to all classes and grades and occupations—language, the meaning of which is impressed upon all by the daily habits and necessities of all, may be wrested from its established and popular import in reference to the common concerns of life, there can be little stability or safety in the regulations of society.[18]

Although Sutherland elaborated on this rule in *Thind*, he also cited it in *Ozawa* as a basis for rejecting scientific definitions of race.[19]

A wide variety of scholars in fields as diverse as law, history, literary studies, cultural studies, and religious studies have nonetheless interpreted the Court's opinions in *Ozawa* and *Thind* to be founded on a contradictory logic that betrays a racial ideology predisposed to only view Europeans as "white." According to this interpretation of the Court's opinions, the Court first interpreted the word *white* as synonymous with the ethnological definition of Caucasian in *Ozawa*. When confronted in *Thind* with a non-European whom ethnologists classified as Caucasian, however, the Court qualified its holding in *Ozawa* and held that the word *white* should be interpreted as synonymous with Caucasian only in its "popular" sense. In Milton Konvitz's 1946 book *The Alien and the Asiatic in American Law*, for example, he states:

> In the *Ozawa* case the court said the test of membership is the Caucasian race. Thind showed he was a Caucasian. But now the court changed its position: the test is whether or not one is a "white person," and one may be a Caucasian (like Thind) and yet not a "white person."[20]

A similar formulation is found in Lon Fuller's 1969 book *The Morality of Law*, in which he writes that the Court became "entangled in its own interpretations" in *Ozawa* and *Thind* by first interpreting the word *white* to mean a person of the Caucasian race "in an attempt to achieve something like scientific exactitude" before claiming that the word should be interpreted only according to its popular sense when confronted with proof that high caste Hindus were Caucasian.[21] Roger Daniels and Harry Kitano make a similar argument in their 1970 book *American Racism*,[22] as does Paul Rundquist in his 1975 dissertation, arguing that the Court only interpreted the word *white* according to its popular sense in *Thind* after making a "false start" in *Ozawa*: "The Supreme Court established one standard, and when faced with an opportunity to apply it a short time later, denied that it had ever enacted the standard and abandoned it in favor of still another standard."[23] Many recent scholars offer similar interpretations, often following the version in Ian Haney López's 1996 book *White by Law*.[24]

It is certainly tempting to view the Court's opinions in *Ozawa* and *Thind* as products of the highly racist and xenophobic era of the 1920s. According to Thomas Gossett, racist theories achieved an importance and respectability in the 1920s that they had not had since the Civil War.[25] In *Plessy v. Ferguson* (1896), the Supreme Court claimed that "legislation is powerless to eradicate racial instinct, or to abolish distinctions based upon physical differences,"[26] and during the period surrounding World War I this belief in "racial instincts" and a fear of immigrants combined to create a particularly racist and xenophobic climate. In President Wilson's 1915 State of the Union address, for example, he warned that the greatest threats to the nation's security had been "uttered within our own borders" by citizens "born under other flags but welcomed under our generous naturalization laws,"[27] and the Bolshevik Revolution and the Red Scare that followed inflamed this tendency. During the period surrounding World War I, Americanization efforts perpetuated a racism that believed race could be discovered by "intuition,"[28] much like the Supreme Court's reference to "racial instincts" in *Plessy* or its reference to the "common understanding" of race in *Thind*.

In contrast to the interpretation of *Ozawa* and *Thind* as founded on a contradictory logic, however, other scholars have noted that this interpretation is belied by Sutherland's rejection of scientific definitions of race in favor of ordinary usage in *Ozawa*. As Mark Weiner writes in *Americans without Law*, for example, a significant number of the arguments in *Ozawa* "centered on issues addressed by anthropologists and other students of human variation and classification," which Sutherland ignored. According to Weiner, Sutherland "chose, that is, not to rely on social science or a scientific standard in determining who was and was not a white person."[29] As Dudley McGovern observed shortly after the Court issued its opinions in the cases, the only difference between them is that in *Thind* "the word *popularly* is italicized."[30] Previous scholars have also overlooked the fact that Sutherland's opinion in *Ozawa* expressly approved of two lower court cases that had held Indians to be racially eligible for naturalization. In *Ozawa*, Sutherland included *In re Mozumdar* and *In re Mohan Singh*, both holding that Indians were "free white persons" for purposes of naturalization, among a list of lower court opinions that had held that the phrase *free white persons* included "only a person of what is *popularly* known as the Caucasian race."[31] After listing these opinions in *Ozawa*, Sutherland expressly approved of them by stating that "we see no reason to differ" with their conclusions.[32] The Court also expressly approved of *In re Ellis*, a lower court case that had held a Syrian to be "white" for purposes of naturalization.[33] When Sutherland wrote three months later in *Thind* that "we are unable to agree with the District Court, or with other lower federal courts, in the conclusion that a native Hindu is eligible for naturalization,"[34] he neglected to identify the other opinions the Court disagreed with or why the Court itself expressly approved of two of them in *Ozawa*.

Although previous scholars have not addressed this contradiction, litigants and courts in later racial eligibility cases were quick to point it out. For example, in proceedings filed after *Thind* to cancel the naturalization certificates of Akhay Mozumdar and Mohan Singh—the applicants whose cases the Supreme Court had expressly approved of in *Ozawa*—both Mozumdar and Singh objected to their cancellations on the basis that the Court had expressly approved of the district court opinions that had granted their naturalizations.[35] In another case, when a Palestinian naturalization applicant argued that *Ozawa* had approved of *Ellis*—a case with circumstances indistinguishable from his own—the government responded that because the Court "withdrew" its approval of *Mozumdar* and *Singh* in *Thind* the district court should also "extend this withdrawal of approval to the *Ellis* case."[36] The Court's previous approval of *Mozumdar* and *Singh* in *Ozawa* precludes any conclusion that the Court was predisposed to classify Indians as racially ineligible for naturalization.

In contrast to Ian Haney López's claim in *White by Law* that the Supreme Court abandoned scientific definitions of race in *Thind* when "science failed to reinforce popular beliefs about racial difference,"[37] it is also important to consider how unstable popular beliefs were regarding the racial classification of Indians both historically and in the early twentieth century. Apparently following Johann Friedrich Blumenbach's *On the Natural Varieties of Mankind*, for example, the 1797 *Encyclopedia Britannica* defined the "white" racial classification to include "those of Asia on this side of the Oby, the Caspian, Mount Imaus, and the Ganges; likewise the natives of the north of Africa, of Greenland and the Esquimaux," demonstrating that during the same decade that the original naturalization act was passed the British publisher of the *Encyclopedia Britannica* considered the people of northern India, the Middle East, and North Africa to be included within the "white" race along with certain Inuit tribes of North America.[38] This racial classification of Indians also persisted into the late nineteenth century, as reflected in the geography textbooks used in American schools of the time, which included Indians in the "white," or Caucasian, racial classification.[39] It was also a commonplace in many circles in the United States during the early twentieth century that Indians were "white." During debates regarding a proposed amendment to the Asiatic Barred Zone in the Immigration Act of 1917 that would have excepted "white persons" living in certain geographical areas of exclusion, for example, some senators raised concerns that "Hindus claim . . . to be white persons of the Aryan race."[40] During a World War I trial of Indian and German defendants in federal court in San Francisco for conspiring to ship arms to India, Judge William Van Fleet even interrupted counsel who distinguished the German defendants as "the white skin defendants" in order to correct him by stating that "I think these defendants are all of the Caucasian race."[41]

Moreover, the vast majority of lower courts had found Indians to be "free white persons" for purposes of naturalization before *Thind*. In 1919, the United States District Court for the Southern District of California wrote:

> I am advised by counsel for petitioner herein, and his statement is not challenged by the Government, that Hindus have been admitted to citizenship in the Southern District of Georgia, the Southern District of New York, the Northern District of California and the Eastern District of Washington by the courts of the United States and by the Superior Court of California in both San Francisco and Los Angeles.[42]

In addition, a list produced to the United States Senate Committee on Immigration in 1926 indicates that sixty-seven Indians had been granted naturalizations since 1908.[43] Thus, *Thind* ignored rather than reinforced at least some popular beliefs about racial difference and overruled numerous lower court decisions finding Indians to be "free white persons" for purposes of naturalization.

This is not to suggest either that Indians did not face racial discrimination or that they were uniformly classified as "white" in European and American thought, but only that popular beliefs regarding their racial classification in the United States were far from uniform. From the time the British East India Company began to rule the Indian subcontinent in the late eighteenth century, Indians were reviled as "exceedingly depraved," one writer describing them as the most "degenerate, crafty, superstitious, litigious, and wicked a people, [of] any race of people in the known world," a description particularly aimed at the higher castes of India, and another writer analogizing their "great depravity" in contrast to Europeans to "the difference of the natural color of the two races."[44] Similarly, in the early nineteenth century French missionary Abbé Dubois wrote in his *Letters on the State of Christianity in India* that "Hindoos, and above all, a Brahmin . . . must be considered as a kind of moral monster" who is "immersed in . . . an abyss of darkness" with the aim of bringing other tribes "under their uncontrolled bondage."[45] In 1906, a feature article in the *Puget Sound American* invoked the imaginary of a "yellow peril" by describing "Hindu hordes invading the state" as a "dusky peril" that would "prove a worse menace to the working classes than the

'Yellow Peril' that has so long threatened the Pacific Coast,"[46] and a letter to the editor on the same page warned that most Indians "have been soldiers under the British government and are well versed in the use of fire-arms," with a "habit of running amuck, when annoyed, in which case a number of innocent people get butchered."[47] Indian philosophers who immigrated to the United States in the early twentieth century were also framed as a peril, as reflected in Elizabeth Reed's 1914 book *Hinduism in Europe and America*, in which Reed described Indian swamis, gossains, and gurus as "insidious emissaries of the East" who "creep into houses and lead captive silly ['white'] women" under their "hypnotic influence," leaving "many a desolated home" in their wake.[48] Such sources attributed relatively high transitivity to the actions of Indians, particularly those belonging to high castes, depicting them as dangerous.

Why did the Supreme Court reverse the majority of lower court opinions regarding the racial eligibility of Indians for naturalization in *Thind*, including two that the Court had expressly approved of during the same term in *Ozawa*? Why did Sutherland not address the fact that *Thind* withdrew the Court's approval of these opinions or the status of the other opinions that the Court approved of in *Ozawa*? In *Ozawa*, the Court largely deferred to the consistency of lower court precedent on Japanese racial eligibility for naturalization, so why did it not in *Thind*? The basis for the Court's decision in *Thind* was not a choice between the ordinary and scientific usage of racial classifications, as Sutherland argued in his opinion and previous scholars have claimed, but a disagreement about the ordinary usage of the word *white*. The word clearly included Indians in many Western circles, so why did Sutherland not address this disagreement or offer any evidence to support the Court's choice between inconsistent usages of the word? These questions, combined with *Thind*'s political activities as a founding member of the Ghadr Party, warrant revisiting the conclusion reached by many Indians that *Thind* was a political decision influenced by British pressure to restrict the activities of Indian independence activists who sought American citizenship in order to avoid arrest, deportation, and prosecution in India.[49] As already noted, Thind blamed the British rather than American authorities for the Court's decision, and in an article written from New York for India's *Modern Review*, the American-born wife of another Indian whose racial eligibility for naturalization had been challenged wrote that "it may be safely asserted that in the Thind case, the Supreme Court rendered a '*political decision*' at the request of the Government of the United States and *for other considerations involving foreign governments.*"[50] Although previous studies have considered the international dimension of Asian exclusion laws and the general significance of the Ghadr Party to Indian naturalizations in the United States, none have specifically considered the significance of Thind's political activities to his naturalization case.[51]

THIND THE GHADRITE

The arguments and evidence presented in *Thind* must be understood in the context of Thind's role as one of the foundational members of the Ghadr Party (the word *Ghadr* meaning "revolution" or "mutiny" in Hindi), an Indian independence movement based in San Francisco that advocated an armed revolution against the British government in India modeled on the American Revolution.[52] One writer describes the Ghadr Party as "an incongruous mixture of Sinn Fein, Marxian socialism, and the romantic nationalism of the Italian patriot, Mazzini."[53] Although the primary objective of the party was to secure India's independence from British rule, the party also framed itself as part of a global anti-imperialist struggle among revolutionaries in all of the former British colonies.[54] Thus, the party united in solidarity with revolutionary groups throughout the world who claimed to resist systems of imperial oppression.[55] The founding leader of the party, Har Dayal, who inspired Thind to join the party at the University of California at Berkeley, wrote favorably of the Bolshevik Revolution, and American intelligence documents reveal that federal authorities believed the Ghadrites might join the Bolshevists.[56]

Despite identifying himself as a "high-caste Hindu, of full Indian blood" in his naturalization case, Thind was a Sikh born in the Amritsar District of the Punjab, which was part of the Sikh Empire until the British imposed imperial control over the region in the nineteenth century.[57] After graduating from college in India, Thind traveled to the Philippines and immigrated to the United States in 1913.[58] He initially worked in the lumber mills of the Pacific Northwest, settling in Astoria, Oregon, but soon moved to San Francisco where he attended the University of California at Berkeley and became one of the founding members of the Ghadr Party.[59] He supported the party by giving speeches in support of Indian independence throughout the Pacific Northwest and was eventually appointed secretary general of the party in Oregon.[60] Although Thind's case was certified to the

Supreme Court on the question of his racial eligibility for naturalization, archival documents reveal that the government's motivation for opposing Thind's racial eligibility for naturalization was his participation in political activities for the Ghadr Party.[61] The government informed the district court of Thind's political activities and of British and American intelligence interest in the Ghadr Party that began when many of the party's leaders were prosecuted in federal court in San Francisco in what is known as the Hindu–German conspiracy trial for conspiring with the German government to ship arms to India to support an armed rebellion against the British government in India during World War I.[62]

The ideology of the Ghadr Party was in part the culmination of a political consciousness among Indian immigrants who considered the racial discrimination they faced in North America to be a necessary consequence of the fact that India remained a colony under British rule rather than a sovereign nation. If they secured independence for India, Indian immigrants believed, their status in North America would drastically improve. They often complained that the British refused to assist them in securing equal rights in North America while pressuring North American authorities to restrict their activities and oppose the naturalization of Indian independence activists such as Thind. As this belief about the relationship between British imperialism and their status in North America grew, Indian immigrants became increasingly committed to the cause of Indian independence as a means to establish their civil rights in North America and viewed their civil rights struggles in North America, including their struggle for racial eligibility for naturalization in the United States, as inseparable from their struggle for Indian independence.[63]

The attention of British and American intelligence officials was quickly drawn to the Ghadr Party's advocacy of violence against the British government in India. Intelligence documents reveal that both governments closely monitored the party's leadership, including Thind, whom British intelligence identified as "the soul of the revolutionary movement in Astoria," sent to Oregon "to preach sedition."[64] Thind supported the *Ghadr* journal by collecting subscriptions and mailing issues abroad, and he managed the journal while editor Ram Chandra was in prison for participating in the Hindu–German conspiracy.[65] Among the British government's earliest efforts to suppress the Ghadr Party's activities was to seek to have leaders of the party extradited from the United States to British jurisdictions where they could be prosecuted, imprisoned, or executed for sedition.[66] The British government similarly pressured the United States to deny the application for naturalization of Ghadr leader Taraknath Das on racial grounds.[67] This and similar cases reflect the Bureau of Naturalization's use of discretion to object to an applicant's racial eligibility for naturalization when it had concerns regarding his character.

In the summer of 1918, Thind applied for naturalization in Washington State and was initially granted a naturalization certificate, but less than a week later the decision was reversed after a Bureau of Naturalization examiner contested Thind's racial eligibility for naturalization.[68] The following spring, Thind filed a new application in Oregon and the Bureau of Naturalization again opposed his petition on racial grounds, but it also informed the court of Thind's political activities as a leader of the Ghadr Party.[69] After the court dismissed the government's objections and granted Thind's application for naturalization, United States attorneys initiated a proceeding to cancel his naturalization certificate as "illegally procured."[70] Following a trial in which the government presented evidence of Thind's racial classification and political activities, Judge Wolverton denied the government's petition to cancel Thind's naturalization, citing previous precedent that had held Parsi, Armenian, and Hindu applicants to be "free white persons" for purposes of naturalization. Before explaining his holding regarding Thind's racial eligibility for naturalization, however, Wolverton addressed Thind's political activities.[71]

When he heard Thind's case, Wolverton had been a judge for more than twenty-five years and had already published another judicial opinion interpreting the racial eligibility provisions of the naturalization act in *Ellis*, holding that a Syrian applicant was a "free white person" and therefore racially eligible for naturalization.[72] Unlike Wolverton's decision in *Thind*, which was reversed by the Supreme Court, his opinion in *Ellis* was among the lower court opinions that the Court had expressly approved of in *Ozawa*.[73] In his opinion in *Thind*, Wolverton began by rejecting the government's concerns regarding Thind's character, writing that Thind's deportment had been that of a good citizen,

> unless it be that his alleged connection with what is known as the Gadhr Party or Gadhr Press . . . and the defendants Bhagwan Singh and others, prosecuted in federal court in San Francisco for a conspiracy to violate the neutrality laws of this country, has rendered him an undesirable citizen.

Wolverton explained that Thind was on friendly terms with Ghadr leaders Ram Chandra and Ram Singh, both defendants in the Hindu–German conspiracy trial, and that Thind had frequently visited Ghadr leader Bhagwan Singh in prison following Singh's conviction for his role in the conspiracy. Wolverton noted that Thind "stoutly denies . . . that he was in any way connected with the alleged propaganda of the Ghadr Press to violate the neutrality laws of this country, or that he was in sympathy with such a course." He also indicated, however, that while Thind did "not [admit] that he favors an armed revolution," he "frankly admits . . . that he is an advocate of India for the Indians, and would like to see India rid of British rule."[74]

The evidence regarding whether or not Thind advocated the use of violence against the British government in India is mixed. Although Thind denied that he "favored" an armed revolution and a biography published by Thind's son claims that Thind shunned violence as a means of achieving Indian independence, it is difficult to reconcile Thind's activities as a leader of the Ghadr Party with a philosophy of nonviolence.[75] British intelligence documents reflect that Thind gave speeches in support of Indian independence years after his naturalization case in which he suggested that violence against the British government in India was at least inevitable, remarking in one speech that if the British continued to oppress the Indians "we will break them to smithereens." He also criticized Gandhi's philosophy of nonviolence and spoke favorably of the benefits that Japan derived from defeating Russia in the Russo-Japanese War.[76] Despite accepting Thind's disavowal of violence, Wolverton notes that Thind's affection for the constitution, laws, customs, and privileges of the United States was a recent development and "obviously, he has modified somewhat his views on the subject."[77]

Although Sutherland did not address Thind's political activities in his opinion in *Thind*, the Supreme Court was apprised of them through Wolverton's opinion, which was included in the briefs filed with the Court.[78] The conflict over Indian independence was also apparent in the parties' briefs, particularly their citation of British authorities regarding the Indian caste system.[79] As a result of the relatively recent headlines regarding the Ghadr Party, including those regarding the Hindu–German conspiracy trial, many perceived the party to be a terrorist organization.[80] In Lothrop Stoddard's 1921 book *The Rising Tide of Color Against White World Supremacy*, for example, he remarked that "Hindu extremists" had "hatched terroristic plots" against the British government in India during World War I,[81] and the British government labeled the Ghadrites anarchists, a political faction whose followers had assassinated President William McKinley in 1901 and targeted numerous politicians, newspaper editors, and businessmen with bombs in 1919, including the bombing of United States Attorney General A. Mitchell Palmer's home.[82] In this context, Thind's political activities are unlikely to have gone unnoticed by the Court and they provide a crucial context for understanding his case.

THIND'S ASSERTION OF HIGH CASTE PRIVILEGE

The central theme of Thind's Supreme Court brief was that as a "high-caste Hindu, of full Indian blood," he was a descendent of the original Aryan race that invaded India from Central Asia in antiquity, that due to the caste restrictions on intermarriage his ancestors had remained pure Aryans, and that he was therefore "white" according to both ordinary and scientific usage of the word.[83] When British Orientalist Sir William Jones published his finding that Sanskrit and European languages had a common linguistic origin in 1786, it led to the theory of an Aryan race to which both Indians and Europeans belonged. Based on this conclusion, Orientalists hoped that the study of Sanskrit would result in an "Oriental Renaissance" as important as the study of newly discovered Greek texts during the fifteenth century.[84] As Edward Said argues in his classic study of Orientalism, European depictions of Asia created "a relationship of power, of domination, of varying degrees of a complex hegemony,"[85] and Thind sought to turn this relationship to his advantage by citing prominent Orientalists in his case. He cited Sir William Jones and German philologist Franz Bopp and quoted at length from German philologist Max Müller's *Survey of Languages* and *Home of Aryans*, including Müller's claim that "there was a time when the first ancestors of the Indians, the Persians, the Greeks, the Romans, the Slavs, the Celts and the Germans were living together within the same enclosures—nay, under the same roof." Thind also cited German geographer Oscar Peschel's *Races of Men*, Irish linguist Augustus Keane's *Man Past and Present* and *The World's Peoples*, British linguist James Anderson's *The Peoples of India*, and the *Encyclopedia Britannica*, all of which reflected the Aryan invasion theory of Indian civilization and corroborated his claim that high caste Hindus were "white."[86]

According to such sources, an Aryan race from Central Asia invaded India prior to India's Vedic age and conquered the dark-skinned Dravidians of India before migrating west to Europe. Accordingly, the ancestors of Indians and Europeans once lived "under the same roof," as Max Müller put it.[87] Some variations of the theory still have currency, although recent archaeological evidence suggests that the people identified as Aryans may have peacefully migrated to India, while others claim that Dravidians inhabited the Indus Valley at the height of India's Vedic age and that Dravidian was the original substratum of Vedic Sanskrit.[88] The British apparently sponsored the Aryan invasion theory out of a desire to create a common bond with the high caste Hindus who ruled India and to suggest that the great works of India's Vedic age were attributable to European ancestors, but a controversy quickly emerged over the implications of the theory for India's sovereignty.[89]

While Thind conceded that the linguistic basis of the Aryan racial classification was not definitive proof of ancestry, he argued that the fact that the Aryans had invaded the Indian subcontinent and conquered the indigenous people there indicated that high caste Hindus were descendants of the invading Aryans. The ancestors of high caste Hindus could not have learned the Aryan language from any other race, Thind claimed, because "as far back as history goes the Aryans themselves have been the conquering race":

> There being no evidence whatsoever that the so-called Aryans of India were ever conquered by any other race, then the fact that they speak the Aryan language is very strong evidence that they have sprung from the primordial Aryan race who spoke the primordial Aryan language.[90]

Like Ozawa's arguments that foregrounded the agentive potency of the Japanese, these passages of Thind's brief foregrounded the invading and conquering actions of Aryans in ancient India, attributing relatively high transitivity to Indians.

In addition, Thind emphasized the fact that Hindu religious law strictly prohibited marriage outside of one's caste. He cited the fact that the caste restrictions on intermarriage could be found in the Institutes of Manu, one of the oldest and most sacred Hindu religious texts. As a result of the strict observance of caste restrictions on intermarriage, he claimed, not only did high caste Hindus descend from primordial Aryan ancestors but they had remained a pure type of the race through the modern era. The fact that the caste system prevailed in India to a degree unsurpassed elsewhere and that it was "reprehensible for one of a higher caste to marry one of a lower caste," he claimed, proved an "effective barrier to prevent a mixture of the Aryan with the dark races of India."[91] This argument invoked a familiar analogy between India's caste system and Western racial segregation and exclusion laws.[92] Thind claimed, however, that because the Indian caste system preserved the racial purity of high caste Hindus better than measures designed to preserve European racial purity, high caste Hindus even possessed a preeminent claim to whiteness.

In fact, Thind's brief took this argument to its logical extreme by casting doubt on the racial purity of European Americans. The brief first compared the Aryan invaders of India to the European invaders of North America, arguing that the Aryans were like "the Caucasian people of this country who have taken possession and driven out the native red men," and that due to caste restrictions on intermarriage high caste Hindus regarded "the aboriginal Indian Mongoloid in the same manner as the American regards the negro, speaking from a matrimonial standpoint." It is unclear whether in making this argument Thind sought to create an identification with the Court by appealing to a common racial prejudice toward non-"whites," or, if so, whether such an argument could have worked, but Thind pressed his claim even further by criticizing the "melting pot" effect in American history. He claimed that although "there are a great many more distinct races in India than there are in the United States," there was "no 'melting pot' in India in the sense that we use the term in the United States."[93] It was not high caste Hindus in India but European colonists in the United States, Thind claimed, who had diluted their blood through intermarriage with non-"white" people.

The claim that high caste Hindus possessed a preeminent claim to whiteness by virtue of their Aryan ancestry and the strict observance of caste restrictions on intermarriage was a commonplace among Indian nationalists, and this claim gave caste a unique significance in the struggle for Indian independence.[94] As historian Harold Isaacs notes, Indian nationalists of the early twentieth century internalized the racial supremacy of the Aryan invasion theory of ancient Indian civilization and conceived of themselves as "more 'white' than the 'whites,' indeed, as descendants from the 'pure Aryan family' of prehistoric times," endowed with a sort of Mayflower status in relation to whiteness.[95] Because many Indian nationalists believed their claim to Aryan racial purity undermined the racial ideology of British imperialism, by the early twentieth century British imperialist and Indian nationalist myths of the Aryan had merged.[96] A 1916 *Ghadr* pamphlet regarding the Asian exclusion policies of the United States proclaimed the Aryan identity of high caste Hindus as evidence of their whiteness,[97] and a 1936 pamphlet published to contest the Court's decision in *Thind* reiterated the claim that the Sikhs of the Punjab were "the purest high type of Aryan blood without any mixture at all . . . purer than the mixed white races of America," and that "no race, no nationality, no group of people, anywhere on the face of the earth, is as pure in its blood as the people of India."[98] A spiritual adviser inspired Ghadr founder Har Dayal "to go to America and propagate the ancient culture of the Aryan race,"[99] and one of the earliest political journals published for Indians in North America bore the simple title *Aryan*.[100] By turning Orientalist scholarship against Western ideology, Indian claims of Aryanism relied on a form of peritrope, or turning of an opponent's arguments against them.[101]

As Jennifer Snow notes, it is a peculiar irony of ideological history that the Aryan racial classification, which was originally developed to recognize the ancient kinship between Indians and Europeans, became so divisive during the era of British imperialism as metaphors of hierarchy and domination became prevalent in racial discourse.[102] Rather than foreground the agentive potency of caste, Thind could have adopted a strategy that foregrounded inclusion such as that expressed in Max Müller's claim that Europeans and Indians had once lived "under the same roof."[103] The idealist strain of Orientalist scholarship had been embraced by American intellectuals such as Ralph Waldo Emerson, Walt Whitman, and Henry David Thoreau, whose interest in Indian religion and philosophy had inspired Thind as a student.[104] Thind could, alternatively, have cited Sikhism's rejection of racial and caste distinctions or the egalitarian ideals of the Indian independence movement.[105] Within a framework of racial hierarchy, Thind could even have drawn upon the British racial ideology of "martial races" formed in the wake of the 1857 Indian rebellion against the British government, in which the British elevated the Sikhs to the status of a "martial race" in recognition of their support of the British during the rebellion, while representing high caste Hindus as weak and effeminate due to their devotion to caste.[106]

Although the Indian nationalism reflected in Thind's arguments paralleled Ozawa's Japanese nationalism, in Thind's case it is not surprising that he would have viewed his naturalization case as more broadly interconnected with the Indian independence movement to which he was committed. His membership in the Ghadr Party and the statements he made about his case make it apparent that he perceived the legal obstacles to immigration and naturalization in the United States to be a consequence of India's status as a British colony rather than a sovereign nation. Other Indians had used the opportunity of a public trial to critique Western racial ideology. This is how some of the Ghadr leaders used their opportunity to speak in the Hindu–German conspiracy trial, critiquing British rule in India as a justification of their actions, and it is consistent with the Ghadr Party's adoption of a primarily critical stance toward British imperialism without any plan for a post-British future.[107] In his naturalization case, Thind's arguments expressed an Indian nationalism and critique of Western racial ideology that extended far beyond the naturalization question.

Participants in judicial cases have many motives to employ discourse directed to less pragmatic ends than those traditionally assigned to legal discourse, and it would be surprising if Thind did not recognize that speaking in a public forum on an equal basis with the United States government provided a unique opportunity to confront the Western racial ideology at the heart of the racial eligibility provisions of the naturalization act rather than confine himself to a narrow juridical logic. As J. Justin Gustainis writes of the trial of the Catonsville Nine, who were tried for entering a draft board office during the Vietnam War and burning draft files:

> The trial augmented the act of burning the draft records by providing a forum and a legitimacy that could not be present in the act itself . . . The legitimacy came from placing the act within an explicitly argumentative process, a process which granted each side (prosecution and defense) equal time. The deviant stance of a handful of radicals thus became proportional to the official position of the state, and the arguments of the protesters were presented within a framework which was self-consciously rational.[108]

The Catsonville Nine used their trial to publicly protest the Vietnam War, addressing wider audiences and issues than those involved in the question of whether they had illegally burned draft files. Similarly, Patricia Roberts-Miller writes that John Quincy Adams neglected wider issues in his argument to the Supreme Court in the *Amistad* case regarding the ownership of kidnapped Africans sold into slavery who ultimately seized the slave ship that carried them. According to Roberts-Miller, Adams narrowly addressed the rights of the African defendants to freedom without addressing the broader question of slavery, as abolitionists had hoped. Although Adams's speech was passionate, he attacked neither slavery nor slaveowners and, perhaps as a result, "failed to persuade the justices of the inherent injustice of slavery, or the universal rights of humanity, the right of a state to forbid slavery within its borders, or even that descendants of slaves . . . have any rights."[109]

The status that Indian independence activists sought in the early twentieth century required not only the elimination of British rule in India but a change in the structures of social power protected by Western racial ideology. In this respect, *Thind*'s strategy of turning Orientalism against the Western powers might be viewed as an element of what Homi Bhabha calls "sly civility," in which the colonized subject resists the mode of address proffered by the imperial ruler.[110] As Harold Gould describes the Ghadr Party's prospects of fomenting an armed revolution against the British government in India, it was "little more than a touching, quixotic fantasy."[111] *Thind*'s strategy before the Supreme Court shared this quixotic quality, but by turning Orientalism against its creators he did more than illuminate the instability of the racial categories in the naturalization act. He also expressed the global anti-imperialist views of the Ghadr Party, challenging the broader implications of Western racial ideology. Like Ozawa's stance before the Supreme Court, however, by foregrounding the agentive potency of high caste Hindus Thind likely undermined his case by reinforcing negative associations of the Indian caste system such as those advanced in the government's Supreme Court brief.

BURKE, KIPLING, AND THE NEGATIVE ASSOCIATIONS
OF CASTE IN THE GOVERNMENT'S BRIEF

The government's citation of British sources regarding the Indian caste system in *Thind* offers a powerful validation of Indian immigrants' belief that the racial discrimination they faced in North America was a necessary consequence of India's status as a colony under British rule rather than a sovereign nation. In contrast to Thind's emphasis on caste as proof that high caste Hindus were "free white persons" for purposes of naturalization, the government appealed to British sources that emphasized the "unalliability" of India's caste system as evidence that high caste Hindus were alien to the "white" race and a threat to Western civilization.[112] The government's brief began by conceding that the Orientalists who concluded that Indians and Europeans shared a common ancestry "seem to afford little ground for challenge," perhaps reflecting the fact that this conclusion was a commonplace at the time. Similarly, the government did not directly challenge Thind's claim that the caste restrictions on intermarriage had preserved the biological purity of high caste Hindus from antiquity through the modern era.[113] Instead, the government claimed that a cultural and political gulf separated Indians from Europeans, a gulf particularly exemplified by India's dependency on the caste system. According to the government, "though high caste Hindus may have kept their blood pure for centuries, nevertheless, the centuries have removed them far from political fellowship with the white men of the Western World."[114]

The claim that India's caste system was to blame for the fact that India remained under British rule was as much a commonplace of British imperialism as the claim that high caste Hindus were "more 'white' than the 'whites'" was a commonplace of Indian nationalism.[115] While some Europeans admired the stability they believed the caste system provided to Indian society, others cited its oppressiveness and blamed it for India's rejection of Western civilization.[116] To support its claim that a cultural and political gulf separated Indians and Europeans, the government explicitly appealed to the ideology of ruling and subject races by reference to the British East India Company, arguing that in 1790 and thereafter,

> British domination in India was really exercised by the British East India Company, [the] people of India were a subject-race, and, while the ideals of liberty, equality and fraternity were being preached in Europe and America, there is no reason to believe that any one seriously extended their applications to the people of India, or believed that those people were of the kind to be assimilated in citizenship in Western civilization.[117]

This passage reflects the central theme of the government's brief, in which the subject status of Indians was offered as proof that they were not "free white persons" for purposes of naturalization.

Drawing on the negative associations of the Indian caste system, the government also offered a three-and-a-half page block quotation from Edmund Burke's address to the House of Lords in the eighteenth-century trial of Warren Hastings.[118] Once the Governor-General of India, Hastings was impeached by the House of Commons after Burke charged him with high crimes and misdemeanors for his conduct in India.[119] In the passage of Burke's speech that the government quoted, Burke claimed that Indians were "the most unalliable to any other part of mankind," without the "convivial bond" of society, and specifically identified caste as a wide gulf that separated the Indian and British people, "that gulf which manners, opinions, and laws have radicated in the very nature of the people." Due to caste restrictions, Burke claimed, Indians rejected contact with any other people, and "this circumstance renders it difficult for us to enter with due sympathy into their concerns, or for them to enter into ours, even when we meet on the same ground."[120] This severance of Indians from any basis of sympathy is particularly important, because as Ernest Renan notes of national solidarity, "suffering in common unites more than joy does," and where national memories are concerned "griefs are of more value than triumphs, for they impose duties, and require a common effort."[121]

In the section of Burke's speech quoted by the government, he also claimed that due to the Indian caste system, "without great danger to his situation, religion, rank, and estimation, [no Indian] can ever pass the sea; and this forbids, forever, all direct communication between that country and this."[122] Indeed, according to Burke the Indian caste system was the most impenetrable enclave in the history of the world:

> Their blood, their opinions, and the soil of their country make one consistent piece, admitting no mixture, no adulteration, no improvement . . . but in proportion as their laws and opinions were concentrated within themselves, and hindered from spreading abroad, they have doubled their force at home.[123]

An agentive potency attributed to caste emerges in these pages of the government's brief through the use of verbs such as *radicated* and *hindered*, depicting caste as a transitive force that simultaneously enslaved Indians and prohibited society with outsiders. As Jennifer Snow writes, the government's brief in *Thind* "made strategic use of the echoes set up by 'caste' itself, negative ideas about caste practices that were well established in scholarship alongside the ideal of caste as preserver of racial purity."[124]

As the capstone of the government's argument that a cultural and political gulf separated Indians and Europeans, it also directly asserted the racial superiority of Europeans to Indians by drawing on the Western racial ideology of white supremacy contained in Rudyard Kipling's poem "The White Man's Burden":

> Whatever the Hindu may be to the ethnologist . . . in the popular conception he is alien to the white race and part of the "white man's burden." This phrase of Kipling, the great poet of the imperial destinies of the white race, has become part of the language and understanding of the English-speaking race. And, while the problem of British rule in India is not our affair, whatever may be the white man's burden, the Hindu does not share it, rather he imposes it.

In this passage, the government dismissed the racial classifications of ethnology as irrelevant rather than incorrect and focused instead on the "popular conception" of Indians as alien to the "white" race, citing Rudyard Kipling's poem "The White Man's Burden," originally subtitled "The United States and the Philippine Islands." In Kipling's poem, he depicts the inhabitants of imperial colonies as a threat to Western civilization.[125] Although Kipling's poem is often interpreted as an endorsement of American imperialism, it warns imperialists of the danger posed by the imperial subject, to which the poem attributes relatively high transitivity: "sullen peoples, / Half-devil and half-child," whose "sloth and heathen Folly" would frustrate the imperial reader and "bring all your hopes to nought."[126] By arguing that Indians did not share the "white" man's burden but "imposed" it, the government attributed transitivity to Indians in their relationship with Europeans and thereby severed them from the solidarity of imperial suffering that the poem imagines.[127] The government did not appeal to the perceived degradation and effeminacy of India's caste system but to the threat it posed, depicting Indians as what Falguni Sheth calls the "unruly," a "threat to the coherence of a polity" that "needs to be domesticated or at least managed in order for the state to maintain control of its population."[128]

SUTHERLAND'S DISTORTIONS

Justice Sutherland's opinion in *Thind* was marked by a number of distortions that raise troubling questions. Despite the government's concession that Indians and Europeans shared a common ancestry, Sutherland challenged both the linguistic basis of the Aryan racial classification and the conclusion that if Indians had descended from a "white" ancestor they had maintained their racial purity through the centuries. In support of the latter argument, he also distorted the *Encyclopedia Britannica* entry that he cited as the only authority for his historical claim in order to elide the fact that the entry actually contradicts his argument. Further, although Sutherland applied the ordinary usage rule as he had in *Ozawa*, he evaded the fact that in *Thind* the Court was withdrawing its express approval of lower court precedent that had also applied the same rule to hold Indians racially eligible for naturalization in *Ozawa*. Finally, Sutherland neglected the arguments and evidence that Thind advanced regarding ordinary usage and misleadingly suggested that Thind had relied only on scientific evidence.[129]

The Supreme Court's motives are difficult to discern in any case, but the combined absence of a reasoned opinion and the distortion of the arguments and evidence in Sutherland's opinion in *Thind* suggest the conclusion reached by many Indians that the decision was a political one. As political scientist Robert Dahl writes of the Supreme Court:

> To consider the Supreme Court of the United States strictly as a legal institution is to underestimate its significance in the American political system . . . As a political institution, the court is highly unusual, not least because Americans are not quite willing to accept the fact that it is a political institution and not quite capable of denying it; so that frequently we take both positions at once. This is confusing to foreigners, amusing to logicians, and rewarding to ordinary Americans who thus manage to retain the best of both worlds.[130]

During the early decades of the Cold War, a mode of Supreme Court criticism arose that sought to distinguish democratic legal institutions from those of totalitarian regimes based on the claim that in a democracy courts published opinions with ample arguments and evidence to support them. In a prominent example of this mode of criticism, Alexander Bickel and Henry Wellington critique the Supreme Court for "the formulation of results accompanied by little or no effort to support them in reason, in sum, of opinions that do not opine and of . . . orders that quite frankly fail to build the bridge between the authorities they cite and the results they decree."[131] According to such critics, when an opinion fails to fulfill its persuasive responsibility it simply does not make law "in the sense which the term 'law' must have in a democratic society."[132]

Sutherland began his opinion by noting that the linguistic basis of the Aryan race theory did not necessarily prove that Indians and Europeans shared a common ancestry. The fact that people spoke a common language provided no "assurance," Sutherland argued, that the "so-called Aryan language" was not spoken by a variety of races living closely together.[133] In addition, Sutherland rejected Thind's claim that high caste Hindus had maintained their racial purity by adhering to the caste restrictions on intermarriage, concluding that even if the Aryan invaders of India were originally "white," their contemporary descendants were a mixed-race people:

> The type may have been so changed by intermixture of blood as to justify an intermediate classification. Something very like this has actually taken place in India. Thus, in Hindustan and Berar [provinces of northeastern India] there was such an intermixture of the "Aryan" invader with the darkskinned Dravidian.
>
> In the Punjab and Rajputana [provinces of northwestern India where Thind was born], while the invaders seem to have met with more success in the effort to preserve their racial purity, intermarriages did occur producing an intermingling of the two and destroying to a greater or less degree the purity of the "Aryan" blood. The rules of caste, while calculated to prevent this intermixture, seem not to have been entirely successful.

In these passages, Sutherland argued that even if Indians and Europeans shared a common ancestry Indians had failed to preserve their racial purity through the centuries because they had intermarried with the dark-skinned Dravidians of the Indian subcontinent in violation of the caste restrictions on intermarriage, citing as his only authority for this historical claim the 1910 *Encyclopedia Britannica* entry on Hinduism. One can hear in this argument a rejection of Thind's claim that high caste Hindus were purer than the descendants of European colonists in North America, or "more 'white' than the 'whites.'"[134]

This intermarriage argument betrays significant anxiety when considered in its rhetorical context, not only because the issue was not contested by the government but because the 1910 *Encyclopedia Britannica* entry on Hinduism represents the racial classification of the high caste Hindus of *Thind*'s birthplace in the Punjab as considerably more uncertain than Sutherland suggested. In fact, the entry suggests that the Aryan invaders of northwestern India had more success in preserving the purity of their ancestry than Sutherland described and explicitly states that they dealt with the Dravidians "the way the white race usually deals with the coloured race— they kept them socially apart."[135] In contrast to Sutherland's statement that the invaders of northwestern India only met with "more success" in preserving the purity of their ancestry, the *Encyclopedia Britannica* states that they "seem to have been *signally successful* in their endeavor to preserve their racial purity, probably by being able to clear a sufficiently extensive area of the original occupants for themselves with their wives and their children to settle upon."[136] Sutherland's use of the qualified language *more* and *not . . . entirely,* in contrast to the *Encyclopedia Britannica*'s use of the word *signally*—meaning "in a signal or striking manner; conspicuously, notably, remarkably, pre-eminently"[137]—suggests that he distorted the entry to bolster his argument. Although it is true, as Sutherland noted, that the *Encyclopedia Britannica* concludes that some intermarriages with Dravidians probably occurred among the high caste Hindus of northwestern India, the entry immediately qualifies this conclusion by stating that "it must be confessed . . . that our information regarding the development of the caste-system is far from complete," a qualification Sutherland neglected.[138] To adequately support his intermarriage argument without resorting to distortion, Sutherland would have had to have cited a more obscure and less reputable source such as the American eugenicist Madison Grant, who wrote in his 1916 book *The Passing of the Great Race* that "there remains not one recognizable trace of the blood of the white conquerors who poured in through the passages of the Northwest" provinces of India, and "the boast of the modern Indian that he is of the same race as his English ruler" is "entirely without basis in fact."[139]

The burden of proof Sutherland applied for establishing whiteness in *Thind* is also nearly impossible to carry, reminiscent of the "one-drop" rule of the nineteenth and early twentieth centuries, which classified people as "black" based on even the slightest African ancestry.[140] Once again, Madison Grant offered a striking example of the rule shortly before *Thind*, extending the rule to Indians and other racial groups by remarking in *The Passing of the Great Race* that "the cross between a white man and an Indian is an Indian; the cross between a white man and a negro is a negro; the cross between a white man and a Hindu is a Hindu; and the cross between any of the three European races and a Jew is a Jew."[141] Not only did Sutherland appear unsatisfied with the *Encyclopedia Britannica's* conclusion that the high caste Hindus of northwestern India had been "signally successful" in observing the caste restrictions on intermarriage, but he concluded that high caste Hindus were not "white" based on his finding that the rules of caste had not been "entirely" successful and that intermarriage had occurred "to a greater or less degree."[142] This reasoning appears to conflict with the unanimous opinion of lower courts in mixed race cases at the time that an applicant only needed to be more "white" than not to be racially eligible for naturalization.[143]

Only after Sutherland rejected Thind's claim that Indians and Europeans shared a common ancestry did he address the government's argument that Indians were not "free white persons" because a cultural and political gulf separated them from Western civilization. With regard to this gulf, Sutherland argued that the naturalization act was originally only intended to include "the type of man whom [the authors of the act] knew as white" and that because in 1790 immigration to the United States was almost exclusively from the British Isles and northwestern Europe, these were the people intended by the phrase *free white person*. According to Sutherland, the succeeding years brought immigrants "from Eastern, Southern and Middle Europe, among them the Slavs and the dark-eyed, swarthy people of Alpine and Mediterranean stock, and these were received as unquestionably akin to those already here and readily amalgamated with them,"[144] but he provided no evidence to support these historical conclusions or to distinguish Indian immigrants from the European immigrants he identified.

In the passages of Sutherland's opinion directed to the cultural and political gulf between Indians and Western civilization, he conceived of whiteness as a social and sexual knowledge or kinship by referring to the immigrants who the original authors of the naturalization act intended by the phrase *free white person* as that they "knew" or received as "akin" to the people of northwestern Europe. He also added an ethno-religious dimension to his argument by using a biblical allusion, writing that "it was these immigrants—bone of their bone and flesh of their flesh—and their kind whom they must have had affirmatively in mind."[145] The phrase *bone of their bone and flesh of their flesh* alluded to the creation story in the biblical book of Genesis, in which God took one of Adam's ribs and used it to create Eve, whom Adam then referred to as "bone of my bone and flesh of my flesh."[146] Although this biblical allusion and the language of knowledge and kinship is less direct than the government's citation of Burke's speech from the trial of Warren Hastings and Kipling's "The White Man's Burden," it implied that high caste Hindus were culturally and politically alien to Western civilization by suggesting a relationship between whiteness and Judeo-Christianity, in contrast to Thind's citation of Hindu religious law.

Finally, Sutherland concluded his opinion with language that echoed the "separate but equal" doctrine first endorsed by the Supreme Court in *Plessy v. Ferguson* (1896).[147] Despite his conclusion that Indians were inassimilable with American life, Sutherland wrote that the Court did not consider them unequal but simply different:

> It is very far from our thought to suggest the slightest question of racial superiority or inferiority. What we suggest is merely racial difference, and it is of such character and extent that the great body of our people instinctively recognize it and reject the thought of assimilation.[148]

If Thind's appeal to his high caste status was intended to persuade the Court of his cultural and political identification with Western civilization, the Court likely interpreted it as inconsistent with the "separate but equal" doctrine. Nothing could more clearly make this point than to contrast Thind's reliance on caste with the Court's assertion in *Plessy* that "there is no caste here."[149] While Thind's arguments had asserted a popular analogy between India's caste system and Western racial segregation and exclusion laws, Sutherland rejected the analogy.[150] In doing so, he also suggested that the Indian caste system was itself proof of Indian inassimilability.

When Sutherland's opinion in *Thind* is read in its rhetorical context, it is decidedly opaque. Sutherland vaguely challenged the validity of the Aryan racial classification and alternatively argued that the Aryans of ancient India intermarried with dark-skinned Dravidians, neither of which the government had contested, and he distorted the only source he offered to support his intermarriage argument. In addition, *Thind* overruled the majority of lower court opinions regarding Indian racial eligibility for naturalization, which had relied on the ordinary usage rule to find Indians eligible for naturalization, but it neither acknowledged that the courts holding Indians eligible for naturalization had relied on the ordinary usage rule nor specifically cited the cases.[151] Instead, Sutherland merely stated that the Court disagreed with any lower courts that had reached contrary conclusions: "We are unable to agree with the District Court, or with other lower federal courts, in the conclusion that a native Hindu is eligible for naturalization under section 2169."[152] In addition, Sutherland falsely implied that Thind's arguments relied solely on ethnological evidence despite the fact that his brief explicitly referenced the ordinary usage rule and cited seven of the opinions that the Court had relied on in *Ozawa*, including both *Mozumdar* and *Singh*, which had held that ordinary usage of the word *white* included Indians.[153] Far from interpreting the word *white* as equivalent to the ethnological definition of Caucasian in *Ozawa* and then adopting an ordinary usage interpretation in *Thind*, the Court neglected to address the ethnological evidence in *Ozawa* or the evidence of ordinary usage in *Thind*.

SAKHARAM PANDIT'S REVERSAL OF CASTE

The Court's decision in *Thind* had a profound impact on Indian immigrants in the United States during the more than two decades between the Court's decision and the congressional grant of racial eligibility for naturalization to natives of the Indian subcontinent in 1946. Almost immediately after *Thind*, the California attorney general began proceedings to revoke Indian land purchases under California's alien land law, which prohibited land ownership by anyone "ineligible to citizenship."[154] The alien land laws of western states incorporated the racial eligibility provisions of the naturalization act and the judicial precedent interpreting them by adopting the phrase *ineligible to citizenship*. As a consequence, Indians either lost their land or had to register it under the name of a "white" friend or associate who acted as a "front man" and usually collected a fee. Although some Indians were able to register their land under the names of their children, who were American citizens through birthright citizenship, few Punjabis had wives in the United States and they were therefore less likely to have children born as citizens.[155] The year after *Thind*, the Immigration Act of 1924 also also prohibited any alien "ineligible to citizenship" from entering the United States. By incorporating the interpretations of *Ozawa* and *Thind*, the act effectively barred Japanese and Indian immigration by race, reinforcing and expanding on the Immigration Act of 1917, which had barred the entry of natives of the Asiatic Barred Zone covering most of Asia, India, and the Arabian Peninsula.[156] Because Indian immigrants were "ineligible to citizenship," they were also denied access to federal relief programs during the Great Depression.[157]

Perhaps most dramatically, within weeks of *Thind* the Bureau of Naturalization began filing proceedings to cancel naturalization certificates that had been previously obtained by Indians in the United States, based on the assertion that the certificates had been "illegally procured."[158] Such cancellation proceedings resulted in the cancellation of at least forty-two naturalization certificates issued to immigrants from the Indian subcontinent, although the bureau exercised its discretion to exempt at least ten Indians from such proceedings due to their status as United States military veterans. Many of the naturalization certificates canceled by such proceedings had been held for five to ten years or longer, some as long as sixteen years, and the proceedings had a traumatic impact on those who lost their citizenship.[159] When Vaishno Das Bagai was forced to sell his property under California's alien land law and was denied a passport to visit his family in India due to his naturalization certificate being canceled, he committed suicide. In a letter he left to his wife and sons, he wrote of the effort he had made to become a model American. Without his naturalization certificate, he was unable to buy a home or return to India without acquiring a British passport, which he refused to do due to his allegiance to the Indian independence movement. He complained of being left effectively interned in the United States, "obstacles this way, blockades that way, and the bridges burnt behind."[160]

The decision to file cancellation proceedings was not without controversy within the Bureau of Naturalization. In a series of memoranda from Chief Naturalization Examiner Henry Hazard to Commissioner of Naturalization Raymond Crist, Hazard argued that the decision to institute cancellation proceedings was discretionary and he emphasized the importance of determining whether those targeted with such proceedings had served in the United States military during World War I, noting that the bureau had already used its discretion to decide that cancellation proceedings "are not to be instituted in the cases of World War veterans on account of race." In support of his position, Hazard echoed the State Department's concerns with the racial eligibility provisions of the naturalization act, writing that "this is peculiarly a time when the United States should be careful in maintaining friendly relations." He specifically referred to "racial antagonisms which exist already throughout the world between the white and the non-white races" and to diplomatic tensions over the racial eligibility provisions of the naturalization act "possibly adding to the complications of international relationships."[161]

Consistent with the bureau's focus on character rather than nativity, Hazard also noted that while the bureau might have had a duty to "attack the record" of any Japanese or Indian citizen shown to be of "bad moral character," there were "urgent reasons" why the bureau should not file cancellation proceedings

> where the record is in every respect regular so far as the course of the proceedings is concerned, as to the . . . showing of good moral character, attachment to the principles of this Government, and other qualifications required.

In a surprisingly rare discussion of the injustice of the proceedings, Hazard also argued that

> to pursue at this time a course which would result in the revocation of these naturalization certificates granted in some cases many years ago, and where the persons naturalized may have acquired valuable vested rights of property, and high standing as reputable citizens of this country, impresses me as being unfair, undemocratic, and contrary to every American principle of fair play.[162]

Thus, in the proceedings to cancel naturalization certificates of Indians after *Thind* the bureau manipulated the racial eligibility provisions of the naturalization act in order to denaturalize those whose character was considered objectionable.

The most important of the post-*Thind* cancellation cases is *United States v. Pandit* (1925), filed within months of the Supreme Court's decision in *Thind*. It was the first cancellation case to be dismissed, and after the dismissal was upheld by the United States Court of Appeals for the Ninth Circuit the Supreme Court denied certiorari in the case. The following year, the Supreme Court also reversed the cancellation of another Indian's naturalization certificate after a different federal appeals court wrote in its opinion in the case that the Court's refusal to grant certiorari in *Pandit* "in no sense indicates its approval of that decision," a reversal that suggests the Court more substantially approved of *Pandit* than a denial of certiorari might necessarily indicate.[163] As precedent, *Pandit* led the Bureau of Naturalization to stop filing cancellation proceedings, and according to testimony given to a subsequent congressional hearing the government restored the naturalization certificates of Indians whose certificates had been cancelled before *Pandit*.[164]

In addition to its importance as precedent, however, the defendant introduced a novel rhetorical strategy in the case that provides a useful contrast to Thind's rhetorical strategy and further supports the conclusion that caste played an important role in the Supreme Court's racial classification of Indians for purposes of naturalization.

Sakharam Pandit was born in Ahmedabad in northwestern India, approximately 1,200 miles south of Thind's birthplace in Amritsar. A Hindu of the Brahmin caste, Pandit obtained a Bachelor of Arts degree from the English university in Bombay, India, and obtained a doctorate degree from a prestigious orthodox Sanskrit university in Benares, India, which secured his admission to all of the learned institutions of India. He moved to the United States from England in 1906 and filed his declaration of intention to become a United States citizen in Chicago in 1911. After moving to California, Pandit filed his application for naturalization in Los Angeles Superior Court. The Bureau of Naturalization opposed Pandit's naturalization based on the claim that he was racially ineligible for naturalization, and a trial was held in which the government presented evidence and cross-examined Pandit and a number of witnesses that Pandit had called. After considering the case for nine months, Judge Willis Morrison granted Pandit's application over the bureau's objection, but the government did not appeal the decision. According to Pandit, as he was leaving the clerk's office with his naturalization certificate the naturalization examiner remarked to him, "Well, Mr. Pandit, now that you are a citizen, you may be required to go on military duty on the Mexican border where men are wanted at the present time."[165] One of the more peculiar examples of the propensity of racial eligibility discourse to focus on perceived threats to the nation, this remark reflects an imaginary in which defense of the nation's territorial integrity against external threats was a defining feature of citizenship.

After Pandit obtained his naturalization certificate, he studied law, obtained a California law license, and became a California notary public. He was later admitted to practice law in the United States District Court for the Southern District of California and in the United States Court of Appeals for the Ninth Circuit. He purchased a home valued at $15,000 (equivalent to more than $200,000 today) and married an American-born wife of mixed English and French ancestry named Lillian Stringer, a marriage that was only legal under California's miscegenation law if both Sakharam and Lillian were "white." Before the couple was married, Lillian filed an application in the United States land office to obtain 320 acres of desert land in the

Imperial Valley of California and spent $1,500 in reclamation work, and after they were married the couple spent another $500 of community property on reclamation work. As a consequence of renouncing his allegiance to India, becoming an American citizen, and marrying a "white" American-born wife, Pandit lost the privileges of his high caste status in India, his doctoral degree, and his right to an inheritance of ancestral land worth between $130,000 and $280,000 (equivalent to more than $1 million today), and his sister disinherited him. Shortly after the Supreme Court issued its opinion in *Thind*, however, the government petitioned to cancel the naturalization certificate that Pandit had held for more than nine years, on the basis that after *Thind* it was clear that his naturalization certificate had been "illegally procured" because he was racially ineligible for naturalization.[166]

Although many if not all Indians could have told similar stories of becoming outcast as a result of renouncing their allegiance to India and becoming an American citizen, Pandit's decision to foreground this as the theme of his case was a novel rhetorical strategy in the racial eligibility cases. As the central premise of Pandit's case, to which he devoted more than half of his answer, he asserted a defense known as equitable estoppel, a broad equitable defense that prevents a party from changing its position after another has justifiably relied on the position to such an extent that it would be unfair to allow the party to change its position.[167] According to Pandit, he had justifiably relied on the finality of the 1914 judgment granting him a naturalization certificate to such an extent that it would be unfair to allow the government to cancel it after a decade. To support this claim, he foregrounded the fact that he had become an "outcast" in Indian society as a result of renouncing his allegiance to India, becoming an American citizen, and marrying a "white" American-born woman. If his naturalization certificate were canceled, he argued, he would become stateless, "a man without a country, greatly to defendant's damage and to his irreparable injury."[168]

During an evidentiary hearing in the case, Pandit testified that when he became a United States citizen he was a Brahmin and belonged to the highest Brahmin subcaste, the highest caste status in Indian society. When he renounced his allegiance to India, however, he became an outcast in Indian society who could no longer associate with any but the untouchables. He could not even associate with the members of his own family:

> An outcaste has no social standing at all, and the higher one's caste
> originally, the lower he falls, on the theory that those who are

high ought to know better than those who are lower. An outcaste cannot have any social position at all, not only with the caste to which he belongs, but in all castes of Hindu society. All he can do is to associate with the so-called "Hill Tribes," the aboriginal people, a kind of negroid stock, with which the Hindus have no social intercourse whatever.

If my certificate of naturalization should be canceled, and I should return to India, I couldn't associate with my own family now. They would not even eat with me, and, of course, there is no possibility of any other social relation; in fact, even any water touched by me would be considered polluted by my own mother, if she were living, and she would not drink it, no matter how much she loved me, because that is against the rules. And in the matter of social status, that is a matter of birth, and once lost, is lost forever.[169]

In this testimony and throughout his case, Pandit reversed the positions that the parties had adopted with regard to caste in *Thind*, appealing to the negative associations of caste to create sympathy for his status as an American citizen rather than foregrounding it as proof of his whiteness. By framing himself as a victim of the Indian caste system, suffering at the hands of Kipling's "sullen peoples" whose sloth and folly "bring all your hopes to nought," Pandit claimed to share rather than impose the "white man's burden,"[170] severing himself from the negative associations of caste and creating a bond of unity with Western civilization against a shared external threat.

Without a country to return to, Pandit claimed, if his naturalization certificate were canceled he would become stateless and his wife would lose her citizenship and become stateless under the Cable Act of 1922, which automatically revoked the citizenship of any American woman who married an alien "ineligible to citizenship."[171] In addition, Pandit would lose his California law license and his appointment as a notary public and he and his wife would both lose their home and property pursuant to California's alien land law and federal requirements for the purchase of government property, leaving them with no means of earning a living. Finally, he had argued that he had renounced his right of inheritance to ancestral property in India, was disinherited by his family, and had lost his Indian doctoral degree in reliance on his American citizenship.[172] Like Vaishno Das Bagai, Pandit claimed that if his naturalization certificate were canceled both he and his wife would be left stateless and effectively interned in the United States.[173]

When *Pandit* was filed, it was assigned to Judge Benjamin Bledsoe until he resigned from the bench to run in the Los Angles mayor's race while the case was pending. Bledsoe had issued judicial opinions in several racial eligibility cases after World War I. In *Singh*, one of the lower court opinions that the Supreme Court expressly approved in *Ozawa*, Bledsoe held that Indians were "free white persons" and therefore racially eligible for naturalization.[174] Several years later, he published a judicial opinion in the consolidated cases of *In re Song* and *In re Mascarenas*, holding that a Korean veteran of the United States military was racially ineligible for naturalization and was not eligible for the exemption from the racial eligibility provisions of the naturalization act for certain veterans under the Naturalization Act of 1918 and that a Filipino veteran of the United States military had failed to follow the procedural requirements for the exemption.[175] Before he resigned, Bledsoe rejected Pandit's motion to dismiss the government's complaint, citing the decision in an earlier cancellation proceeding holding that naturalization certificates issued to those racially ineligible for naturalization were "illegally procured."[176]

When Bledsoe resigned, the case was assigned to Judge Paul McCormick, appointed to the federal court by President Coolidge in 1924 after serving as an assistant district attorney in Los Angeles County, as a judge on the California Superior Court for Los Angeles County, and as an associate justice of the District Court of Appeals of California. McCormick would later become chief judge of the court and decide *Méndez v. Westminster School District* (1949), in which he held that the practice of segregating Mexican schoolchildren in Orange County, California, was an unconstitutional denial of equal protection, often cited as an important precursor to the Supreme Court's opinion in *Brown v. Board of Education* (1954).[177] In *Pandit*, the government moved to strike all of Pandit's defenses—or effectively remove them from the trial record—and McCormick granted the motion as to all defenses except for Pandit's equitable estoppel defense. This left the question of whether the government was equitably estopped from canceling Pandit's naturalization certificate as the only issue in the case.[178] During a hearing, McCormick noted that although he believed Pandit to belong to the group that the Supreme Court had held racially ineligible for naturalization in *Thind*, Justice Sutherland's opinion in *Thind* indicated that a court might refuse to cancel the naturalization certificate of such individuals in special circumstances. Like the Bureau of Naturalization's policy toward the racial eligibility provisions of the naturalization act, McCormick appeared to interpret the provisions to be more concerned with individual character than nativity.

After considering the arguments and evidence, McCormick dismissed the government's case and adopted Pandit's equitable estoppel defense in its entirety to explain his decision. He discussed Pandit's arguments at length from the bench and later repeated Pandit's argument nearly verbatim in his written findings of fact and conclusions of law. During his comments from the bench, McCormick particularly emphasized the effect that canceling Pandit's naturalization certificate would have on Pandit's marriage and the undesirable prospect of rendering the couple stateless.[179] As he concluded his explanation of his ruling during the oral hearing, McCormick placed special emphasis on Pandit's statelessness argument by remarking that while "under the application of cold legal principles" the argument might not be sufficient to justify dismissing the government's petition, it appealed to the "conscience of the court" because

> it is the intent of this country to have all aliens who come here lawfully and conduct themselves properly, become citizens, become members of the American family, to identify themselves with this country in a substantial and patriotic manner, and do so by becoming American citizens. It is much better to have aliens citizens of the United States than it is to have foreigners in the United States.

According to McCormick, a court of equity should interpret the law in such a way as to encourage desirable aliens to become American citizens "rather than ostracizing them from our political family," suggesting that the United States would treat them differently than the Indian caste system. The court was not justified in canceling Pandit's citizenship after years of exemplary conduct, McCormick argued, because "this man is now a member of the national family."[180]

In a curious procedural occurrence, the Ninth Circuit upheld Judge McCormick's decision in *Pandit* based on the defense of res judicata—the rule that a final judgment in one case bars later actions involving the same dispute[181]—despite the fact that Judge McCormick struck Pandit's res judicata defense from his pleadings. The prefatory statement published with the Ninth Circuit's opinion, however, recited all of the factual premises of Pandit's equitable estoppel defense, which would have been irrelevant to a res judicata defense. The appellate court also distinguished its earlier opinion in *Mozumdar v. United States* (1924), in which it had reached the opposite conclusion, by the fact that the same arguments had not been presented or considered in *Mozumdar*, and yet the defense of res judicata had been presented in *Mozumdar*.[182] Considering the district and appellate court records of *Pandit* and *Mozumdar* in their entirety, there is substantial evidence that the different outcomes in the two cases is attributable to Pandit's equitable estoppel defense. The result was that although both Judge McCormick and the Ninth Circuit concluded that Pandit was not a "free white person" based on the Supreme Court's precedent in *Thind*, Judge Morrison's original order finding that Pandit was a "free white person" when he granted Pandit's naturalization certificate was never declared void. Thus, Pandit remained a lawyer and notary public, he could own land under California's alien land law, his marriage to Lillian Pandit remained legal under California's miscegenation law, and her citizenship could not be revoked under the Cable Act of 1922.[183]

STATELESSNESS AND ASYLUM IN RACIAL ELIGIBILITY DISCOURSE

In 1935, Thind petitioned for naturalization a third time after Congress passed the Nye-Lea Act, which made World War I veterans eligible for naturalization regardless of race, and he was finally granted American citizenship without objection nearly two decades after he first petitioned for naturalization.[184] During a 1933 speech given shortly before he obtained his citizenship, Thind expressed his lingering bitterness toward the United States, stating that

> America, by far the best of all the Christian lands, sided with perfidious Albion to insult India in the matter of citizenship, we being the only Aryans excluded. Our compatriots in California have trouble after trouble with local authorities in the Imperial Valley in connection with their leasing of land. Any Oriental who expects justice from the West, America included, should be examined for his sanity.[185]

It is important that Thind referred to Britain by the poetic designation *Albion,* from the Latin *albus,* or "white." The name is believed to have originally been a reference to the white cliffs of Dover, England, but Thind's usage may have suggested a racial meaning, particularly when contained in the phrase *perfidious Albion*—from the French *la perfide Albion*—an expression that associated Britain with treachery toward foreigners.[186] This passage from Thind's speech offers a succinct summary of his arguments before the Supreme Court, identifying himself as Aryan and attributing America's actions to Britain, with which the United States merely "sided." The speech expressed the perception of many Indians that their racial eligibility for naturalization in the United States depended on India's status as a British colony rather than a sovereign nation.

According to Falguni Sheth, race is instantiated through sovereign power that confronts a threat to the coherence of a polity that must be domesticated or managed in order for the state to maintain control of its population.[187] She writes that the most important element of racial division is not the fact of division but

> the identification of something unruly, which is at once the essence of race, but also something that reveals itself to be apprehended in precisely the way that it is thrust forth by the context, the apparatus in which it is located. In other words, race is predicated on something that is always-already-threatening.[188]

For Sheth, race is the method by which sovereign power transforms the "unruly" into a set of categories "by which to divide populations against themselves—biopolitically, culturally, socially, etc."[189] Not only does Sheth identify race with the assessment of threats through the concept of the "unruly," but she describes racial difference as the product of a process that sounds remarkably like the appeal to unify against a shared external threat by describing race as a tripartite dynamic in which racial difference is contingent on a third group, either an intermediary between a dominant and subordinate group or as an outsider "which enables a formerly subordinate group to—provisionally, momentarily—appear to be allied with a dominant population."[190]

Applying her philosophy to Asian Indians in North America during the early twentieth century, Sheth places particular emphasis on the Supreme

Court's opinion in *Thind*. Although she claims that the threat Thind posed in the case was to the status of being a Caucasian—a conclusion irreconcilable with the Court's express approval of two cases holding Indians to be "free white persons" in *Ozawa*—Sheth includes in her general contextualization of *Thind* the fact that British and American intelligence officials treated the Ghadr Party as an insurgency. She does not mention Thind's own political activities as a leader of the Ghadr Party, however, nor the fact that those activities specifically motivated the government to oppose his naturalization. According to Sheth, Indians first came to the attention of American officials because they were perceived to be a threatening or unruly population based on differences in skin color, dress, accent, and economic competition. The threat that these differences were perceived to pose was amplified, however, by "their 'unusual' political subjectivity":

> They were Indian Nationals and British colonial subjects in the midst of nationalist struggles. The deliberate decision to agitate while in the U.S. leads to their perception as insurgents and anarchists and exacerbates the concern that they may be political traitors.[191]

While Sheth is one of the only commentators to note the relationship between *Thind* and the Indian independence movement, she neglects the role that Thind's own political activities as a founding member of the Ghadr Party and his rhetorical strategy before the Supreme Court served in amplifying the threat Indian nationalists were perceived to pose. She also fails to account for the fact that the vast majority of Indians who applied for naturalization before *Thind* were successful, the Court's approval of two cases finding that Indians were "free white persons" for purposes of naturalization three months earlier in *Ozawa*, the government's use of its prosecutorial discretion to exempt Indian veterans of the United States military from cancellation proceedings after *Thind*, or Sakharam Pandit's success in preserving his American citizenship and ending the government's practice of denaturalizing Indians in *Pandit*. These considerations indicate that Indian racial classification for purposes of naturalization was considerably more unstable, reflecting the constantly shifting and intensely political process of racial formation that Michael Omi and Howard Winant describe.[192]

In *Constructing the Political Spectacle*, Murray Edelman claims that a predictable discourse and a continuity in "power, privileges, and relative resources" emerges out of longstanding enmities. The commonly recurring language that arises from such longstanding enmities, Edelman argues, creates a continuity in public support for social structures of power that its audience finds valuable regardless of whether the enemy actually presents a threat. Through this "dramaturgy of enmity," as Edelman calls it, "unequal relationships become stabilized, each group learning its expected form of action and each episode in the sequence of hostilities rationalizing later ones and long-standing differences in material resources and privilege."[193] The longstanding enmity between Indians and Europeans served to stabilize power, privilege, and relative resources in both societies through the unifying force of consistent and predictable enmities. Colonial subjects served this function in Europe, while British imperialists served a similar unifying function for Indians. The arguments In *Thind* revolved around this dramaturgy of enmity as the parties cited competing authorities regarding the significance of the caste system to Indian racial classification. Rather than finding common ground, however, Thind reinforced the longstanding enmity between Indians and Europeans by advancing a rival "white" supremacy to critique Western racial ideology. Reflecting the ideology of the Ghadr Party, Thind's strategy was more of a critique than an affirmative vision of a shared future.

As previously noted, Ernest Renan claims that the most important experiences that build national identity are common regrets and suffering, because "suffering in common unites more than joy does," and where national memories are concerned "griefs are of more value than triumphs, for they impose duties, and require a common effort." According to Renan, a nation is "the culmination of a long past of endeavors, sacrifice, and devotion," and "to have performed great deeds together, to wish to perform still more—these are the essential conditions for being a people." Moreover, Renan concludes that these shared experiences can be understood "in spite of differences of race and language."[194] In contrast to the rhetorical strategies of the applicants in *Ozawa* and *Thind* which both foregrounded the agentive potency of their racial groups as proof of their whiteness, rhetorical strategies that framed Asian immigrants as sharing in the nation's grief, suffering in common with the nation, or making sacrifices for the nation succeeded not only in *Pandit* but in several other important racial eligibility cases after *Thind*, as well as in legislative debates regarding extensions of racial eligibility for naturalization to the natives of allied nations in Asia during World War II and ultimately in the legislative debates regarding the decision to remove the racial eligibility provisions from the naturalization act in 1952.

In particular, the appeal to statelessness that was advanced in *Pandit* also appeared prominently in other racial eligibility cases before the racial eligibility provisions of the naturalization act were removed by the Immigration and Nationality Act of 1952. As Hannah Arendt writes, the rise of mass statelessness during the early twentieth century as a result of World War I and World War II reveals how superfluous individuals became in the history of nations organized on the basis of the sovereign power to exclude.[195] According to Arendt, although the right of asylum existed from antiquity to provide refuge, protection, and sanctuary to exiles and the persecuted, the modern nation-state viewed the right of asylum to conflict with the rights of the state. In individual instances the right continued to function, but it "cannot be found in written law, in no constitution or international agreement, and the Covenant of the League of Nations never even so much as mentioned it."[196] Although the first statutory protection of refugees in the United States was a provision in the Immigration Act of 1917 that exempted immigrants seeking admission to the United States "to avoid religious persecution" from the act's literacy test,[197] formal legal protections for refugees were not adopted until the United Nations Convention Relating to the Status of Refugees recognized such protection in 1951 and the United Nations Protocol Relating to the Status of Refugees recognized them in 1967, both documents defining a refugee as a person who was stateless due to a "well-founded fear of being persecuted," and the United States did not incorporate this language into its domestic law until it was included in the Immigration and Nationality Act of 1980.[198]

Despite the absence of formal legal protections for refugees during the early twentieth century, however, the appeals to statelessness in *Pandit* and later racial eligibility cases reveals the impulse to provide refuge, sanctuary, and asylum to the oppressed. Importantly, the appearance of this form of appeal in racial eligibility cases also reveals the fact that statelessness creates a more powerful pull of sympathy when it is attributed to an adversary rather than an ally. The majority of refugees who have been admitted to the United States came from sites of Cold War conflict in accordance with foreign policy interests, and decisions regarding asylum applications have often been informed by the State Department. Thus, asylum is more likely to be granted to those who complain of persecution by the nation's adversaries than to those who complain of persecution by its allies, even if the mistreatment suffered is similar.[199] In *Pandit*, although India was not an adversary of the United States its people were imagined as "unruly" colonized subjects in part due to their continued adherence to the caste system.[200] Although Pandit generally appealed to the negative associations of caste in the Western imagination, it is also important that he framed the caste system as targeting him for exclusion on the specific basis that he had become an American citizen and married a "white" American-born woman, or what Judge McCormick called his membership in the American "family."[201] He became identified as part of the American family, as McCormick put it, by sharing in the common suffering, grief, and sacrifice of the nation, allowing him to transcend or suspend perceived racial differences in order to retain his citizenship even if at the cost of reinforcing the negative associations of caste.

Although the right of asylum was not formally recognized during the early twentieth century, Hannah Arendt claims that it "led a somewhat shadowy existence as an appeal in individual exceptional cases for which normal legal institutions did not suffice."[202] We can see this shadowy existence in how contingent the racial classifications under the naturalization act were on perceived threats to the nation and on rhetorical strategies such as Pandit's that positioned naturalization applicants as exceptional cases for which normal legal provisions did not suffice. Arendt cites examples of mass denaturalizations during the early twentieth century such as the Belgian laws of 1922 and 1934 that "canceled naturalization of persons who had committed antinational acts during the war," the Italian (1926), Egyptian (1926), French (1927), and Turkish (1928) laws that allowed for the denaturalization of persons who were "a threat to the social order" or who "committed acts contrary to the interests" of the state, and the Austrian and German laws of 1933 that allowed the state to denationalize any citizen living abroad, much as Russian decrees had since 1921.[203] Although Arendt writes that prior to World War II only totalitarian or half-totalitarian dictatorships "resorted to the weapon of denaturalization with regard to those who were citizens by birth" while after the war even free democracies such as the United States were resorting to such measures with Cold War proposals to strip communists of their birthright citizenship,[204] she neglects the provision of the Cable Act of 1922 that denaturalized any American woman who married a person "ineligible to citizenship" as a means of furthering the nation's Asian exclusion policy.[205] The effect of such proceedings on women such as Lillian Pandit, as well as the effect of the proceedings instituted after *Thind* to strip even naturalized citizens of citizenship rights they had long held, express the same sovereign right to exclude in order to protect national interests as the laws Arendt cites. The following chapters examine other appeals to the exception of statelessness in order to avoid the effect of this sovereign right to exclude in cases contemporary with *Pandit* and surrounding World War II.

3

THE ARMENIAN GENOCIDE,
MARTYRDOM, AND *CARTOZIAN*

On April 23, 2014, Turkey's President Recep Tayyip Erdoğan expressed an unprecedented but considerably qualified condolence to the descendants of Armenians who died in what Erdoğan referred to as "the events of 1915," a reference to what is more commonly known as the Armenian Genocide. In a statement that comes closer to Turkish recognition of the genocide than any to date, Erdoğan stated that "we wish that the Armenians who lost their lives in the context of the early twentieth century rest in peace, and we convey our condolences to their grandchildren."[1] Between 1894 and 1896, Turkish massacres of the Armenian minority in the Ottoman Empire resulted in the deaths of approximately 100,000–250,000 Armenians in the Hamidian massacres, named after Sultan Abdul Hamid II, also called the Red Sultan or the Bloody Sultan for his brutality toward Armenians. Following the rise of the Young Turks after the turn of the twentieth century, another 15,000–25,000 Armenians were massacred in Adana, Turkey, in the spring of 1909, and experts estimate that Ottoman Turks massacred or marched to their deaths 1–1.5 million Armenians during World War I. Although the Armenian Genocide has become established as a canonical genocide alongside other genocides such as the Holocaust and Rwanda, for decades Turkey so effectively censored public discourse regarding the Armenian Genocide that it was called the "forgotten genocide," the "unremembered genocide," the "hidden holocaust," or the "secret genocide."[2]

Despite Erdoğan's expression of condolence to Armenians for "the events of 1915," as he described the Armenian Genocide, Turkey continues to deny both the scale of Armenian deaths during World War I and the characterization of them as genocide.[3] In his April 23, 2014, statement, Erdoğan also sought to frame the war as a "shared pain," stating that "the last years of the Ottoman period were a difficult period, full of suffering for Turkish, Kurdish, Arab, Armenian and millions of other Ottoman citizens, regardless of their religion or ethnic origin," suggesting a false equivalence between the general impact of the war and the deaths of 1–1.5 million Armenians. Warning that "using the events of 1915 as an excuse for hostility against Turkey and turning this issue into a matter of political conflict is inadmissible," Erdoğan called for a joint historical commission to investigate the events and ended his statement by paying tribute to "all Ottoman citizens who lost their lives in the same period and under similar conditions."[4] In a peculiar example of genocide denial, Erdoğan avoided using the word *genocide* even as he denied its propriety in describing the massacre of Armenians during the war, dismissing the utterance of the word itself as inadmissible.

Although Raphael Lemkin did not coin the word *genocide* until the 1940s, his early thinking on the subject was deeply influenced by the Armenian Genocide,[5] and the phrase *crimes against humanity* was originally coined to refer to the Armenian Genocide.[6] The first war crimes tribunals in Turkish history were convened to prosecute Ottoman officials for their treatment of Armenians during the war,[7] but under the pressure of Turkish nationalism the tribunals were suddenly abandoned and the major powers stopped publicly confronting Turkey about the issue.[8] According to Robert Balakian, by denying the genocide, "the Turkish government was, in effect, conducting a campaign against American history as well; for what had been America's first, major international human rights campaign was being subverted by crude power politics."[9] Although twenty-six countries and forty-three states in the United States have recognized the Armenian Genocide either by legislation or proclamation, under diplomatic pressure from Turkey the United States government has yet to recognize it.[10] On March 4, 2010, after the United States House of Representatives foreign affairs committee voted 23–22 to recognize the Armenian Genocide, Turkey's deputy chairman for external affairs publicly warned of "major consequences" if the resolution was accepted by the full House of Representatives, to include downgrading the diplomatic relationship between the United States and Turkey "at every level," affecting "everything from Afghanistan to Pakistan to Iraq to the Middle East process."[11]

Testimony regarding the Armenian Genocide and refugee crisis that it caused served a crucial function in the 1924 trial of Armenian immigrant

Tatos Cartozian, whose naturalization the government opposed based on the assertion that Armenians were Asian and therefore not "free white persons" for purposes of naturalization. In support of the government's assertion that Armenians were Asian rather than European, it cited the fact that the commissioner of immigration classified Armenian immigration as coming from "Turkey in Asia" rather than "Turkey in Europe."[12] During the late nineteenth and early twentieth century, Armenians were commonly referred to as an "Oriental nation,"[13] and the Asiatic Exclusion League opposed their immigration based on the conclusion that they were not "free white persons" but "Western Asiatics" because they were "so deeply tinged with Mongol blood that they have all the instinct and traits of their forebears in eastern Asia—cunning, duplicity, lying and the usual code of Asiatic morality and attendant vices."[14] As such virulent rhetoric suggests, the Armenians who began immigrating to the United States in greater numbers to flee Turkish persecution in the early twentieth century faced substantial racial discrimination in local communities. In Fresno, California, where a large Armenian immigrant community resided, Armenians were referred to as "Fresno Niggers," excluded from churches and social centers, prohibited from owning or leasing land through restrictive land covenants,[15] and excluded from labor unions because they were considered "foreigners."[16]

With regard to Armenian racial eligibility for naturalization, the Bureau of Naturalization had previously deferred to the precedent set by an opinion published in 1909 by Judge Francis Lowell of the United States Circuit Court for the Circuit of Massachusetts in *In re Halladjian*, holding four Armenians to be racially eligible for naturalization,[17] but toward the end of the Supreme Court's opinion in *Thind* Justice Sutherland commented that in light of the 1870 legislative debates rejecting the proposal to remove the word *white* from the naturalization act "there is much in the origin and historic development of the statute to suggest that no Asiatic whatever was included."[18] To the extent that Sutherland's comment related to issues beyond the facts of *Thind* it constituted what is known as dicta, a statement of a court that is not required for resolving a case and is therefore not considered binding legal precedent.[19] Lower courts took notice of this dicta in *Thind*, however, and shortly after *Thind* Commissioner of Naturalization Raymond Crist suggested to Secretary of Labor James Davis that the Bureau of Naturalization should reconsider its policy of leaving the racial eligibility of particular groups to determination by the courts. In light of *Thind*, Crist wrote, it seemed desirable that the admissibility to citizenship of members of other Asiatic races, such as Afghans, Syrians, Armenians, Turks, Kurds, Arabs, and Bedouins, should be tested by means of cancelation proceedings, with a view of having the issue taken to the United States Supreme Court in order that the correct interpretation of the law may be obtained.[20]

None of the groups identified in Crist's letter had been held racially ineligible for naturalization in any published judicial opinion, and of the groups mentioned in the letter only the Armenians faced a new test case regarding their racial eligibility for naturalization.

Coming as it did during the refugee crisis that followed the Armenian Genocide of World War I, the government's renewed challenge to Armenian racial eligibility for naturalization in *Cartozian* is particularly surprising. Because the Immigration Act of 1924 prohibited any alien "ineligible to citizenship" from entering the United States, the case effectively determined the racial eligibility of Armenians for immigration as well.[21] The Treaty of Sèvres initially awarded territory to establish an independent Armenia, but after Turkish nationalists gained independence for Turkey they renegotiated the terms of postwar peace in the Treaty of Lausanne, establishing the current borders of Turkey with no territory awarded to Armenians. Although the United States Senate refused to ratify the Treaty of Lausanne, after the other major powers accepted it the treaty prevailed as the final negotiation of Turkey's postwar borders.[22] Because the Treaty of Lausanne was negotiated and signed while *Cartozian* was pending and was ratified by the other major powers shortly after the trial but before Judge Wolverton issued his opinion, the postwar negotiations for an independent Armenia and the failure of Allied efforts to secure it provide a crucial context for understanding the importance of *Cartozian* to Armenians. The government's decision to challenge Armenian eligibility for naturalization in the United States at such a vulnerable time profoundly shocked the Armenian community. The Armenian weekly review *Gotchag* wrote that the case was of great concern to all Armenians, "rich and poor, educated and uneducated, big and small,"[23] and the *Washington Post* noted that it seemed "strange to raise the question of eligibility at this late hour."[24] The case threatened Armenian refugees not only with the diplomatic abandonment of postwar negotiations for an independent Armenia, but with exclusion by their closest ally, the United States.

Pretrial correspondence regarding *Cartozian* between the lead defense counsel and the Bureau of Naturalization reveals that the bureau reassured Armenians that it conceived of the case as a friendly test case intended to help clarify the racial eligibility of Armenians for naturalization in response to conflicting rulings after some courts had concluded that the Court's dicta in *Thind* indicated that all historical inhabitants of Asia such as the Armenians were racially ineligible for naturalization.[25] Referring to a December 28, 1923, meeting with Commissioner of Naturalization Raymond Crist, Cartozian's lawyer M. Vartan Malcolm wrote to Crist:

> I trust our conference has cleared the atmosphere and has resulted in a mutual understanding. We have no desire to make propaganda and everything has been done to discourage mass meetings and other public demonstrations. We realize that while the suit commenced by the Government is friendly, and on every level I have heard the expression of the hope that we may and will win, still the issues involved are grave. Common prudence, therefore, requires that no effort should be spared to meet these issues quietly but intelligently. I trust that you will do all in your power to assist our Committee and me in this task.[26]

This correspondence suggests that some initial conflict existed regarding the government's renewed challenge to Armenian racial eligibility for naturalization, but that Crist and others assured Malcolm that the government would do all it could to help the Armenians secure a favorable ruling.

The National Archives has preserved a nearly complete record of the trial, including a 167-page transcript of a two-day trial, a 97-page transcript of four expert depositions taken before trial and introduced into the trial record, trial exhibits, and other documents, making the case a particularly valuable example of the discursive practices of racial formation in racial eligibility discourse.[27] No more complete record of the arguments and evidence advanced to determine whether a specific individual was eligible under the racial eligibility provisions of the naturalization act has been discovered. Despite the nearly complete record in the case, however, previous studies of *Cartozian* largely subordinate it to the study of the earlier precedent of *Halladjian*.[28] Further, those who have discussed *Cartozian* have largely limited their comments to the arguments and evidence discussed in Judge Wolverton's published judicial opinion regarding the assimilability of Armenians with contemporary Europeans, including ethnographic and statistical evidence of previous Armenian marriages to Europeans and Armenian naturalizations in the United States. John Tehranian argues, for example, that *Cartozian* epitomizes the performative aspects of whiteness reflected in the racial eligibility cases and concludes that "performance of whiteness and perceived assimilatory capacity played a critical role in the court's decision."[29] Similarly, Phillip Lothyan examines evidence of census figures regarding the number of Armenian naturalizations in the United States, evidence of affinities between European and Armenian languages, and evidence that Armenians intermarried and readily assimilated with Europeans.[30] Ian Haney López mentions the case only in passing to note that Franz Boas provided expert testimony,[31] and Matthew Frye Jacobson and Ariela Gross give the case a similar treatment.[32]

The trial transcript not only reveals the claim that Armenians readily assimilated with contemporary Europeans, however, but the corresponding claim that Armenians were inassimilable with the Turks, Kurds, and Syrian Muslims of Asia Minor as proven by their historical persecution by these groups. The latter argument reflected a powerful appeal to unify against a shared external threat by foregrounding fears of Turkish, and more broadly Islamic, aggression toward Western civilization both historically and during World War I and the interwar period. As Beyza Tekin describes the imagination of Turks in early medieval Europe, they were "the Muslim warrior who fought against the Christian knights during the Crusades . . . a distant enemy, the bloodthirsty warrior, the cruel, blasphemous aggressor of Christendom, the infidel occupier of the holy sites,"[33] and in Shakespeare's *Richard II* the Bishop of Carlisle associates the Turks with blackness and Saracens when he informs parliament of the Duke of Norfolk's death:

> Many a time hath banish'd Norfolk fought
> For Jesus Christ in glorious Christian field
> Streaming the ensign of the Christian cross
> Against black pagans, Turks, and Saracens.[34]

In *Halladjian*, Judge Francis Lowell quoted the last two lines of this passage when he described the Armenians who fled Turkish conquest in the eleventh century to form the Armenian Kingdom of Cilicia.[35] According to Beyza Tekin, as late as World War I the Turks were still imagined as "an unstable territory, the domain of aggression and cruelty, the realm of 'arbitrary violence' and 'Oriental despotism,'" in part due to their frequent massacres of Armenians and other Ottoman subjects.[36] The Asiatic Exclusion League racially classified Turks as Mongolian and even claimed they were racially ineligible for naturalization under the provision of the Chinese Exclusion Act that prohibited courts from granting citizenship to the Chinese, believing the act also barred "persons of Mongolian descent,"[37] and Lothrop Stoddard listed the Ottoman Turks as one of four outstanding racial groups in the "brown world" while citing "Islam's warlike vigor" as a threat to Western civilization.[38] During World War I, American war propaganda reinforced these historical divisions between European Christianity and Islam by thematically invoking the imagery of the Crusades to frame the war as one between "white" Christians and dark barbarian "Huns," and after the war tensions lingered between Turkey and the United States over Turkey's alliance with Germany during the war, its opposition to an independent Armenia after the war, and its continued massacres of Armenians and American missionaries.[39] Although most authorities had held Turks and other groups from the Middle East to be "free white persons" for purposes of naturalization, their racial eligibility for naturalization faced local challenges and the Supreme Court's dicta in *Thind* that "no Asiatic whatever" might be racially eligible for naturalization cast renewed doubt on their eligibility.[40]

In *Cartozian*, the defense exploited fears of Turkish and Islamic aggression throughout the trial. Many witnesses testified that the Turks forced Armenians to convert to Islam "during the massacres," referring to the Turkish massacres of Armenians that escalated from the 1890s through the Armenian Genocide.[41] Indeed, most Armenian immigrants who came to the United States during the early twentieth century fled persecution in the Ottoman Empire.[42] Other witnesses testified that Europeans admired Armenians as "the great defenders of the Christian religion," who withstood "the onslaught of Mohammedanism" at the hands of the Turks, and of how Armenians fought alongside American troops during World War I. References to the Crusades, the Hamidian massacres, and the Armenian Genocide appeared frequently during the trial, depicting Armenians as Christian martyrs who had defended Western values by suffering at the hands of "black pagans, Turks, and Saracens."[43] According to the defense, the historical persecution of the Armenians by Turks, Kurds, and Syrian Muslims proved that that Armenians were not truly Asian despite residing in Asia for centuries.

These historical conflicts and tensions are more evident in the trial transcript than in Judge Wolverton's published judicial opinion. As Robert

Ferguson writes, because trial transcripts reflect complete records of court proceedings in which everything that is said is spontaneously recorded, transcripts reveal, "as nothing else quite can, the real preoccupations in the flow of legal argument," supplying a better perspective for understanding "the formulation of story that lies at the center of all courtroom proceedings." If transcripts are "decidedly more opaque, less accessible, and less dramatic than final opinions," Ferguson writes,

> they are richer in the range of commentary that they include, and they tell us much about the choices made in a final opinion. As complete records of court proceedings, transcripts register the conflict in the advocacy system in ways that a judicial decision ignores in the name of judgment.[44]

In *Cartozian*, the trial transcript reveals the broad range of discursive practices of racial formation employed in the case and provides crucial context for understanding Wolverton's opinion.

This chapter examines the *Cartozian* trial in the context of the existential crisis for Armenian refugees after the Armenian Genocide left many Armenians stateless. The chapter begins with a rhetorical analysis of the defense's trial arguments, which depicted Armenian history as a story of Turkish, Kurdish, and Syrian Muslim persecution of Armenians in Asia Minor as a basis for concluding that Armenians were not truly Asian. The chapter then compares the defense's trial arguments with Wolverton's published judicial opinion, particularly Wolverton's adoption of the defense's historical claim regarding the conflict between the Armenians and their Islamic neighbors as a central justification for his conclusion that Armenians were racially eligible for naturalization. The chapter concludes by discussing martyrdom as a common form of appeal to unify against a shared external threat in which a victim's death is framed in a larger context of meaning as well as how the defense's story of Armenian religious persecution in Asia Minor advanced such an appeal.

THE CARTOZIAN TRIAL: A STORY OF PERSECUTION AND MARTYRDOM

Although the number of Armenians who died during World War I gives the wartime period a particular gravity, Vahakn Dadrian notes that the Armenian

Genocide was "punctuated by a history of accumulative tensions, animosities, and attendant sanguinary persecutions . . . anchored on a constantly evolving and critically escalating perpetrator-victim conflict" extending deep into Anatolian history.[45] Many observers have claimed that Turkish violence toward Armenians in the Ottoman Empire was a result of the rising nationalisms of the early twentieth century and volatile national boundaries in the Balkans, Anatolia, Ukraine, and the Caucasus. According to Cathie Carmichael, for example, previously tolerated minorities in these areas, including the Armenians, never made the transition from subject to citizen, and population elimination in Europe and Western Asia during the nineteenth and twentieth centuries occurred because some groups never obtained full citizenship rights.[46] The resolution of nationality and citizenship conflicts by violent population elimination also inspired future eliminationists, as reflected in the question Adolf Hitler is reputed to have put to German troops before the invasion of Poland after telling them to kill all of the men, women, and children they found: "Who, after all, speaks today about the annihilation of the Armenians?"[47] As this question suggests, eliminationist campaigns frequently targeted the historical as well as the material existence of minority populations.

Immediately after World War I, Armenian immigration to the United States increased as refugees fled the oppression and violence they faced in Turkey. Soon thereafter Armenian applications for naturalization increased, rising by 60 percent between 1920 and the time of *Cartozian*, in part to avert the statelessness that they faced and to secure passports to travel in order to help loved ones who were dislocated abroad.[48] The Armenian refugee crisis also prompted the earliest statutory protection for refugees in the United States, a provision in the Immigration Act of 1917 that exempted immigrants "seeking admission to the United States to avoid religious persecution in the country of their last permanent residence" from the act's literacy test,[49] an exemption that was specifically designed to protect Armenians and Russian Jews affected by the war. In a 1924 habeas corpus proceeding regarding Ossana Soghanalian's request for an exemption to the literacy test under this provision, the record showed that "the Turks killed her father and mother, and killed or deported all the Christians in Hadjin, that she was seized and kept in a harem for 3 1/2 years, until she was saved by the Allied armies," and that she pleaded that "'if the government of the United States sends me back, I will throw myself overboard, as I have no place to go.'"[50] The Armenians represent one of the largest and most distinctive examples of stateless people that resulted from either World War I or World War II.

Apparently as a result of the fact that the government's renewed objection to Armenian racial eligibility for naturalization was a friendly test case brought to clarify their eligibility, the government presented virtually no evidence but rested its case after introducing only a small amount of documentary evidence and brief testimony regarding the fact that the commissioner of immigration classified Armenians as originating in "Turkey in Asia" rather than "Turkey in Europe."[51] The government also introduced George Washington's remark in his Farewell Address to the American people that "with slight shades of difference, you have the same Religion, Manners, Habits, and political principles," a statement from John Quincy Adams's writings expressing the doctrine of manifest destiny in which he states his belief that "the whole continent of North America appears to be destined by Divine Providence to be peopled by one nation, speaking one language, professing one general system of religious and political principles, and accustomed to one general tenor of social usages and customs," and William Darby's 1819 travel narrative *A Tour from the City of New-York, to Detroit, in the Michigan Territory.* The government claimed that these works were relevant because they reflected "who the Fathers regarded as white persons; and that is exactly in line with the decision of Justice Sutherland, of the Supreme Court."[52] The government's case was consistent both with the Bureau of Naturalization's historical interpretation of the phrase *free white person* to mean those who belonged to Western civilization and its policy of taking no position on the racial eligibility of particular groups but merely informing courts of applicants' race and of previous judicial precedent.

Beyond introducing this documentary evidence, the government claimed that Judge Wolverton could take judicial notice of "historical, geographical and ethnological matters and works and authorities" to determine whether Armenians were "free white persons" for purposes of naturalization, a position with which Wolverton and the defense initially agreed. Judicial notice allows courts to rely on the existence and truth of facts without the need for formal proof when certain facts are universally regarded as established by common notoriety, such as laws, historical events, or geographical features.[53] The government claimed that because the Supreme Court declared in *Thind* that the racial eligibility provisions of the naturalization act should be interpreted in accordance with "common understanding," racial classifications did not require formal proof but were among the universally established facts which a court could simply look up in reference works such as the *Encyclopedia Britannica* entry that Justice Sutherland distorted in *Thind.*[54] If the court could take judicial notice of racial classifications, however, it would have rendered the *Cartozian* trial almost unnecessary. Although Wolverton initially agreed that he might consult sources outside the trial record, he later changed his mind, stating in his opinion that "I have confined my investigation to the testimony in the record, and have made no attempt at independent investigation respecting race, color, assimilation, or amalgamation."[55] Because the government presented almost no evidence and Wolverton declined to consult sources outside of the trial record, the case was decided almost entirely on the arguments and evidence presented by the defense.

As reflected in the trial transcript, the defense presented a tripartite case for Armenian whiteness: (1) Armenians descended from Aryan ancestors who migrated to Asia Minor in the seventh century BCE in one of the many Aryan invasions of Central Asia, (2) unlike descendants of the Aryan invaders of the Indian subcontinent whom the Court rejected as non-"white" in *Thind* based on the conclusion that they had violated the caste restrictions on intermarriage, Armenians had remained "white" due to a geographical, religious, and linguistic isolation in Asia Minor even more successful than the isolation produced by the Indian caste system, and (3) Armenians culturally assimilated with contemporary Europeans as evidenced by Armenian Christianity, their affinity for the people of the Russian Caucasus who were the original inspiration for Johann Friedrich Blumenbach's Caucasian racial classification, and intermarriages between Armenians and Europeans. Because *Cartozian* was filed shortly after the Supreme Court issued its opinion in *Thind*, and, like Thind, the defense claimed whiteness through one of the many Aryan invasions of Central Asia, a central problem for the defense was to distinguish the isolation they claimed for Armenians in Asia Minor from that claimed for high caste Hindus in *Thind*. To establish such unparalleled isolation, the defense thematically foregrounded persecution of the Armenian Christian minority in the Ottoman Empire by Turks, Kurds, and Syrian Muslims, including references to the Hamidian massacres of the 1890s and the Armenian Genocide of World War I, as a result of which the Armenians would be a displaced and stateless people if they were held racially ineligible for naturalization in the United States. This historical argument provided the link between the defense's claims of ancient Aryan descent and contemporary assimilability with Europeans, without which the case could not have been distinguished from *Thind*.

The claim that Armenians descended from Aryan ancestors who originated in Europe and migrated to Asia Minor in the seventh century BCE reflected what was known as the classical hypothesis of Armenian origins. The defense supported its claim through the expert testimony of Columbia anthropologist Franz Boas, Harvard ethnologist Roland Dixon, and M. Vartan Malcolm, one of Cartozian's lawyers, who authored *The Armenians in America*. These witnesses cited a host of ethnological, archaeological, philological, geographical, historical, and travel authorities, beginning with the fifth-century BCE Greek historian Herodotus's *Histories* and the first-century BCE Greek geographer Strabo's *Geography*, as support for the conclusion that Armenians descended from Phrygian colonists belonging to the Alpine subdivision of the Caucasian race who migrated to Asia Minor from Europe in the seventh century BCE.[56] Although this was the prevailing hypothesis of Armenian origins, the defense distorted its reliability, the homogeneity it reflected, and the marginality of alternative hypotheses. The history of Armenian origins in Strabo's *Geography*, for example, is premised on mythology and claims that Armenia was founded by the consolidation of a host of heterogeneous people from Central and Western Asia.[57] Similarly, in M. Vartan Malcolm's book *The Armenians in America* he acknowledges that some scholars identified the Armenians with the non-Aryan Hittites of the Bible.[58] In a 1925 article on Armenian mythology in the encyclopedic *Mythology of all Races*, Mardiros Ananikian also argues that the original inhabitants of the Armenian plateau, known as Urartrians, belonged to the same people as the Hittites.[59] Despite the weakness of the classical hypothesis of Armenian origins, however, it was the prevailing theory at the time and endorsed by many authorities.

The appearance of ethnological and philological evidence in a racial eligibility case so soon after the Supreme Court had rejected scientific definitions of race in *Ozawa* and *Thind* may be surprising, but the appearance of Franz Boas as an expert witness in the case provides some insight into the relevance the defense claimed for the scientific authorities it referred to or introduced during the trial. Often referred to as the Father of American Anthropology, Boas was a pioneer of social anthropology and particularly well known for opposing the racial determinism of eugenicists by introducing cultural relativism into anthropology and debunking the idea that Western civilization was superior to other societies. Thus, Boas believed neither in any essential racial characteristics nor in the superiority of "whites" to other racial groups. In fact, according to Lee Baker, white supremacists rank Boas among those who have done the most to damage "white" interests, depicting him as "the man who somehow singlehandedly perpetuated the myth that all races

have an equal potential for achieving intelligence and developing civiliza-
tions."[60] In *Cartozian*, Boas testified as an ethnohistorian, and the scientific
authorities he and other witnesses cited were offered to supplement rather
than supersede evidence regarding ordinary usage of racial classifications.

Premised on the classical hypothesis of Armenian origins, the defense
claimed that despite residing in Asia Minor for centuries Armenians had
remained racially pure due to an unprecedented isolation, which had
"preserved their individuality, their religion, and their national characteristics, as against the conquering Turks, more than probably any other
people."[61] Roland Dixon testified, for example, that the Armenians had maintained an unprecedented homogeneity due to the tremendous pressure applied
to assimilate them by the Turks and other Islamic people of Asian Minor:

> The Armenians retained their nationality and national charac-
> teristics against the tremendous pressure brought to bear upon
> them by these conquerors for many centuries. They were prac-
> tically the first nation to be converted to Christianity, and they
> have retained their faith in the face of tremendous odds from
> the early fourth century to the present time.[62]

The defense also asked Franz Boas to read the following excerpt into the
record from Felix von Luschan's work *Die Tachtadschy*, in which von Luschan
wrote that the racial homogeneity of Armenians was absolutely unparalleled:

> The homogeneity of this people . . . is interesting because it shows
> that owing to the striking geographical, linguistic and religious
> isolation of Armenia during its development and florescence,
> the type has remained pure and has been consolidated to such
> an extent that even today, many centuries after the fall of the
> empire, it has remained almost entirely uniform.[63]

When one witness was asked if he had ever known of any marriages between
Armenians and Turks or Kurds, he replied, "I have never heard of it," and
when another was pressed whether there were not some Armenian Muslims
he replied "not one."[64] In this and similar testimony throughout the trial,
the defense argued that unlike high caste Hindus in India, Armenians not
only shared a biological ancestry with Europeans but had maintained their
racial purity due to an unprecedented geographical, linguistic, and religious

isolation that even surpassed that of the Indian caste system. Unlike *Thind*, however, in *Cartozian* this isolation was framed not as unalliable to Western civilization but as imposed by a shared external threat.

Despite the local prejudice against Armenian immigrants that led to conflicting rulings regarding their racial eligibility for naturalization, the claim that Armenians were persecuted by the Turks, Kurds, and Syrian Muslims of Asia Minor invoked Islamophobic prejudices that were a particularly powerful source of American identification with Armenians during the late nineteenth and early twentieth century.[65] When Americans began establishing Christian missionaries and schools in the Ottoman Empire in the nineteenth century, Christian communities in the United States developed a powerful religious identification with Armenians. As Judge Francis Lowell noted in *Halladjian*, in the European imagination Armenia was "continuously associated with the place and landscape of the Bible," particularly Armenia's national symbol, Mount Ararat, the site of God's covenant with Noah in the biblical book of Genesis and located in Armenia by Renaissance cartographers.[66] Recognizing this mythic power of Armenia in mid-nineteenth-century America, Walt Whitman wrote in his poem to the peoples of the world, "*Salut au Monde*," in *Leaves of Grass*,

> You thoughtful Armenian pondering by some stream of the
> Euphrates! You peering amid the ruins of Nineveh!
> You ascending Mt. Ararat![67]

The early twentieth century became an era of popular epithets about the Armenians, referring to them as the "Christian people of ancient Eden" and "guides to the Crusaders."[68] They were also commonly referred to as "the starving Armenians" in recognition of the starvation that flowed from their treatment by the Turks. After a charity drive spread news of this epithet, American children were often told to remember "the starving Armenians" when admonished to clean their plates.[69] As President Herbert Hoover later commented of the period, "the name Armenia was in the front of the American mind" and "known to the American schoolchild only a little less than England."[70]

As a result of this powerful identification with Armenians, many Americans were shocked by the Armenian Genocide of World War I and the genocide denial that followed. Immediately after the war, books and films about the Armenian Genocide proliferated. Most notably, in 1918, Henry Morgenthau published his memoirs of service as American ambassador to Turkey under the title *Ambassador Morgenthau's Story*,[71] including a lengthy chapter entitled "The Murder of a Nation" in which he recounts horrific details of the Armenian Genocide, describing it as "one of the most hideous chapters of modern history" and lamenting that "the whole history of the human race contains no such horrible episode."[72] The same year that *Ambassador Morgenthau's Story* was published, Aurora Mardiganian's struggle to survive her forced march across Anatolia was published as a book and adapted to silent film under the title *Ravished Armenia*, reflecting the first time genocide was depicted on screen.[73] As a result of these and other works depicting the Armenian Genocide during the early postwar period, the events were fresh in the nation's memory.

The trial transcript reveals that both the Hamidian massacres of the 1890s and the more recent Armenian Genocide of World War I were frequent topics of testimony. Two Armenian witnesses testified that they and their parents had escaped from Turkey during the Hamidian massacres to seek refuge in the United States.[74] According to M. Vartan Malcolm, Armenians came to the United States in larger numbers during the 1890s because of the sympathy that the American missionaries showed to them. "From that time on," Malcolm explained, "these people have come here because of their religious persecution by the Turks and because they found friends among the American missionaries in Turkey."[75] The dramatic increase in Armenian applications for naturalization in the United States since 1920, Malcolm testified, was due to the fact that Armenians, particularly bachelors "whose parents have been driven out of their home land through the last Turkish massacres and the war, needed a passport and other protections to go back and find their lost loved ones."[76] Likewise, during the testimony of James Barton, foreign secretary of the American Board of Commissioners for Foreign Missions who headed the relief expedition in Turkey after World War I, Barton referenced Turkish deportations of Armenians during the war.[77]

In one of the most poignant moments of the trial, at the end of Malcolm's first day of testimony he explained to Judge Wolverton that although President Wilson had awarded Armenians territory for an independent Armenia in the Treaty of Sèvres, "today the entire Armenian people are scattered all over the Near East, and the possibility of Armenians going back to the old country is absolutely dead."[78] When Wolverton asked if the Armenians had any governmental organization in Turkey, Malcolm explained, "we have no Armenia, your Honor" and "there is no Armenia now," adding,

> I must state that we lost a million Armenians during the war. There were before the war four million Armenians in all the world. We lost one quarter of the entire population. No other nation has lost so many as the Armenians. And there are now in all the world about two and a half million Armenians, and most of them are in the Caucasus. They took refuge there in order to save themselves.[79]

When asked if Syria was more populous than Armenia, another witness responded "well, certainly, because the Armenians have been decimated in their numbers, and scattered broadcast."[80] The defense emphasized that due to these conditions, if their eligibility for American citizenship was denied Armenian refugees would be rendered stateless, a "people without a country," explaining that because Armenians who left Turkey forfeited all of their rights and the Turkish government would not issue them passports they could not travel without an American passport.[81] The verbs *scattered* and *decimated* in this testimony attributed particularly high transitivity to the actions of the Turks, Kurds, and Syrian Muslims who were implicitly the agents of the actions, and the word *refuge* similarly suggests violent acts from which Armenians sought protection.

By appealing to the prospect of statelessness, the defense's strategy remarkably paralleled Pandit's claim that he would be an outcast in Indian society and rendered stateless if his naturalization certificate were cancelled. In *Cartozian*, however, Armenians were framed as martyrs who suffered Turkish persecution because they would not recant their Christian faith, the defense frequently reiterating the claim that the Armenians were "the oldest Christian nation" and had remained devoutly Christian through the centuries.[82] This was a familiar narrative at the time regarding Armenian history in the Ottoman Empire. In an article published in *The New Armenia* shortly before *Cartozian*, for example, Herbert Lee wrote that "when . . . we remember that these [Armenians] were slain *because* they would not deny Christ, may we not assert that here is the supreme call to every Christian in the world?"[83] This depiction of Armenians created an appeal to unify against the shared external threat of Turkish and Islamic aggression, framing Armenian affinity with Europeans as the cause of their persecution in Asia Minor much as Pandit had framed his decision to become an American citizen and marry a "white" American-born woman as the cause of his ostracism by the Indian caste system. In *Cartozian*, numerous witnesses testified regarding the positions of Armenians in Christian churches in Armenia, Europe, and the United States, including a number of witnesses who were ministers, pastors, or Sunday school teachers, and the defense's tabulation of hundreds of responses to a questionnaire distributed to Armenian American men listed detailed Christian affiliations for most of the respondents.[84] Paul Rohrbach testified that Armenians in Venice and Vienna belonged to the Armenian Church, which he described as "a very old branch of Christendom," and that the Armenian monasteries in Venice and Vienna had "very large libraries and a very noted printing office" used for "the most difficult printing work in the eastern language of Europe."[85] Similarly, James Barton testified that the Armenians were "pastors of our churches" and "recognized as a Christian race."[86] The defense also exploited the crusading imaginary of European Christianity by eliciting testimony to support the epithet that Armenians had been "guides to the crusaders" by asking witnesses what effect the Crusades had on the Armenians.[87] One witness even attributed the downfall of the last kingdom of Armenia to the fact that "Armenians had given all of their men protectors and a great deal of the resources of their country" to the European crusaders.[8]

The defense's association of Christianity with whiteness and Islam with blackness is particularly disturbing in light of the fact that Armenian efforts to achieve a "white" status by depicting Turks, Kurds, and Syrian Muslims as non-"white" for purposes of naturalization was a dubious legal premise. As previously noted, although the Supreme Court's dicta in *Thind* that "no Asiatic whatever" might be racially eligible for naturalization cast renewed doubt on the racial classification of Turks, Syrians, and other groups from the Middle East, most authorities had held such groups to be racially eligible for naturalization. The defense simply adopted the useful fiction that Turks, Kurds, and Syrian Muslims were not "white" as a foil against which to establish Armenian whiteness by focusing on the segregation of the groups in Asia Minor. Yet if the Armenians were as inassimilable with their Islamic neighbors in Asia Minor as they claimed and these groups were not only racially eligible for naturalization but entitled to birthright citizenship under the Fourteenth Amendment, this strategy could just as easily have suggested that Armenians were not assimilable with contemporary Americans. The First Amendment to the United States Constitution prohibits the establishment of a national religion, and by the early twentieth century religious life in the United States was significantly more diverse than Christianity.[89] Numerous courts held that applicants from Islamic,

Zoroastrian, Hindu, Sikh, and Buddhist religious backgrounds were racially eligible for naturalization, not to mention the children born to these and other groups in the United States who were entitled to birthright citizenship under the Fourteenth Amendment.

In order to meet the almost impossible standard of racial purity that Justice Sutherland adopted in *Thind*, the defense struggled throughout *Cartozian* with what Kenneth Burke calls the "paradox of purity" or the "paradox of the absolute," implicit in "any term for a *collective* motivation, such as a class, nation, the 'general will,' and the like," where the collective motive only becomes "pure" by negating any individual motive.[90] The defense could only prove that Armenians had retained their racial purity despite residing in Asia for centuries by establishing that they had remained in a state of proportionately pure isolation from their Islamic neighbors in Asia Minor, resulting in such hyperbole as the claim that there was "not one" Armenian Muslim.[91] The hyperbolic claims of purity that resulted from this paradox were not only evident in the defense's claim that Armenians were absolutely inassimilable with their Islamic neighbors in Asia Minor, however, but in its corresponding claim that Armenians were absolutely assimilable with contemporary Europeans. In support of the latter claim, the defense offered a wealth of evidence including Armenians' proximity to the people of the Caucasus region of southwestern Russia who formed the original inspiration for Johann Friedrich Blumenbach's Caucasian racial classification, Armenian Christianity, marriages between Armenians and contemporary Europeans, evidence regarding previous Armenian naturalizations in the United States, and evidence of Armenian membership in American churches and professional, civic, and fraternal organizations.[92] Even in conjunction with such evidence, however, the defense often highlighted Armenian support of the American war effort, citing Armenians who served in the United States military, the national guard and state defense corps, and draft and exemption boards, as well as one Armenian who was appointed by President Wilson to serve as a Four Minute Man to speak in support of America's participation in the war and one who served as war work secretary of the Y.M.C.A.[93] Judge Wolverton appeared to have been receptive to these arguments, at times himself expressing interest in the question of Armenian military service. During the testimony of Martin Fereshetian, for example, Wolverton interjected to ask Fereshetian if he had been in the war, and when Fereshetian replied that he was exempt but had asked to serve anyway, Wolverton asked him to confirm that he had not claimed an exemption on account of his nationality.[94] Thus, even when evidence of Armenian assimilability with contemporary Europeans was introduced in the case it was often inseparable from appeals to unify against a shared external threat.

To establish that Armenians readily assimilated with contemporary Europeans, the defense also offered evidence that Armenian immigrant communities in Europe and the United States did not form enclaves, and this testimony at times employed particularly disturbing metaphors of disappearance, loss, and consumption that suggested a continuation of the eliminationist campaign the Armenians had only recently escaped in the war. When asked about Armenian "colonies" in Europe, for example, M. Vartan Malcolm testified that an Armenian colony in Lemberg, Poland, that had once numbered approximately 200,000 Armenians had become assimilated into the Polish population to such an extent that when he visited Lemberg a decade before the trial he found "no trace" of the Armenian colony there with the exception of "the great buildings which these Armenians had built, and the names of the streets in a certain section of the town," because "the entire colony had disappeared by assimilating with the native population."[95] Similarly, Malcolm testified that the oldest Armenian colony in Europe, which was in Holland, had "disappeared, and there are no traces of it left," that an Armenian colony in Marseilles, France, too, had "disappeared," and that Armenian colonies in Italy and England "have been lost within the native populations."[96] Franz Boas read from a French writer explaining that the Armenians had probably not "played an important part in [French] national history and demography" because immediately upon their arrival they "submerged themselves in the great French family" and were "devoured" by the French nation,[97] and one Armenian witness testified that as soon as Armenians learned to speak English, they immediately separated from each other and became "very readily consumed in American life."[98]

The language of this testimony suggests that the assimilability of Armenians was considered proportionate to the "decay" of Armenian immigrant communities in Europe.[99] The metaphors of disappearance, loss, and consumption not only reflected the historical elimination of Armenians but negated Armenian national agency by depicting them as the targets of the actions of Europeans, much like their agency is negated by their depiction as victims of Turkish persecution. As Richard Hovannisian remarked to the Permanent Peoples' Tribunal during its session on the Armenian Genocide in 1985, one result of the Allies' failure to establish an independent Armenia after World War I was a life of exile and dispersion for Armenians, who were "subjected to inevitable acculturation and assimilation on five continents and facing an indifferent and even hostile world that preferred not to remember."[100] The defense's strategy in *Cartozian* not only reflected an acceptance of this fate, but denied the suffering of forced acculturation and assimilation that is a continuing harm of the Armenian Genocide.

WOLVERTON'S ADOPTION OF THE DEFENSE'S HISTORICAL CLAIM

Judge Wolverton did not issue his opinion in *Cartozian* until over a year after the trial. As previously noted, Wolverton had already issued two opinions interpreting the racial eligibility provisions of the naturalization act. Although the Supreme Court reversed his decision in *Thind*,[101] in *Ozawa* the Court expressly approved of *Ellis*, in which Wolverton had held that a Syrian applicant was a "free white person" and therefore racially eligible for naturalization. In *Ellis*, Wolverton had relied almost exclusively on the government's admission that the applicant was "white" while rejecting the government's claim that the phrase *free white person* in the naturalization act included only those "whites" who at the time that the act was passed either lived in Europe or on the North American continent and were "inured to European governmental institutions." Wolverton briefly cited Daniel Brinton's *Races and Peoples*, Augustus Keane's *The World's Peoples*, and Joseph Deniker's *The Races of Man*, noting that from these sources the United States attorney admitted that the applicant was "a member of what is known as the white or Caucasian race," an admission Wolverton found sufficient to render Syrians racially eligible for naturalization.[102] In *Thind*, Wolverton simply relied on previous precedent that had held Armenians, Asian Indians, and Parsis to be "free white persons" for purposes of naturalization.[103]

In *Cartozian*, Wolverton relied neither on a government admission nor on precedent but on the defense's theory of the case. The defense's case provided the basic structure of Wolverton's opinion: (1) Armenians descended from Aryan ancestors who migrated to Asia Minor in the seventh century BCE, (2) Armenians had remained "white" due to their geographical, linguistic, and religious isolation in Asia Minor, and (3) Armenians readily assimilated with contemporary Europeans. After beginning his argument with the premise that Armenians descended from ancient ancestors who belonged to the Alpine subdivision of the Caucasian race, Wolverton offered a highly condensed version of the defense's historical claim of Turkish, Kurdish, and Syrian Muslim persecution to justify the conclusion that Armenians had remained "white" despite residing in Asia for centuries. In contrast to the detail given these historical claims by the defense, however, Wolverton reduced them to the following sentence:

> Although the Armenian province is within the confines of the Turkish Empire, being in Asia Minor, the people thereof have always held themselves aloof from the Turks, Kurds, and allied peoples, principally, it might be said, on account of their religion, though color may have had something to do with it.[104]

Although this sentence offered a highly condensed historical claim and was buried in the middle of Wolverton's opinion, it was the most important sentence in the opinion, because without it the case could not have been distinguished from *Thind*.

The central action of this crucial sentence in Wolverton's opinion is reflected in the phrase *the people thereof . . . held themselves aloof*, particularly the single word *aloof*. By condensing a historical claim of Armenian persecution in Asia Minor to the brief reflexive statement that they "held themselves aloof" from the Turks, Kurds, and allied peoples of the region, Wolverton avoided directly attributing responsibility for the historical conflict to those groups but attributed relatively low transitivity to the Armenians. The action in the phrase *held themselves aloof* referred to a real rather than a threatened or hypothetical action and placed the Armenians in the role of the actor, but it did not clearly indicate a transfer of action between the participants because the action was reflexive. The Armenians did not do anything to the Turks, Kurds, and allied peoples, and it is even unclear whether the sentence referred to an action or an internal state, or, if an action was referred to, what the action was. In addition, by qualifying the phrase *held themselves aloof* with the adverb *always* it is clear that the action was neither sudden nor completed but ongoing. The Armenians had not done anything so much as they had always refrained from society with their Islamic neighbors.

Perhaps most importantly, it is unclear that any action Wolverton's sentence depicted was a deliberate one. The word *aloof* primarily refers to an act of avoidance, which admits of varying degrees of voluntariness. It originally derives from "a loof," a combination of the preposition *a*, referring to motion toward something, and the noun *loof*, referring to the palm of the hand. The combined form *a loof* came to refer to the injunction to a rudder operator of a ship to "keep your loof" in the act of turning the ship toward the wind and away from a dangerous reef or shore. From this arose the sense of avoiding, "steering clear of," or "giving a wide berth to" anything threatening with which one might otherwise come in contact, as in the exhortation to "keep aloof." The word may also describe a lack of sympathy or community with a person or group to which one might otherwise be drawn, in the sense of someone who stands "coldly aloof."[105] The latter is more often associated with the verb *hold,* or alternatively *stand* or *keep,* as in the phrases, *stood aloof, kept aloof, held aloof,* or Wolverton's phrase *held themselves aloof.* This sense of "aloof" may also refer to a person ignoring pleas of help or appeasement, as when Laertes tells Hamlet in the final act of Shakespeare's *Hamlet* "I stand aloof, and will no reconcilement,"[106] or may suggest a resistance offered to seduction, resembling its use as an injunction to turn a ship toward the wind so that it does not drift. Moreover, Wolverton's hesitation in claiming only that "it might be said" that Armenian isolation in Asia Minor was "principally" due to religion but that color "may" have had "something" to do with it further obscured the causality of the action.[107] Interpreting the latter language is complicated by the fact that the social stratification of the Ottoman *millet* system was based on religious rather than racial difference and the fact that the trial included no explicit discussion of color having anything to do with the relationship between the Armenians and their Islamic neighbors in Asia Minor.[108]

The actions foregrounded by Wolverton's sentence were more the unstated actions of the Turks, Kurds, and allied peoples reflected in the defense's trial arguments that form the rhetorical context of the opinion: the "tremendous pressure brought to bear upon [the Armenians] by these conquerors for many centuries,"[109] the "religious persecution" they faced,[110] the violence that created a situation in which they were "scattered all over the Near East,"[111] "decimated in their numbers, and scattered broadcast,"[112] their parents "driven out of their home land through the last Turkish massacres and the war."[113] These highly transitive actions provided the motive for the Armenians to "hold themselves aloof" from their Islamic neighbors in the history of Asia Minor, and only such extreme actions would justify the conclusion that Armenian isolation in Asia Minor surpassed even that of high caste Hindus in India. Although Wolverton avoided involving the court in directly attributing responsibility for the historical conflict between the Armenians and their Islamic neighbors in Asia Minor to the Turks, Kurds, and allied peoples, his opinion is, critically, premised on the defense's historical claim regarding the conflict.

Previous scholars have almost exclusively focused on evidence of Armenian assimilability with contemporary Europeans addressed in the second half of Wolverton's opinion. Based on the Supreme Court's opinion in *Thind*, it is difficult to imagine that the Court would endorse assimilability alone as a sufficient basis for finding a group that had resided in Asia for centuries racially eligible for naturalization, but a focus on this evidence alone also neglects both the historical claim at the heart of the opinion and the fact that Wolverton only relied on assimilability evidence to corroborate an earlier and more figural argument that he introduced regarding Armenians' affiliation with the Russian people of the Caucasus region of southwestern Russia. Specifically, after advancing his historical claim of Armenian isolation in Asia Minor, Wolverton argued that Armenians were assimilable with contemporary Europeans based on Armenians' geographical and political proximity to the people of the Caucasus region of southwestern Russia who inspired Johann Friedrich Blumenbach's Caucasian racial classification:

> Whatever analogy there may be or may exist between the Caucasian and the white races that may be of assistance in the present controversy, the alliance of the Armenians with the Caucasians of Russia has ever been very close. Indeed, the Armenians have for many generations, possibly centuries, occupied territory in Caucasian Russia, have intermingled freely and harmoniously with that people, and the races mix and amalgamate readily and spontaneously.[114]

In contrast to Wolverton's emphasis on this analogy, the defense barely mentioned it during the trial. Although Franz Boas quoted a passage from Blumenbach's *On the Natural Variety of Mankind* in which Blumenbach explains that he named the Caucasian racial classification after Mount Caucasus because he considered the people of that region "the autochthones of mankind,"[115] the transcript is otherwise silent on the history of the Caucasian racial classification. The only time the relationship between the Armenians and the Russian people of the Caucasus region was referred to during the trial was when M. Vartan Malcolm testified that the Armenians "took refuge [in the Caucasus] in order to save themselves" during World War I, connecting the analogy to Armenian flight from persecution.[116]

Immediately after advancing his analogy between the Caucasian and "white" races, Wolverton found that the tripartite argument laid out in the

first half of his opinion was sufficient to determine the racial classification of Armenians, stating that "the status of the [Armenian] people thus
evolved is *practically conclusive* of their eligibility to citizenship in the United
States, seeing that they are of Alpine stock, and so remain to the present
time, without appreciable blending with the Mongolian or other kindred
races."[117] Wolverton referred to additional evidence of Armenian assimilability with contemporary Europeans only after remarking, "but to pursue
the inquiry further, it may be confidently affirmed that Armenians are white
persons, and moreover that they readily amalgamate with the European and
white races."[118] The rest of Wolverton's opinion then catalogued testimony
and statistical evidence that was introduced by James Barton, Franz Boas,
Roland Dixon, Mrs. Otis Floyd Lamson, M. Vartan Malcolm, and Paul
Rohrbach regarding Armenian assimilability with contemporary Europeans,
including statistical evidence introduced by Boas and Malcolm.[119] Because
Wolverton had already set forth the heart of his argument in the first half
of the opinion, the testimony and statistical evidence in the second half of
the opinion functioned only as an appendix of additional evidence.

SHARED SUFFERING AND MARTYRDOM

The Bureau of Naturalization originally intended to appeal Wolverton's
decision to the United States Supreme Court, but after President Harding's
unexpected death the Coolidge administration decided not to appeal.[120]
The record of the proceedings in *Cartozian* is the most complete available
of the arguments and evidence advanced in a single racial eligibility case
at the trial court level, and because it occurred soon after the Court's opinions
in *Ozawa* and *Thind* it offers a unique glimpse into how those opinions
were approached as precedent by lower courts. The transcript reveals that
the trial was largely devoted to the defense's presentation of evidence
and that Wolverton adopted the defense's theory of the case almost in its
entirety, even declining to consult sources outside the record as he had originally indicated he would. The defense focused on a strategy of unification
against a shared external threat in the form of the Turks, Kurds, and Syrian
Muslims whom it depicted as historical persecutors of the Armenians in Asia
Minor, invoking historical memories of the Crusades and the imaginary
of dangerous Mongolian invaders of medieval Europe such as Attila the
Hun, Genghis Khan, and Tamerlane, which had recently been invoked
in American war propaganda during World War I,[121] as well as continuing

tensions between the United States and Turkey after the war. The defense also appealed to the prospect of Armenian statelessness created by the Armenian Genocide of World War I, a strategy that paralleled the appeal to statelessness in *Pandit* and reflected the increasingly conflicted relationship between race, nation, and sovereignty in the postwar period.

The defense's strategy also highlights the significance of martyrdom as a form of an appeal to unify against a shared external threat. The defense depicted Armenian suffering at the hands of Turks, Kurds, and Syrian Muslims as the suffering of Christian martyrs who were persecuted as a result of their adherence to their faith. By positing a necessary relationship between Christianity and Western civilization while depicting Islam as essentially foreign and hostile to that civilization, the defense established Armenians' suffering in Asia Minor as a consequence of their European identity. Like the historical memories of the Crusades invoked in war propaganda during World War I, Armenian martyrdom was a commonplace at the time. In an article published shortly before *Cartozian*, for example, Herbert Lee wrote that "when . . . we remember that [Armenians] were slain *because* they would not deny Christ, may we not assert that here is the supreme call to every Christian in the world?"[122] Shortly after the trial, Mardiros Ananikian similarly dedicated an essay on Armenian mythology in *The Mythology of all Races* to "the memory of the Armenian hosts which fought in the last war for freedom and of the great army of martyrs who were atrociously tortured to death by the Turks."[123] By depicting martyrs as witnesses to a common cause that unites a community through suffering, martyrdom has the transcendent effect suggested by Herbert Lee's claim that Armenian martyrdom was a "call to every Christian in the world."[124] In *Cartozian*, the defense depicted Armenian martyrdom as a rallying cry for solidarity with European Christians.

Many scholars have noted that the willingness of individuals to sacrifice themselves, often to the point of their lives, coalesces the boundaries of national and group identity.[125] In her study of the rhetorical strategies of martyrologists during the French Reformation, Nikki Shepardson claims that the rhetoric of martyrdom in martyrological texts of the period reflects a significance that extended beyond the martyr's individual conscience by serving "to console and unite the faithful, while at the same time defining their world view vis-à-vis persecution."[126] The creation of Huguenot communal identity during the French Reformation, Shepardson writes, was "intrinsically tied to the shared experience of persecution and suffering" through representations of martyrdom. According to Shepardson, the purpose of martyrological narratives is to "respond to the needs of a fledgling community struggling for their existence and sense of identity," and the depictions of martyrdom found in such texts bound the Huguenot community together on a psychological level and created a powerful sense of solidarity by defining it as a "community of suffering." This solidarity, Shepardson notes, provided equality for those included in the community regardless of age, class, gender, or nationality, through "the universality of martyrdom—a phenomenon transcendent of the traditional boundaries and hierarchies within a community."[127] Depictions of martyrdom incorporated the individual experiences of the Huguenot community into a "larger, more profound, and meaningful context" by emphasizing "the faithful's responsibility not only to God, but the individual's responsibility to the community as well."[128]

Like the transcendent function of Huguenot martyrdom during the French Reformation, the defense's strategy in *Cartozian* incorporated the historical suffering of Armenians in Asia Minor into a larger context of meaning. By depicting Armenians as martyrs for European Christianity, the defense positioned Armenians as belonging to Western civilization despite residing in Asia for centuries and emphasized the need for American solidarity with Armenians against Turkish and Islamic aggression. This strategy foregrounded the hostile actions of Turks, Kurds, and Syrian Muslims in order to amplify the importance of transcending any perceived conflict between Armenian immigrants and local communities in the United States. The Ghadr Party to which Thind belonged had also adopted the rhetoric of martyrdom by echoing a long Sikh tradition of martyrdom that celebrated the martial glory and sacrifices of Sikh martyrs,[129] often running advertisements in its journal *Ghadr* calling for "heroic soldiers" to fight in Hindustan with the reward of "martyrdom,"[130] but the source of Ghadrite suffering was not an adversary but an ally of the United States. In *Cartozian*, by contrast, the defense foregrounded the hostile actions of a nation that had recently been a wartime adversary of the United States and of a broader group of people that invoked historical Islamophobic prejudices among European Americans, appealing to statelessness at the hands of America's adversaries much like the successful claims of political asylum applicants.[131] Accordingly, the defense's strategy in *Cartozian* provides another example in racial eligibility discourse of an incipient form of the "well-founded fear of persecution" standard of later political asylum law.

4

WORLD WAR II ALLIANCES IN ASIA AND
THE END OF RACIAL ELIGIBILITY FOR NATURALIZATION

During the two decades after the Supreme Court denied certiorari in *Pandit*, courts published only six judicial opinions regarding the racial eligibility provisions of the naturalization act. In contrast to the two decades before *Pandit*, when thirty-eight published opinions and numerous unpublished opinions were issued in racial eligibility cases, the evidence suggests that after *Pandit* fewer cases arose regarding the racial eligibility provisions of the act. This decline in cases appears to be a result, in part, of the fact that the racial eligibility of natives of the most populous areas of Asia—China, Japan, and India—had already been decided by the Chinese Exclusion Act and the Court's opinions in *Ozawa* and *Thind*. In addition, after the Immigration Act of 1917 prohibited immigration from the Asiatic Barred Zone and the Immigration Act of 1924 introduced a discriminatory immigration quota system that privileged immigration from northern Europe and prohibited the admission to the United States of all aliens "ineligible to citizenship," fewer Asians were eligible to immigrate to the United States and most decisions regarding the racial eligibility provisions of the naturalization act were shifted to immigration authorities and special immigration courts.[1] Not only was further immigration from India prohibited following *Thind*, but the discriminatory quota system of the Immigration Act of 1924 effectively excluded most Armenian immigration despite the fact that they remained racially eligible for immigration. The total quota for Turkey, for example, was one hundred people per year.[2] The judicial opinions that were published in racial eligibility cases after *Pandit* also raised no novel issues but simply applied existing precedent. Three of the opinions

involved procedural questions regarding cancellations of naturalization certificates granted to two Asian Indians and a Filipino,[3] two of the opinions
involved so-called "mixed-blood" cases regarding persons of mixed Chinese
and Hindu descent,[4] and one involved an Afghan immigrant whom the
court held racially ineligible for naturalization based on the conclusion that
he "approximates to Hindus."[5]

After the passage of the Immigration Act of 1924, however, the United
States Board of Immigration Appeals (hereinafter BIA) issued a series
of written opinions interpreting the racial eligibility provisions of the naturalization act in cases arising out of decisions by border agents excluding
immigrants from admission to the United States based on the conclusion
that they were not "free white persons" and were therefore racially ineligible
to citizenship. These interpretations of the racial eligibility provisions of the
nationality act can be found both in cases in which the racial classification
appears to have been uncontested and occupied a relatively insignificant
place in the opinions and in cases in which the racial classification was the
central issue addressed by the opinion. In a number of cases between 1944
and 1947, the BIA issued opinions containing unexplained findings that
various immigrants were persons of the "white race" while mostly discussing other issues. These cases included findings that natives and citizens
of Canada, Mexico, Hungary, Italy, and Portugal belonged to the "white
race," without indicating how the BIA arrived at its racial classifications.[6] In
other opinions issued as late as 1952, however, the BIA focused almost
entirely on the racial classification of Afghan, Arab, Kalmyk, Tatar, Thai,
and Vietnamese immigrants, seeking to justify its interpretation of the racial
eligibility provisions of the nationality act by reference to judicial precedents
such as *Ozawa* and *Thind*.

As a result of the relatively small number of published judicial opinions
and the absence of novel issues raised in those that were published, racial
eligibility discourse after *Pandit* has received little attention by previous
scholars. Ian Haney López's *White by Law*, for example, stops with the
Court's opinion in *Thind* based on the conclusion that the published
judicial opinions in later racial eligibility cases reflected no new "racial
rationales."[7] This neglect of racial eligibility discourse after *Thind* obscures
a number of significant developments during the World War II era that
ultimately undermined the Asian exclusion policy reflected in the racial
eligibility provisions of the naturalization act before they were removed
in 1952. The Nationality Act of 1940 extended racial eligibility for citizenship

to "races indigenous to the Western Hemisphere," making natives of the Western Hemisphere born outside the territorial limits of the United States racially eligible for naturalization, and six years later Congress modified this to include "races indigenous to the continents of North or South America or adjacent islands."[8] In 1942, Congress passed the Second War Powers Act which provided expedited naturalization without regard to race for those who served honorably in the United States military during World War II, and the same year an Asian Indian naturalization applicant filed a petition for writ of certiorari in the United States Supreme Court urging for the first time that the Court reconsider and overrule *Thind*.[9] In 1943, the Chinese Exclusion Repeal Act was overwhelmingly supported by both the executive and legislative branches of the United States government, extending racial eligibility for naturalization to "Chinese persons or persons of Chinese descent,"[10] and by 1944 some federal district courts had concluded that in light of the legislative changes to racial eligibility for naturalization the Court's opinion in *Thind* was no longer binding precedent and the racial eligibility provisions of the nationality act should be broadly interpreted "so as to promote friendlier relations between the United States and other nations."[11] In 1945, Immigration and Naturalization Service lawyer Charles Gordon argued in the *Pennsylvania Law Review* that the United States should end its Asian exclusion policy, citing the need for strong alliances in the war and the uncomfortable association of the racial eligibility provisions of the naturalization act with the Nazi Nuremberg laws,[12] and in 1946 Congress passed the Filipino and Indian Naturalization Act, explicitly extending racial eligibility for naturalization to "Filipino persons or persons of Filipino descent" and "persons of races indigenous to India."[13] By 1946, the Japanese were the largest and most readily identifiable group to remain racially ineligible for naturalization.

These changes to the racial eligibility provisions of the naturalization act during the World War II and early Cold War coincided with a dramatic revision of America's history of race relations that arose in response to World War II. In Justice Frank Murphy's concurring opinion in the United States Supreme Court's opinion in *Hirabayashi v. United States* (1944), in which the Court upheld the constitutionality of curfews that formed part of the internment of Japanese Americans after Pearl Harbor, Murphy praised the history of racial equality in the United States. Although he did not mention the Court's precedents in *Ozawa* and *Thind*, he implicitly repudiated the attribution of inassimilability to Asian immigrants:

Distinctions based on color and ancestry are utterly inconsistent with our traditions and ideals . . . To say that any group cannot be assimilated is to admit that the great American experiment has failed, that our way of life has failed . . . Today is the first time, so far as I am aware, that we have sustained a substantial restriction of the personal liberty of citizens of the United States based upon the accident of race or ancestry.[14]

In this statement, Murphy neglected both the Court's holdings that racially limited those who could become citizens—including the Court's holdings in *Ozawa*, *Thind*, and *Toyota* that Japanese, Hindu, and Filipino persons were racially ineligible for naturalization—as well as the restrictions on the citizenship of racial minorities imposed by Jim Crow laws. Perhaps Murphy did not consider such laws to be as "substantial" a restriction on personal liberty as the forced relocation and detention of Japanese Americans, but his claim is surprising in light of the growing questions regarding the constitutionality of segregation during the following decade that culminated in the Court's opinion in *Brown v. Board of Education* (1954).[15]

Far from an anomaly, however, Justice Murphy's account of American race relations in *Hirabayashi* expressed a growing idealism that emerged during World War II regarding the relationship between American war propaganda, which framed the war as a global fight for democracy led by the United States, and the principle of racial equality. This idealism often included revisionist histories of American race relations that elided the nation's history of racial discrimination in order to project an image of national unity. During legislative debates regarding the Chinese Exclusion Repeal Act of 1943, for example, Tennessee representative John Jennings claimed that the United States had "always been friendly to the people of China," and Pennsylvania representative James Wright asked, "Do you think America, with the traditional respect it has for human rights—America, the traditional champion of liberty—should imitate the Germans and Japs—should put herself in the position of saying to a proud civilized people, the Chinese, 'You are not fit to come here and live'?"[16] In his 1945 article in the *Pennsylvania Law Review*, Charles Gordon asked how the nation could square its racial exclusion policy with "our advocacy of the principles of equality upon which our nation was founded—equality of opportunity, equality before the law, and equal treatment for all men so far as consistent with the public interest."[17] During World War II, the image of the United States as a model of democracy emerged in direct response to anti-American propaganda that highlighted the nation's history of racial discrimination, and efforts to combat this propaganda substantially impacted racial eligibility discourse. Although previous scholars have explored the galvanizing influence that the Cold War had on the civil rights movement in the United States,[18] none have explored the similar influence that World War II had on racial eligibility for naturalization.

Prior to World War II, appeals to abstract principles of equality were surprisingly absent in racial eligibility discourse. Although in 1870 Senator Charles Sumner advanced the principle of equality reflected in the Declaration of Independence's proclamation that "all men are created equal" during the legislative debates regarding his proposal to remove the racial eligibility provision from the naturalization act, references to the principle of equality and the Declaration's proclamation that "all men are created equal" nearly vanished in debates regarding racial eligibility for naturalization between 1870 and World War II. When Takuji Yamashita appealed to the principle of equality at the turn of the twentieth century in support of his application for a license to practice law in the state of Washington which depended on his racial eligibility for naturalization, the Washington attorney general openly mocked him for relying on "the worn out star spangled banner orations, based upon the Declaration of Independence that all men are created equal."[19] Similar appeals are not even evident in most of the briefs and judicial opinions in racial eligibility cases. Until 1942, no one even argued that the racial eligibility provisions of the naturalization act violated the principle of equal protection reflected in the United States Constitution.[20]

During World War II, however, the principle of equality, and particularly the Declaration of Independence's proclamation that "all men are created equal," suddenly emerged as a commonly expressed unifying device in the context of the existential threat presented by the war. At the beginning of Frank Capra's 1942 film *Prelude to War,* the first of seven films he produced during World War II in cooperation with the United States Office of War Information in a series entitled "Why We Fight," the narrator explains that the free world became free through men of vision, including Moses, Mohammed, Confucius, and Christ, who "all believed that in the sight of God all men were created equal, and from that there developed this spirit among men and nations which is best expressed in our own declaration of freedoms: 'We hold these truths to be self-evident, that all men are created equal.'" The film describes this principle of equality as "the cornerstone upon which our nation was built."[21] The Declaration's proclamation of equality also played an important role in racial eligibility discourse during World War II and the early Cold War, cited in legislative debates regarding the Chinese Exclusion Repeal Act and the Filipino and Indian Naturalization Act as well as in the final published judicial opinion in a racial eligibility case.

This chapter examines how the compelling need for alliances in Asia to defeat the Japanese during World War II and Soviet communism during the early Cold War led authorities to reconsider racial exclusion in immigration and naturalization. I begin by examining legislative debates regarding the extension of racial eligibility for naturalization to the Chinese, Asian Indians, and Filipinos during and shortly after World War II, particularly the appearance of appeals to unify against Japanese aggression in the Pacific during the war and the spread of Soviet communism after the war. I then examine how these legislative changes led courts to question the Supreme Court's opinion in *Thind* and adopt a more inclusive interpretation of racial eligibility for naturalization to suit foreign policy goals, both in judicial opinions and in opinions issued by the BIA holding that Tatar and Kalmyk refugees from the Soviet Union were "free white persons" for purposes of naturalization despite their historical classification as Mongolians and Asian origins. I conclude by considering how the Declaration of Independence's proclamation that "all men are created equal," frequently cited as a unifying device during this period, itself depends on the amplification of a shared external threat in the statement of grievances at the heart of the document.

PEARL HARBOR AND THE CHINESE EXCLUSION REPEAL ACT

It took more than sixty years to repeal the Chinese Exclusion Act, and the legislation that repealed it was specifically proposed to strengthen the nation's alliance with China to defeat Japan during World War II. During the interwar period and the early years of the war, Japanese hostility toward the United States was fueled in part by the defeat of Japan's racial equality proposal to the League of Nations during the Paris Peace Conference, the Court's decision in *Ozawa*, and the ban on aliens "ineligible to citizenship" from entering the United States in the Immigration Act of 1924, the latter effectively abrogating the bilateral Gentlemen's Agreement regarding Japanese immigration to the United States.[22] When the details of the

Immigration Act of 1924 were negotiated in Congress, the Japanese ambassador to the United States warned of "grave consequences" if any exclusionary measures should target Japan. Congressional leaders perceived the ambassador's warning to be a veiled threat of war, which only galvanized congressional resolve to support the immigration act.[23] The State Department recognized the hostility such a racial restriction on Japanese immigration was likely to engender and warned President Coolidge of the danger, but Coolidge signed the Immigration Act of 1924 anyway.[24] Soon after the act was passed, Rumanian writer and educator Savel Zimand wrote in *The New York Times* that the racial exclusion issue had assumed such importance in Japan that "it is apt to become in the near future a menace to world peace,"[25] and Raymond Buell, president of the nonprofit Foreign Policy Association, wrote in 1934 that "the Japanese people are even more indignant over the treatment accorded Orientals by the United States than are the American people over Japanese imperialism."[26]

In *Cold War Civil Rights*, Mary Dudziak documents the negative impact that America's race relations had on its image abroad during the Cold War period of the 1950s and early 1960s and the influence this consideration had on the civil rights movement in the United States. As civil rights crises became foreign affairs crises, Dudziak writes, the relationship between civil rights and Cold War propaganda developed into a story of a struggle over the narrative of race and democracy.[27] Her analysis largely focuses on the relationship between the United States and the newly independent African nations during the early Cold War, however, and is almost entirely limited to the treatment of African Americans. The treatment of Asian Americans surrounding World War II and the early Cold War period has been largely unexplored, but also had a significant impact on the narrative of race and democracy in the United States. The nation's conflicts involving Asia and Asian Americans were often inextricably intertwined with the growing tensions between the United States, Japan, and Asia over the nation's Asian exclusion laws, reflected in part in the racial eligibility provisions of the naturalization act and their incorporation into the ban on those "ineligible to citizenship" from entering the United States in the Immigration Act of 1924.[28] These issues were uniquely illuminated during the World War II period.

Although discussions of race during World War II often focus on the racial ideology of Nazi Germany, the war in the Pacific also had a significant impact on racial ideology. After Pearl Harbor, leaders on both sides of the Pacific presented the war in terms of a race war between the Orient and Occident, leading historian John Dower to argue that this framing of the war in the Pacific gave rise to an obsession with extermination on both sides, a "war without mercy" that was far more savage than anything in the European theater of the war.[29] Given this framing of the war in the Pacific, the Asian exclusion laws of the United States became a major theme of Japanese propaganda during World War II. During legislative debates regarding the Chinese Exclusion Repeal Act, Minnesota representative Walter Judd referred to the Japanese ambassador's warning that the ban on Japanese immigration in the Immigration Act of 1924 would have "grave consequences" and noted that "the Americans at Bataan and Iwo Jima would admit there have been rather 'grave consequences,'" which he claimed confirmed his repeated warning that war with Japan was inevitable from the time the Immigration Act of 1924 was passed.[30] Because the war in the Pacific was framed as a race war and Asians decried the humiliation of being allied with a country that declared them racially ineligible for immigration and naturalization, the Asian exclusion laws became a crucial political issue during the war.[31]

In particular, the Japanese government relentlessly focused on the Asian exclusion laws in its propaganda throughout Asia during the interwar period and World War II. In 1942, Pearl Buck reported that Japan was telling Asians in the Philippines, China, India, Malaysia, and Russia that "every lynching, every race riot gives joy to Japan" because they gave credence to Japan's message that "white" America was false to its claim that it fought on the side of democracy.[32] According to a typical Tokyo broadcast:

> The few Chinese who are temporarily permitted to enter the United States . . . are forced to undergo the most humiliating and discourteous treatment and detention at the various immigration stations . . . The Chunking authorities must also know that the Chinese are rigidly excluded from attaining American citizenship by naturalization, a right which is accorded to the lowliest immigrant from Europe.[33]

As Chinese, Indian, and Burmese nationalists formed independent armies to collaborate with the Japanese during the war, American officials began to fear Japan's capacity to finally achieve the pan-Asian alliance it had sought throughout the first half of the century and threaten the West with a war in which the "white" races would be outnumbered.[34] Accordingly, officials considered it a matter of military expediency to combat such propaganda by repealing the Chinese Exclusion Act. During legislative debates regarding the repeal act, for example, Massachusetts representative John McCormack appealed to the claim made by a United States Navy commander that the act was "worth 20 divisions to the Japanese army," and Utah senator Elbert Thomas remarked that the act was "a military action just as surely as is winning a battle in Italy."[35]

The House Committee on Immigration and Naturalization held public hearings regarding the Chinese Exclusion Repeal Act between May 19 and June 3, 1943, featuring testimony from witnesses such as Pearl Buck, the Library of Congress's Asia expert Arthur Hummel, religious leaders, and military commanders.[36] The House debated the act on October 20, 1943, the Senate debated it on November 26, 1943, and it was signed into law on December 17, 1943. During the debates regarding the act, legislators explicitly identified the need to combat the Japanese, who were described as "our most contemptible enemy" and "America's most dangerous enemy," "vicious" and "treacherous," "shrewd, conniving . . . propagandists," guilty of many "atrocities and dastardly machinations."[37] Representative McCormack referred to the "savagery of our enemy, Japan," and to Japanese "encroachment upon [China's] sovereignty," Nebraska representative Carl Curtis referred to the Japanese "drive to break down the resistance of the Chinese," and Texas representative Ed Gossett referred to the Japanese "bending every effort to knock China out of the war or to greatly weaken the Chinese war effort."[38] In all of these statements, not only did the speakers explicitly label the Japanese as dangerous enemies, but they foregrounded the threat that the Japanese posed to both the United States and China by attributing a relatively high degree of transitivity to Japanese actions. The words *vicious, treacherous, shrewd,* and *conniving* suggested the deliberate actions of an actor toward a distinct target significantly affected by the actions, as did the qualities of being *contemptible* and *dastardly.* The verbs *break down* and *knock* added relatively high completeness and punctuality to Japanese actions, and the reference to *encroachment* on China's sovereignty highlighted their threat to China's territorial sovereignty. In this and similar language during the debates, Chinese exclusion was subordinated to the transcendent threat the Japanese were perceived to pose.

These attributions of relatively high transitivity to Japanese actions were not isolated, but appeared throughout the debates. In another example,

Representative McCormack stated that "the Tokyo radio never hesitates to seize a single opportunity to besmirch America to China," and he referred to Japanese propaganda as a "poison" being circulated among those

> who saw their brothers and sons die while struggling to keep high the flag we love [in the Philippines.] Japan has rid Burma, French Indochina, Thailand, and the Dutch East Indies of white authority. She has given these peoples the illusion of liberty and has made them in their present state of dependency fertile fields for dissatisfaction with America as evidenced particularly by our Exclusion Act. Race hatred is the master weapon of the Nippon as well as the Nazi. It is our greatest threat to world peace.[39]

In these statements, the verbs *seize, besmirch, circulate, rid,* and *made* all attributed high transitivity to Japanese actions by framing their actions as the deliberate, completed, and punctual actions of an unaffected actor toward distinct and significantly affected targets. Representative McCormack even depicted race hatred as a "weapon" that threatened world peace.

In contrast to these amplifications of the Japanese threat, legislators praised the Chinese during the debates. After decades during which all natives of the Far East had been indiscriminately denigrated in racial eligibility discourse, in the context of the war in the Pacific the Chinese and Japanese were suddenly depicted as starkly different. Illinois representative Adolph Sabath, for example, stated that the Chinese were "so much different from the Japanese that there is no comparison." According to a letter from the National Conference of Christians and Jews that Sabath read into the record, "the Chinese people, by their heroic resistance to Japan, have certainly proved themselves a great and noble people," and Sabath's own remarks regarding the character of the Chinese reflected a virtual encomium to Chinese heroism during the war: "The Chinese people cannot be charged with being derelict or disloyal. They cannot be charged with not being law abiding. It cannot be charged that they are repugnant and dishonest." New York representative Hamilton Fish described China as "a very gallant and heroic nation that has been fighting for the last 6 years, almost without arms, against one of the strongest and mightiest armies in the world," and other legislators praised Chinese "heroism" and "bravery" in the Pacific.[40] This sudden unity of the United States and China against a shared external threat inspired Missouri representative William Elmer to remark that only as a result of the Japanese attack on Pearl Harbor had the people once regarded as "Chinese devils" suddenly become "Chinese saints."[41]

Importantly, these depictions of Chinese heroism also attributed relatively low transitivity to Chinese actions. In Representative Fish's remark that the Chinese "have been fighting . . . against one of the strongest and mightiest armies in the world," for example, he used the verb *fighting* intransitively.[42] Similarly, Representative Judd remarked that "the Chinese have endured over 6 years of bombings and invasion, famine, disease, dislocation of all normal life, uncontrolled inflation, enforced migration of over 50,000,000 people, and a year and a half of almost complete blockade,"[43] and Nebraska representative Carl Curtis remarked that the Chinese had "withstood bombings, executions, hunger, disease, and all the terrible ravages of war," being attacked by "a savage enemy, who possesses the mechanized monsters of war."[44] Representative Sabath stated that although "peaceful China has suffered at the hands of [Japan] . . . she continues under great disadvantage and handicap to defend herself."[45] In these statements, the aggressive actions of the Japanese and their effect on the Chinese are amplified while Chinese actions are depicted as defensive and intransitive. Relatively little action is transferred from the Chinese to any target in these descriptions, and to the extent any action is transferred it is compelled by the aggressive actions of the Japanese.

These and other speakers in the debates also framed the defensive actions of the Chinese and their sacrifices as performed specifically on behalf of "salutary internationalism" and "the American principles of equality of opportunity for life, liberty, and happiness for all mankind."[46] In President Roosevelt's letter urging Congress to pass the Chinese Exclusion Repeal Act, he declared that China had stood "alone in the fight against aggression" and continued her struggle "against very great odds,"[47] language remarkably similar to that of witnesses in *Cartozian* regarding the conflict between Armenians and their Islamic neighbors in Asia Minor. In a similar statement of the overwhelming odds the Chinese faced, Texas representative Ed Gossett stated that China

> has suffered more than two and one-half million casualties to her military personnel, and approximately 10,000,000 casualties in civilian personnel. All of her great industries have been destroyed, her leading cities looted and occupied by the enemy, her schools and churches destroyed, yet China has fought on.[48]

The contrasting depictions of Japanese aggression and Chinese heroism during the debates powerfully appealed to the impulse to unify against a shared external threat.

This appeal was not only implicit throughout the debates but was often explicitly stated. In a letter from New York representative Martin Kennedy to China's First Lady Soong May-ling, which Kennedy read into the record, for example, Kennedy called the Chinese "a people which have shared with us the common danger,"[49] and in the United States Senate debates Utah senator Elbert Thomas appealed to China's "common participation in a common effort" with the United States.[50] Other legislators similarly explained their calls for cooperation with China by citing the existential crisis of the war. Representative Judd, for example, argued against isolationism in the face of the crisis presented by the war:

> No one will dispute that this Nation is in the most critical hour in its whole history. The feeling of self-sufficiency and self-confidence with which we have always approached our problems is not wholly justified under the present circumstances.[51]

Similarly, Washington congressman Warren Magnuson referred to the Chinese as "brothers in arms," arguing that the Chinese Exclusion Repeal Act was undoubtedly supported by "our soldiers and sailors and marines returning from the Pacific war front, fighting side by side, maybe literally side by side, with Chinese as brothers in arms," who would expect Congress to put "our brothers in arms on an equal basis with all the other allies."[52] During the debates in the United States Senate, Florida senator Charles Andrews also referred to the Chinese as "comrades in arms."[53]

In remarkable contrast to the racial eligibility discourse of the previous century, such appeals often found expression in appeals to the principle of equality, particularly in references to the American Revolution and the Declaration of Independence's proclamation that "all men are created equal." Representative Kennedy, for example, stated that he would vote in favor of the act "because of the principle that is involved, and that is the principle of equal treatment to all men."[54] Representative Judd compared America's alliance with the Chinese to the American Revolution, stating that "we who are the descendants of 1776 ought to know of people who fought in the snow with bare, bleeding feet for such things as equality." In fact, Judd claimed that the principle of equality was more important than providing material aid to the Chinese: "The chief thing is the principle of being treated as equals."[55] Likewise, Arizona representative John Murdock stated that "Thomas Jefferson threw out something we all give lip service to, when he said in the Declaration of Independence that all men are created equal," and Murdock referenced the Lincoln–Douglas debates of 1858 regarding the relationship between the Declaration's proclamation of equality and slavery. Washington representative John Coffee also referred to the Declaration, arguing that "this is an opportunity to demonstrate to the world that we recognize the Chinese as brothers, insofar as we are willing to exemplify the Declaration of Independence where it states, 'All men are created equal.'"[56] Representative McCormack noted that Chinese children are taught to believe that Americans believe "all men are created equal, with rights and privileges which the State did not create, but which the State is bound to protect."[57] In these statements, legislators expressed unity against a shared external threat by referring to the nation's founding in which American colonists unified against the British during the Revolutionary War.[58]

The legislative debates regarding the Chinese Exclusion Repeal Act mirrored the glorification of the Chinese in American public discourse after Pearl Harbor.[59] In contrast to the negative stereotypes of the Chinese that had been prevalent in the United States for almost a century, depicting them as "heathen Chinee," "mice-eaters," and "Chinks," after Pearl Harbor the Chinese were suddenly depicted as a brave and honorable people due to their status as allies in the war. As one Chinese American remarked, "World War II was the most important historic event of our times" because for the first time "we could make it in American society." Similarly, another Chinese American recalled, "all of a sudden, we became part of an American dream" and were "accepted by Americans as being friends because at that time, Chinese and Americans were fighting against the Japanese and the Germans and the Nazis."[60] In 1943, Vice President Henry Wallace declared that China had been "one of the chief inspirers of, and indirectly one of the creators of, western democracy," exerting a powerful influence on the democratic concepts found in the United States Constitution,[61] and as previously mentioned Frank Capra's Office of War Information film *Prelude to War* lists Confucius among the men of vision who freed the world.[62] This new imaginary of the Chinese was also reflected in American war films such as the 1943 film *Mission to Moscow*, in which a Chinese official and Russian doctor remark during United States ambassador Joseph Davies's tour of a Moscow hospital treating Chinese civilians that "if our three countries would be united, we could stop all this" and "the three of us must face this common enemy together."[63] In the 1944 film *The Purple Heart*, a young Chinese man heroically kills his father in a Japanese courtroom after his father gives false testimony against American pilots put on trial for taking part in the Doolittle Raid.[64] Although these new attitudes toward the Chinese did not continue for long once the war ended, during the war the national perception of the Chinese fundamentally changed in a manner that was reflected prominently during the legislative debates regarding the Chinese Exclusion Repeal Act. As a result of this sentiment, the United States extended racial eligibility for naturalization to the Chinese and altered the nation's Asian exclusion policy to such an extent that the end of the policy seemed imminent.

JUDICIAL CASES AFTER THE CHINESE EXCLUSION REPEAL ACT

Given the central role that Chinese exclusion played in the continued existence of the racial eligibility provisions of the naturalization act after the Civil War, the judiciary believed the Chinese Exclusion Repeal Act cast doubt on congressional intent regarding the viability of the racial eligibility provisions of the nationality act, including the interpretation of the phrase *free white person* in the act. In a racial eligibility case decided the year after Congress passed the Chinese Exclusion Repeal Act, for example, Judge Paul McCormick of the United States District Court for the Southern District of California, who had presided in *Pandit*, questioned the continuing authority of *Thind* in a case regarding the racial eligibility for naturalization of a "native and citizen of Palestine . . . of the Arabian race":

> To interpret the words "white persons" as found in the existing statute applicable to this petition in the manner stated by the Supreme Court in the *Thind* decision would, in my opinion, render ineffectual provisions now present in the law relating to certain Asiatics and to descendants of races indigenous to the Western Hemisphere, and would also tend to introduce confusing and contradictory interpretations of the statute under construction. Such results should be avoided if possible.
>
> We think that the amendments to applicable law subsequent to the *Thind* decision evince a Congressional intent to depart from the meaning attributed to the term "white persons" by the framers of the original statute in 1790.[65]

Many concluded that the authority of *Thind* and other racial eligibility cases was undermined by the legislative changes to racial eligibility for naturalization during the war to such an extent that the basis for denying almost any application on the basis of race was uncertain.

The same month as the legislative debates regarding the Chinese Exclusion Repeal Act, the Immigration and Naturalization Service also referred to changing attitudes toward race in an article denouncing a federal district court's decision that had denied the racial eligibility of an Arab for naturalization based on the conclusion that Arabs were "part of the Mohammedan world and . . . a wide gulf separates their culture from that of the predominately Christian peoples of Europe."[66] In its October 1943 *Monthly Review,* the Immigration and Naturalization Service devoted an entire article to "The Eligibility of Arabs to Naturalization" in which the service denounced the Michigan court's decision, surveyed contrary decisions holding Arabs to be "free white persons," noted that the longstanding administrative policy of the United States had been to not object to Arab racial eligibility for naturalization, and concluded by warning that the recent decision to the contrary was deplored "because it comes at a time when the evil results of race discrimination are so disastrously apparent."[67] Similarly, commentators such as Charles Gordon wrote of the widespread discontent that arose with the racial eligibility provisions of the nationality act during the war.[68]

In an April 1944 judicial opinion in *Ex Parte Mohriez,* Judge Charles Wyzanski of the United States District Court for the District of Massachusetts relied in part on the Immigration and Naturalization Service's October 1943 *Monthly Report* to support the conclusion that an Arab applicant was a "free white person" for purposes of naturalization, commenting that "both the learned and the unlearned would compare the Arabs with the Jews towards whose naturalization every American Congress since the first has been avowedly sympathetic." Wyzanski recited the contributions of Arabs to European history and culture, including their contributions to the Greek foundations of Western thought, and wrote:

> The names of Avicenna and Averroes, the sciences of algebra and medicine, the population and the architecture of Spain and of Sicily, the very words of the English language, remind us as they would have reminded the Founding Fathers of the action and interaction of Arabic and non-Arabic elements of our culture. Indeed, to earlier centuries as to the twentieth century, the Arab people stand as one of the chief channels by which the

traditions of white Europe, especially the ancient Greek traditions, have been carried into the present.

In the final paragraph of the opinion, Wyzanski wrote that the Chinese Exclusion Repeal Act suggested the racial eligibility provisions of the nationality act should be interpreted more inclusively. Like the legislators in the debates regarding the Chinese Exclusion Repeal Act, Wyzanski cited the Declaration of Independence's proclamation that "all men are created equal" to make his point:

> It may not be out of place to say that, as is shown by our recent changes in the laws respecting persons of Chinese nationality and of the yellow race, we as a country have learned that policies of rigid exclusion are not only false to our professions of democratic liberalism but repugnant to our vital interests as a world power. In so far as the Nationality Act of 1940 is still open to interpretation, it is highly desirable that it should be interpreted so as to promote friendlier relations between the United States and other nations and so as to fulfill the promise that we shall treat all men as created equal.[69]

In this concluding passage of the last published judicial opinion in a racial eligibility case, Wyzanski summed up the new interpretive approach to the naturalization act that arose out of World War II.

Despite the conclusion that congressional intent regarding racial eligibility for naturalization was uncertain, however, the nation's Asian exclusion policy was not entirely negated by the legislative changes of World War II. The Japanese were still considered racially ineligible for naturalization until the racial eligibility provisions were completely eliminated in 1952. The United States Court of Appeals for the Ninth Circuit upheld a ruling by the BIA shortly after the war, for example, that a woman of "one-half white and one-half Japanese blood" was not entitled to admission to the United States because the woman was racially ineligible for naturalization despite her marriage to an American soldier during the American occupation of Japan after World War II.[70] Similarly, Vietnamese, Samoans, and other Pacific islanders were held to be racially ineligible for naturalization after the war.[71] The importance of nationality to racial eligibility for naturalization was also more explicitly discussed in racial eligibility cases during the period. In a 1948 case, the BIA narrowly interpreted the phrase *Chinese persons or persons of Chinese descent* to hold that a person born in Germany of a German mother and of a father who was a native of Thailand but "predominantly Chinese in blood" was neither a "free white person" nor of "Chinese descent" based in part on the BIA's consideration of the legislative debates regarding the Chinese Exclusion Repeal Act. The BIA interpreted the debates to evince only an intention to extend racial eligibility for naturalization to contemporary Chinese nationals and their progeny who had been allies during the war rather than to those with more historical Chinese ancestry, writing that "the House report makes it clear that the bill was concerned with the people of China, and that the House intended to limit the benefits of the measure to them."[72] The repeal of Chinese exclusion had not yet negated the racial eligibility provisions of the nationality act in their entirety, but the war brought more explicit recognition of the relationship between race, nation, and sovereignty in racial classifications under the act.

THE EFFECT OF V-J DAY ON THE FILIPINO AND INDIAN NATURALIZATION ACT

The power of the appeal to unify against a shared external threat in racial eligibility discourse is particularly illustrated by a shift that occurred in legislative debates that spanned the end of the war regarding the racial eligibility of natives of India for naturalization. During the legislative debates regarding the Chinese Exclusion Repeal Act, some questioned why racial eligibility for naturalization should be extended to the Chinese and not to the people of the Philippines and India who were also important allies in the Pacific. Although a 1918 act extended eligibility for naturalization to Filipinos who served honorably in the United States military, most Filipinos remained racially ineligible for naturalization following the United States Supreme Court's opinion in *Toyota*, just as the natives of India were under *Thind*. Like Filipinos under the 1918 act, some natives of India who served in the United States military gained admission under the Nye-Lea Act of 1935, but the rest remained racially ineligible for naturalization even after the Chinese Exclusion Repeal Act.[73] The Filipino and Indian Naturalization Act, which extended racial eligibility for naturalization to "Filipino persons or persons of Filipino descent" and to "persons of races indigenous to India," was proposed the same year that the Chinese Exclusion Repeal Act was signed into law but was not passed until after the war ended. Although the House Committee on Immigration and Naturalization held hearings on the act during the war, the Senate did not debate the act until October 10, 1945, after the war had ended. As a result, the legislative debates regarding the act spanned both the war and postwar periods. Significantly, both debates appealed to the need to unify against a shared external threat, but when the threat posed by the Axis powers ended with the war, legislators simply substituted the threat of Soviet communism in the postwar debates. This shift in the enmities relied on in support of a change in racial eligibility for naturalization marks one of the clearest examples of the power that the appeal to unify against a shared external threat had in racial eligibility discourse.[74]

The Filipino and Indian Naturalization Act originated as two separate acts regarding natives of the Philippines and India, respectively, but the debates found in the *Congressional Record* are limited to the proposal regarding natives of India. As a result, this chapter refers to the Filipino and Indian Naturalization Act in the form it was finally passed but only examines legislative debates regarding the portion of the act that extended racial eligibility for naturalization to natives of India. Although the act was initially motivated by the same concerns that had motivated the Chinese Exclusion Repeal Act—to strengthen Asian alliances in the Pacific and "dull the edge of Jap propaganda" to win World War II[75]—once Japan surrendered some objected that the measure was no longer necessary. Ohio representative Edward McCowen, for example, argued that in contrast to the justification of the Chinese Exclusion Repeal Act as a necessary measure to keep China in the war, "Indians are not now fighting Japan."[76] Similarly, Connecticut representative Clare Boothe Luce acknowledged that although at the time of the initial hearings regarding the act much was made of the strategic value of India's assistance in the war, "that reason of military expediency was disposed of by VJ-day."[77] Congress only passed the act after postwar debates stressed the importance of strengthening India's alliance to combat the influence of Soviet communism.

In a letter to the House Committee on Immigration and Naturalization which was read into the record during the wartime debates, President Roosevelt stated that he considered the extension of racial eligibility for naturalization to natives of India, like the Chinese Exclusion Repeal Act, an important enactment that "will help us to win the war and to establish a secure peace." He specifically praised the services of the Indian army during the war:

> I am sure that your committee is aware of the great services that India has rendered to the United Nations in their war against the Axis. The Indian army, raised entirely by voluntary enlistment, has fought with great skill and courage in Europe, Africa, and Asia.

Following President Roosevelt's death, President Truman endorsed President Roosevelt's position by a separate letter. Similarly, a letter from Attorney General Francis Biddle was introduced into the record in which Biddle declared that the act was particularly desirable "in view of the important contributions both of men and material that India has made in the present war."[78] During the postwar debates, New York representative Emanuel Celler even argued that India's participation in the war should be recognized despite the fact that the war had ended. India had the largest volunteer army of all of the Allies during the war, Celler noted, and it would be inconsistent to abandon them as soon as they were no longer needed:

> The Indians reason thusly: we were brothers in war. We were allies in battle. Why should we not be brothers and allies in peace? They say, "We helped you open the Burma Road. Our aviators went through blood, sweat, and tears with your aviators. Why should America continue to look upon us as inferior during peace? If we were good enough in war, we should be good enough for you in peace.[79]

Likewise, Illinois representative Everett Dirksen noted that Indians "fought shoulder to shoulder with the American doughboy and the British Tommy against the common enemy" during the war, and "died in the elephant grass of Burma along with other soldiers in the interest of victory."[80] The weakness of this appeal was simply that the threat no longer existed after the war ended.

Although these and other participants in the postwar debates appeared to regret the implications of what Pennsylvania representative James Fulton called "forgetting already the people who helped us and fought alongside us not longer than a few months ago,"[81] they placed greater emphasis on the need to secure India's alliance against Soviet communism and amplified the threat that the spread of communism posed in the Cold War that emerged after World War II ended. Illinois representative Noah Mason, for example, argued that the act was critical to winning the "tug of war between Uncle Sam and Joe Stalin" in Asia:

> We all know the effort Stalin is making today, through his
> Communist agents all over the world, to undermine MacArthur
> and to weaken Uncle Sam's position in Asia. The work of his
> agents in both China and India is witness to this fact. We must
> do what we can to offset his efforts in these two countries, each
> of which has some 400,000,000 people.

Like the depictions of the Japanese in the legislative debates regarding the
Chinese Exclusion Repeal Act, this statement amplified the threat of Soviet
communism by attributing higher transitivity to communist actions with
the verbs *undermine* and *weaken* compared to the action of the United
States to merely "offset" those actions. The territorial sovereignty implicated
in Mason's argument was more explicitly reflected in the further claim that
the need to establish good will in India arose because "Communist influence is beginning to permeate India," suggesting an action of penetrating
or invading from outside.[82]

In contrast to these depictions of communist influence, Illinois representative Dirksen attributed relatively low transitivity to similar American
efforts to spread influence in Asia:

> If we expect to protect ourselves against what is freely referred
> to as the Communist ideology in the world; if we expect not only
> to safeguard ourselves but to translate democratic ideals in other
> corners of the earth, how can you best do it than to start build-
> ing upon a foundation of good will? So, in proportion as we
> do this, we shall gain a respectful hearing among those people,
> and instead of becoming willing converts to some ideology with
> which we do not agree, there will be an opportunity for us to
> have the language and also the message of America find a place
> in those far-off corners.[83]

In this statement, the reflexive clauses *protect ourselves* and *safeguard ourselves* did not indicate a transfer of action between distinct participants but
an act to preserve existing relationships. Similarly, the action described in the
clauses *translate democratic ideals, gain a respectful hearing,* and *have the language and . . . the message of America find a place,* suggested an invitation
and collaboration rather than a transfer of action between distinct participants in which the target was significantly more affected than the actor.

In contrast to the communist ideology, which was depicted as alien and aggressive, American actions were depicted as familiar and peaceful.

While the Soviet Union had not yet successfully tested its first nuclear weapon at the time of the postwar debates regarding the Filipino and Indian Naturalization Act, the spread of Soviet communism was also explicitly framed as an existential threat in light of the inevitability of nuclear proliferation. California representative Horace Voorhis argued that racial discrimination was more perilous than ever due to the nuclear threat:

> We are living in a world in which it is altogether possible for any nation large or small within the course of a reasonable period of time to equip itself with weapons of war against which there is no known defense, weapons of war capable of almost wiping out the civilization of a whole nation by a surprise attack. Against that situation only one known defense exists, a moral, spiritual, and religious advance among mankind in the next few years that is in some degree comparable to the scientific advance of the atomic bomb . . .
>
> Whatever you or I may like to do, whatever may be the easy attitude for us to take toward this, that or the other person or group of persons . . . in this hour we shall either attain a reasonable approximation to human brotherhood on this earth or face the imminent possibility of the virtual destruction of human civilization, if not a large part of the human race itself. We live in a new age. It is almost impossible for us to realize how completely the bomb that blasted Hiroshima erased, likewise, the old familiar world in which men once lived. The whole world is now united in one fate, for good or ill, to an extent never before dreamed possible.[84]

In these remarks, although the actions Voorhis described were only hypothetical, they were otherwise as transitive as any imaginable. His appeal to unify against the threat of nuclear destruction suggested the line from W. H. Auden's poem "September 1, 1939," written as a commentary on the beginning of World War II, "We must love one another or die."[85]

Also addressing the national security issue, Representative Luce stated that after the war there was "going to be a great deal of shopping around, so to speak, among the Asiatic peoples, particularly colonial peoples, for political ideologies." Luce cited experts who testified that "in the years ahead it will matter greatly to us, in terms of our own national security, whether the Asiatic countries veer toward democracy as we know it, or toward the Soviet brand of democracy." She argued that the fact that official Soviet communist ideology seemed to "make room for men of all colors" was "a most potent political fact in the world," perhaps "the most potent one of all." Communism even appealed to "some few American Negroes," Luce observed, because it seemed to "promise a quick end to the spiritual humiliations and economic handicaps they must suffer simply because they were born, with a black skin," and "the colored peoples of Asia, those who are still under white masters, will be inclined, all other forces being equal, to do their ideological shopping in Moscow."[86] Accordingly, Luce argued that a vote for the Filipino and Indian Naturalization Act would strengthen national security by transcending racial divisions both domestically and internationally.[87]

Despite acknowledging the "spiritual humiliations and economic handicaps" of non-"whites," however, Luce's remarks also reflected the quality of a jeremiad lamenting the loss of America's moral leadership on racial equality:

> In India and in the colonial world America, once the hope of all enslaved peoples of every color, race, and creed, is slowly coming to be viewed, at worst, as a nation of dollar imperialists, of hypocritical coexploiters with other imperialistic nations, of the black, brown, and yellow man. And at best, as a country which, in spite of its vast power and professed ideals, does not practice what it preaches abroad. Yet, more and more today, colonial peoples are looking for inspiration and economic salvation toward Russia rather than toward us, as did all the world, including Russia, from 1776 until the time of Versailles. The loss of moral leadership implied by such a reorientation of the colonial peoples of Europe and Asia, and, yes, Africa, too, toward Soviet ideals can be, I repeat, a very great tragedy for our Nation and for the cause of our democracy and our freedom everywhere in the world.

While Luce expressed enthusiasm for the principle of equality in these remarks, she also minimized America's lengthy history of racial discrimination toward colonial subjects such as the Asian exclusion policy of immigration and naturalization.

Luce even specifically distorted the legal history of immigration and naturalization in the United States by claiming that the original principle of the nation's immigration and naturalization laws reflected the principle of equality expressed in the Declaration of Independence's proclamation that "all men are created equal." Toward the end of her remarks, Luce stated that "as I understand it, the original principle behind our immigration laws was the principle that any man . . . was eligible for entry and citizenship, regardless of race, color, or creed," based on the principle that "all men, regardless of color, race, or creed, are judged alike, not only in the eyes of God, but in the eyes of Uncle Sam," a principle that Luce claimed was abandoned by the Asian exclusion laws which put "the Hitlerian principle" of race discrimination in its place.[88] Whatever the scope of the racial eligibility provisions of the original naturalization act, it is difficult to reconcile Luce's remarks with the restriction of eligibility for naturalization to "free white persons" by the First Congress. The original principle Luce referred to simply served her purpose of rewriting the history of immigration and naturalization in the United States to depict it as more harmonious than it was in response to wartime exigencies that made that history politically inexpedient. Her reference to "all men, regardless of color, race, or creed" being "judged alike" alluded to the Declaration of Independence's proclamation that "all men are created equal," which functioned as a unifying device against the existential crisis presented by the war.

THE BIA'S CLASSIFICATION OF TATAR AND KALMYK REFUGEES FROM THE SOVIET UNION AS "WHITE" DURING THE EARLY COLD WAR

In two opinions issued by the BIA in 1950 and 1951 racially classifying displaced Tatar and Kalmyk refugees from the Soviet Union as "free white persons" within the meaning of the nationality act, the threat of Soviet communism reflected in the debates regarding the Filipino and Indian Naturalization Act was also amplified. Although the BIA is an administrative court hearing appeals from immigration courts to which Congress has delegated authority under Article II of the United States Constitution rather than part of the judicial branch under Article III of the United States Constitution, the BIA's opinions in these cases were among the latest to interpret the racial eligibility provisions of the nationality act. The opinions are also particularly remarkable given that both the Tatars and Kalmyks were historically classified as Mongolians with Asian origins. From their first appearance in Russian history through World War II, Tatars faced racial discrimination in Russia, and they continue to in areas of Russia and Crimea today.[89] In 1916, Madison Grant described the Tatars of southeastern Russia as "Mongoloid tribes" that had "maintained their type . . . by religious and social differences," and in 1921 Lothrop Stoddard classified them as part of the "brown world."[90] The narrator of Arthur Koestler's 1941 novel *Darkness at Noon*, set during World War II, twice refers to a character with "slit Tartar eyes" and "slanting Tartar eyes,"[91] and the Stalinist deportations of World War II forcibly relocated both the Volga and Crimean Tatars due to the suspicion that they were likely to collaborate with advancing German troops given their persecution under Soviet rule.[92] In 1951, Harold Lamb compared the Russian Tsar Ivan Vasilyevich, known as Ivan the Terrible, to Ottoman Sultan Suleiman I, concluding that "of the two, Ivan was more the Asiatic, his ancestors having been under Tatar and eastern influence for two and a half centuries."[93] With regard to the Kalmyks, they were once even described as the epitome of the Mongolian type. In 1676, Jean-Baptiste Tavernier wrote in a popular travel narrative that the Kalmyks were "the ugliest and most deformed people under the sun" and "the most hideous and brutal," and Petrus Camper later argued that the Kalmyk skull epitomized Asian man.[94] Although many Russians, including Vladimir Lenin, had Kalmyk ancestors, in the early twentieth century Kalmyk ancestry was often considered to detract from a person's "Russianness," and, like the Tatars, many Kalmyks were forcibly relocated during World War II.[95] In 1950, a *New York Times* article regarding the settlement of Kalmyk refugees to Paraguay from a German displaced persons camp repeatedly associated the Kalmyks with Asia, Mongolians, and Genghis Khan, noting that they "trace their ancestry back to the invasion armies of the great Mongolian empire" and had faced "firm barriers" to their settlement "because most countries have refused to admit Mongolians."[96]

Both of the BIA opinions holding Tatars and Kalmyks to be "free white persons" described the oppressive actions of the Soviet Union toward the Tatar and Kalmyk minorities, particularly the forced relocation of the groups during the Soviet deportations of World War II, reflecting the effect that the perceived threat of Soviet communism had on the interpretation of the racial eligibility provisions of the nationality act. In both of the BIA cases, the refugees were issued visas by consular officers under the Displaced Persons Act of 1948 before their admissibility was questioned on the basis of their racial eligibility for naturalization. The end of the 1940s saw the rise of the McCarthy era and hearings on the film industry before the House Un-American Activities Committee, and by 1951 Julius and Ethel Rosenberg had been arrested for allegedly passing atomic secrets to the Soviet Union and Communist Party leaders had been prosecuted for alleged violations of the Smith Act, which prohibited actions deemed subversive, such as advocating the overthrow of the government.[97] The Displaced Persons Act of 1948 provided accelerated and preferential immigration to the United States to those defined as a refugee or displaced person under the Constitution of the International Refugee Organization as well as certain people in Germany, Austria, and Italy who were victims of persecution by the government of Nazi Germany and certain natives of Czechoslovakia fleeing communist persecution.[98] In a message from President Truman to Congress regarding aid for refugees and displaced persons in 1952, Truman wrote of the success of the Displaced Persons Act and recommended passage of similar measures when it expired, remarking that "the flight and expulsion of people from the oppressed countries of Eastern Europe" affected "the peace and security of the free world" and was of concern to the United States "because of our long-established humanitarian traditions." He referred to those affected as "victims of oppression who are escaping from communist tyranny behind the Iron Curtain," "fugitives from Soviet terror," and "friends of freedom," and insisted that "our common defense requires that we make the best possible use not only of the material resources of the free world but of our human resources as well." He also proposed that "as under the Displaced Persons Act, there should be no religious, racial or other discrimination in the selection of immigrants."[99] Like Judge Wyzanski's opinion in *Mohriez*, the BIA's opinions regarding Tatar and Kalmyk refugees from the Soviet Union appear to have adopted a more inclusive interpretation of the racial eligibility provisions of the nationality act in order to "promote friendlier relations between the United States and other nations" and protect "our vital interests as a world power,"[100] in this instance the Cold War foreign policy interests of the United States reflected in the Displaced Persons Act.

The first of the two opinions was issued on July 12, 1950, in *In re S—*, in which the BIA held that a "native and citizen of Russia of the Tartar race, born in Ufa, Russia," and "a Mohammedan by religion," was a "free white person" within the meaning of the nationality act.[101] Given the discriminatory basis of the word *Tartars,* I use the *Tatar* spelling except where quoting directly from the BIA's opinion.[102] The BIA wrote that the appellant in the case, "a soldier in the Russian army from 1941 to January 1945, when he was captured by the German Army," was sent to a camp in Austria where "he stated that he was born in Istanbul, Turkey, to avoid repatriation to Russia," and since then had been housed in a displaced persons camp in Germany.[103] The appeal came to the BIA after the appellant's eligibility for the visa issued to him by a consular officer under the Displaced Persons Act was disputed by a Board of Special Inquiry and by the acting assistant commissioner of immigration, who concluded that because Tatars were "members of the Mongolian race originating in Turkestan, a region of central Asia," they were not "free white persons" and were racially ineligible for naturalization and therefore for admission to the United States under the Immigration Act of 1924.

The BIA rejected the Immigration Service's claim that Tatars were not "free white persons," however, arguing that Tatars had become "more or less Europeanized" by association and intermarriage with the people of eastern European Russia for centuries and by life under oppressive Soviet rule since the Bolshevik Revolution:

> Although the Tartars were originally considered Asiatic barbarians of the Mongolian variety, the majority of Tartars have for several centuries lived in eastern Russia, have become civilized and partially absorbed or assimilated by association and intermarriage. In language and religion, they may be designated as near Eastern or closely related to that portion of western Asia bordering on southwestern Russia . . . The Tartar group have become absorbed into the mass of Eastern Russian peoples and more or less Europeanized in blood and custom, even though the racial traces are still discernible. The Soviet rule during the past 33 years has probably hastened the process of integration, since the Soviet Government requires all communities to speak Russian, in addition to their own traditional language.

This passage foregrounded the transitive actions of the Russian and Soviet people, who "absorbed," "assimilated," and "Europeanized" the Tatars, and who "hastened the process" of Tatar integration by "requiring" them to speak Russian. The BIA attributed an even higher degree of transitivity to the actions of the Soviet government, however, by describing the Soviet pogroms targeting Tatars, writing that the people of Ufa, the appellant's birthplace, were "reportedly being systematically displaced or exterminated and replaced by a special military class of so-called Russianized Cossacks or trusted members of the Red Army's communist youth organization."[104]

After offering these historical narratives, the BIA cited judicial precedent finding that racial groups in nearby Asia Minor such as Arabs, Syrians, Armenians, and Afghans were held to be "free white persons" and specifically cited a 1945 BIA opinion finding that an Afghan was a "free white person" despite the fact that "some Afghans have some Mongoloid and Indian strains."[105] The BIA also attached an appendix to its opinion in S— that outlined the racial origins and historical background of the Tatars, classifying them within the Mongolian racial division related to the Turks and Huns and explicitly tracing the history of the Ufa region from the eighth century through the time of Genghis Khan, Tamerlane, Ivan the Terrible, Peter the Great, and Catherine the Great:

> The adherence of the present inhabitants of the Idel-Ural sector to the Moslem faith appears to date back to 1395, when they were conquered by Timus of Tamerlane and Samarkand, an ardent Mohammedan zealot. Upon Tamerlane's death in 1405, the empire vanished and reverted to minor tribal chiefs; the process of stabilization and assimilation then began, progressing very slowly from the advent of rising Russian power under Ivan the Terrible in the sixteenth century through the twentieth century of the Romanov and Soviet regimes. The process of Europeanizing Russia began about 1700 by command of Tsar Peter I, "The Great," and was continued by Catherine the Great, who made Russia a great world power for the first time.[106]

The appendix also specially noted the fact that since the Soviet Union was established "that government has permitted very few visitors in the eastern and southeastern portions of European Russia," and therefore "statistics cannot readily be verified and represent a reliable estimate."[107]

The long association of Tatars with Mongolians of Asian origin whose racial traces the BIA recognized as "still discernible" makes it difficult to imagine them being classified as "free white persons" before the legislative developments of World War II and the early Cold War. None of the groups previously classified as "free white persons" within the meaning of the racial eligibility provisions of the naturalization act had been historically classified as Mongolian, making the BIA's opinion in *S—* unprecedented in the history of racial eligibility discourse. Although at times the Mongolian ancestry of Finns, Hungarians, and others had been noted, their Mongolian ancestry was considered far more distant and marginal than that of the Tatars. From the time of Reconstruction until Pearl Harbor, racial eligibility discourse had foregrounded Mongolian hostility to Western civilization, particularly during the nineteenth and early twentieth centuries, when the image of dangerous Mongolian invaders held an archetypal power in the Western mind.[108] As a result of this imaginary, descriptions of Mongolian ancestry had almost always accompanied findings of racial ineligibility for naturalization.

What made it possible for the BIA to racially classify Tatars as "free white persons" were the legislative changes of World War II and the broader concern for strengthening international alliances against the spread of Soviet communism during the Cold War. This led President Truman to argue, for example, that "our common defense requires that we make the best possible use not only of the material resources of the free world but of our human resources," with no room for "religious, racial or other discrimination."[109] This motive meant that descriptions of Tatar assimilation into Russian and Soviet society served two conflicting purposes, both of which are evident in *S—*. On the one hand, because Tatars were recognized as a Mongolian people of Asian origin, their assimilation into Russian life and culture was essential to finding that they had become part of Western civilization, but on the other hand it was necessary to establish that they were not communists. Thus, although the BIA noted that the Tatars were "more or less Europeanized in blood and custom, even though the racial traces are still discernible" and "Soviet rule during the past 33 years has probably hastened the process of integration," it also wrote that the appellant lied about his birthplace to avoid repatriation to the Soviet Union and that the Tatars of the appellant's birthplace were suffering persecution by the Soviet government to the point of being "systematically displaced or exterminated."[110] At no point in the opinion was high transitivity attributed to the actions of Tatars, but instead it was attributed to the actions of the Russian and Soviet governments.

The BIA's approach to racially classifying a Tatar refugee from the Soviet Union in *S—* was duplicated in a BIA opinion the following year holding that two Kalmyk immigrants from the Soviet Union were "free white persons" and therefore racially eligible for naturalization and admission to the United States. In *In re R—*, a Kalmyk husband and wife, natives of Russia, applied for immigration under the Displaced Persons Act of 1948 and, like the Tatar immigrant in S—, were initially granted a visa by a consular officer but later excluded by a board of special inquiry and by the assistant commissioner of immigration based on the conclusion that Kalmyks were racially ineligible for naturalization because they were not "members of the white race." The BIA opinion noted that the couple was married in Bulgaria "according to the Buddhist rite, which is their religion," and that both were stateless, having "fled from Russia about 1920, after resisting the communist revolutionary forces." The opinion indicated that the man had served in the cavalry of the Russian Tsar, but his first wife and two children had "died of starvation in Russia in 1922" and the woman's first husband was "shot by the revolutionaries in 1918."[111] Counsel for the couple argued that even if they did have a predominance of Kalmyk blood, which they disputed, the Kalmyk ethnic group had been "identified with European people by several generations of affinity, education, cultural activity, and 33 years of Soviet rule in Russia and is, therefore, a member of the white race."[112] The BIA agreed with the couple's counsel, holding that despite the fact that the Kalmyks of southeastern European Russia were "admittedly of Mongolian" and "Asiatic" origin, they were "free white persons" within the meaning of the nationality act.

The BIA began its opinion in R— with a historical narrative of the Kalmyks' settlement in southeastern European Russia:

> During the opening years of the 17th century, a small group of Kalmuks migrated from their original habitat in central Asia to southeastern European Russia. They ultimately settled in that portion of Russia which lies between the mouth of the Don River and the mouth of the Volga River. About the middle of the 17th century, this group of Kalmuks took an oath of allegiance to the Tsar, submitted to Russian rule, and thereafter served as the official protectors of the southeastern borders of European Russia from infringement by warring tribes. Although the Kalmuks were considered to be seminomadic in their habits prior to the 1917 revolution, they have settled on land and carried on their occupation of herding on collective farms under Soviet rule. They have also been taught how to read the Russian language.

The actions of the Kalmyks are attributed relatively low transitivity in this passage and their whiteness is partly established by their role as "protectors of the southeastern borders of European Russia from infringement by warring tribes," highlighting their defense of European borders against invasion by external enemies. The BIA also indicated that because the Kalmyks had been landowners before the Bolshevik revolution and spoke primarily Russian, "it would seem that the Kalmuks, after residing in European Russia for 300 years, have become partially integrated with the other ethnic groups of Russia."[113]

As in S—, the BIA then cited prior judicial precedent holding that Arabs, Armenians, Syrians, and Afghans were "free white persons" as well as its opinion in S— holding that Tatars were "free white persons." The BIA concluded that the Kalmyks of southeastern European Russia were "members of the so-called European race, in spite of their Asiatic origin."[114] The BIA also attached an appendix to its opinion in R—, outlining the nativity and historical background of the Kalmyks. The appendix classified Kalmyks within the Mongolian racial division that included the Turks and Huns but also outlined at some length the Soviet government's recent pogrom that had targeted Kalmyks:

> On February 11, 1943, the Soviet Politbureau and the State Committee of Defense, in joint conference, determined that the Kalmuks should be displaced and deported, because they opposed the oppressive Soviet regime and, hence, were considered wanting in loyalty, dangerous to the State. This order was actually executed on February 22, 1944 (Red Army Day), when without warning and at gun-point, the Kalmuk population was herded into unheated railroad cars. Since they were sent on their journey in locked cars, without benefit of food or water, many died en route, while the rest were scattered in various spots of the Soviet Union. This action, by which the helpless Kalmuk minority group was forced to migrate east, was ratified, or legalized in retrospect, by Soviet government decree in 1946.

In this passage, the BIA attributed high transitivity to the actions of the Soviet government, the verbs *determined, executed, herded, sent, scattered, forced, ratified,* and *legalized* all reflecting the deliberate, completed, and punctual actions of an unaffected actor with a high degree of agency toward distinct targets who were significantly affected by the actions. An editor's note appended to R— also noted that after the Central Office's opinion the

BIA had issued an opinion in the unreported case of *In re A*—, holding that "a person of stock (Tadjik or Tadshik) originating in the Turan area, east coast of the Caspian Sea, of a group of families settled in the Ukraine in 1931 by the Soviet Government," was a "free white person" and therefore racially eligible for naturalization and admission to the United States.[115] Like the BIA's focus on Soviet pogroms in *S*— and *R*—, the phrase *settled . . . by the Soviet Government* foregrounded the violent Soviet pogrom that had targeted Tadjiks.

Unlike *S*—, however, the BIA's decision in *R*— was contested by the Immigration Service's Central Office which returned the case to the BIA for reconsideration based on the Central Office's conclusion that "the Kalmuks have only been settled in European Russia for a little over 300 years," which it considered "a comparatively short time in the history of western civilization." The Central Office also claimed that in light of the 1911 *Dictionary of Races and Peoples*' description of the Kalmyks as "more Asiatic" than the Tatars in appearance and culture, "while it is true that 33 years of Soviet rule may have hastened the process of integration, it does not follow that the characteristics of this group, as set forth in a compilation made in 1911, have been materially altered in such short space of time." The Central Office distinguished *S*— by arguing that there was a substantial difference between the Tatars and Kalmyks insofar as the Kalmyks were more closely related to "the Mongols of northern China."[116] This internal disagreement regarding the racial classification of Kalmyks in light of their historical classification as Mongolian and their Asian origins further highlights how unprecedented it was to classify them as "free white persons."

On reconsideration, the BIA again held that the Kalmyks of southeastern European Russia were "free white persons" and therefore racially eligible for naturalization and admission to the United States. The BIA challenged the Central Office's reliance on the historical classification of Kalmyks as Mongolian as a basis on which to conclude that they were not "free white persons," writing that the word *Mongol* could be applied to numerous European people as well:

> The Kalmuks of southeastern European Russia are admittedly of Mongolian origin, as are the Tartars of the same general area but these parallel racial groups have both become fused with the rest of the racial minorities of southeastern European Russia by a gradual process of association and intermarriage. Thus, both the

Kalmuks and Tartars have become "more or less Europeanized in blood and custom, even though the racial traces are still discernible."[117]

In addition, the BIA appealed to the geographical interpretation of the racial eligibility provisions of the nationality act, writing that because the Kalmyks in question inhabited "a part of Europe," its members were "in a better position to contend that they are 'white persons' than the Afghans, Armenians, Syrians, and non-European Arabs," and that the phrase *white persons* as commonly understood included "all races living in Europe, even though some of the southern and eastern European races included are technically classified as Mongolian or Tartaric in origin."[118]

In contrast to the judicial opinions in earlier racial eligibility cases involving Europe's borders with India and the Middle East, in *S—* and *R—* the BIA was faced with defining Europe's border with China against the invading Mongol hordes that originally inspired the development of the nation's Asian exclusion policy in the nineteenth century. The BIA justified its racial classification in the cases by, on the one hand, arguing that the Tatars and Kalmyks were on the European side of the political struggle surrounding Russia's border with China while, on the other hand, arguing that they were on the side of Western Europe in the emerging Cold War with Soviet communism. The language in which whiteness is defined in *S—* and *R—* also went farther to openly acknowledge the instability of racial classifications. In both cases, the BIA was content to write that the Tatar and Kalmyk refugees were "*more or less* Europeanized in blood and custom, even though the racial traces are still discernible,"[119] a conclusion that stands in stark contrast to earlier racial eligibility discourse in which almost any Mongolian ancestry suggested the imaginary of dangerous Mongolian invaders that the racial eligibility provisions of the naturalization act were believed to be specifically designed to exclude. In the changed circumstances of the Cold War, however, refugees fleeing Soviet persecution were held to be "free white persons" despite retaining discernible traces of racial difference.

THE IMMORTAL DECLARATION IN TIMES OF CRISIS

During World War II and the early Cold War, the racial eligibility provisions of the nationality act came into conflict with the nation's foreign policy goals as reflected in the legislative debates regarding the Chinese

Exclusion Repeal Act and the Filipino and Indian Naturalization Act, the BIA's opinions in *S—* and *R—*, and the removal of the racial eligibility provisions of the nationality act in 1952. Toward the end of the war, Immigration and Naturalization Service lawyer Charles Gordon wrote of the importance of the war to racial eligibility for naturalization:

> In time of war many things can be seen quite clearly. Under the stress of a great common adventure, we are able to shed some of our misconceptions and to recognize some of our mistakes. Thus it has transpired that an increasing public sentiment has challenged the validity of racial exclusions in our naturalization laws.[120]

In support of his proposal to eliminate the racial eligibility provisions of the nationality act, Gordon not only cited the need for help from the residents of Asia and the Pacific Rim to defeat the Japanese during the war but noted that the Nazi Nuremberg laws appeared to be the only other example of a modern nation that had limited eligibility for citizenship by race. Referring to this parallel, Gordon wrote that "certainly we do not want to be associated in any way with the pernicious and discredited Nazi dogma of racial superiority."[121] Although Gordon's assessment neglected the laws and administrative practices of former British dominions such as Australia, New Zealand, and Canada, which imposed racial barriers to immigration and naturalization closely paralleling those in the United States,[122] his association of the racial eligibility provisions of the nationality act with the racial supremacy theories of Nazi Germany was an uncomfortable association that frequently arose during World War II.

In Milton Konvitz's *The Alien and the Asiatic in American Law*, published the year after World War II ended at roughly the same time as the legislative debates regarding the Filipino and Indian Naturalization Act, Konvitz also supported his argument for increasing civil liberty protections for Asian immigrants to the United States by referring to the negative example of Nazi Germany, noting that "the smallness of a minority group is not always a factor tending to eliminate prejudice or intolerance [as] shown tragically by the history of the Jews in Germany under Hitler." Like Gordon, Konvitz claimed that the United States and Nazi Germany were the only modern nations to impose racial eligibility requirements for naturalization and quoted a remark by former Commissioner of Immigration and Naturalization Earl Harrison that "we all agree that this is not very desirable company."[123] The

Immigration and Naturalization Service's comment in its October 1943 *Monthly Review* that a federal judicial decision denying an Arab's petition for naturalization on the basis of race was deplored in part "because it comes at a time when the evil results of race discrimination are so disastrously apparent" also reflects this wartime sentiment.[124] These and other associations of the Asian exclusion laws of the United States with the Nazi Nuremberg laws reflected the recognition during World War II that the racial eligibility provisions of the nationality act were inexpedient because they inspired hostility by valued allies. This sentiment extended into the Cold War and ultimately led to the elimination of the racial eligibility provisions of the nationality act.

In contrast to the indiscriminate depiction of all Asians as dangerous Mongolian invaders to be feared throughout the earlier history of racial eligibility discourse, during and after World War II the people of China, India, and the Philippines became differentiated as the Japanese were depicted as an enemy so threatening that the United States was compelled to ally with other Asians to survive. This shift in the nation's Asian exclusion policy was accompanied by changes in depictions of Asians and of the nation's history of race relations as more harmonious than they actually were, often accompanied by references to the proclamation that "all men are created equal" in the Declaration of Independence—sometimes referred to as the "immortal declaration"—as proof of the nation's commitment to equality. References to the Declaration's proclamation of equality also continued to a lesser extent in the racial eligibility discourse during the Cold War. The need for cooperation during the Cold War figured prominently not only in the Filipino and Indian Naturalization Act and the BIA's opinions in *S—* and *R—*, but in legislative debates regarding the Immigration and Nationality Act of 1952. The 1952 act finally eliminated the racial eligibility provisions of the nationality act by providing that the "right of a person to become a naturalized citizen . . . shall not be denied . . . because of race."[125] Although the act was criticized by many and even initially vetoed by President Truman for continuing the discriminatory quota system of the Immigration Act of 1924, by removing the racial eligibility provisions of the nationality act the 1952 act effectively removed the 1924 act's bar on the admission of Asians to the United States on the basis that they were "ineligible to citizenship." After 1952, Asian immigrants were at least able to fill the small quotas allotted to Asian nations and were no longer explicitly stigmatized by race, however racially discriminatory the quota system remained.

As early as 1943, Representative Judd proposed removing the racial eligibility provisions from the nationality act consistent with the Chinese Exclusion Repeal Act, and the House of Representatives debated such a bill in 1949. In legislative debates regarding the proposed elimination of the racial eligibility provisions from the nationality act in both 1949 and 1952, legislators amplified the contributions of Asians to the Allied effort during the war and the importance of the legislation to fighting the spread of Soviet communism. The participants in these debates framed Asian actions during World War II and the early Cold War as sacrifices made on behalf of the United States, just as they had during the debates regarding the Chinese Exclusion Repeal Act and the Filipino and Indian Naturalization Act.[126] Representative Sabath argued, for example, that "we are now rewarding them, in part, for their deeds on behalf of Americanism,"[127] and Illinois representative Sidney Yates argued that "just as they assumed the obligations of citizens by giving their blood, their lives, and their substance to protect our democratic ideals, so, comparably, they are entitled to enjoy the benefits which citizenship bestows."[128] Representative Judd also remarked that it was crucial that the United States provide moral support to Asia to "help build up their will to fight with us and the free nations of the world against the glacier of tyranny moving out of the Soviet Union over parts of Asia," a remark that followed the pattern of framing Soviet expansionism as a dangerous invasion.[129] As in the legislative debates regarding racial eligibility for naturalization during World War II, New York representative Adam Clayton Powell Jr. also cited the Declaration's proclamation of equality in his opposition to the discriminatory quota system contained in the 1952 act, arguing that "it is clear that they are based on a rejection of the principle stated in the Declaration of Independence that all men are created equal."[130]

In these circumstances, the Declaration's proclamation of equality functioned as a commonplace of cooperation in a time of crisis, but it is important to understand how contingent the document's proclamation is on the existence of a shared external threat. In historian Carl Becker's study of the Declaration, he writes that despite the subordinate role that the list of grievances against King George III plays in the Declaration's structure compared to the more frequently cited preamble and concluding paragraphs, "the list of grievances is of the highest importance in respect to the total effect which the Declaration aims to produce" because it effectively differentiates the aggression of the English king from the suffering of the American colonists:

In this drama the king alone acts—he conspires, incites, plunders; the colonists have the passive part, never lifting a hand to burn stamps or destroy tea; they suffer while evils are sufferable. It is a high literary merit of the Declaration that by subtle contrasts Jefferson contrives to conjure up for us a vision of the virtuous and long-suffering colonists standing like martyrs to receive on their defenseless heads the ceaseless blows of the tyrant's hand.[131]

Becker attributes this effect to the fact that each charge in the Declaration's list of grievances begins with the phrase *he has,* foregrounding the king's actions:

> "he has refused to assent"; "he has forbidden his governors"; "he has refused to pass laws"; "he has called together legislative bodies"; "he has refused for a long time." . . . Nothing could be more effective than these brief, crisp sentences, each one the bare affirmation of a malevolent act. Keep your mind on the king, Jefferson seems to say; he is the man: *"he has refused"; "he has forbidden"; "he has combined"; "he has incited"; "he has plundered"; "he has abdicated."*[132]

While Becker's observation may help us understand the central function of the Declaration's list of grievances, what makes the list particularly effective is not merely the use of the active voice but the fact that it attributes high transitivity to the king's actions.

In fact, many of the clauses Becker cites from the Declaration's list of grievances are from the beginning of the list, which attributes relatively low transitivity to the king's actions. As the list of grievances proceeds, it attributes increasingly high transitivity to the king's actions with the effect of building the case against the king to a crescendo:

> He has plundered our seas, ravaged our Coasts, burnt our towns, and destroyed the lives of our people. He is at this time transporting large Armies of foreign Mercenaries to compleat the works of death, desolation and tyranny . . . He has constrained our fellow Citizens taken Captive on the high Seas to bear Arms against their Country, to become the executioners of their friends and Brethren . . . He has excited domestic insurrections amongst us, and has endeavoured to bring on the inhabitants

of our frontiers, the merciless Indian Savages, whose known rule of warfare, is an undistinguished destruction of all ages, sexes and conditions.

The final clauses of the list of grievances attribute significantly higher transitivity to the king's actions than those at the beginning, which claim only that the king has "refused his Assent to Laws," "called together legislative bodies at places unusual, uncomfortable, and distant," and "refused for a long time" to elect legislative representatives. These statements frame the actions negatively in terms of mere failures to act, reflect little agentive potency or effect on the colonists, and lack the completeness and punctuality of verbs such as *plundered, ravaged, burnt,* or *destroyed.*

The transitivity attributed to the king's actions gradually increases as the list proceeds, beginning with claims that the king has not only failed to act but has "obstructed the Administration of Justice," "sent hither swarms of Officers to harass our people," "combined with others to subject us to a jurisdiction foreign to our constitution," and supported legislation for "cutting off our trade," "imposing taxes on us," "transporting us beyond Seas to be tried for pretended offences," "taking away our Charters, abolishing our most valuable Laws, and altering fundamentally the Forms of our Governments." These clauses indicate a transfer of action between participants with higher agency, purpose, and effect on the colonists than the failures to act that form the basis of the list's beginning lines. The list then ends with the actions highest in transitivity by claiming that the king has "plundered," "ravaged," "burnt," "destroyed," and ultimately sought to annihilate the colonists by exciting slave rebellions and inciting American Indians to genocide. In Thomas Jefferson's *Autobiography,* he writes that during the Revolutionary War "the pressure of an external enemy hooped us together,"[133] and the gradual amplification of the king's transitive actions toward the colonists in the Declaration of Independence is a particularly powerful statement of the shared suffering that cemented the colonists into a new nation.

In his book *Enemyship,* Jeremy Engels writes that during the American Revolution "unity was premised as much on the danger of an external enemy as it was on shared ideals such as life, liberty, and the pursuit of happiness." He could alternatively or additionally have mentioned the shared ideal of equality expressed in the Declaration's proclamation that "all men are created equal." Although Engels suggests that shared ideals and the danger of an external enemy represent alternative appeals to unity, they may instead

be mutually constitutive. The unifying power of the Declaration's proclamation of equality, at least, is contingent on the presence of a shared external threat. During times of crisis, the Declaration's proclamation that "all
men are created equal" expresses a powerful call to unify against a shared
external threat. As William Smith notes in his study of the Declaration,
when "confronted with a crisis, it is the commonplace by which men act,"
and our problem has been "to understand this commonplace as an argument to meet a crisis."[134] To the extent that the equality proclaimed in the
Declaration's preamble is contingent on the presence of a shared external
threat, the fear amplified by the list of grievances is the premise of equality
rather than an alternative appeal. As Frederick Douglass remarked in his
speech "What Is the Slave to the 4th of July?": "The blessings in which you,
this day, rejoice, are not enjoyed in common—the rich inheritance of justice,
liberty, prosperity and independence, bequeathed by your fathers, is shared
by you, not by me." Those who were proclaimed equal in the Declaration
were those compelled to unify in common defense against a shared external threat, or, in Justice Taney's language in *Dred Scott*, those "whose rights
and liberties had been outraged by the English government."[135]

The conclusion that the unifying power of the Declaration's proclamation
of equality is contingent on the presence of a shared external threat might
explain the fact that recitations of the Declaration's proclamation of equality
as an appeal to unify during interwar periods are relatively absent, ineffec-
tive, or even openly mocked, such as when the Washington attorney general
criticized Takuji Yamashita for relying on "the worn out star spangled banner
orations, based upon the Declaration of Independence that all men are
created equal." During World War II, however, the Declaration's proclamation
of equality was aligned with the great scriptural traditions of the world and
heralded as a definitive statement of the character and ideals of the nation.
It appeared frequently in legislative debates regarding the Chinese Exclusion
Repeal Act and the Filipino and Indian Naturalization Act as well as in
the final lines of Judge Wyzanski's opinion in the last published judicial
opinion in a racial eligibility case. The proclamation expresses the commonplace of unifying against a shared external threat and therefore holds
a power proportionate to the existence of such a threat, but in the absence
of such a threat the words quickly become only a "worn out star spangled
banner oration."[136]

CONCLUSION

Simone Weil's essay on Homer's *Iliad*, "The *Iliad*, or the Poem of Force," written in late 1940 after the fall of France and first published in the December 1940 and January 1941 issues of the Marseilles literary monthly *Cahiers du Sud*, is a powerful expression of the desire to transcend human division during World War II. Weil begins her essay with the simple statement that "the true hero, the true subject, the center of the *Iliad* is force." According to Weil, in the *Iliad* "the human spirit is shown as modified by its relations with force, as swept away, blinded by the very force it imagined it could handle, as deformed by the weight of the force it submits to."[1] Force is not a condition of the Greeks or the Trojans alone in the poem, Weil claims, but is "common to all men," resulting in "the friendship between comrades-at-arms . . . the final theme of The Epic," expanding to encompass "the friendship that floods the hearts of mortal enemies" and before which "the distance between benefactor and suppliant, between victor and vanquished, shrinks to nothing." In Weil's reading of the *Iliad*, Homer offers an eloquent if optimistic expression of unity against a shared external threat, substituting the threat of violence itself for group enmities.

Significantly, in Weil's description of the events depicted in the *Iliad* she attributes relatively low transitivity to human actions—depicting them as "modified," "swept away," "blinded," and "deformed" by force, even "flooded" by friendship—and claims that the poem's theme of "incurable bitterness" in response to the violence that the poem depicts proceeds from a "tenderness that spreads over the whole human race." According to Weil, the *Iliad* views both victor and vanquished as counterparts of the poet, whom the reader can barely distinguish as a Greek or Trojan. It is the shared suffering of those on both sides of the war that makes the *Iliad* more powerful than all other Western literature. In the *Iliad*, shared suffering is a precondition of love and justice:

> He who does not realize to what extent shifting fortune and necessity hold in subjection every human spirit, cannot regard as fellow-creatures nor love as he loves himself those whom chance separated from him by an abyss. The variety of constraints pressing upon man give rise to the illusion of several distinct species that cannot communicate. Only he who has measured the dominion of force, and who knows not to respect it, is capable of love and justice.[2]

For Weil, only through the common struggle against violence itself can we transcend human conflict.

While it may be overly optimistic to hope that humanity will become so embittered by violence that the distance between victor and vanquished will "shrink to nothing,"[3] Weil appeals to the positive dimension of unity against a shared external threat. In Kenneth Burke's "The Rhetoric of Hitler's 'Battle,'" a critical review in 1939 of Adolf Hitler's *Mein Kampf,* Burke argues that in contrast to Hitler's "sinister unifying" around the symbol of the "villainous Jew," Americans should unify against Hitlerism itself in an "anti-Hitler Battle."[4] The desire for unity is so powerful, Burke writes, that "people are always willing to meet you halfway if you will give it to them by fiat, by flat statement, regardless of the facts," but if attained honestly the desire for unity is "genuine and admirable." It is only when unity is attained "by emotional trickeries that shift our criticism from the accurate locus of our trouble" that it becomes dangerous, because in such circumstances it is not true unity.[5] People may need both an enemy and a goal, Burke concludes, and Hitlerism represents "no purely fictitious 'devil-function' made to look like a world menace by rhetorical blandishments, but a reality whose ominousness is clarified by the record of its conduct to date."[6] Similarly, in Jeremy Engels's study of calls to unify against a shared external threat during the Revolutionary War he argues that before the war the strategy was used to create a more democratic world and defend the revolution but after the war it became a technique of governing that sought to suppress democracy by promoting an ideal of citizenship as "orderly, deferential, and virtuous."[7] In Burke's *A Rhetoric of Motives,* he writes that rhetorical activity operates in the ambiguous space between identification and division, the struggle between "us" and "them,"[8] and the appeal to unify against a shared external threat is a powerful source of identification that can be evaluated only in specific situations. In racial eligibility discourse, while such appeals reinforced and amplified racial discrimination in naturalization they also expanded the scope of those racially eligible for naturalization and ultimately led to the removal of the racial eligibility provisions from the nationality act.

The appeal to unify against a shared external threat has not only been the focus of scholars of enemy construction such as Kenneth Burke and Jeremy Engels, but has also been emphasized by scholars of racial formation. In Jeffrey Cohen's study of how historical narratives composed by Britain's clerical elite during the twelfth century rhetorically constructed a homogeneous Anglo-Saxon race out of a heterogeneity of races in Britain, Cohen notes that external threats of violence served as an important "sorting practice" through which historians "limned and thereby solidified the borders of collective identities" by rendering Welsh, Irish, Scots, and Jews as barbarians or beasts so that England envisioned itself as "under siege at its borders by bellicose Welsh and Scots, and at its center by homicidal Jews."[9] With regard to racial eligibility for naturalization in the United States, Matthew Frye Jacobson claims that the racial eligibility cases played a crucial role in what he calls the "crucible of empire," by which the whiteness of the probationary "white" races of Europe such as the Irish, Greeks, Italians, and Slavs was confirmed as American expansion into the Pacific and the imaginary of the natives encountered there as "savages" dissolved the distinctions often made between European "whites" at the turn of the twentieth century.[10]

As the present study demonstrates, however, the appeal to unify against a shared external threat was far more widespread in racial eligibility discourse than the imagined threats arising out of the nation's imperial expansion into the Pacific. Accordingly, the racial eligibility cases reflect not only a "crucible of empire," but many crucibles. While the imagined threat of Pacific natives may have confirmed the whiteness of Europeans whose racial classification was initially considered suspect, racial eligibility discourse reflected a wide variety of real and imagined threats employed to confirm or disconfirm the racial eligibility for naturalization of immigrants from all corners of the globe. As Murray Edelman writes, "Enemies are sometimes substituted for others to keep a cognitive structure credible and vital," different enemies succeeding one another "as times change and fashions in naming threats change with them . . . though new enemies also coexist with the older ones."[11] According to the imaginaries of participants in racial eligibility discourse, the threat that the British posed during the Revolutionary War confirmed the whiteness of the French,[12] the threat that pirates from the Barbary states posed to American merchant vessels in the eighteenth century disconfirmed the whiteness of Parsis,[13] the threat that outsiders posed to the integrity of the nation's borders during the territorial expansions of the nineteenth century confirmed the whiteness of Mexicans,[14] the threat that the Central Powers posed during World War I confirmed the racial eligibility for naturalization of American Indian, Filipino, and Puerto Rican veterans and eventually American Indians and World War I veterans,[15] the threat posed by the Indian caste system disconfirmed Bhagat Singh Thind's whiteness but confirmed the validity of Sakharam Pandit's naturalization,[16] the threat posed by Turkish aggression following World War I confirmed the whiteness of Armenians,[17] and the threat posed by the Axis Powers during World War II confirmed the racial eligibility for naturalization of "races indigenous to the continents of North or South America or adjacent islands,"[18] "Chinese persons or persons of Chinese descent,"[19] and World War II veterans.[20] Finally, the threat of Soviet communism during the early Cold War not only confirmed the whiteness of Tatar, Kalmyk, and Tadjik refugees from the Soviet Union and the racial eligibility for naturalization of Filipinos and natives of the Indian subcontinent,[21] but ultimately led to the removal of the racial eligibility provisions from the nationality act.

The prominence of the appeal to unify against a shared external threat as a means of subordinating perceived racial divisions to national interests in racial eligibility discourse suggests that it may be a particularly persuasive discursive practice in racial identity formation, and the frequent use of transitivity to amplify external threats in the appeal indicates that transitivity plays an important role in the construction of enemies. According to Åshlid Næss, the distinctness of the participants in a clause is the centrally defining feature of transitivity. The most transitive clause is one in which two participants are not only physically distinct but also "play maximally distinct roles in the event in question," or one in which the actor and target are defined "in maximal opposition to each other."[22] A transitive actor is typically defined as the volitional instigator of the action identified by a verb, and therefore "the property of instigating or causing an event is central to our whole understanding of what an agent is," while the target is the participant affected by the action "which in some ways undergoes a change of state as a result of the event."[23] Reflecting transitivity's rhetorical quality, these categories only designate thematic or participant roles or types of relation rather than inherent properties of the participants, but the relationship that transitivity designates is one of opposition.[24] The features of transitivity described by linguists are also found in many of the attributes of enemies identified in the existing scholarship on the construction of enemies. For example, Robert Ivie describes how war is typically depicted as "a necessary evil forced upon a reluctant nation by the aggressive acts of an enemy," whose acts are "conveyed as 'voluntary' and 'initial' in contrast to a reaction that was 'involuntary' and 'defensive.'" The enemy, according to Ivie, "initiated, led, caused, and threatened the conflict," while the target "only responded, followed, and protected important interests and allies."[25] The speakers in the examples of justificatory rhetoric that Ivie quotes also frequently foreground the actions of enemies by using highly transitive verbs such as *strangled, ravaged, crippled, scarred, attacked, exiled, overwhelmed, subverted, breached,* and *destroyed,*[26] all the deliberate, completed, and punctual actions of an unaffected actor with a high degree of agency toward distinct targets who were significantly affected by them.

If, as political theorists have claimed, fear of enemies is always present in political group formation and during crises that threaten the group because the primacy of self-preservation transcends barriers to group formation,[27] one powerful illustration of this principle may be the earliest example of citizenship, which is often traced to the military elites of ancient Greek Sparta who are famous for the stand of three hundred Spartans against the Persian army at Thermopylae. The citizenship of Spartan military elites, called "Spartiates," afforded them the benefits of equality, land ownership, and slave labor while requiring a rigorous military training program, government service, and taking meals together in common messes. The Spartiates referred to each other as *Homoioi,* meaning "equals" or "peers," and their primary duty was to defend and govern the state. Derek Heater writes that the poetry of the seventh century BCE poet Tyrtaeus, a sort of poet laureate of Sparta, paints a portrait of the soldier "risking his life for his city," which reflects "the new citizenly state of mind, in sharp contrast to the heroes of Homer, who fought valiantly for their personal glory."[28] One of Tyrtaeus's surviving poems describes the courage of a typical soldier in relatively intransitive terms, focusing on the wounds he sustains rather than the violence he commits:

> With a sudden rush he turns to fight the rugged battalions
> of the enemy, and sustains the beating waves of assault.
> And he who so falls among the champions and loses his sweet life,
> so blessing with honor his city, his father, and all his people,

with wounds in his chest, where the spear that he was facing
 has transfixed
that massive guard of his shield, and gone through his breast-
 plate as well,
why, such a man is lamented alike by the young and the elders,
and all his city goes into mourning and grieves for his loss.[29]

As this passage reflects, the citizenly state of mind was specifically cultivated by war memorials that foregrounded the wounds that soldiers received in battle while defending the city-state.[30]

Fear of enemies also played a particularly important role in racial eligibility discourse at the nation's founding and during crises that threatened it. The collective naturalization provisions of the nation's territorial expansion treaties did not discriminate on the basis of race, and as a result of the Civil War the Fourteenth Amendment provided birthright citizenship without regard to race and Congress expanded racial eligibility for naturalization to "aliens of African nativity and persons of African descent." The conflict between the Asian exclusion policy that followed the Civil War and the desire for unity during World War I and World War II led to numerous exemptions for Asian veterans and to legislative extensions of racial eligibility for naturalization to natives of China, India, the Philippines, and North and South America in order to strengthen the nation's military alliances.[31] In *Pandit* and *Cartozian* after World War I, and in *S—* and *R—* after World War II, the decision to foreground the potential statelessness of Asian Indian, Armenian, Tatar, and Kalmyk immigrants also invoked the newly emerging category of stateless persons that arose out of the world wars and the development of political asylum law that followed. Like the fear of enemies, offering asylum to fugitives has often been associated with the founding of political groups. One of the mythical founders of Rome was believed to have made the Palatine Hill an asylum, for example, and based on this myth Romans believed their ancestors were outlaws and refugees who found asylum there.[32] Similarly, the ancient Israelites established cities of refuge under Joshua and Moses for those who had committed homicide, and most ancient Greek temples offered asylum to fugitives. Although these institutions more closely resemble the religious right of sanctuary that emerged in Christian churches in medieval Europe, offering temporary protection to fugitives to prevent a rush to judgment, modern political asylum grants aliens fleeing persecution the right to permanently relocate in a new nation.[33]

Despite the absence of formal legal protections for refugees in the United States until the late twentieth century, both before and after the American Revolution political and religious refugees from Europe—particularly English Puritans and French Huguenots—sought refuge in the American colonies and later in the newly formed nation. Before the American Revolution, English officials even lured Protestants from rival nations to settle in the colonies by promising them, among other things, religious toleration and the "rights of Englishmen." As Marilyn Baseler notes, however, asylum offers were discretionary and "could be revoked at will, when they no longer served the interests of the mother country."[34] The American colonists similarly promoted the idea that the new nation would be a refuge from persecution, as reflected in Thomas Paine's challenge to protect freedom and "prepare in time an asylum for mankind."[35] Like English asylum offers, however, the early protections afforded refugees in the United States were "ad hoc and situation-specific," providing the executive branch with tremendous discretion.[36] Moreover, studies have shown that formal asylum provisions have mostly benefited those who have complained of persecution by the nation's adversaries rather than its allies.[37] Thus, although the United States incorporated the "well-founded fear of persecution" language of the United Nations Convention Relating to the Status of Refugees into the Immigration and Nationality Act of 1980, determinations of whether fear is "well-founded" under the act favor those who identify threats from the nation's adversaries.[38] In other words, if the right of asylum once "led a somewhat shadowy existence as an appeal in individual exceptional cases for which normal legal institutions did not suffice," as Hannah Arendt noted in the mid-twentieth century,[39] it still does. The concepts of refuge, sanctuary, and asylum more often exist as appeals in individual exceptional cases than as elements of normal legal institutions.

The basis of such discretion is the doctrine of sovereignty articulated in the Supreme Court's opinion in *Chae Chan Ping* (1889), in which the Court offered one of its most important articulations of plenary power by holding that the government possessed an unlimited power to revoke certificates granting Chinese immigrants who had left the country permission to return because the power to exclude foreigners was an "incident of sovereignty." In support of this conclusion, the Court invoked the imaginary of dangerous Mongolian invaders by describing the Chinese as a "great danger" that threatened to overrun the West Coast with "crowded millions of China" in "an Oriental invasion."[40] Sumi Cho and Gil Gott reference the Court's opinion as an example of what they call "the racial contingency of sovereignty," which reflects their claim that sovereignty "developed homologously with the structures of societal racial formation" insofar as the most important legal principles on which the nation was founded—national sovereignty, federalism, separation of powers, and plenary power—are the product of "a racialized history in which race and law were mutually constituted."[41] Among other examples, Cho and Gott reference the Insular Cases, which determined whether Puerto Rico, Cuba, the Philippines, and Guam could become part of the United States after the Spanish–American War, noting that opposition to the statehood of the newly acquired islands was premised on the racialization of their residents. According to Cho and Gott, like plenary power and other central legal principles on which the United States was founded, eligibility for statehood depended on the "racialized, imperial logic of the day." Accordingly, they write, sovereign power is "utterly racial in origin and development."[42]

The prominence of appeals to unify against a shared external threat in racial eligibility discourse raises particularly important questions about the tension between sovereignty and legality. The challenges that crises pose to legality have been discussed by numerous scholars in a wide variety of disciplines and contexts, particularly referring to the theories of exception found in the works of Carl Schmitt and Giorgio Agamben. A prominent political theorist of Weimar and Nazi Germany, Carl Schmitt claimed that sovereignty is a limit concept that can only be understood when a crisis threatens the existence of the state. In Schmitt's famous definition of sovereignty, the sovereign is "he who decides in the emergency situation."[43] This decisionist formulation of sovereignty concludes that the emergency powers of a sovereign constitute law despite the exceptional circumstances in which they arise,[44] or emergency powers are legal by virtue of the fact that the sovereign exercises them, a conclusion many have found to be an unacceptable assessment of what they consider the lawless rule by fiat of totalitarian regimes such as Nazi Germany. In Giorgio Agamben's critique of Schmitt, Agamben argues that the state of exception is "a suspension of the legal order itself" rather than a form of law.[45] He also claims that despite being depicted as exceptional, however, the exercise of emergency power has increasingly become the norm as the "voluntary creation of a permanent state of emergency . . . has become one of the essential practices of contemporary states."[46] The relationship between emergency powers and law may be even more pervasive than Agamben claims, however, given the ubiquity of the tension between law and expediency in ordinary legal reasoning. According to Austin Sarat, by devoting so much attention to the dispute between Schmitt and Agamben scholars have neglected "the myriad of ways in which law imagines, anticipates, and responds to emergencies, ways in which sovereign prerogative is either irrelevant or operates within the terrain of ordinary legal procedures."[47]

In colonial law, permanent states of exception also existed under the guise of ordinary legal procedures. With important implications for the relationship of race and sovereignty, some scholars have argued that the state of exception reveals the inner logic of colonial law. According to Achille Mbembe, for example, "the colony represents the site where sovereignty consists fundamentally in the exercise of power outside the law (*ab legibus solutus*) and where 'peace' is more likely to take on the face of a 'war without end.'" In early and late modernity, Mbembe writes, one of the characteristic imaginaries of sovereignty is "the perception of the existence of the Other as an attempt on my life, as a mortal threat or absolute danger whose biophysical elimination would strengthen my potential to life and serenity," and the lawlessness of the colony is made possible by the "racial denial of any common bond between the conqueror and the native."[48] Similarly, Ngũgĩ wa Thiong'o concludes that the state of exception was the true nature of colonial law, describing how colonial authorities depicted the allowance of customary law as a concession to native people while justifying a dual system of justice that treated Europeans as citizens and natives as subjects. In some instances, as Mbembe notes, colonial authorities even provided for democratic law in European areas and martial law in native areas.[49] Going even farther, Anthony Anghie argues, much like Sumi Cho and Gil Gott's claim that sovereign power is "utterly racial in origin and development,"[50] that sovereignty can only be understood "in terms of its complex relationship with the colonial encounter and the constellation of racial and cultural distinctions it generated and elaborated," an encounter that was premised on the conclusion that only European states could be sovereign while non-European states were "deemed to be lacking in sovereignty and hence excluded from the family of nations and of law."[51] In the colonial encounter, Anghie writes, "native sovereignty is accommodated largely to the extent that this is compatible with the interests of colonial powers,"[52] a conclusion that parallels Derrick Bell's interest convergence thesis which predicts that "the interest of blacks in achieving racial equality will be accommodated only when it converges with the interest of whites."[53]

Perhaps because race, sovereignty, and enmity are so closely aligned, the instability caused by what Ioannis Evrigenis describes as the "sudden and radical transformation of others from enemies to allies and vice versa" in political group formation is evident both in racial eligibility discourse and in the contradictory gains of the civil rights movement.[54] In one of the early critiques of the contradictory gains of the civil rights movement, Derrick Bell explains the failure of the Supreme Court's decision in *Brown v. Board of Education* (1954) as a result of the fact that the opinion was motivated more by the desire to protect America's image during the Cold War to combat Soviet propaganda than by the principle of equality. Accordingly, Bell argues, commitment to the opinion faded once the Cold War ended.[55] The interest convergence thesis that Bell uses to explain *Brown* only forms one side of a two-sided coin that he calls "racial fortuity," however, the other side of which is "involuntary racial sacrifice." At the Constitutional Convention, Bell writes, the Framers sacrificed black hopes for freedom in order to secure the support of slave owners. He analogizes racial fortuity to a third party who is the intended beneficiary of a contract to which they are not a signatory. In general, if the benefit conferred on a third party beneficiary is a direct benefit, then the third party beneficiary can sue for breach of the contract, but if it is only incidental to the contract it cannot. According to Bell,

> racial policy actions may be influenced, but are seldom determined, by the seriousness of the harm blacks are suffering, by the earnest petitions they have argued in courts, by the civil rights bills filed in legislative chambers, or even by impressive street protests.

This is true, Bell claims, because "none of these change blacks' status as fortuitous beneficiaries." Although legal developments such as the Emancipation Proclamation, *Brown*, or the Civil Rights Act are often justified as remedies for discrimination, they came about because those who made them "saw that they, those they represented, or the country could derive benefits that were at least as important as those blacks would receive." In other words, Bell concludes, blacks were not necessary parties to such policy changes but only fortuitous beneficiaries of them.[56]

In what has become a new subgenre of scholarship on race and law, many scholars have expanded on Bell's thesis to explain how civil rights reforms were influenced by Cold War foreign policy considerations.[57]

In *Cold War Civil Rights*, for example, Mary Dudziak argues that during the Cold War the relationship between civil rights and Cold War propaganda developed into a struggle over the narrative of race and democracy as the conflict between the United States and the Soviet Union to win the hearts and minds of third world peoples in the Cold War turned civil rights crises into national security crises. Despite the gains of the civil rights movement in securing the Supreme Court's decision in *Brown*, Dudziak concludes, the deployment of the National Guard to enforce *Brown* in Little Rock, Arkansas, and the passage of the Civil Rights Act of 1964 and the Voting Rights Act of 1965, the Cold War was "simultaneously an agent of repression and an agent of change."[58] While advocating civil rights, the Truman administration also tried to suppress the activities of African American activists such as Josephine Baker and Malcolm X when they traveled abroad.[59] Similarly, Gerald Horne and Carol Anderson have documented how the anticommunist sentiment of the Cold War associated support for human rights with communism, legitimated only a limited version of civil rights reforms, and influenced the National Association for the Advancement of Colored People to abandon its anti-imperialist position.[60] As Dudziak notes, the United States government's response to the civil rights movement was driven in part by whether activists supported the government's progressive story of improved American race relations, which it considered pivotal to its Cold War propaganda efforts.[61]

After *Brown*, Little Rock, and civil rights legislation helped the United States government secure international confidence that it was part of the solution to civil rights crises, the nation's commitment to civil rights waned. Subsequently, as Michael Kreen writes, United States officials "fell back into old habits, biases, and theories with disturbing ease."[62] Thus, although the Cold War helped motivate civil rights reforms it also "limited the field of vision to formal equality, to opening the doors of opportunity, and away from a broader critique of the American economic and political system."[63] Consistent with Bell's concept of "racial fortuity," the civil rights advances of the Cold War appear to have been merely fortuitous outcomes of the struggle between the United States government and the Soviet Union to convince third world peoples that they would treat them equally. Once this burden was satisfied by adopting formal laws that espoused equality, the nation shifted its attention to other matters and discouraged further discussions of race. In many ways, racial eligibility discourse prefigured the contradictory gains of the civil rights movement during the Cold War and forms part of the same story. While Bell's interest convergence thesis may explain this phenomenon, it is important to recognize that interest convergence is rhetorically constructed in appeals to unify against a shared external threat. The United States government's retreat from civil rights reforms after securing its image among third world peoples during the Cold War may be explained, for example, by David Kertzer's observation that the transcendent power of enemies is fragile and temporary because it creates "solidarity without consensus."[64]

In response to Sumi Cho and Gil Gott's conclusion that sovereignty is "utterly racial in origin and development,"[65] Debra Bassett objects that this conclusion may be overinclusive because sovereign power includes activities such as rationing water or declaring a state of emergency during economic crises that bear no obvious relationship to race.[66] If sovereignty is not exclusively racial in origin and development, however, the reverse may be true—that racial classifications are primarily sovereignal. After all, the debate regarding whether or not the state of exception is an aberration or endemic to law remarkably parallels the debate regarding whether racism is aberrant or normal and whether "the state *is* inherently racial."[67] Postcolonial theorists have noted the European presumption that natives lacked sovereignty in colonial encounters as well as how much European settlers depended on the state of exception in colonial law,[68] and Cheryl Harris notes that whiteness and property "share a common premise—a conceptual nucleus—of a right to exclude."[69] The Supreme Court also held this power of racial exclusion to be an "incident of sovereignty" in *Chae Chan Ping*.[70] The homologous relationship between race and sovereignty offers one explanation of the prominence of appeals to unify against a shared external threat in racial eligibility discourse, illustrating the political quality of racial formation that Michael Omi and Howard Winant describe.[71]

Despite the preference of modern legal theory for the formal analysis of legal doctrine to the exclusion of rhetorical considerations,[72] legal discourse offers a wealth of material for the study of the relationships that constitute identity, power, and legitimacy in the practice of legal advocacy and lend themselves to the transformative practice of demystifying the symbolic authority of legal doctrine.[73] This is imperative when social systems of oppression such as race intersect and struggle for recognition with other sources of legal norms, and a critical rhetorical approach is particularly suited to understanding the role of discursive practices in creating, sustaining, and opposing such systems.[74] Such an approach shifts the focus to how "symbols come to possess power—what they 'do' in society as contrasted to what they 'are,'"[75] or to the performative dimension of discursive practices "on those occasions, and by those speakers, we think of as legal."[76] By considering the discursive practices of the many participants in racial eligibility discourse, it is apparent that the strategy of foregrounding shared external threats as a means of transcending perceived racial divisions was often more important to racial classification than legal doctrine due to the rapid shifts in the nation's geopolitical enmities and alliances during the early twentieth century and the closely intertwined relationship between race, nation, and sovereignty.

NOTES

NAB   National Archives Building, Washington, DC
NAPAR   National Archives and Records Administration
             Pacific Alaska Region, Seattle, Wash.
NAPR (LN)   National Archives and Records Administration
             Pacific Region, Laguna Niguel, Calif.
NAPR (SB)   National Archives and Records Administration
             Pacific Region, San Bruno, Calif.
RG   Record Group

INTRODUCTION

1. See Transcript of Evidence at a–d, 104, United States v. Cartozian, No. E-8668 (D. Or. May 8–9, 1924), in Civil and Criminal Case Files, District of Oregon (Portland), Records of the District Courts of the United States, RG 21, NAPAR (Cartozian Trial Transcript); United States v. Cartozian, 6 F.2d 919 (D. Or. 1925).

2. Cartozian Trial Transcript at 60–61.

3. See Transcript of the Depositions of Dr. Paul Rohrbach, Roland Dixon, Dr. James Barton, and Dr. Franz Boas at 36, 77, 88, United States v. Cartozian, No. E-8668 (D. Or. Apr. 5, 8–9, and 11, 1924), in Significant Civil and Criminal Case Files, 1899–1925, District of Oregon (Portland), Records of U.S. Attorneys and Marshals, RG 118, NAPAR.

4. U.S. Const. Art. I, § 8.

5. See *Naturalization Act of 1790*, 1st Cong., 2nd Sess., *Statutes at Large of the United States of America* 1 (1790): 103; *Naturalization Act of 1795*, 3rd Cong., 2nd Sess., *Statutes at Large of the United States of America* 1 (1795): 414; *Naturalization Act of 1802*, 7th Cong., 1st Sess., *Statutes at Large of the United States of America* 2 (1802): 153; *Naturalization Act of*

1804, 8th Cong., 1st Sess., *Statutes at Large of the United States of America* 2 (1804): 292; *Naturalization Act of 1824*, 18th Cong., 2nd Sess., *Statutes at Large of the United States of America* 4 (1824): 69; *Naturalization Act of 1828*, 20th Cong., 1st Sess., *Statutes at Large of the United States of America* 4 (1828): 310; *Naturalization Act of 1870*, 41st Cong., 2nd Sess., *Statutes at Large of the United States of America* 16 (1870): 254; *Naturalization Act of 1875*, 43rd Cong., 2nd Sess., *U.S. Statutes at Large* 18 (1875): 316; Darrell Smith, *The Bureau of Naturalization: Its History, Activities and Organization* (Baltimore: Johns Hopkins Press, 1926).

6. See *Nationality Act of 1940*, 76th Cong., 3rd Sess., U.S. Statutes at Large 54 (1940): 1137; *Chinese Exclusion Repeal Act of 1943*, 78th Cong., 1st Sess., *U.S. Statutes at Large* 57 (1943): 600; *Filipino and Indian Naturalization Act of 1946*, 79th Cong., 2nd Sess., *U.S. Statutes at Large* 60 (1946): 416.

7. Only a few of the cases addressed the extension of the act to non-"white" racial classifications. One case addressed the meaning of the phrase *aliens of African nativity and persons of African descent,* see *In re* Cruz, 23 F. Supp. 774 (E.D.N.Y. 1938) (holding that an applicant who was three-quarters Native American and one-quarter African was not of sufficient "African descent" to be eligible under the act), one case addressed the meaning of the phrase *indigenous to the Western Hemisphere,* U.S. Department of Justice, Immigration and Naturalization Service, "Summaries of Recent Court Decisions," *Monthly Review* 1 (1944): 44 (reporting a ruling that a Polynesian born on the Society Islands was neither a "free white person" nor a descendant of a race "indigenous to the Western Hemisphere"), and one case addressed the meaning of the phrase *persons of Chinese descent,* see *In re* B—, 3 I. & N. Dec. 304 (B.I.A. 1948) (holding that a person born in Germany of a German mother, but of a father who was Siamese and "predominantly Chinese in blood," was neither a "white person" nor a "person of Chinese descent").

8. For a list of published judicial opinions addressing the racial eligibility provisions of the naturalization act, see Ian Haney López, *White by Law: The Legal Construction of Race* (New York: New York University Press, 1996). In addition to the cases identified by López, the United States Board of Immigration Appeals issued a series of opinions in racial eligibility cases under § 13(c) of the Immigration Act of 1924, which prohibited the admission to the United States of any alien "ineligible to citizenship" as defined in part by the racial eligibility provisions of the naturalization act.

See *Immigration Act of 1924*, 68th Cong., 1st Sess., *U.S. Statutes at Large* 43 (1924): 153, 162, 168. See also *In re* S—, 1 I. & N Dec. 174 (B.I.A. 1941) (holding that a native and citizen of Iraq, whose parents were "full-blooded Arabians" and whose ancestors "came from Turkish stock," was a "white person"); *In re* K—, 2 I. & N. Dec. 253 (B.I.A. 1945) (holding that a native and citizen of Afghanistan, "of the Afghan race," was a "white person"); *In re* B—, 3 I. & N. Dec. 304 (B.I.A 1948) (holding that a person born in Germany of a German mother, but of a father who was Thai and "predominantly Chinese in blood," was neither a "white person" nor a "person of Chinese descent"); *In re* S—, 4 I. & N. Dec. 104 (B.I.A. 1950) (holding that a native and citizen of Russia "of the Tartar race, born in Ufa, Russia," was a "white person"); *In re* R—, 4 I. & N. Dec. 275 (B.I.A. 1951) (holding that natives of Russia "whose blood was found to be predominantly that of the Kalmuk race" were "white persons"); *In re* J— W— F—, 6 I. & N. Dec. 200 (B.I.A. 1954) (holding that a native of the Philippines, but "racially Chinese (full blood)" was not a "white person").

9. See Michael LeMay and Elliott Barkan, eds., *U.S. Immigration and Naturalization Laws and Issues: A Documentary History* (Westport, CT: Greenwood, 1999), 33–34, 51–54, 108–12, 148–51; Ronald Takaki, *Strangers From a Different Shore: A History of Asian Americans*, rev. ed. (1989; rpt., New York: Little, Brown, 1998), 14.

10. See, e.g., Michael Bobelian, *Children of Armenia: A Forgotten Genocide and the Century-Long Struggle for Justice* (New York: Simon and Schuster, 2009), 110; Takaki, *Strangers From a Different Shore*, 13, 101–102, 271–72, 300; California School Law of 1860 and California Political Code of 1880, quoted in Joyce Kuo, "Excluded, Segregated and Forgotten: A Historical View of the Discrimination of Chinese Americans in Public Schools," *Asian American Law Journal* 5 (1998): 190 n. 56, 198 n. 115.

11. See, e.g., Takaki, *Strangers from a Different Shore*, 15, 271–72, 297.

12. See, e.g., Gabriel Chin, "Twenty Years on Trial: Takuji Yamashita's Struggle for Citizenship," in *Race on Trial: Law and Justice in American History*, edited by Annette Gordon-Reed (Oxford: Oxford University Press, 2002), 103–17; Lucy Salyer, "Baptism by Fire: Race, Military Service, and U.S. Citizenship Policy, 1918–1935," *Journal of American History* 91 (2004): 856; Takaki, *Strangers From a Different Shore*, 14–15. The 1922 Cable Act also provided that any American woman who married a person "ineligible to citizenship" would cease to be a citizen of the United States, effectively

discouraging the intermarriage of American-born women to immigrants who were racially ineligible for citizenship. See *Cable Act of 1922*, 67th Cong., 2nd Sess., *U.S. Statutes at Large* 42 (1922): 1021.

13. Not only was judicial rhetoric central to many of the canonical works of classical rhetoric, but numerous scholars in rhetorical and legal studies have traced a variety of legal doctrines to the rhetorical tradition, particularly the rules of legal evidence and procedure. See, e.g., Alessandro Giuliani, "The Influence of Rhetoric on the Law of Evidence and Pleading," *The Juridical Review*, new ser., 7 (1962): 216–51; Hanns Hohmann, "The Dynamics of Stasis: Classical Rhetorical Theory and Modern Legal Argumentation," *The American Journal of Jurisprudence* 34 (1989): 171–97; Richard Schoeck, "Rhetoric and Law in Sixteenth-Century England," *Studies in Philology* 50 (1953): 110–27; Barbara Shapiro, "Classical Rhetoric and the English Law of Evidence," in *Rhetoric and Law in Early Modern Europe*, ed. Victoria Kahn and Lorna Hutson (New Haven: Yale University Press, 2001). The close relationship between rhetoric and law is also recognized by contemporary scholars in rhetorical studies, who frequently cite and review legal scholarship. See, e.g., Eugene Garver and Philip Keith, eds., "Focus on James Boyd White," *Rhetoric Society Quarterly* 21, no. 3 (1991) (special issue devoted to the work of legal scholar James Boyd White); Geoffrey Klinger, review of *Rhetorical Knowledge in Legal Practice and Critical Legal Theory*, by Francis Mootz III, *Argumentation and Advocacy* 44 (2008): 160–64; Todd McDorman, review of *Troubling Confessions: Speaking Guilt in Law and Literature*, by Peter Brooks, *Argumentation and Advocacy* 38 (2002): 189–92; Sean O'Rourke, "The Rhetoric of Law," review of *Metaphor and Reason in Judicial Opinions*, by Haig Bosmajian, *Political Literacy: Rhetoric, Ideology, and the Possibility of Justice*, by Frederic Gale, and *The Rhetoric of Law*, edited by Austin Sarat and Thomas Kearns, *Rhetoric Review* 14 (1995): 213–20; Sean O'Rourke, "The Rhetoric of Legal Scholarship," review of *The Law of the Other: The Mixed Jury and Changing Conceptions of Citizenship, Law and Knowledge*, by Marianne Constable, and *Reinterpreting Property*, by Margaret Radin, *Rhetoric Society Quarterly* 26 (1996): 119–23; Catherine Prendergast, review of *Brown v. Board of Education: A Civil Rights Milestone and Its Troubled Legacy*, by James Patterson, *Rhetoric Review* 53 (2001): 170–73.

14. Gerald Wetlaufer, "Rhetoric and Its Denial in Legal Discourse," *Virginia Law Review* 76 (1990): 1591.

15. James Stratman, "Legal Rhetoric," in *Encyclopedia of Rhetoric and Composition: Communication from Ancient Times to the Information Age*, ed. Theresa Enos (New York: Routledge, 2010).

16. See generally Jeffrey Walker, *Rhetoric and Poetics in Antiquity* (Oxford: Oxford Univ. Press, 2000), 7–10; Chaïm Perelman and Lucie Olbrechts-Tyteca, *The New Rhetoric: A Treatise on Argumentation*, trans. John Wilkinson and Purcell Weaver (Notre Dame: University of Notre Dame Press, 1969), 47–51.

17. Stratman, "Legal Rhetoric," 383.

18. David Cairns, *Advocacy and the Making of the Adversarial Criminal Trial 1800–1865* (Oxford: Clarendon Press, 1998), xi.

19. James Boyd White, *Heracles' Bow: Essays on the Rhetoric and Poetics of the Law* (Madison: University of Wisconsin Press, 1985), 33, 33 n. 2.

20. Marouf Hasian Jr., Legal Memories and Amnesias in America's Rhetorical Culture (Boulder: Westview, 2000), 2, 13.

21. Celeste Condit and John Lucaites, *Crafting Equality: America's Anglo-African Word* (Chicago: University of Chicago Press, 1993), xii.

22. John Lucaites, "Between Rhetoric and 'The Law': Power, Legitimacy, and Social Change," review of *A Guide to Critical Legal Studies*, by Mark Kelman, *Interpreting Law and Literature: A Hermeneutic Reader*, edited by Sanford Levinson and Steven Mailloux, and *The Critical Legal Studies Movement*, by Roberto Unger, *Quarterly Journal of Speech* 76 (1990): 446.

23. James Boyd White, "'Our Meanings Can Never Be the Same': Reflections on Language and Law," *Rhetoric Society Quarterly* 21, no. 3 (1991): 72, 75.

24. See Thomas Sloane, ed. *Encyclopedia of Rhetoric* (New York: Oxford University Press, 2001), s.v. "Law" (noting that American legal realism and Critical Legal Studies have "been informed by and addressed to the rhetorical dimensions of legal governance"); Hasian, *Legal Memories*, 9 (noting that Critical Legal Studies appears to take "the notion of rhetoric and the role of the public in the formation of judicial principles" seriously); William Wiethoff, "Critical Perspectives on Perelman's Philosophy of Legal Argument," *Journal of the American Forensic Association* 22 (1985): 8 (noting that Perelman's new rhetoric and Critical Legal Studies both see "a salutary role for rhetorical method in jurisprudence").

25. Jerome Frank, "What Courts Do in Fact, Part One," *Illinois Law Review* 26 (1932): 645.

26. Ibid., 662.

27. Ibid., 655.

28. Ibid.; Jerome Frank, "What Courts Do in Fact, Part Two," *Illinois Law Review* 26 (1932): 764.

29. Frank, "What Courts Do in Fact, Part One," 653–54.

30. See, e.g., Peter Gabel and Paul Harris, "Building Power and Breaking Images: Critical Legal Theory and the Practice of Law," *New York University Review of Law and Social Change* 11 (1982): 376.

31. Roberto Unger, "The Critical Legal Studies Movement," *Harvard Law Review* 96 (1983): 584; cf. Lucaites, "Between Rhetoric and 'The Law,'" 435–49.

32. See, e.g., *Encyclopedia of Rhetoric*, s.v. "Law"; Hasian, *Legal Memories*, 9; Wiethoff, "Critical Perspectives on Perelman's Philosophy of Legal Argument," 94.

33. See Lucaites, "Between Rhetoric and 'The Law,'" 446–47.

34. See Kimberlé Crenshaw, Neil Gotanda, Gary Peller, and Kendall Thomas, eds. *Critical Race Theory: The Key Writings That Formed the Movement* (New York: The New Press, 1995), xiii; Richard Delgado, "Liberal McCarthyism and the Origins of Critical Race Theory," *Iowa Law Review* 94 (2009): 1505–45.

35. *Critical Race Theory*, xiii; Francisco Valdes, Jerome Culp, and Angela Harris, "Battles Waged, Won, and Lost: Critical Race Theory at the Turn of the Millennium," introduction to *Crossroads, Directions, and a New Critical Race Theory*, ed. Francisco Valdes, Jerome Culp, and Angela Harris (Philadelphia: Temple University Press, 2002), 1–2.

36. Catherine Prendergast, "Race: The Absent Presence in Composition Studies," *CCC* 50, no. 1 (1998): 37–38.

37. Raymie McKerrow, "Critical Rhetoric: Theory and Praxis," *Communication Monographs* 56 (1989): 91, 101.

38. Ibid., 102–107.

39. Michael Lacy and Kent Ono, introduction to *Critical Rhetorics of Race*, ed. Michael Lacy and Kent Ono (New York: New York University Press, 2011), 4–7.

40. See, e.g., Sanford Levinson, "The Rhetoric of the Judicial Opinion," in *Law's Stories: Narrative and Rhetoric in the Law*, ed. Peter Brooks and Paul Gewirtz (New Haven: Yale University Press, 1996).

41. Frank, "What Courts Do in Fact, Part One," 653–54.

42. Rogers Smith, review of *White by Law: The Legal Construction of Race*, by Ian F. Haney López, *The American Journal of Legal History* 42 (1998): 66.

43. See, e.g., *In re* Halladjian, 174 F. 834 (C.C.D. Mass. 1909); *In re* Mozumdar, 207 F. 115 (E.D. Wash. 1913); *Ex parte* Shahid, 205 F. 812 (E.D.S.C. 1913); *In re* Dow, 213 F. 355 (E.D.S.C. 1914); United States v. Thind, 261 U.S. 204 (1923); United States v. Cartozian, 6 F.2d 919 (D. Or. 1925); *Ex parte* Mohriez, 54 F. Supp. 941 (D. Mass. 1944); *In re* S—, 4 I. & N. Dec. 104 (1950); *In re* K—, 4 I. & N. Dec. 275 (1951).

44. *In re* Singh, 246 F. 496, 498–500 (E.D. Pa. 1917).

45. *In re* Balsara, 171 F. 294, 295 (C.C.S.D.N.Y. 1909).

46. *Ex parte* Mohriez, 54 F. Supp. 941, 942 (D. Mass. 1944).

47. Cf. David Zarefsky, "Reflections on Making the Case," in *Making the Case: Advocacy and Judgment in Public Argument*, ed. Kathryn Olson, Michael Pfau, Benjamin Ponder, and Kirt Wilson (East Lansing: Michigan State University Press, 2012), 11–12.

48. Michael Omi and Howard Winant, "Racial Formation," in *Race Critical Theories: Text and Context*, ed. Philomena Essed and David Theo Goldberg (Oxford: Blackwell, 2002), 123–24.

49. Howard Winant, *Racial Conditions: Politics, Theory, Comparisons* (Minneapolis: University of Minnesota Press, 1994), 112.

50. Raymie McKerrow, foreword to *Critical Rhetorics of Race*, ix.

51. Michael Lacy and Kent Ono, introduction to *Critical Rhetorics of Race*, 4.

52. Thomas Nakayama and Robert Krizek, "Whiteness: A Strategic Rhetoric," *Quarterly Journal of Speech* 81 (1995): 293.

53. López, *White by Law*, xiv.

54. See, e.g., Elise Boddie, "Racial Territoriality," *UCLA Law Review* 58 (2010): 401, 406; see also Henri Lefebvre, *The Production of Space*, trans. Donald Nicholson-Smith (1991; repr. Oxford: Blackwell, 1995); Lorraine Code, *Rhetorical Spaces: Essays on Gendered Locations* (New York: Routledge, 1995); Cheryl Harris, "Whiteness as Property," *Harvard Law Review* 106 (1993): 1707–14; Roxanne Mountford, "On Gender and Rhetorical Space," *Rhetoric Society Quarterly* 31, no. 1 (2001): 41–71.

55. Matthew Frye Jacobson, *Whiteness of a Different Color: European Immigrants and the Alchemy of Race* (Cambridge: Harvard University Press, 1998), 142.

56. Omi and Winant, "Racial Formation," 124–28.

57. López, *White by Law*, 2–3.

58. Ibid., 34.

59. Barbara Biesecker, "Of Historicity, Rhetoric: The Archive as Scene of Invention," *Rhetoric & Public Affairs* 9, no. 1 (2006): 124.

60. Charles Morris, "The Archival Turn in Rhetorical Studies; Or, the Archive's Rhetorical (Re)turn," *Rhetoric & Public Affairs* 9, no. 1 (2006): 115; see Charles Morris, "Archival Queer," *Rhetoric & Public Affairs* 9, no. 1 (2006): 145–51.

61. Ann Stoler, "Colonial Archives and the Arts of Governance," *Archival Science* 2 (2002): 90, 97.

62. National Archives and Records Administration, "National Archives History," https://www.archives.gov/about/history (accessed Sept. 5, 2016).

63. *Naturalization Act of 1870*, 41st Cong., 2nd Sess., 42, *Congressional Globe* (July 4, 1870), pt. 6:5152 and 5155–57. Senator Sumner's proposed amendment provided: "And be it further enacted, That all acts of Congress relating to naturalization be, and the same are hereby, amended by striking out the word 'white' wherever it occurs, so that in naturalization there shall be no distinction of race or color." Ibid., 5121.

64. Ibid., 5158.

65. *In re* Rodriguez, 81 F. 337, 340 (W.D. Tex. 1897).

66. *Chinese Exclusion Repeal Act of 1943*, 78th Cong., 1st Sess., *Congressional Record* 89 (Oct. 20, 1943), 8573, 8579, 8581, 8597, 8600.

67. Ibid., 8573–98.

68. Ibid., 8577.

69. Ibid., 8590.

70. *In re* R——, 4 I. & N. Dec. 275, 276, 280, 286 (B.I.A. 1951).

71. See generally Charles Gordon, "The Racial Barrier to American Citizenship," *University of Pennsylvania Law Review* 93 (1945): 248; LeMay and Barkan, *U.S. Immigration and Naturalization Laws and Issues*, 116–18, 121–22.

72. Gordon, "The Racial Barrier to American Citizenship," 246.

73. See Salyer, "Baptism by Fire," 854, 858.

74. See ibid., 856–62.

75. *Chinese Exclusion Repeal Act of 1943*, 78th Cong., 1st Sess., *Congressional Record* 89 (Oct. 20, 1943), 8577.

76. Ariela Gross, *What Blood Won't Tell: A History of Race on Trial in America* (Cambridge: Harvard University Press, 2008), 8–9.

77. John Tehranian, *Whitewashed: America's Middle Eastern Minority* (New York: New York University Press, 2009), 5.

78. López, *White by Law*, 22–25.

79. See Janice Okoomian, "Becoming White: Contested History, Armenian American Women, and Racialized Bodies," *MELUS* 27 (2002): 214.

80. See Ozawa v. United States, 260 U.S. 178, 189–190 (1922).

81. See *Shahid*, 205 F. at 812; see also *In re* Dow, 213 F. 355 (E.D.S.C. 1914). The decisions in these cases were later reversed by *Dow v. United States*, 226 F. 145 (4th Cir. 1915). See generally Sarah Gualtieri, "Becoming 'White': Race, Religion and the Foundations of Syrian/Lebanese Ethnicity in the United States," *Journal of American Ethnic History* 20, no. 4 (2001): 41–42.

82. See, e.g., United States v. Balsara, 180 F. 694, 696 (2d Cir. 1910); *Mozumdar*, 207 F. at 117; *In re* Singh, 257 F. 209, 212 (S.D. Cal. 1919); *In re* Sallak, No. 14876 (N.D. Ill., East. Div., June 27, 1924), in Significant Civil and Criminal Case Files, 1899–1925, District of Oregon (Portland), Records of U.S. Attorneys and Marshals, RG 118, NAPAR (holding that an applicant "born in Palestine" was a "white person"); *S*—, 1 I. & N. Dec. 174; *Ex parte* Mohriez, 54 F. Supp. 941, 942 (D. Mass. 1944); *In re* Shaikhaly, No. 119332 (S.D. Cal. Dec. 20, 1944), in Folder 119332, Contested Naturalizations, Southern District of California, Central Division (Los Angeles), RG 21, NAPR (LN) (holding that "a native and citizen of Palestine . . . of the Arabian race," was a "white person"); *K*—, 2 I. & N. Dec. 253; *R*—, 4 I. & N. Dec. 275.

83. Tehranian, *Whitewashed*, 51–54.

84. See James Jasinski, *Sourcebook on Rhetoric: Key Concepts in Contemporary Rhetorical Studies* (Thousand Oaks, CA: SAGE, 2001): s.v. "Transcendence."

85. Kenneth Burke, *A Rhetoric of Motives*, Calif. ed. (Berkeley: University of California Press, 1969), xiii; see generally *Encyclopedia of Rhetoric*, s.v. "Identification."

86. Kenneth Burke, *Dramatism and Development* (Barre, MA: Clark Univ. Press, 1972), 28–29.

87. Ioannis Evrigenis, *Fear of Enemies and Collective Action* (Cambridge: Cambridge University Press, 2008), 1–2.

88. See Murray Edelman, *Constructing the Political Spectacle* (Chicago: University of Chicago Press, 1988), 66.

89. Jeremy Engels, *Enemyship: Democracy and Counter-Revolution in the Early Republic* (East Lansing: Michigan State University Press, 2010), 13.

90. Ibid., 22.

91. Åshlid Næss, *Prototypical Transitivity* (Amsterdam: John Benjamins, 2007), 42; see also C. V. Chvany, "Foregrounding, 'Transitivity,' Saliency

in Sequential and Nonsequential Prose," *Essays in Poetics* 10, no. 2 (1985): 1–26; Michael Halliday, *Halliday's Introduction to Functional Grammar*, 4th ed., rev. by Christian Matthiessen (London: Routledge, 2013), 347; Paul Hopper and Sandra Thompson, "Transitivity in Grammar and Discourse," *Language* 56, no. 2 (1980): 251–53.

92. See Robert Bell, Matthew McGlone, and Marko Dragojevic, "Bacteria as Bullies: Effects of Linguistic Agency Assignment in Health Message," *Journal of Health Communication* 19, no. 3 (2013): 340–58; Robert Bell, Matthew McGlone, and Marko Dragojevic, "Vicious Viruses and Vigilant Vaccines: Effects of Linguistic Agency Assignment in Health Policy Advocacy," *Journal of Health Communication* 19, no. 10 (2014): 1178–93; Matthew McGlone, Robert Bell, Sarah Zaitchik, and Joseph McGlynn III, "Don't Let the Flu Catch You: Agency Assignment in Printed Educational Materials about the H1N1 Influenza Virus," *Journal of Health Communication* 18, no. 6 (2012): 740–56.

93. See Andreea Ritivoi, "Talking the (Political) Talk: Cold War Refugees and Their Political Legitimation through Style" and Christopher Eisenhart, "Reporting Waco: The Constitutive Work of Bureaucratic Style," in *Rhetoric in Detail: Discourse Analyses of Rhetorical Talk and Text*, ed. Barbara Johnstone and Christopher Eisenhart (Philadelphia: John Benjamins, 2008), 33–79.

94. Evrigenis, *Fear of Enemies*, 1–2; see also Neal Wood, "Sallust's Theorem: A Comment on 'Fear' in Western Political Thought," *History of Political Thought* 16, no. 2 (1995): 174–89.

95. Evrigenis, *Fear of Enemies*, 5.

96. Ibid., 93.

97. Wood, "Sallust's Theorem," 181, 184.

98. Harold Laski, *Studies in the Problem of Sovereignty* (New Haven: Yale University Press, 1917), 12–14, 17, 19–20.

99. See Robert Cover, "*Nomos* and Narrative," in *Narrative, Violence, and the Law: The Essays of Robert Cover*, ed. Martha Minow, Michael Ryan, and Austin Sarat (Ann Arbor: University of Michigan Press, 1995), 95–96, 102, 128, 139–41.

100. Scott Lyons, "Rhetorical Sovereignty: What Do American Indians Want from Writing?" *CCC* 51, no. 3 (2000): 450–51, 456.

101. Sumi Cho and Gil Gott, "The Racial Sovereign," in *Sovereignty, Emergency, Legality*, ed. Austin Sarat (Cambridge: Cambridge University Press, 2010), 212–13.

102. Falguni Sheth, *Toward a Political Philosophy of Race* (Albany: State University of New York Press, 2009), 30.

103. Omi and Winant, *Racial Formation in the United States*, 82; cf. Winant, *Racial Conditions*, 112.

104. Hannah Arendt, *The Origins of Totalitarianism*, new ed. with additional prefaces (New York: Harcourt Brace, 1973), 280–81.

CHAPTER 1. MONGOLIAN INVADERS,
THE BUREAU OF NATURALIZATION, AND *OZAWA*

1. *In re* Yup, 1 F. Ca. 223, 223–24 (C.C.D. Cal. 1878).

2. Quoted in *In re* Halladjian, 174 F. 834, 838 (C.C.D. Mass. 1909).

3. United States v. Balsara, 180 F. 694, 696 (2d Cir. 1910).

4. Michael Keevak, *Becoming Yellow: A Short History of Racial Thinking* (Princeton: Princeton University Press, 2011), 4, 27, 36–37, 41–42, 124; cf. Harold Isaacs, *Scratches on Our Minds: American Views of China and India* (1958; repr. Armonk, NY: M. E. Sharpe, 1980), 67 (noting that "some of America's first and most important leaders acquired a highly respectful view indeed of the merits of Chinese civilization and even thought it worthy of emulation in their own new world").

5. See Roy Malcolm, "American Citizenship and the Japanese," *Annals of the American Academy of Political and Social Science* 93 (1921): 78.

6. See John Tchen, *New York Before Chinatown: Orientalism and the Shaping of American Culture, 1776–1882* (Baltimore: Johns Hopkins University Press, 1999), 76, 136, 231–32.

7. *Boston Daily Advertiser*, July 22, 1870.

8. See *Halladjian*, 174 F. at 843–44 ("While an exhaustive search of the voluminous records of this court, sitting as a court of naturalization, has been impossible, yet some early instances have been found where not only western Asiatics, but even Chinese, were admitted to naturalization."); cf. *In re* Chang, 24 P. 156 (Cal. 1890) (writing that "a person of Mongolian nativity" exhibited a "license admitting him to practice as an attorney and counselor at law in all the courts of the state of New York, issued by the supreme court of that state . . . ; also, a certificate of naturalization, issued by the court of common pleas of the city of New York, November 11, 1887").

9. "The Treatment of the Chinese Question," *Daily Evening Bulletin (San Francisco)*, March 28, 1879; see also William Bernard, "The Law, The

Mores, and The Oriental," *Rocky Mountain Law Review* 10 (1938): 115–16 (noting that by 1910 the United States census recorded more than a thousand Chinese who had been naturalized); Malcolm, "American Citizenship and the Japanese," 78 (writing that before the Chinese Exclusion Act of 1882 "a very considerable number of Chinese were naturalized, the naturalization courts apparently including them in 'white persons'").

10. See John Wigmore, "American Naturalization and the Japanese," *American Law Review* 28 (1894): 824–27; cf. Gretchen Murphy, "How the Irish Became Japanese: Winnifred Eaton's Racial Reconstructions in a Transnational Context," *American Literature* 79 (2007): 33–35.

11. William Griffis, "Are the Japanese Mongolian?" *North American Review* 197 (1913): 721; see also "Think Government Can't Debar Knight," *New York Times*, July 16, 1909 (noting that "the Japanese have always contended that they are not Mongolian"); cf. Raymond Buell, "Some Legal Aspects of the Japanese Question," *The American Journal of International Law* 17 (1923): 29–49.

12. *Halladjian*, 174 F. at 843–45; see also Ronald Takaki, *Strangers from a Different Shore: A History of Asian Americans*, rev. ed. (1989; rpt., New York: Little, Brown, 1998), 207.

13. See H. G. Wells, *The Outline of History: Being a Plain History of Life and Mankind* (New York: Macmillan, 1920), 1:147.

14. Brief for the United States at 33, Ozawa v. United States, No. 1 (U.S. Supr. Ct. Sept. 19, 1922); Brief for Petitioner at 59, Ozawa v. United States, No. 1 (U.S. Sup. Ct. Dec. 9, 1918).

15. See Ozawa v. United States, 260 U.S. 178 (1922).

16. See, e.g., Walter Nugent, *Habits of Empire: A History of American Expansionism* (2008; repr. New York: Vintage, 2009), 65–68.

17. See "Treaty of Amity, Settlement and Limits Between the United States of America and His Catholic Majesty, the King of Spain," Feb. 22, 1819, *Statutes at Large of the United States of America* 8 (1819): 252; *An Act for the establishment of a territorial government in Florida*, 17th Cong., 1st Sess., *Statutes at Large of the United States of America* 3 (1822): 654; *Joint Resolution for annexing Texas to the United States*, 28th Cong., 2nd Sess., *Statutes at Large of the United States of America* 5 (1845): 797 and *Joint Resolution for the Admission of the State of Texas into the Union*, 29th Cong., 1st Sess., *Statutes at Large of the United States of America* 9 (1845): 108; "Treaty of Peace, Friendship, Limits and Settlement between the United States of America and the Mexican Republic," Feb. 2, 1848, *Statutes at Large*

of the United States of America 9 (1848): 922; "Treaty With Mexico," Dec. 30, 1853, *Statutes at Large of the United States of America* 10 (1853): 1031.

18. See Scott v. Sandford, 60 U.S. 393, 529 (1856) (*Dred Scott*) (McLean, dissenting).

19. *In re* Rodriguez, 81 F. 337, 337, 349 (W.D. Tex. 1897); cf. *In re* M—, 2 I. & N. Dec. 196 (B.I.A. 1944). For a historical account of the *Rodriguez* case and the Texas politics that motivated the challenge to Rodriguez's racial eligibility for naturalization, see Martha Menchaca, *Naturalizing Mexican Immigrants: A Texas History* (Austin: University of Texas Press, 2011).

20. *Black's Law Dictionary*, 6th ed., s.v. "Jus soli."

21. U.S. Const. amend. XIV, § 1. Two years earlier, the Civil Rights Act of 1866 provided that "all persons born in the United States and not subject to any foreign power, excluding Indians not taxed, are hereby declared to be citizens of the United States." *Civil Rights Act of 1866*, 39th Cong., 1st Sess., *U.S. Statutes at Large* 14 (1866): 27.

22. Elk v. Wilkins, 112 U.S. 94, 102–103 (1884).

23. United States v. Wong Kim Ark, 169 U.S. 649, 693–94 (1897).

24. See, e.g., *In re* Burton, 1 Ala. 111, 113–14 (1900); *In re* Camille, 6 F. 256 (C.C.D. Or. 1880).

25. *Dred Scott*, 60 U.S. 393, 403–407, 415–20.

26. See *Oxford English Dictionary*, 2nd ed., s.v. "Outrage, *v.*1."

27. Sumi Cho and Gil Gott, "The Racial Sovereign," in *Sovereignty, Emergency, Legality*, ed. Austin Sarat (Cambridge: Cambridge University Press, 2010), 194–204.

28. See *Indian Citizenship Act of 1924*, 68th Cong., 2nd Sess., *U.S. Statutes at Large* 43 (1924): 253; Kevin Brunyeel, "Challenging American Boundaries: Indigenous People and the 'Gift' of American Citizenship," *Studies in American Political Development* 18 (2004): 30.

29. See "Treaty with the Cherokees," July 8, 1817, *Statutes at Large of the United States of America* 7 (1817): 156; "Treaty with the Choctaws," Sept. 5, 1820, *Statutes at Large of the United States of America* 7 (1820): 210; "Treaty with the Choctaws," Jan. 20, 1825, *Statutes at Large of the United States of America* 7 (1825): 234; "Treaty with the Choctaws," Sept. 27, 1830, *Statutes at Large of the United States of America* 7 (1830): 333; "Treaty with the Cherokees," Dec. 29, 1835, *Statutes at Large of the United States of America* 7 (1835): 478; "Treaty with the Cherokees," March 1, 1836, *Statutes at Large of the United States of America* 7 (1836): 488; "Treaty with the Stockbridge Indians," Nov. 24, 1848, *Statutes at Large of*

the United States of America 9 (1848): 955; "Treaty with the Wyandots," Jan. 31, 1855, *Statutes at Large of the United States of America* 10 (1855): 1159; "Treaty with the Pottawatomies," Nov. 15, 1861, *Statutes at Large of the United States of America* 12 (1861): 1192; "Treaty with the Ottawa Indians," June 24, 1862, *Statutes at Large of the United States of America* 12 (1862): 1237; "Treaty with the Kickapoo Indians," June 28, 1862, *Statutes at Large of the United States of America* 13 (1862): 623; "Treaty with the Pottawatomies," March 29, 1866, *Statutes at Large of the United States of America* 14 (1866): 763; "Treaty with the Delaware Indians," July 4, 1866, *Statutes at Large of the United States of America* 14 (1866): 793; "Treaty between the United States of America and the Senecas, Mixed Senecas and Shawnees, Quapaws, Confederated Peorias, Kaskaskias, Weas, and Piankeshaws, Ottawas of Blanchard's Fork and Roche de Bauf, and certain Wyandottes," Feb. 23, 1867, *Statutes at Large of the United States of America* 15 (1867): 513; "Treaty with the Pottawatomies," Feb. 27, 1867, *Statutes at Large of the United States of America* 15 (1867): 531; "Treaty with the Sioux," April 29, 1868, *Statutes at Large of the United States of America* 15 (1868): 635.

30. *Oklahoma Organic Act of 1890*, 51st Cong., 1st Sess., *U.S. Statutes at Large* 26 (1890): 81, 99–100.

31. See, e.g., Jeanette Wolfley, "Jim Crow, Indian Style: The Disenfranchisement of Native Americans," *American Indian Law Review* 16 (1991): 173–79.

32. *Dawes Act of 1887*, 49th Cong., 2nd Sess., *U.S. Statutes at Large* 24 (1887): 388, 390; see Wolfley, "Jim Crow, Indian Style," 178.

33. See *Indian Citizenship Act of 1919*, 66th Cong., 1st Sess., *U.S. Statutes at Large* 41 (1919): 350; *Indian Citizenship Act of 1924*, 68th Cong., 2nd Sess., *U.S. Statutes at Large* 43 (1924): 253; see also Brunyeel, "Challenging American Boundaries," 31 n. 5; Wolfley, "Jim Crow, Indian Style," 179–80.

34. See, e.g., Wolfley, "Jim Crow, Indian Style," 181–92.

35. *In re* Minook, 2 Ala. 200, 202 (1904) (emphasis added).

36. Ibid., 212–20. By contrast, an Alaska state court that found a native Indian of British Columbia racially ineligible for naturalization because he was not a "free white person" cited the Alaska treaty's provision relating to "uncivilized" tribes and referred to the practice of treating the Indian tribes as "unfriendly to our government, living under conditions of barbarism." *Burton*, 1 Ala. 111, 113–14.

37. *Minook*, 2 Ala. 200, 212–20.

38. *In re* Nian, 21 P. 993, 993–94 (Utah 1889).

39. *Hawaiian Organic Act of 1900*, 56th Cong., 1st Sess., *U.S. Statutes at Large* 31 (1900): 141; Patrick Hanifin, "To Dwell on the Earth in Unity: *Rice, Arakaki,* and the Growth of Citizenship and Voting Rights in Hawai'i," *Hawaii Bar Journal* 5, no. 13 (2002): 29–31; see also Charles Gordon, "The Racial Barrier to American Citizenship," *University of Pennsylvania Law Review* 93 (1945): 247.

40. Hanifin, "To Dwell on the Earth in Unity," 22 n. 66; Campbell Gibson and Kay Jung, *Historical Census Statistics on Population Totals by Race, 1790 to 1990, and by Hispanic Origin, 1970 to 1990, for The United States, Regions, Divisions, and States* (Washington, DC: U.S. Census Bureau, 2002), table 26. In 1901, the United States District Court for the District of Hawaii recognized that a Chinese person arriving in Honolulu from China was an American citizen because he had been born in Hawaii prior to annexation and was therefore naturalized by the Hawaiian Organic Act of 1900. See United States v. Ching Tai Sai, 1 U.S. Dist. Ct. Haw. 118 (1901); see also *In re* MacFarlane, 11 Haw. 166, 172–76 (Haw. 1897).

41. *Jones-Shafroth Act of 1917*, 64th Cong., 2nd Sess., *U.S. Statutes at Large* 39 (1917): 951; *Act of Feb. 25, 1927*, 69th Cong., 2nd Sess., *U.S. Statutes at Large* 44 (1927): 1234.

42. See generally Gordon, "The Racial Barrier," 247; Hanifin, "To Dwell on the Earth in Unity," 15–44; Michael Lemay and Elliott Barkan, eds., *U.S. Immigration and Naturalization Laws and Issues: A Documentary History* (Westport, CT: Greenwood, 1999), 87, 112–13, 156.

43. *In re* Singh, 246 F. 496, 498–500 (E.D. Pa. 1917).

44. Matthew Frye Jacobson, *Whiteness of a Different Color: European Immigrants and the Alchemy of Race* (Cambridge: Harvard University Press, 1998), 203–22.

45. Ibid., 225–26.

46. Ibid., 233; see also Murphy, "How the Irish Became Japanese."

47. *Naturalization Act of 1870*, 41st Cong., 2nd Sess. 42 *Congressional Globe* (July 4, 1870), pt. 6:5156.

48. *Yup*, 1 F. Ca. at 224.

49. See, e.g., *In re* Halladjian, 174 F.834, 841 (C.C.D. Mass. 1909); *Ex parte* Shahid, 205 F. 812, 814 (E.D.S.C. 1913) ("Nor would 'free white persons' mean an 'Aryan' race, a word of much later coinage, and practically unknown to common usage in 1790, and one still more indefinite than Caucasian, and which would exclude all Semitics, viz., Jews and Arabians,

and also all Europeans, such as Magyars, Finns, and Basques, not included in the Aryan family."); *Ex parte* Dow, 211 F. 486, 488 (E.D.S.C. 1914) ("If racial determination or definition is to be given to the expression as limiting it to the Caucasian races, and the Caucasian race is to be determined philologically by the tongue spoken as Indo-European, then there are a number of European peoples who would be excluded, such as the Magyars, the Finns, the Turks, the Basques, and the Lapps."); *In re* Dow, 213 F. 355, 359 (E.D.S.C. 1914) ("This philological development led to the coining of the word 'Aryan,' taken from the Vedic or old Sanscrit and Zend, . . . and excluded from the 'Aryan brotherhood' of whites the Magyars, the Finns, and the Turks because they spoke tongues of the Ugric or Turanian group."); Arthur William Hoglund, *Finnish Immigrants in America 1880–1920* (Madison: University of Wisconsin Press, 1960), 114.

50. Keevak, *Becoming Yellow*, 70–76.

51. Ibid.

52. S. Wells Williams, *The Middle Kingdom: A Survey of the Geography, Government, Literature, Social Life, Arts, and History of the Chinese Empire and Its Inhabitants*, rev. ed., vol. 1 (London: W. H. Allen, 1883), 45.

53. Theodore Lothrop Stoddard, *The Rising Tide of Color Against White World Supremacy* (New York: Charles Scribner's Sons, 1921), 146.

54. Keevak, *Becoming Yellow*, 76, 124–25.

55. People v. Hall, 4 Cal. 399, 402 (Cal. 1854).

56. See Randolph Lapp, *Blacks in Gold Rush California* (New Haven: Yale University Press, 1977), 209.

57. See *California School Law of 1860* and *California Political Code of 1880*, quoted in Joyce Kuo, "Excluded, Segregated and Forgotten: A Historical View of the Discrimination of Chinese Americans in Public Schools," *Asian American Law Journal* 5 (1998): 190 n. 56, 198 n. 115.

58. See Takaki, *Strangers From a Different Shore*, 101–102.

59. "Anti-Chinese Uprising," *Daily Evening Bulletin* (San Francisco), March 4, 1882.

60. "Asiatic Invaders," *Daily Evening Bulletin* (San Francisco), May 18, 1886.

61. Edward Gilliam, "The African Problem," *North American Review* 139 (1884): 429.

62. Asiatic Exclusion League, *Proceedings of the Asiatic Exclusion League* (June 1910), at 35, in Asiatic Exclusion League, *Proceedings of the Asiatic Exclusion League, 1907–1913* (New York: Arno Press, 1977); see also *Oxford English Dictionary*, 2nd ed., s.v. "Mongolianize."

63. See Pierton Dooner, *Last Days of the Republic* (San Francisco: Alta, 1880); Abwell Whitney, *Almond-Eyed: A Story of the Day* (San Francisco: A. L. Bancroft, 1878); Robert Woltor, *Truthful History of the Taking of Oregon and California in the Year A.D. 1899* (San Francisco: A. L. Bancroft, 1882); see generally David Seed, "Constructing America's Enemies: The Invasions of the USA," *The Yearbook of English Studies* 37, no. 2 (2007), 64–84; Edlie Wong, *Racial Reconstruction: Black Inclusion, Chinese Exclusion, and the Fictions of Citizenship* (New York: New York University Press, 2015), 124–66; William Wu, *The Yellow Peril: Chinese Americans in American Fiction, 1850–1940* (Hamden, CT: Archon, 1982), 30–40.

64. Dooner, *Last Days of the Republic*, 105, 131, 189, 194–98.

65. Lorelle, "The Battle of the Wabash: A Letter from the Invisible Police," *Californian* 2, no. 10 (1880): 374–75.

66. Quoted in Wong, *Racial Reconstruction*, 151–53; see also Kevin Jenks, "Before the 'Yellow Peril,'" *Social Contract* 6, no. 4 (1996).

67. Philip Nowlan, *Armageddon 2419 A.D.* (1928; repr. Project Gutenberg, 2010), http://www.gutenberg.org/files/32530/32530-h/32530-h. htm (accessed Aug. 16, 2016); Philip Nowlan, *The Airlords of Han* (1929; repr. Project Gutenberg, 2010), http://www.gutenberg.org/files/25438/25438-h/25438-h.htm (accessed Aug. 16, 2016).

68. *Naturalization Act of 1870*, 41st Cong., 2nd Sess. 42, *Congressional Globe* (July 4, 1870), pt. 6:5152 and 5155–57.

69. *Naturalization Act of 1870*, 41st Cong., 2nd Sess., *Statutes at Large of the United States of America* 16 (1870): 254.

70. *In re* Po, 7 Misc. 471, 472 (City Ct. N.Y. 1894).

71. See, e.g., Bessho v. United States, 178 F. 245, 246 (4th Cir. 1910) ("The attention of the legislative branch of the government was thus particularly called to the point we are now considering, and the action then taken by it is most significant, and clearly indicates that the Congress then intended to exclude all persons of the Mongolian race from the privileges of the naturalization laws."); see also, e.g., *In re* Saito, 62 F. 126, 127 (C.C.D. Mass. 1894).

72. Chae Chan Ping v. United States, 130 U.S. 581, 595–96, 606–07 (1889).

73. Cho and Gott, "The Racial Sovereign," 190–91.

74. The primary meaning of "horde" given by the *Oxford English Dictionary* is "a tribe or troop of Tartar or kindred Asiatic nomads, dwelling in tents or wagons, and migrating from place to place for pasturage, *or*

for war or plunder," and the etymology of the word also suggests this. *Oxford English Dictionary*, 2nd ed., s.v. "Horde" (emphasis added).

75. *Chinese Exclusion Act of 1882*, 47th Cong., 1st Sess., *U.S. Statutes at Large* 22 (1882): 58.

76. *Po*, 7 Misc. at 472.

77. *Rodriguez*, 81 F. at 349.

78. See generally Darrell Smith, *The Bureau of Naturalization: Its History, Activities and Organization* (Baltimore: Johns Hopkins Press, 1926).

79. See United States Customs and Border Protection, "U.S. Immigration and Naturalization Service—Populating a Nation: A History of Immigration and Naturalization," http://www.cbp.gov/about/history/legacy/immigration-history (accessed Aug. 13, 2014); *Report to the President of the Commission on Naturalization, Appointed by Executive Order March 1, 1905* (Washington, DC: GPO, 1905).

80. *Naturalization Act of 1906*, 59th Cong., 1st Sess., *U.S. Statutes at Large* 34 (1906): 596.

81. Ibid., 599–603.

82. Ibid., 601.

83. For a discussion of the diversity of views among courts regarding the proper scope of jurisdiction in cancellation proceedings, see generally United States v. Kamm, 247 F. 968 (E.D. Wash. 1918); Oscar Trelles and James Bailey, eds., *Immigration and Nationality Acts: Legislative Histories and Related Documents, 1950–1978* (Buffalo: W. S. Hein, 1977), 1:760.

84. See, e.g., United States v. Gokhale, 26 F.2d 360 (2d Cir. 1928); United States v. Javier, 22 F.2d 879 (D.C. Cir. 1927); Mozumdar v. United States, 299 F. 240 (9th Cir. 1924); United States v. Ali, 20 F.2d 998 (E.D. Mich. 1927); United States v. Ali, 7 F.2d 728 (E.D. Mich. 1925); United States v. Khan, 1 F.2d 1006 (W.D. Penn. 1924); United States v. Mozumdar, 296 F. 173 (S.D. Cal. 1923); Sato v. Hall, 217 P. 520 (Cal. 1923).

85. *In re* Mudarri, 176 F. 465, 466 (D. Mass. 1910).

86. A. Rustem Bey, "Thinks Law Unfair," *Washington Post*, Nov. 3, 1909.

87. Earlene Craver, "On the Boundary of White: The *Cartozian* Naturalization Case and the Armenians, 1923–1925," *Journal of American Ethnic History* 28 (2009): 30–56; "Turkey Will Protest," *Washington Post*, Nov. 1, 1909; A. Rustem Bey, "Thinks Law Unfair," *Washington Post*, Nov. 3, 1909; "Conflicting Views Taken of Asiatic Exclusion," *Dallas Morning News*, Nov. 6, 1909; see also "Aliens Refused Naturalization," *Duluth* (MN) *News Tribune*, Sept. 29, 1909; "Race Row Up to Courts," *Washington*

Post, Nov. 4, 1909; "Way Paved for Syrians," *Grand Forks* (ND) *Daily Herald*, Dec. 15, 1909.

88. Conflicting Views Taken of Asiatic Exclusion," *Dallas Morning News*; see also "Aliens Refused Naturalization," *Duluth* (MN) *News Tribune*; "Race Row Up To Courts," *Washington Post*.

89. *Immigration Act of 1917*, 64th Cong., 2nd Sess., *Congressional Record* 54 (Dec. 12, 1916): 222.

90. Correspondence from Secretary of Commerce and Labor Charles Nagel to Chief of the Naturalization Division Richard Campbell dated Nov. 9, 1909, in Box 1573, Records of the Immigration and Naturalization Service of the United States, RG 85, NAB.

91. Memoranda from Chief of the Naturalization Division Richard Campbell to Chief Naturalization Examiners dated Dec. 3, 1909, in Records of the Immigration and Naturalization Service of the United States, RG 85, Box 1573, NAB; cf. Correspondence from Commissioner of Naturalization Richard Campbell to Secretary of Labor William Wilson dated March 22, 1913, in Box 1573, Records of the Immigration and Naturalization Service of the United States, RG 85, NAB; ("The Department preferred a cessation of the practice of raising the question in any way as to whether aliens applying for citizenship came within the provisions of section 2169. With that understanding, I have to report that there has been no action since that time upon the part of this office to question the admissibility of Asiatics, other than Chinese who are plainly forbidden, and Japanese, who had been decided by a number of courts to be not white persons.").

92. See, e.g., *In re* Mozumdar, 207 F. 115, 116 (E.D. Wash. 1913) ("The questions propounded by the Naturalization Examiner, representing the government, simply brought out the fact that the applicant is a native of India, and that his ancestors for generations before him were natives of that country.").

93. Nagel also indicated that he discussed the policy with President William Taft and that Taft approved of it. See Correspondence from Secretary of Commerce and Labor Charles Nagel to Chief of the Naturalization Division Richard Campbell dated Nov. 9, 1909, in Records of the Immigration and Naturalization Service of the United States, RG 85, Box 1573, NAB.

94. Correspondence from Charles Nagel to Justin Kirreh dated Nov. 13, 1909, in Records of the Immigration and Naturalization Service of the United States, RG 85, Box 1573, NAB.

95. *Halladjian*, 174 F. 834, 841–43.

96. *Ozawa*, 260 U.S. at 198; see, e.g., Dow v. United States, 226 F. 145, 146 (4th Cir. 1915) ("In 1790, . . . immigration to this country was almost altogether from Europe; and doubtless the act of 1790 was intended mainly to provide for naturalization of aliens from Europe, and to deny naturalization to negroes."); United States v. Balsara, 180 F. 694, 695 (2d Cir. 1910) (writing that congressmen in 1790 "probably has principally in mind the exclusion of Africans, whether slave or free, and Indians, both of which races were and had been objects of serious public consideration," and that that Syrian interveners as amici curiae "contend that the words 'free white persons' were used simply to exclude slaves and free negroes"); *In re* Singh, 257 F. 209, 211 (S.D. Cal. 1919) ("There is nothing that I can discover to indicate anywhere that either the colonies originally or the United States government later, when the federal statute was passed, had in mind the exclusion from citizenship of any other persons than those referred to, to wit, negroes, Indians, and unfree whites."); *In re* Mozumdar, 207 F. 115, 117 (E.D. Wash. 1913) ("In the original naturalization act the expression 'free white persons' was doubtless primarily intended to include the white emigrants from Northern Europe, with whom the Congress of that day was familiar, and to exclude Indians and persons of African descent or nativity."); Brief for Petitioner at 42, Ozawa v. United States, No. 1 (U.S. Sup. Ct. Dec. 9, 1918) ("At the time the original law was passed, . . . there can be no question but white was used in counter distinction from black, and 'free white persons' included all who were not black.").

97. Shahid, 205 F. at 812 ("In color, [the applicant] is about that of a walnut, or somewhat darker than is the usual mulatto of one-half mixed blood between the white and the negro race."); *In re* Nian, 21 P. 993, 993 (Utah 1889); see also *Halladjian*, 174 F. 834, 835 (finding that four Armenian applicants were all "white persons in appearance, not darker in complexion than some persons of north European descent traceable for generations"); *In re* Najour, 174 F. 735, 735 (C.C.N.D. Ga. 1909) (noting that the applicant "is not particularly dark, and has none of the characteristics or appearance of the Mongolian race").

98. United States v. Dolla, 177 F. 101, 102 (5th Cir. 1910).

99. Brief for Petitioner at 65, Ozawa v. United States, No. 1 (U.S. Sup. Ct. Dec. 9, 1918).

100. *In re* R—, 4 I. & N. Dec. 275, 285 (B.I.A. 1951).

101. See, e.g., Singh, 246 F. at 497–98.

102. *Ex parte* Dow, 211 F. 486, 487 (E.D.S.C. 1914); see also *In re* Dow, 213 F. 355, 357–58.

103. *Ozawa*, 260 U.S. at 197.

104. R—, 4 I. & N. Dec. at 285 (emphasis added).

105. See, e.g., Correspondence from Judge Adam Cliffe of the United States District Court for the Northern District of Illinois to M. Vartan Malcolm dated Oct. 30, 1924, in Transcript of Evidence, United States v. Cartozian, No. E-8668 (D. Or. June 10, 1925), Civil and Criminal Case Files, District of Oregon (Portland), Records of the District Courts of the United States, RG 21, NAPAR; "Judge Edings Grants Citizenship to Das," *Maui News*, Jan. 4, 1918; *Mozumdar*, 207 F. at 117; *In re* Alverto, 198 F. 688, 690 (E.D. Pa. 1912); *In re* Young, 198 F. 715, 716 (W.D. Wash. 1912); *Halladjian*, 174 F. at 840; *Saito*, 62 F. at 127–28; *Yup*, 1 F. Ca. at 223–24; *In re* Yamashita, 70 P. 482, 483 (Wash. 1902); *Nian*, 21 P. at 993–94. With regard to the relationship between the Aryan and Caucasian racial classifications, see, e.g., John Clarke, *Oriental Enlightenment: The Encounter Between Asian and Western Thought* (London: Routledge, 1997), 55–59; Wendy Doniger, *The Hindus: An Alternative History* (New York: Penguin, 2009), 85–102; Raymond Shwab, *The Oriental Renaissance: Europe's Rediscovery of India and the East, 1680–1880*, trans. Gene Patterson-Black and Victor Reinking (New York: Columbia University Press, 1984), 32; Thomas Trautmann, *Aryans and British India* (Berkeley: University of California Press, 1997), 11–13, 23–26; Romila Thapar, "Imagined Religious Communities? Ancient History and the Modern Search for a Hindu Identity," *Modern Asian Studies* 23, no. 2 (1989): 226; *Meyers Konversationslexikon*, 4th ed., 1885–90.

106. See, e.g., *Dow*, 226 F. at 146 ("It is reasonably certain that congressmen [in 1790] had no knowledge of Blumenbach's classification of the races of men published in 1781."); *Dow*, 213 F. at 358–60 ("Very few agree as to what peoples are members of the Caucasian race . . . Ethnologists and philologists do not agree . . . as to who are the white races. They will rank different peoples as 'Aryans' or 'Indo-Europeans' or 'Semites' or 'Hamites,' differing even as to who are included in these; but when it comes to 'white' no agreed classification exists."); *Mudarri*, 176 F. at 466–67 ("What may be called . . . the Caucasian-Mongolian classification is not now held to be valid by any considerable body of ethnologists. To make naturalization depend upon this classification is to make an important result depend upon the application of an abandoned scientific theory, a course of proceeding which surely brings the law and its administration into disrepute."); *In re* Balsara,

171 F. 294 (C.C.S.D.N.Y. 1909) (commenting that serious objections existed to interpreting "white" to include "all branches of the great race or family known to ethnologists as the Aryan, Indo-European, or Caucasian" because it "would bring in, not only the Parsees, . . . which is probably the purest Aryan type, but also Afghans, Hindoos, Arabs, and Berbers").

107. Brief for Appellant at 12, United States v. Thind, No. 3745 (9th Cir. Sept. 28, 1921).

108. Brief for Petitioner at 62–77, Ozawa v. United States, No. 1 (U.S. Sup. Ct. Dec. 9, 1918); Brief of Respondent at 8–23 and 34–49, United States v. Thind, No. 202 (U.S. Sup. Ct. Dec. 30, 1921).

109. *Ozawa*, 260 U.S. at 197; *Thind*, 261 U.S. at 208–10.

110. Brief Submitted by the Appellant at 5, United States v. Balsara, No. 186 (2d Cir. 1909–1910); Brief for the United States at 20–21, United States v. Thind, No. 202 (U.S. Sup. Ct. Dec. 30, 1921); cf. *In re* Ellis, 179 F. 1002, 1003 (D. Or. 1910).

111. *Halladjian*, 174 F. at 837.

112. Untitled Department Memorandum dated Aug. 13, 1931, in Box 1573, Records of the Immigration and Naturalization Service of the United States, RG 85, NAB; cf. *Dolla*, 177 F. at 101 (noting that the government opposed the naturalization of a man who was born and raised in Calcutta, India, to parents who were natives on Afghanistan on the ground that he was a "native of India").

113. In a 1924 case involving a Palestinian applicant, for example, one federal judge wrote:

> If we look at the map we find that the place where this man was born is on a parallel of longitude which runs West of Moscow. This is some distance West of Armenia but even in the case of Armenia the line of longitude runs only a short distance to the East of Moscow.

Decision at 2, *In re* Sallak, No. 14876 (N.D. Ill, June 27, 1924), in Significant Civil and Criminal Case Files, 1899–1925, District of Oregon (Portland), Records of U.S. Attorneys and Marshals, RG 118, NAPAR. Similarly, the Board of Immigration Appeals included the precise latitude and longitude of the Russian towns where two Kalmyk immigrants were born in an opinion addressing their racial eligibility for naturalization:

St. Potavoskaja (47°19" N., 43°18" E.) and St. Vlasovskaja (47°13" N., 42°20" E.) are about midway between Rostov and the Sea of Azov on the west and Astrakhan and the Caspian Sea on the east, in that area of eastern European Russia which lies north of the Caucasus Mountains.

R—, 4 I. & N. Dec. 275, 275 n.2.

114. Brief for the United States at 20–21, United States v. Thind, No. 202 (U.S. Sup. Ct. Dec. 30, 1921).

115. Michael Omi and Howard Winant, "Racial Formation," in *Race Critical Theories: Text and Context*, ed. Philomena Essed and David Theo Goldberg (Oxford: Blackwell, 2002), 123.

116. *Ellis*, 179 F. at 1003.

117. *Oxford English Dictionary*, 2nd ed., s.v. "White, adj." and "White Man."

118. Orlando Patterson, *Freedom, Vol. I: Freedom in the Making of Western Culture* (New York: Basic Books, 1991), 3–4; see also Martin Japtok, "'The Gospel of Whiteness': Whiteness in African American Literature," *American Studies* 49 (2004): 491.

119. *Ellis*, 179 F. at 1003–1004.

120. Brief Submitted by the Appellant at 126-27, United States v. Balsara, No. 186 (2d Cir. 1909–1910).

121. *Dred Scott*, 60 U.S. at 403–407 and 415–20; *Singh*, 246 F. at 498–500.

122. In 1943, the Immigration and Naturalization Service noted in an article in its *Monthly Review* regarding Arab racial eligibility for naturalization that it had long been the administrative policy of the United States not to object to Arab naturalizations on racial grounds. U.S. Department of Justice, Immigration and Naturalization Service, "The Eligibility of Arabs to Naturalization," *Monthly Review* 1 (1943): 16.

123. Correspondence from Secretary of Commerce and Labor Charles Nagel to O'Brien, Boardman, Platt & Littleton dated Nov. 18, 1909, in Box 1573, Records of the Immigration and Naturalization Service of the United States, RG 85, NAB.

124. See *Naturalization Act of 1918*, 65th Cong., 2nd Sess., *U.S. Statutes at Large* 40 (1918): 542; Lucy Salyer, "Baptism by Fire: Race, Military Service, and U.S. Citizenship Policy, 1918–1935," *Journal of American History* 91 (2004): 856–62. In some instances, courts that concluded they had no discretion but

to deny soldier petitions also expressed powerful sympathy for their cause. See, e.g., "Think Government Can't Debar Knight," *New York Times*, July 16, 1909.

125. See Salyer, "Baptism by Fire," 859–61.

126. Memorandum from Chief Naturalization Examiner Henry Hazard to Commissioner of Naturalization Raymond Crist dated June 19, 1924, in Box 1573, Records of the Immigration and Naturalization Service of the United States, RG 85, NAB; cf. Memorandum from Chief Naturalization Examiner Henry Hazard to Commissioner of Naturalization Raymond Crist dated June 19, 1924, ibid.

127. Memorandum from Chief Naturalization Examiner Henry Hazard to Commissioner of Naturalization Raymond Crist dated May 21, 1924, in Box 1573, Records of the Immigration and Naturalization Service of the United States, RG 85, NAB.

128. See U.S. Senate Committee on Immigration, *Hearings on S.J. Res. 128, Providing for the Ratification and Confirmation of Naturalization of Certain Persons of the Hindu Race*, 69th Cong., 2nd sess. (Washington, DC: GPO, 1926), 7.

129. See Salyer, "Baptism by Fire," 862–64; Toyota v. United States, 268 U.S. 402 (1925).

130. Ian Haney López, *White by Law: The Legal Construction of Race* (New York: New York Univ. Press, 1996), 2–3.

131. Sumi Cho and Gil Gott, "The Racial Sovereign," in *Sovereignty, Emergency, Legality*, ed. Austin Sarat (Cambridge: Cambridge University Press, 2010), 212–13.

132. Falguni Sheth, *Toward a Political Philosophy of Race* (Albany: State University of New York Press, 2009), 30.

133. Brief Submitted by the Appellant at 126–27, United States v. Balsara, No. 186 (2d Cir. 1909–1910).

134. Paul Hopper and Sandra Thompson, "Transitivity in Grammar and Discourse," *Language* 56, no. 2 (1980): 251–53.

135. Åshlid Næss, *Prototypical Transitivity* (Amsterdam: John Benjamins, 2007), 77.

136. Brief Submitted by the Appellant, United States v. Balsara, No. 186 (2d Cir. 1909–1910), 126–27.

137. *Dred Scott*, 60 U.S. at 407, 420.

138. See Brief for Appellee, Ozawa v. United States, No. 2888–2889 (9th Cir. May 29, 1917), at 2, in Box 1068, Records of the U.S. Courts of Appeals, RG 276, NAPR (SB).

139. Brief by Takao Ozawa (typewritten copy) at 1–7 and 14–21, *In re* Ozawa, No. 274 (Terr. Haw. May 29, 1915), in Folder 1, Box 9, Naturalization Case Files, District Court for the Territory of Hawaii, Records of the District Courts of the United States, RG 21, NAPAR (SB) (Ozawa District Court Brief).

140. Quoted in Brief for Appellee at 7–9, Ozawa v. United States, No. 2888–2889 (9th Cir. May 29, 1917), in Box 1068, Records of the U.S. Courts of Appeals, RG 276, NAPR (SB).

141. See *Ozawa*, 260 U.S. at 189.

142. See Brief for Petitioner, Ozawa v. United States, No. 1 (U.S. Sup. Ct. Dec. 9, 1918) (Ozawa's Supreme Court Brief); Brief for the United States, Ozawa v. United States, No. 1 (U.S. Supr. Ct. Sept. 19, 1922); "Defers Again Japanese Case: U.S. Solicitor General Asks to Postpone Argument in Citizenship Rights," *Washington Post*, Sep. 30, 1920.

143. Gerald Horne, "Race from Power: U.S. Foreign Policy and the General Crisis of White Supremacy," in *Window on Freedom: Race, Civil Rights, and Foreign Affairs 1945–1988* (Chapel Hill: University of North Carolina Press, 2003), 50; see also Gurdev Deol, *The Role of the Ghadar Party in the National Movement* (New Delhi, India: Sterling, 1969), 25–26.

144. See generally Craver, "On the Boundary of White," 30–56; cf. Stoddard, *The Rising Tide of Color*, 10, 21–22, 28–32.

145. Sean Brawley, *The White Peril: Foreign Relations and Asian Immigration to Australasia and North America 1919–78* (Sydney: University of New South Wales Press, 1995), 13; see generally Edwin James, "Europeans Incline to Side With Japan: Old World Diplomats Take Issue With American Exclusion Law," *New York Times*, June 5, 1924; Savel Zimand, "Color Issue Breeds Unrest in the East," *New York Times*, Oct. 26, 1924; cf. Stoddard, *The Rising Tide*, 42.

146. Brawley, *White Peril*, 14; see also Stoddard, *The Rising Tide of Color*, 42–43.

147. Brawley, *White Peril*, 15–17.

148. Ibid., 16–17.

149. Ibid., 26.

150. Quoted in Brawley, *White Peril*, 28.

151. See Margaret MacMillan, *Paris 1919: Six Months That Changed the World* (New York: Random House, 2002), 321.

152. Brawley, *White Peril*, 18, 36–44.

153. See, e.g., ibid., 43.

154. Ozawa's District Court Brief at 29–30.

155. Brief for the United States at 1–2, *In re* Ozawa, No. 274 (Terr. Haw. May 29, 1915), in Folder 2, Box 9, Naturalization Case Files, District Court for the Territory of Hawaii, Records of the District Courts of the United States, RG 21, NAPAR (SB).

156. Brief for Appellant at 59–68, Ozawa v. United States, No. 2888–2889 (9th Cir. May 29, 1917), in Box 1068, Records of the U.S. Courts of Appeals, RG 276, NAPR (SB) (Ozawa's Ninth Circuit Brief); Ozawa's Supreme Court Brief at 52, 60–62.

157. Ozawa's Ninth Circuit Brief at 80–83; Ozawa's Supreme Court Brief at 75–78.

158. Ozawa's Ninth Circuit Brief at 68–79; Ozawa's Supreme Court Brief at 60–78.

159. Ozawa's Supreme Court Brief at 62–77.

160. Ozawa's Ninth Circuit Brief at 77–79; Ozawa's Supreme Court Brief at 62–77.

161. See, e.g., Asiatic Exclusion League, *Proceedings of the Asiatic Exclusion League* (Jan. 1908), at 10–11, Asiatic Exclusion League, *Proceedings of the Asiatic Exclusion League* (June 1908), at 12, in Asiatic Exclusion League, *Proceedings of the Asiatic Exclusion League*; Stoddard, *The Rising Tide of Color*, 20–21, 48–53, 130–38.

162. Takaki, *Strangers from a Different Shore*, 180, 207, 209.

163. Ozawa's Ninth Circuit Brief at 81 (emphasis added); Ozawa's Supreme Court Brief at 62–83 (emphasis added).

164. See *Oxford English Dictionary*, 2nd ed., s.v. "Assimilate."

165. Næss, *Prototypical Transitivity*, 77–81.

166. *Dred Scott*, 60 U.S. at 403–407, 415–20; *Singh*, 246 F. at 498–500.

167. Brief for the United States at 31, Ozawa v. United States, No. 1 (U.S. Supr. Ct. Sept. 19, 1922).

168. Ibid., 31–37, 54.

169. Brief Filed by the Attorney General of the State of California as Amicus Curiae at 120–24, Ozawa v. United States, No. 1 (U.S. Supr. Ct. Oct. 4, 1922).

170. See Susan Brewer, *Why America Fights: Patriotism and War Propaganda from the Philippines to Iraq* (New York: Oxford University Press, 2009), 46–86.

171. Stoddard, *The Rising Tide of Color*, 130–31, 137, 231.

172. *Ozawa*, 260 U.S. at 195–96 (emphasis added) (citing *In re* Camille, 6 F. 256 (C.C.D. Or. 1880); *In re* Saito, 62 Fed. 126 (C.C.D. Mass. 1894); *In re* Nian, 21 P. 993 (Utah 1889); *In re* Kumagai, 163 Fed. 922 (W.D. Wash. 1908); *In re* Yamashita, 10 P. 482 (Wash. 1902); *In re* Ellis, 179 F. 1002 (D. Or. 1910); *In re* Mozumdar, 207 F. 115 (E.D. Wash. 1913); *In re* Singh, 257 F. 209 (S.D. Cal. 1919); and *In re* Charr, 273 Fed. 207 (W.D. Mo. 1921)).

173. *Ozawa*, 260 U.S. at 198.

174. William Sumner, *Folkways: A Study of the Sociological Importance of Usages, Manners, Customs, Mores, and Morals* (New York: Ginn, 1906), 12–13.

175. Muzafer Sherif and Carolyn Sherif, "Research on Intergroup Relations," in *The Social Psychology of Intergroup Relations*, ed. William Austin and Stephen Worchel (Monterey, CA: Brooks/Cole, 1979), 11; see generally, e.g., Catherine Cottrell, "Different Emotional Reactions to Different Groups: A Sociofunctional Threat-Based Approach to 'Prejudice,'" *Journal of Personality and Social Psychology* 88 (2005): 770–89; Susan Fiske, "What We Know Now About Bias and Intergroup Conflict, the Problem of the Century," *Current Directions in Psychological Science* 2 (2002): 123–28; Muzafer Sherif, O. J. Harvey, B. Jack White, William Hood, and Carolyn Sherif, *The Robbers Cave Experiment: Intergroup Conflict and Cooperation* (1961; repr. Middletown, CT: Wesleyan Univ. Press, 1988); Mark Van Vugt, David De Cremer, and Dirk Janssen, "Gender Differences in Cooperation and Competition: The Male Warrior Hypothesis," *Psychological Science* 18 (2007): 19–23; Masaki Yuki and Kunihiro Yokota, "The Primal Warrior: Outgroup Threat Priming Enhances Intergroup Discrimination in Men But Not Women," *Journal of Experimental Social Psychology* 45 (2009): 271–74; see generally Jay Jackson, "Realistic Group Conflict Theory: A Review and Evaluation of the Theoretical and Empirical Literature," *Psychological Record* 43 (1993): 395–415.

176. Jackson, "Realistic Group Conflict Theory," 398, 405.

177. Sherif, "Research on Intergroup Relations," 259.

178. See, e.g., Chris Hedges, *War Is a Force That Gives Us Meaning* (New York: Anchor, 2002); Anthony Lloyd, *My War Gone By, I Miss It So* (New York: Atlantic Monthly, 1999).

179. Hedges, *War Is a Force*, 9, 45, 74.

180. Ibid., 115–16.

181. Ibid., 7.

182. See Lawrence LeShan, *The Psychology of War: Comprehending Its Mystique and Its Madness* (Chicago: The Noble Press, 1992), 28.

183. See Lloyd, *My War Gone By.*

184. Robert Ivie, "Images of Savagery in American Justifications for War," *Communication Monographs* 47 (1980): 290.

185. LeShan, *Psychology of War*, 35–36.

186. Elias Canetti, *Crowds and Power* (New York: Viking 1962), 138.

187. See Salyer, "Baptism by Fire," 848.

188. Ibid., 849.

189. See Rogers Smith, *Civic Ideals: Conflicting Visions of Citizenship in U.S. History* (New Haven: Yale University Press, 1997), 16; cf., e.g., Nancy Ford, *Americans All! Foreign-Born Soldiers in World War I* (College Station: Texas A & M University Press, 2001); Gary Gerstle, *American Crucible: Race and Nation in the Twentieth Century* (Princeton: Princeton University Press, 2001); James Jacobs and Leslie Hayes, "Aliens in the U.S. Armed Forces: A Historico-Legal Analysis," *Armed Forces and Society* 7, no. 2 (1981): 187–208.

190. Jacobson, *Whiteness of a Different Color*, 203–22.

191. Derrick Bell Jr., "*Brown v. Board of Education* and the Interest-Convergence Dilemma," *Harvard Law Review* 93 (1980): 523–24.

192. See, e.g., Carol Anderson, *Eyes Off the Prize: The United Nations and the African American Struggle for Human Rights, 1944–1955* (Cambridge: Cambridge University Press, 2003); Thomas Borstelmann, *The Cold War and the Color Line: American Race Relations in the Global Arena* (Cambridge: Harvard University Press, 2003); Mary Dudziak, *Cold War Civil Rights: Race and the Image of American Democracy* (Princeton: Princeton University Press, 2000); Gerald Horne, *Black and Red: W. E. B. DuBois and the African American Response to the Cold War* (Albany: State University of New York Press, 1986); Brenda Plummer, *Rising Wind: Black Americans and U.S. Foreign Affairs, 1935–1960* (Chapel Hill: University of North Carolina Press, 1996); Jonathan Rosenberg, *How Far the Promised Land? World Affairs and the American Civil Rights Movement from the First World War to Vietnam* (Princeton: Princeton University Press, 2006.

193. Elise Boddie, "Racial Territoriality," *UCLA Law Review* 58 (2010): 401, 406; see also Henri Lefebvre, *The Production of Space*, trans. Donald Nicholson-Smith (1991; repr. Oxford, UK: Blackwell, 1995).

194. Cheryl Harris, "Whiteness as Property," *Harvard Law Review* 106 (1993): 1707–14.

195. Cho and Gott, "The Racial Sovereign," 212–13.

196. Sheth, *Toward a Political Philosophy of Race*, 30.

197. Lefebvre, *Production of Space*, 280.

198. *Ellis*, 179 F. at 1003; *Halladjian*, 174 F. at 837.

199. See, e.g., Jessica Mayo, "Court-Mandated Story Time: The Victim Narrative in U.S. Asylum Law," *Washington University Law Review* 89 (2012): 1485–1522; Amy Shuman and Carol Bohmer, "Representing Trauma: Political Asylum Narrative," *Journal of American Folklore* 117 (2004): 394–414.

CHAPTER 2. THE GHADR PARTY AND THE INDIAN CASTE SYSTEM IN *THIND*

1. Correspondence from the Sixth Grade of Herman Klix School to United States Secretary of State Cordell Hull dated Nov. 11, 1937, in Box 1573, Records of the Immigration and Naturalization Service of the United States, RG 85, NAB.

2. Correspondence from Secretary of State Cordell Hull to Secretary of Labor Frances Perkins dated Nov. 26, 1937, in Box 1573, Records of the Immigration and Naturalization Service of the United States, RG 85, NAB; Correspondence from Assistant Naturalization Examiner Henry Hazard to the Principal of Herman Klix School dated Jan. 10, 1938, in Box 1573, Records of the Immigration and Naturalization Service of the United States, RG 85, NAB.

3. Correspondence from Chief Naturalization Examiner Henry Hazard to the Principal of Herman Klix School dated Jan. 10, 1938, in Box 1573, Records of the Immigration and Naturalization Service of the United States, RG 85, NAB.

4. United States v. Thind, 261 U.S. 204, 209 (1923). Although the word *Hindu* primarily refers to an adherent of Hinduism rather than a racial classification, during the early twentieth century the word was used more generally to refer to all of the people of India. See, e.g., *Oxford English Dictionary*, 2nd ed., s.v. "Hindu." Indeed, Thind identified himself as a "high-caste Hindu of full Indian blood" despite belonging to the Sikh religious tradition. See

Brief of Respondent at 2, 15, United States v. Thind, No. 202 (U.S. Sup. Ct. Dec. 30, 1921) (claiming that "Bhagat Singh Thind is a high-caste Hindu of full Indian blood," but also noting that "Bhagat Singh Thind is a Sikh, that being the religion of the inhabitants of the Punjab"); see also Amanda de la Garza, *Doctorji: The Life, Teachings, and Legacy of Dr. Bhagat Singh Thind* (Malibu, CA: David Singh Thind, 2010), 3 (noting that "the men of Thind's family were military Kamboj Sikhs, descended from a people of Iron Age India (circa ninth century B.C.) who are frequently mentioned in ancient Sanskrit literature"). I have tracked the language of historical sources where it is particularly relevant, but otherwise I refer to the people of India as "Asian Indians," "natives of India," or, where the context is sufficient to mark the word as referring to a national rather than a racial group, simply as "Indians."

5. *Thind*, 261 U.S. at 206, 210.

6. Ibid., 213, 215.

7. See Ozawa v. United States, 260 U.S. 178, 197 (1922).

8. Ibid., 215. See Brown v. Board of Education, 347 U.S. 483 (1954); Plessy v. Ferguson, 163 U.S. 537 (1896).

9. See, e.g., Phillip Lothyan, "A Question of Citizenship," *Prologue: Quarterly of the National Archives* 21 (1989): 267–73.

10. Garza, *Doctorji*, 20.

11. See, e.g., Mary Das, "True Status of Hindus Regarding American Citizenship," *Modern Review* 41 (1927): 461–65; Taraknath Das, "India and the League of Nations," *Modern Review* 35 (1924): 163–67; Taraknath Das, "What Is at the Back of Anti-Asianism of the Anglo-Saxon World?" *Modern Review* 35 (1924): 262–68; Taraknath Das, "American Naturalization Law Is Against the Chinese, Japanese and Hindustanees," *Modern Review* 39 (1926): 349–50; Taraknath Das, *Foreign Policy in the Far East* (New York: Longmans, Green, 1936); Taraknath Das, "People of India and U.S. Citizenship," *India Today* (August 1941): 3–4.

12. See Bessho v. United States, 178 F. 245 (4th Cir. 1910); *In re* Young, 195 F. 645 (W.D. Wash. 1912); *In re* Young, 198 F. 715 (W.D. Wash. 1912); *In re* Knight, 171 F. 299 (E.D.N.Y. 1909); *In re* Kumagai, 163 F. 922 (W.D. Wash. 1908); *In re* Saito, 62 F. 126 (C.C.D. Mass. 1894); *In re* Yamashita, 10 P. 482 (Wash. 1902).

13. See *In re Mozumdar*, 207 F. 115 (E.D. Wash. 1913) (holding that a "high-caste Hindu of pure blood," from "Upper India, or what is called Hindustan proper," was a "free white person" for purposes of naturalization);

In re Singh, 246 F. 496, 499 (E.D. Penn. 1917) (holding that a "Hindu" was not a "free white person" for purposes of naturalization); *In re* Mohan Singh, 257 F. 209 (S.D. Cal. 1919) (holding that a "high caste Hindu" was a "free white person" for purposes of naturalization).

14. See, e.g., Caminetti v. United States, 242 U.S. 470, 485–86 (1917). See generally Gustav Endlich, *A Commentary on the Interpretation of Statutes: Founded on the Treatise of Sir Peter Benson Maxwell* (Jersey City: Frederick D. Linn, 1888), 4–5.

15. *Thind*, 261 U.S. at 208–10, 214–15; Brief of Respondent at 8–29, 38–48, United States v. Thind, No. 202 (U.S. Sup. Ct. Dec. 30, 1921). The Aryan race theory was developed before the Caucasian racial classification but later subsumed within the Caucasian classification along with the Semitic and Hamitic racial classifications. See, e.g., *Meyers Konversationslexikon*, 4th ed., 1885–1890.

16. *Thind*, 261 U.S. at 210, 214–15.

17. *Thind*, 261 U.S. at 208–209; see Endlich, *A Commentary on the Interpretation of Statutes*, 4–5.

18. Maillard v. Lawrence, 57 U.S. 251, 261 (1853); see *Thind*, 261 U.S. at 214. In an opinion issued shortly before *Ozawa* and *Thind*, the Court wrote that "statutory words are uniformly presumed, unless the contrary appears, to be used in their ordinary and usual sense, and with the meaning commonly attributed to them." *Caminetti*, 242 U.S. at 485–86.

19. Cf. Michael Omi and Howard Winant, "Racial Formation," in *Race Critical Theories: Text and Context*, ed. Philomena Essed and David Theo Goldberg (Oxford: Blackwell, 2002), 123.

20. Milton Konvitz, *The Alien and the Asiatic in American Law* (Ithaca: Cornell University Press, 1946), 89.

21. Lon Fuller, *The Morality of Law*, rev. ed. (New Haven: Yale University Press, 1969), 161–62.

22. See Roger Daniels and Harry Kitano, *American Racism: Exploration of the Nature of Prejudice* (Englewood Cliffs, NJ: Prentice-Hall, 1970), 53–54.

23. Paul Rundquist, "A Uniform Rule: The Congress and the Courts in American Naturalization, 1865–1952" (PhD diss., University of Chicago, 1975), 210–16; cf. Stanford Lyman, "The Race Question and Liberalism: Casuistries in American Constitutional Law," *International Journal of Politics, Culture, and Society* 5 (1991): 221.

24. See, e.g., Angelo Ancheta, *Scientific Evidence and Equal Protection of the Law* (New Brunswick: Rutgers University Press, 2006), 34–35;

Gross, *What Blood Won't Tell: A History of Race on Trial in America* (Cambridge: Harvard University Press, 2008), 240–41; Sarah Gualtieri, "Becoming 'White': Race, Religion and the Foundations of Syrian/Lebanese Ethnicity in the United States," *Journal of American Ethnic History* 20, no. 4 (2001): 29–58, Matthew Frye Jacobson, *Whiteness of a Different Color: European Immigrants and the Alchemy of Race* (Cambridge: Harvard University Press, 1998), 236; Laura Kang, *Compositional Subjects: Enfiguring Asian/American Women* (Durham: Duke University Press, 2002), 135–36; Desmond King, *Making Americans: Immigration, Race, and the Origins of the Diverse Democracy* (Cambridge: Harvard University Press, 2000), 45–46; Ian Haney López, *White by Law: The Legal Construction of Race* (New York: New York University Press, 1996); Natalia Molina, "'In a Race All Their Own': The Quest to Make Mexicans Ineligible for U.S. Citizenship," *Pacific Historical Review* 79 (2010): 176–78; Sucheta Mazumdar, "Racist Responses to Racism: The Aryan Myth and South Asians in the United States," *South Asia Bulletin* 9 (1989): 50; John Park, *Elusive Citizenship: Immigration, Asian Americans, and the Paradox of Civil Rights* (New York: New York University Press, 2004), 121–27; Kunal Parker, "Citizenship and Immigration Law, 1800–1924," in *The Cambridge History of Law in America*, ed. Michael Grossberg and Christopher Tomlins (Cambridge: Cambridge University Press, 2008), 194–95; David Roediger, *Working Toward Whiteness: How America's Immigrants Became White: The Strange Journey from Ellis Island to the Suburbs* (New York: Basic Books, 2005), 59; Nyan Shah, *Stranger Intimacy: Contesting Race, Sexuality and the Law in the North American West* (Berkeley: University of California Press, 2011), 245–46; Jennifer Snow, "The Civilization of White Men: The Race of the Hindu in *United States v. Bhagat Singh Thind*," in *Race, Nation, and Religion in the Americas*, ed. Henry Goldschmidt and Elizabeth McAlister (New York: Oxford University Press, 2004), 262; Min Song, "Pahkar Singh's Argument with Asian America: Color and the Structure of Race Formation," in *A Part, Yet Apart: South Asians in Asian America*, ed. Lavina Dhingra Shankar and Rajini Srikanath (Philadelphia: Temple University Press, 1998), 93–95; Ronald Takaki, *Strangers From a Different Shore: A History of Asian Americans*, rev. ed. (New York: Little, Brown, 1998), 298–99; John Tehranian, *Whitewashed: America's Middle Eastern Minority* (New York: New York University Press, 2009), 41.

25. Thomas Gossett, *Race: The History of an Idea in America*, new ed. (Oxford: Oxford University Press, 1997), 369.

26. *Plessy*, 163 U.S. 537.

27. President Woodrow Wilson delivering his State of the Union Address to a joint session of Congress on Dec. 7, 1915, 64th Cong., 1st Sess., *Congressional Record* 53 (1915): pt. 1:99.

28. See, e.g., Thomas Adam, *Germany and the Americas: Culture, Politics, and History* (Santa Barbara, CA: ABC-CLIO, 2005), 319; Philip Foner, *History of the Labor Movement in the United States: Postwar Struggles*, 1918–1920 (New York: International Publishers, 1987), 25–26; Gossett, *Race*, 371; William Petersen, Michael Novak, and Philip Gleason, *Concepts of Ethnicity* (Cambridge: Harvard University Press, 1980), 88.

29. Mark Weiner, *Americans without Law: The Racial Boundaries of Citizenship* (New York: New York University Press, 2006), 100–102; see also Donald Braman. "Of Race and Immutability," *UCLA Law Review* 46 (1999): 1403–1404; J. Allen Douglas, "The 'Priceless Possession' of Citizenship: Race, Nation and Naturalization in American Law, 1880–1930," *Duquesne Law Review* 43 (2005): 416–17; Dudley McGovney, "Race Discrimination in Naturalization," *Iowa Law Bulletin* 8 (1923): 152; Dudley McGovney, "Naturalization of the Mixed-Blood—A Dictum," *California Law Review* 22 (1934): 380; cf. Rogers Smith, review of *White by Law: The Legal Construction of Race*, by Ian F. Haney López, *The American Journal of Legal History* 42 (1998): 66 (noting that López "strains to read George Sutherland's opinions in the two Supreme Court cases of the 1920s, *Ozawa* and *Thind*, as more contrasting than they are"). For an interpretation that seeks to bridge these conflicting readings of the cases by arguing that in *Ozawa* the Court evinces an effort to reconcile ordinary usage and scientific definitions of race before abandoning scientific definitions of race altogether in *Thind*, see Mae Ngai, *Impossible Subjects: Illegal Aliens and the Making of Modern America* (Princeton: Princeton University Press, 2004), 44–46.

30. McGovney, "Race Discrimination," 152.

31. See *Ozawa*, 260 U.S. at 197. The Court cites *In re Mozumdar*, 207 F. 115 (E.D. Wash. 1913) (holding that a "high-caste Hindu of pure blood," from "Upper India, or what is called Hindustan proper," is "white" and therefore racially eligible for naturalization) and *In re Mohan Singh*, 257 F. 209 (S.D. Cal. 1919) (holding that a "high caste Hindu" is "white" and therefore racially eligible for naturalization).

Ozawa, 260 U.S. at 197. The Court also omits from its list of approved opinions in *Ozawa* the only published opinion concluding that Indians were not "free white persons" for purposes of naturalization. See *In re* Singh, 246 F. 496, 499 (E.D. Penn. 1917) (holding that a Hindu is not a "free white person" for purposes of naturalization). The Court's omission of this opinion from its list of approved opinions in *Ozawa* suggests that it specifically considered the published opinions of lower courts regarding the racial eligibility of Indians for naturalization and approved only of those that held them eligible.

32. *Ozawa*, 260 U.S. at 197.

33. *Thind*, 261 U.S. at 213.

34. See Defendant's Brief of Points and Authorities in Support of Motion to Dismiss at 5–6, United States v. Mozumdar, No. H-5-J Equity (S.D. Cal. Oct. 15, 1923), in Records of the U.S. Courts of Appeals, RG 276, NAPR (LN); see also Taraknath Das, "Stateless Persons in *the* U.S.A.," *Calcutta Review* 16 (July 1925): 42. Notwithstanding the fact that the Supreme Court had expressly approved of the lower court opinion in the case that had granted Mozumdar's naturalization certificate, his certificate was canceled. See United States v. Mozumdar, 296 F. 173 (S.D. Cal. 1923), *aff'd*, 299 F. 240 (9th Cir. 1924).

35. Decision at 2, *In re* Sallak, No. 14876 (N.D. Ill, June 27, 1924), in Significant Civil and Criminal Case Files, 1899–1925, District of Oregon (Portland), Records of U.S. Attorneys and Marshals, RG 118, NAPAR.

36. López, *White by Law*, 79–80.

37. *Encyclopedia Britannica*, 3rd ed., s.v. "Man," 508; see also Johann Friedrich Blumenbach, *On the Natural Variety of Mankind* (1775), in Johann Friedrich Blumenbach, *The Anthropological Treatises of Johann Friedrich Blumenbach*, trans. and ed. Thomas Bendyshe (London: Longman, Green, Longman, Roberts & Green, 1865), 99 n. 4.

38. Ray Chase and S. G. Pandit, *An Examination of the Opinion of the Supreme Court of the United States Deciding Against the Eligibility of Hindus for Citizenship* (Los Angeles: S. G. Pandit, 1926), 3, 5, 9.

39. *Immigration Act of 1917*, 64th Cong., 2nd Sess., *Congressional Record* 54 (Dec. 12, 1916): 220–22.

40. See Reporter's Transcript, United States v. Bopp, et. al., No. 6133 (N.D. Calif., Feb. 28, 1918), text-fiche, 44:4169, Reel 4, Newspapers & Microforms, University of California at Berkeley Library.

41. *Singh*, 257 F. at 213.

42. See Correspondence from the Commissioner of Naturalization Raymond Christ to Secretary of Labor James Davis dated Oct. 26, 1926, in Senate Committee on Immigration, *Ratification and Confirmation of Naturalization of Certain Persons of the Hindu Race on S.J. Res. 128*, 69th

Cong., 2nd sess. (Washington, DC: GPO, 1926), 1:5–7; cf. "Judge Grants Citizenship to Das," *Mani News (Waiiluku, Ha.)*, Jan. 4, 1918 (discussing a lower court opinion holding a high caste Hindu to be a "free white person" for purposes of naturalization).

43. Charles Grant, *Observations on the State of Society Among the Asiatic Subjects of Great-Britain, Particularly with Respect to Morals; and on the Means of Improving It* (East-India House, 1797), 43–44, 55, 57.

44. Abbé Dubois, *Letters on the State of Christianity in India; in Which the Conversion of the Hindoos Is Considered as Impracticable* (1823; repr. New Delhi, India: Asian Educational Services, 1995), 100–102, 136.

45. "Have We a Dusky Peril?: Hindu Hordes Invading the State," *Puget Sound American* (Bellingham, WA), Sept. 16, 1906.

46. "Keep the Hindus Out, Says Writer," *Puget Sound American* (Bellingham, WA), Sept. 16, 1906.

47. Elizabeth Reed, *Hinduism in Europe and America* (New York: G. P. Putnam's Sons, 1914), iv, 127–33.

48. See, e.g., Correspondence from Commissioner of Naturalization Raymond Christ to Secretary of Labor James Davis dated Oct. 26, 1926, reproduced in Senate Committee on Immigration, *Ratification and Confirmation of Naturalization of Certain Persons of the Hindu Race on S.J. Res. 128,* 69th Cong., 2nd sess. (Washington, DC: GPO, 1926), 1:5.

49. Das, "True Status," 462.

50. With regard to the mutual influence of North American and Australasian legal restrictions on Asian immigration during the nineteenth and twentieth centuries, see generally, e.g., Henry Angus, "The Legal Status in British Columbia of Residents of Oriental Race and Their Descendants," in *The Legal Status of Aliens in Pacific Countries: An International Survey of Law and Practice Concerning Immigration, Naturalization and Deportation of Aliens and Their Legal Rights and Disabilities*, ed. Norman MacKenzie (London: Oxford University Press, 1937); Sean Brawley, *The White Peril: Foreign Relations and Asian Immigration to Australasia and North America 1919–78* (Sydney: University of New South Wales Press, 1995); Tom Clark and Brian Galligan, "'Aboriginal Native' and the Institutional Construction of the Australian Citizen 1901–48," *Australian Historical Studies* 26 (1995): 523–43; David Dutton, *One of Us?: A Century of Australian Citizenship* (Sydney: University of New South Wales Press, 2002); Robert Huttenback, *Racism and Empire: White Settlers and Colored Immigrants in the British Self-Governing Colonies 1830–1910* (Ithaca: Cornell University Press, 1976);

Andrew Markus, *Australian Race Relations 1788–1993* (St. Leonards, Aus.: Allen and Unwin, 1994); Andrew Markus, *Fear and Hatred: Purifying Australia and California 1850–1901* (Sydney: Hale and Iremonger, 1979); Charles Price, *The Great White Walls Are Built: Restrictive Immigration to North America and Australasia 1836–1888* (Canberra: Australian National University Press, 1974); Patricia Roy, *A White Man's Province: British Columbia Politicians and Chinese and Japanese Immigrants, 1858–1914* (Vancouver: University of British Columbia Press, 1989); Shah, *Stranger Intimacy*; W. Peter Ward, *White Canada: Popular Attitudes and Public Policy Toward Orientals in British Columbia* (Montreal: McGill-Queen's University Press, 1978); Myra Willard, *History of the White Australia Policy to 1920* (London: Cass, 1967). With regard to the significance of the Ghadr Party to the racial eligibility cases involving Asian Indians, see, e.g., Garza, *Doctorji*; Harold Gould, *Sikhs, Swamis, Students, and Spies: The India Lobby in the United States, 1900–1946* (Thousand Oaks, CA: SAGE, 2006); Gary Hess, "The 'Hindu' in America: Immigration and Naturalization Policies and India, 1917–1946," *Pacific Historical Review* 38, no. 1 (1969): 68; Charles Gordon, "The Racial Barrier to American Citizenship," *University of Pennsylvania Law Review* 93 (1945): 250; Lothyan, "A Question of Citizenship," 267–73; Stanford Lyman, "The Race Question and Liberalism: Casuistries in American Constitutional Law," *International Journal of Politics, Culture, and Society* 5 (1991), 209; Shah, *Stranger Intimacy*, 242–45; Jennifer Snow, "The Civilization of White Men: The Race of the Hindu in *United States v. Bhagat Singh Thind*," in *Race, Nation, and Religion in the Americas*, ed. Henry Goldschmidt and Elizabeth McAlister (New York: Oxford University Press, 2004): 260.

51. Garza, *Doctorji*, 1–10.

52. Mark Naidis, "Propaganda of the *Gadar* Party," *Pacific Historical Review* 20 (1951): 251.

53. See Harish Puri, *Ghadar Movement: Ideology, Organisation & Strategy* (Amritsar, India: Guru Nanak Dev University, 1983), 72.

54. See, e.g., ibid.

55. See ibid.; Lothyan, "A Question of Citizenship," 269.

56. See Brief of Respondent at 2, 15, United States v. Thind, No. 202 (U.S. Sup. Ct. Dec. 30, 1921); see also Garza, *Doctorji*, 3.

57. See, e.g., Garza, *Doctorji*, 5–6.

58. See, e.g., ibid., 5–13.

59. See, e.g., Gurdev Deol, *The Role of the Ghadar Party in the National Movement* (Delhi: Sterling, 1969), 68, 74–75; Garza, *Doctorji*, 12–13; Puri, *Ghadar Movement*, 72.

60. See, e.g., Lothyan, "A Question of Citizenship," 269.

61. See, e.g., ibid. In 1917, only five years before Thind's case, the Ghadr Party made national headlines when the party's leadership was credited with efforts to organize a violent attack on the British government in India with Germany's assistance in what is often referred to as the Hindu–German conspiracy. See, e.g., Haridas Muzumdar, *America's Contributions to India's Freedom* (Allahabad: Central Book Depot, 1962), 7–9; Takaki, *Strangers from a Different Shore*, 301; Giles Brown, "The Hindu Conspiracy, 1914–1917," *Pacific Historical Review* 17 (1948): 299–310; Don Dignan, "The Hindu Conspiracy in Anglo-American Relations during World War I," *Pacific Historical Review* 40 (1971): 57–76. At the insistence of the British government, one day after the United States declared war in World War I the United States arrested seventeen Ghadr leaders in San Francisco and numerous Indian and German defendants across the country, resulting in the indictment of over 100 defendants by a federal grand jury in San Francisco on charges of violating the neutrality laws of the United States. The federal criminal trial of these defendants in San Francisco lasted 155 days, costing the United States government $450,000 and the British government $2.5 million. See Gould, *Sikhs, Swamis*, 214, 220–21; Puri, *Ghadar Movement*, 100–101; Kushwant Singh and Satindra Singh, *Ghadar 1915: India's First Armed Revolution* (New Delhi: R & K, 1966), 52; Brown, "The Hindu Conspiracy, 1914–1917," 308–309; Karl Hoover, "The Hindu Conspiracy in California, 1913–1918," *German Studies Review* 8 (1985): 258–59; Muzumdar, *America's Contributions*, 9. During opening statements in the trial, the lawyer for one of the Indian defendants publicly denounced British rule in India. "British Rule in India Denounced in Hindu Trial," *Aberdeen Daily American* (Aberdeen, SD), March 1, 1918. The trial was a frequent media spectacle, and on the final day of the trial one of the Indian defendants obtained a gun during the lunch recess and shot and killed one of his codefendants before he was himself shot and killed by a federal marshal. See "Two Killed in Court," *Washington Post*, April 24, 1918; see also Correspondence from Commissioner of Naturalization Raymond Christ to Secretary of Labor James Davis dated Oct. 26, 1926, reproduced in Senate

Committee on Immigration, *Ratification and Confirmation of Naturalization of Certain Persons of the Hindu Race on S.J. Res. 128,* 69th Cong., 2nd sess. (Washington, DC: GPO, 1926), 1:5. See generally Gould, *Sikhs, Swamis,* 214, 220–21; Muzumdar, *America's Contributions,* 9; Puri, *Ghadar Movement,* 100–101; Singh and Singh, *Ghadar 1915,* 52; Brown, "The Hindu Conspiracy, 1914–1917," 308–309; Hoover, "The Hindu Conspiracy," 258–59.

62. See Garza, *Doctorji,* 9; Deol, *The Role of the Ghadar Party,* 44–45; Gould, *Sikhs, Swamis,* 106–107, 134, 138, 146; Puri, *Ghadar Movement,* 61, 118; Takaki, *Strangers from a Different Shore,* 301.

63. See Indian Political Intelligence Files, 1912–1950, British Library, London, Oriental and India Office Collections, available via IDC Publishers BV, microfiche, IPI-13 Fiche 382–392 (1–11), Fiche 410 (29), and Fiche 415 (34). One of the best sources for understanding the Ghadr Party's ideology is the Ghadr Press, based in San Francisco, which was the party's central means of communicating with its global audience. The Ghadr Press primarily published a free monthly journal entitled *Ghadr* which was distributed to subscribers internationally, but it also published a variety of pamphlets, handbills, and articles written for publication in mainstream newspapers as part of its lobbying effort. *See* Ram Chandra, "Hindus Hanged: History of Hindustan Gadar Political Parties in India," reprinted in *Selected Documents on the Ghadr Party,* ed. T. R. Sareen (Inderpuri, New Delhi: Mounto, 1994), 152; Deol, *The Role of the Ghadar Party,* 71, 74, 183; Naidis, "Propaganda of the Gadar Party," 251–60; Puri, *Ghadar Movement,* 74; Singh and Singh, *Ghadar,* 20. The *Ghadr* journal openly advocated the use of violence, beginning with the following mission statement in its inaugural issue:

> Today, there begins in foreign lands, but in our country's language, a war against the British *Raj* . . . What is our name? *Ghadar.* What is our work? *Ghadar.* Where will *Ghadar* break out? In India. The time will soon come when rifles and blood will take the place of pen and ink.

Quoted in Singh and Singh, *Ghadar,* 19. Subsequent issues of the journal reflect even more violent language, inciting its readers to kill all of the "whites," or Europeans, and to fill the rivers with their corpses. See Deol, *The Role of the Ghadar Party,* 76. Another *Ghadr* publication urged readers to "take arms from the troops of native states and, wherever you see the British, kill them." Ibid., 100.

64. See De la Garza, *Doctorji*, 12–14.

65. See, e.g., Correspondence from Commissioner of Naturalization Raymond Christ to Secretary of Labor James Davis dated Oct. 26, 1926, reproduced in Senate Committee on Immigration, *Ratification and Confirmation of Naturalization of Certain Persons of the Hindu Race on S.J. Res. 128,* 69th Cong., 2nd sess. (Washington, DC: GPO, 1926), 1:5; Gould, *Sikhs, Swamis,* 200. These efforts ultimately resulted in the arrest of Ghadr leader Har Dayal in 1914, and although the government's case against Dayal was weak, the threat of extradition to British custody led him to flee to Switzerland before trial. See Gould, *Sikhs, Swamis,* 200.

66. See Correspondence from Commissioner of Naturalization Raymond Christ to Secretary of Labor James Davis dated Oct. 26, 1926, reproduced in Senate Committee on Immigration, *Ratification and Confirmation of Naturalization of Certain Persons of the Hindu Race on S.J. Res. 128,* 69th Cong., 2nd sess. (Washington, DC: GPO, 1926), 1:5; Gould, *Sikhs, Swamis,* 189–90, 275–76; Dignan, "The Hindu Conspiracy," 60–61, 76.

67. See Bill of Complaint in Equity at 1–2, *In re* Thind, No. E-8547 (D. Or. Jan. 8, 1921), in Civil, Criminal and Admiralty Case Files, 1911–1922, Southern District of California, Central Division (Los Angeles), Records of the District Courts of the United States, RG 21, NAPAR.

68. See ibid.; Lothyan, "A Question of Citizenship," 269.

69. See Bill of Complaint in Equity at 1–2, *In re* Thind, No. E-8547 (D. Or. Jan. 8, 1921), in Civil, Criminal and Admiralty Case Files, 1911–1922, Southern District of California, Central Division (Los Angeles), Records of the District Courts of the United States, RG 21, NAPAR; *Naturalization Act of 1906,* 59th Cong., 1st Sess., *U.S. Statutes at Large* 34 (1906): 596.

70. See In re *Thind,* 268 F. at 683.

71. See *Ellis,* 179 F. at 1003; *Ozawa,* 260 U.S. at 197.

72. See *Ozawa,* 260 U.S. at 197 (citing with approval *In re* Ellis, 179 F. 1002, 1003 (D. Or. 1910)).

73. In re *Thind,* 268 F. at 683.

74. Ibid.; De la Garza, *Doctorji,* 10.

75. Indian Political Intelligence Files, 1912–1950, British Library, London, Oriental and India Office Collections, available via IDC Publishers BV, microfiche, IPI-13 Fiche 382–392 (1–11), Fiche 410 (29), and Fiche 415 (34).

76. *Thind*, 268 F. at 683.

77. See Brief of Respondent at 4–8, United States v. Thind, No. 202 (U.S. Sup. Ct. Dec. 30, 1921) (reproducing Judge Wolverton's opinion in its entirety).

78. See Brief of Respondent, United States v. Thind, No. 202 (U.S. Sup. Ct. Dec. 30, 1921); Brief for the United States, United States v. Thind, No. 202 (U.S. Sup. Ct. Jan. 11, 1923).

79. See, e.g., Correspondence from Commissioner of Naturalization Raymond Christ to Secretary of Labor James Davis dated Oct. 26, 1926, reproduced in Senate Committee on Immigration, *Ratification and Confirmation of Naturalization of Certain Persons of the Hindu Race on S.J. Res. 128*, 69th Cong., 2nd sess. (Washington, DC: GPO, 1926), 1:5; "Two Killed in Court," *Washington Post*, April 24, 1918; Ram Chandra, "What Young India Has in Mind: Rumblings of Dissatisfaction the First Warning that the People Have a Vision of a Republican Government," *New York Times*, July 8, 1916.

80. Theodore Lothrop Stoddard, *The Rising Tide of Color against White World Supremacy* (New York: Charles Scribner's Sons, 1921), 80.

81. See, e.g., Chandra, "What Young India Has in Mind."

82. See Brief of Respondent at 8–29 and 38–48, United States v. Thind, No. 202 (U.S. Sup. Ct. Dec. 30, 1921).

83. See John Clarke, *Oriental Enlightenment: The Encounter Between Asian and Western Thought* (London: Routledge, 1997), 55–59; Wendy Doniger, *The Hindus: An Alternative History* (New York: Penguin, 2009), 85–102; Raymond Shwab, *The Oriental Renaissance: Europe's Rediscovery of India and the East, 1680–1880*, trans. Gene Patterson-Black and Victor Reinking (New York: Columbia University Press, 1984), 32; Thomas Trautmann, *Aryans and British India* (Berkeley: University of California Press, 1997), 11–13, 23–26; Romila Thapar, "Imagined Religious Communities? Ancient History and the Modern Search for a Hindu Identity," *Modern Asian Studies* 23, no. 2 (1989): 226.

84. Edward Said, *Orientalism*, 25th Anniversary ed. (New York: Vintage, 1994), 5.

85. Brief of Respondent at 11, United States v. Thind, No. 202 (U.S. Sup. Ct. Dec. 30, 1921).

86. Ibid.

87. See Doniger, *The Hindus*, 85–102; Vasant Kaiwar, "The Aryan Model of History and the Oriental Renaissance," in *Antinomies of Modernity: Essays*

on Race, Orient, Nation, ed. Vasant Kaiwar and Sucheta Mazumdar (Durham: Duke University Press, 2003), 24; Laurie Patton, "Cosmic Men and Fluid Exchanges: Myths of *Ārya*, *Varṇa*, and *Jāti* in the Hindu Tradition," in *Religion and the Creation of Race and Ethnicity: An Introduction*, ed. Craig Prentiss (New York: New York University Press, 2003), 185, 194.

88. See David Lorenzen, "Imperialism and the Historiography of Ancient India," in *India: History and Thought, Essays in Honor of A. L. Basham*, ed. S. N. Mukherjee (Calcutta: Subarnarekha, 1982), 84–102.

89. Brief of Respondent at 18–23, United States v. Thind, No. 202 (U.S. Sup. Ct. Dec. 30, 1921).

90. Ibid., 20.

91. See Snow, "The Civilization of White Men," 266; cf. Nico Slate, *Colored Cosmopolitanism: The Shared Struggle for Freedom in the United States and India* (Cambridge: Harvard University Press, 2012).

92. Brief of Respondent at 18–20, United States v. Thind, No. 202 (U.S. Sup. Ct. Dec. 30, 1921).

93. Harold Isaacs, *Scratches on Our Minds: American Views of China and India* (1958; repr. Armonk, NY: M. E. Sharpe, 1980), 290.

94. Ibid.

95. See, e.g., Patton, "Cosmic Men," 184–85.

96. See "Hindu from America Exclusion," reprinted in *Selected Documents on the Ghadr Party*, ed. Tilak Sareen (New Delhi: Mounto, 1994), 161–66.

97. Pardaman Singh, *Ethnological Epitome of the Hindustanees of the Pacific Coast* (Stockton, CA: The Pacific Coast Khalsa Diwan Society, 1936), 10, 12.

98. Quoted in Gould, *Sikhs, Swamis*, 164.

99. See Singh and Singh, *Ghadar 1915*, 15 n. 23.

100. For a discussion of the peritrope, see Christopher Tindale, *Reason's Dark Champions: Constructive Strategies of Sophistic Argument* (Columbia: University of South Carolina Press, 2010), 83–98. Tindale defines the peritrope to include the following features:

> (1) In its widest sense . . . it "turns the tables" on an opponent. To do this it must take some aspect of the opponent's argument or position and turn it around on them so that the same point made by them can be made against them. The *peritrope*, then, incorporates some aspect of the opposing position in the argumentation. (2) It would follow from this that the strategy is adversarial in nature, even if this is understood in its mildest

form . . . (3) Finally the strategy aims at showing inconsistency or contradiction. (87–88)

101. Snow, "The Civilization of White Men," 265.

102. Brief of Respondent at 11, United States v. Thind, No. 202 (U.S. Sup. Ct. Dec. 30, 1921).

103. Clarke, *Oriental Enlightenment*, 116, 136; De la Garza, *Doctorji*, 5; Shwab, *The Oriental Renaissance*, 401–403.

104. Snow, "The Civilization of White Men," 267

105. See, e.g., Gould, *Sikhs, Swamis*, 78; Heather Streets, *Martial Races: The Military, Race and Masculinity in British Imperial Culture, 1857–1914* (Manchester: Manchester University Press, 2004), 8, 178–79.

106. See, e.g., Mark Naidis, "Propaganda of the *Gadar* Party," 251

107. J. Justin Gustainis, "Crime as Rhetoric: The Trial of the Catonsville Nine," in *Popular Trials: Rhetoric, Mass Media, and the Law*, ed. Robert Hariman (Tuscaloosa: University of Alabama Press, 1990), 178.

108. Patricia Roberts-Miller, "John Quincy Adams's Amistad Argument: The Problem of Outrage; Or, the Constrains of Decorum," *Rhetoric Society Quarterly* 32, no. 2 (2002): 22–23.

109. Homi Bhabha, *The Location of Culture* (New York: Routledge, 1994), 132–44.

110. Gould, *Sikhs, Swamis*, 203.

111. Brief for the United States at 10–14, 19–20, United States v. Thind, No. 202 (U.S. Sup. Ct. Jan. 11, 1923).

112. Ibid., 4.

113. Ibid., 10–14, 19–20.

114. Isaacs, *Scratches on Our Minds*, 290.

115. See Snow, "The Civilization of White Men," 266; cf. Slate, *Colored Cosmopolitanism*, 193.

116. Brief for the United States at 10, United States v. Thind, No. 202 (U.S. Sup. Ct. Jan. 11, 1923).

117. Ibid., 10–14.

118. See generally Sarah Suleri, *The Rhetoric of English India* (Chicago: University of Chicago Press, 1992), 45–46, 65.

119. Brief for the United States at 10–14, United States v. Thind, No. 202 (U.S. Sup. Ct. Jan. 11, 1923).

120. Ernest Renan, "What Is a Nation?," in *Nation and Narration*, ed. Homi Bhabha (New York: Routledge: 1990), 19.

121. Brief for the United States at 10–14, United States v. Thind, No. 202 (U.S. Sup. Ct. Jan. 11, 1923).

122. Ibid., 14.

123. Snow, "The Civilization of White Men," 270.

124. Brief of Respondent at 19, United States v. Thind, No. 202 (U.S. Sup. Ct. Dec. 30, 1921).

125. Rudyard Kipling, "The White Man's Burden," *McClure's Magazine* 12, no. 4 (1899): 4.

126. Brief of Respondent at 19, United States v. Thind, No. 202 (U.S. Sup. Ct. Dec. 30, 1921).

127. Falguni Sheth, *Toward a Political Philosophy of Race* (Albany: State University of New York Press, 2009), 30.

128. See *Thind*, 261 U.S. at 209–15; cf. Brief of Respondent at 24-27, United States v. Thind, No. 202 (U.S. Sup. Ct. Dec. 30, 1921) (citing *In re* Singh, 257 F. 209 (S.D. Cal. 1919), *In re* Mozumdar, 207 F. 115 (E.D. Wash. 1913), *In re* Ellis, 179 F. 1002 (D. Or. 1910), *In re* Kumagai, 163 F. 922 (W.D. Wash. 1908), *In re* Saito, 62 F. 126 (C.C.D. Mass. 1894), *In re* Camille, 6 F. 256 (C.C.D. Or. 1880), and *In re* Yup, 1 F. Cas. 223 (C.C.D. Cal. 1878), all expressly approved of by the Court in *Ozawa*).

129. See Robert Dahl, "Decision-Making in a Democracy: The Supreme Court as a National Policy-Maker," *Journal of Public Law* 6 (1957): 279–95.

130. Alexander Bickel and Henry Wellington, "Legislative Purpose and the Judicial Process: The *Lincoln Mills* Case," *Harvard Law Review* 71 (1957): 1–5.

131. Ibid.; see also, e.g., Henry Hart Jr., "Foreward: The Time Chart of the Justices," *Harvard Law Review* 73 (1959): 100–101; see generally G. Edward White, "The Evolution of Reasoned Elaboration: Jurisprudential Criticism and Social Change," *Virginia Law Review* 59 (1973): 279.

132. *Thind*, 261 U.S. at 210–11.

133. Ibid., 212–13.

134. *Encyclopedia Britannica*, 11th ed., s.v. "Hinduism," 502.

135. Ibid. (emphasis added); *Thind*, 261 U.S. at 212–13 & nn. 8–9.

136. *Oxford English Dictionary*, 2nd ed., s.v. "Signally."

137. *Encyclopedia Britannica*, 11th ed., s.v. "Hinduism," 502–503; *Thind*, 261 U.S. at 212–13 & nn. 8–9.

138. Madison Grant, *The Passing of the Great Race; or, the Racial Basis of European History* (1916; repr. London: Forgotten Books, 2012), 64.

139. See generally Gross, *What Blood Won't Tell*, 13, 44, 88, 100, 106, 163, 297.

140. Grant, *The Passing of the Great Race*, 16.

141. *Thind*, 261 U.S. at 212–13.

142. See, e.g., *In re* Rallos, 241 F. 686 (E.D.N.Y. 1917); *In re* Young, 195 F. 645 (W.D. Wash. 1912); *In re* Young, 198 F. 715 (W.D. Wash. 1912); *In re* Knight, 171 F. 299 (E.D.N.Y. 1909); *In re* Camille, 6 F. 256 (C.C.D. Or. 1880).

143. *Thind*, 261 U.S. at 213.

144. Ibid., 213.

145. *Genesis* 2:23 (King James).

146. *Plessy*, 163 U.S. 537.

147. *Thind*, 261 U.S. at 210–11.

148. *Plessy*, 163 U.S. at 559.

149. See generally Slate, *Colored Cosmopolitanism*.

150. See *Thind*, 261 U.S. at 213; cf. *Mozumdar*, 207 F. 115; *Singh*, 257 F. 209; Correspondence from Commissioner of Naturalization Raymond Christ to Secretary of Labor James Davis dated Oct. 26, 1926, and attached lists of naturalized Hindus, pending cancellation cases, and soldier cases in which cancellation proceedings had not been instituted, reproduced in Senate Committee on Immigration, *Ratification and Confirmation of Naturalization of Certain Persons of the Hindu Race on S.J. Res. 128,* 69th Cong., 2nd sess. (Washington, DC: GPO, 1926), 1:5–7; "Judge Grants Citizenship to Das," *Mani News* (Waiiluku, HA), Jan. 4, 1918.

151. *Thind*, 261 U.S. at 213.

152. See Brief of Respondent at 24–27, United States v. Thind, No. 202 (U.S. Sup. Ct. Dec. 30, 1921) (arguing that while the Caucasian racial classification has been criticized, "it has stood the test of time and amounts to a common-sense, every-day, usable classification," and citing *In re* Singh, 257 F. 209 (S.D. Cal. 1919), *In re* Mozumdar, 207 F. 115 (E.D. Wash. 1913), *In re* Ellis, 179 F. 1002 (D. Or. 1910), *In re* Kumagai, 163 F. 922 (W.D. Wash. 1908), *In re* Saito, 62 F. 126 (C.C.D. Mass. 1894), *In re* Camille, 6 F. 256 (C.C.D. Or. 1880), and *In re* Yup, 1 F. Cas. 223 (C.C.D. Cal. 1878), all expressly approved of by the Court in *Ozawa*). Thind's brief also quotes the following passage from the opinion in *Singh*:

I am advised by counsel for petitioner herein, and his statement is not challenged by the Government, that Hindus have been admitted to citizenship in the Southern District of Georgia, the Southern District of New York, the Northern District of California and the Eastern District of Washington by the courts of the United States and by the Superior Court of California in both San Francisco and Los Angeles.

Brief of Respondent at 24–25, United States v. Thind, No. 202 (U.S. Sup. Ct. Dec. 30, 1921) (quoting *In re* Singh, 257 F. 209, 213 (S.D. Cal. 1919)).

153. See, e.g., Garza, *Doctorji*, 20; Takaki, *Strangers from a Different Shore*, 300.

154. See Takaki, *Strangers From a Different Shore*, 307.

155. *Immigration Act of 1924*. 68th Cong., 1st Sess. *U.S. Statutes at Large* 43 (1924): 153.

156. See Takaki, *Strangers From a Different Shore*, 367.

157. *Naturalization Act of 1906*, 59th Cong., 1st Sess., *U.S. Statutes at Large* 34 (1906): 596.

158. See U.S. Senate Committee on Immigration, *Hearings on S.J. Res. 128, Providing for the Ratification and Confirmation of Naturalization of Certain Persons of the Hindu Race*, 69th Cong., 2nd sess. (Washington, DC: GPO, 1926), 1–2, 6–7.

159. Like Thind and other Asian Indians targeted by the bureau's cancellation proceedings, Bagai was active in the Ghadr Party. See Takaki, *Strangers from a Different Shore*, 299–300; Rani Bagai, "'Bridges Burnt Behind': The Story of Vaishno Das Bagai," Angel Island Immigration Station Foundation, http://www.aiisf.org/stories-by-author/876-bridges-burnt-behind-the-story-of-vaishno-das-bagai (accessed Sept. 13, 2014).

160. See Memoranda from Chief Naturalization Examiner Henry Hazard to Commissioner of Naturalization Raymond Crist dated May 21, May 31, June 4, and June 19, 1924, in Box 1573, Records of the Immigration and Naturalization Service of the United States, RG 85, NAB.

161. See ibid.

162. United States v. Gokhale, 26 F.2d 360, 361 (2d Cit. 1928), *rev'd*, 278 U.S. 662 (1928); United States v. Pandit, 15 F.2d 285 (9th Cir. 1926), *cert. denied*, 273 U.S. 759 (1927).

163. See Transcript of Hearing on Naturalization of Natives of India Now Living in the United States, United States House of Representatives Committee on Immigration and Naturalization, June 21, 1939 at 12, in Box 1573, Records of the Immigration and Naturalization Service of the United States, RG 85, NAB.

164. Transcript of Record at 9, 33–34, 75, United States v. Sakharam Ganesh Pandit, No. 4938 (9th Cir. Aug. 13, 1926), in Records of the U.S. Courts of Appeals, RG 276, NAPR (SB).

165. See ibid., 3–6, 28–29, 36–40; *Naturalization Act of 1906*, 59th Cong., 1st Sess., *U.S. Statutes at Large* 34 (1906): 596.

166. See Bryan Garner, *A Dictionary of Modern Legal Usage*, 2nd ed. (Oxford: Oxford University Press, 1995), 321–22. Although traditionally the government could not be estopped by the courts, many exceptions to this rule emerged, including an exception that the government could be estopped when the plaintiff sought the assistance of a court to protect its rights, and Judge Paul McCormick agreed with Pandit that the government could be estopped in *Pandit*. See David Thompson, "Equitable Estoppel of the Government," *Columbia Law Review* 79 (1979): 551–71; Transcript of Record at 152, United States v. Sakharam Ganesh Pandit, No. 4938 (9th Cir. Aug. 13, 1926), in Records of the U.S. Courts of Appeals, RG 276, NAPR (SB).

167. Defendant's Answer, United States v. Pandit, No. G-111-T (S.D. Cal. March 10, 1924), in Transcript of Record at 25–30b, United States v. Sakharam Ganesh Pandit, No. 4938 (9th Cir. Aug. 13, 1926), in Records of the U.S. Courts of Appeals, RG 276, NAPR (SB).

168. Statement of Testimony Under Equity Rule 75 B, United States v. Pandit, No. G-111-T (S.D. Cal. May 11, 1926), in Transcript of Record at 84–85, United States v. Sakharam Ganesh Pandit, No. 4938 (9th Cir. Aug. 13, 1926).

169. Kipling, "The White Man's Burden."

170. Section 3 of the 1922 Cable Act provided that "any woman who marries an alien ineligible to citizenship shall cease to be a citizen." *Cable Act*, *U.S. Statutes at Large* 42 (1922): 1021.

171. See Defendant's Answer, United States v. Pandit, No. G-111-T (S.D. Cal. March 10, 1924), in Transcript of Record at 21–31 (emphasis added), United States v. Sakharam Ganesh Pandit, No. 4938 (9th Cir. Aug. 13, 1926), in Records of the U.S. Courts of Appeals, RG 276, NAPR (SB).

172. See, e.g., Rani Bagai, "'Bridges Burnt Behind': The Story of Vaishno Das Bagai," Angel Island Immigration Station Foundation, http://www.aiisf.org/ stories-by-author/876-bridges-burnt-behind-the-stor y-of-vaishno-das-bagai (accessed Sept. 13, 2014).

173. See *Singh*, 257 F. 209.

174. See *In re* Song, 271 F. 23 (S.D. Cal. 1921).

175. *Naturalization Act of 1906*, 59th Cong., 1st Sess., *U.S. Statutes at Large* 34 (1906): 596; see Memorandum Opinion, United States v. Pandit, No. G-111-T (S.D. Cal. Feb. 8, 1924), in Transcript of Record at 161–62,

United States v. Sakharam Ganesh Pandit, No. 4938 (9th Cir. Aug. 13, 1926); *United States v. Mozumdar*, 296 F. 173 (S.D. Cal. 1923).

176. See Mendez v. Westminster School District, 64 F. Supp. 544 (C.D. Cal. 1946).

177. See Memorandum Opinion, United States v. Pandit, No. G-111-T (S.D. Cal. Jan. 9, 1925), in Transcript of Record at 163–64, United States v. Sakharam Ganesh Pandit, No. 4938 (9th Cir. Aug. 13, 1926).

178. Findings of Fact and Conclusions of Law, United States v. Pandit, No. G-111-T (S.D. Cal. Jan. 8, 1926), in Transcript of Record at 33–42, United States v. Sakharam Ganesh Pandit, No. 4938 (9th Cir. Aug. 13, 1926).

179. Statement of Testimony Under Equity Rule 75 B, United States v. Pandit, No. G-111-T (S.D. Cal. May 11, 1926), in Transcript of Record at 152–54, United States v. Sakharam Ganesh Pandit, No. 4938 (9th Cir. Aug. 13, 1926).

180. *Black's Law Dictionary*, 6th ed., s.v. "Res judicata."

181. See Mozumdar v. United States, 299 F. 240 (9th Cir. 1924); United States v. Pandit, 15 F.2d 285, 285–86 (9th Cir. 1926), *cert. denied*, 273 U.S. 759 (1927); Defendant's Brief of Points and Authorities in Support of Motion to Dismiss at 17, United States v. Mozumdar, No. H-5-J Equity (S.D. Cal. Oct. 15, 1923); Brief for the Appellant at 20–24, United States v. Mozumdar, No. 4229 (9th Cir. April 17, 1924), and Brief of Appellee at 13–19, United States v. Mozumdar, No. 4229 (9th Cir. April 30, 1924), in Records of the U.S. Courts of Appeals, RG 276, NAPR (SB); Transcript of Record at 21–33, United States v. Pandit, No. 4938 (9th Cir. Aug. 13, 1926), in Records of the U.S. Courts of Appeals, RG 276, NAPR (SB); see also Petition for a Writ of Certiorari to the United States Circuit Court of Appeals for the Ninth Circuit, and Brief in Support Thereof at 3, United States v. Pandit, No. 870 (U.S. Sup. Ct. Jan., 1927).

182. See *Cable Act of 1922*, 67th Cong., 2nd Sess., *U.S. Statutes at Large* 42 (1922): 1021.

183. See Garza, *Doctorji*, 20–21; *Nye-Lea Act*, 74th Cong., 1st Sess., *U.S. Statutes at Large* 49 (1935): 397.

184. Quoted in Garza, *Doctorji*, 20–21.

185. *Oxford English Dictionary*, 2nd ed., s.v. "Albion."

186. See Sheth, *Toward a Political Philosophy of Race*, 30.

187. Ibid., 35.

188. Ibid., 32.

189. Ibid., 164.

190. Ibid., 154.

191. See Omi and Winant, "Racial Formation," 123–24.

192. Murray Edelman, *Constructing the Political Spectacle* (Chicago: University of Chicago Press, 1988), 83.

193. Renan, "What Is a Nation?" 19.

194. Hannah Arendt, *Essays in Understanding 1930–1954*, New York: Schocken Books, 1994), 74; Hannah Arendt, *The Origins of Totalitarianism*, new ed. with additional prefaces (New York: Harcourt Brace, 1973), 296–300.

195. Arendt, *The Origins of Totalitarianism*, 280.

196. *Immigration Act of 1917*, 64th Cong, 2nd Sess., *U.S. Statutes at Large* 39 (1917): § 3.

197. See Christopher Einolf, *The Mercy Factory: Refugees and the American Asylum System* (Chicago: Ivan R. Dee, 2001), 3–10.

198. Philip Schrag, *A Well-Founded Fear: The Congressional Battle to Save Political Asylum in America* (New York: Routledge, 2000), 28–29.

199. Sheth, *Toward a Political Philosophy of Race*, 30.

200. Statement of Testimony Under Equity Rule 75 B, United States v. Pandit, No. G-111-T (S.D. Cal. May 11, 1926), in Transcript of Record at 152–54, United States v. Sakharam Ganesh Pandit, No. 4938 (9th Cir. Aug. 13, 1926).

201. Arendt, *The Origins of Totalitarianism*, 280–81.

202. Ibid., 279 n. 25.

203. Ibid., 279–80.

204. See *Cable Act of 1922*, 67th Cong., 2nd Sess., *U.S. Statutes at Large* 42 (1922): 1021.

CHAPTER 3. THE ARMENIAN GENOCIDE, MARTYRDOM, AND *CARTOZIAN*

1. "Erdogan Issues Statement on 'Events of 1915,'" *Armenian Weekly*, April 23, 2014.

2. See Peter Balakian, *The Burning Tigris: The Armenian Genocide and America's Response* (New York: HarperCollins, 2003), 149.

3. See generally Balakian, *The Burning Tigris*, 11; Donald Bloxham and Fatma Göçek, "The Armenian Genocide," in *The Historiography of Genocide*, ed. Dan Stone (New York: Palgrave Macmillan, 2008), 360; Robert Koolakian, *Struggle for Justice: A Story of the American Committee for*

the Independence of Armenia, 1915–1920 (Dearborn: Armenian Research Center, University of Michigan-Dearborn, 2008), 21–23.

4. "Erdogan Issues Statement on 'Events of 1915,'" *Armenian Weekly*, April 23, 2014.

5. See Peter Balakian, "Raphael Lemkin, Cultural Destruction, and the Armenian Genocide," *Holocaust and Genocide Studies* 27, no. 1 (2013): 57–59.

6. See Balakian, *The Burning Tigris*, 331–47; Adam Jones, *Genocide: A Comprehensive Introduction*, 2nd ed. (New York: Routledge, 2011), 149.

7. Turkey's war crimes proceedings resulted in a number of guilty verdicts and executions before they were abandoned. See, e.g., Vahakn Dadrian, "The Naim-Andonian Documents on the World War I Destruction of Ottoman Armenians: The Anatomy of a Genocide," *International Journal of Middle East Studies* 18 (1986): 311–60; Vahakn Dadrian, "The Turkish Military Tribunal's Prosecution of the Authors of the Armenian Genocide: Four Major Court-Martial Series," *Holocaust and Genocide Studies* 11 (1997): 28–59; see also "The Turkish Military's Prosecution," *Washington Post*, Feb. 13, 1919. The Turkish attorney general who was appointed to prosecute the perpetrators of the Armenian genocide in the Turkish war crimes tribunals after the war himself denounced the crimes against the Armenians as "crimes against humanity." See Dadrian, "The Turkish Military Tribunal's Prosecution," 34.

8. See Balakian, *The Burning Tigris*, 331–47; *see also* Stanford Shaw and Ezel Shaw, *History of the Ottoman Empire and Modern Turkey*, 2 vols. (New York: Cambridge University Press, 1976–77); Richard Hovannisian, "Confronting the Armenian Genocide," in *Pioneers of Genocide Studies*, ed. Samuel Totten and Steven Leonard Jacobs (New Brunswick, NJ: Transaction, 2002), 34.

9. Balakian, *The Burning Tigris*, 386.

10. See "Countries that Recognize the Armenian Genocide," *Armenian National Institute*, http://www.armenian-genocide.org/recognition_countries. html (accessed Sept. 23, 2016); "Genocide Recognition by U.S. States," *Armenian National Committee of America*, http://www.anca.org/genocide/ states_map.php (accessed Sept. 23, 2016).

11. "Turkey threatens 'serious consequences' after US vote on Armenian genocide," *The Guardian*, March 5, 2010, http://www.theguardian.com/ world/2010/mar/05/turkey-us-vote-armenian-genocide (accessed Oct. 14, 2014).

12. See Transcript of Evidence at 8, United States v. Cartozian, No. E-8668 (D. Or. May 8–9, 1924), in Civil and Criminal Case Files, District

of Oregon (Portland), Records of the District Courts of the United States, RG 21, NAPAR (Cartozian Trial Transcript).

13. See, e.g., Kesnin Bey, *The Evil of the East; or, Truths About Turkey* (London: Vizetelley & Co., 1888), 199 (noting the affinity of Armenians with Europeans, but describing Armenians as an "Oriental nation"); National Reform Association, *The World's Moral Problems: Addresses at the Third World's Christian Citizenship Conference* (Pittsburgh: Murdoch-Kerr Press, 1920), 454 (describing Armenians as having a higher literacy rate than "any other Oriental nation that comes to America").

14. Asiatic Exclusion League, *Proceedings of the Asiatic Exclusion League* (March 1910), at 4–5, in Asiatic Exclusion League, *Proceedings of the Asiatic Exclusion League, 1907–1913* (New York: Arno Press, 1977).

15. As late as the 1950s, both President Eisenhower and Vice President Richard Nixon owned property containing anti-Armenian covenants. See Michael Bobelian, *Children of Armenia: A Forgotten Genocide and the Century-Long Struggle for Justice* (New York: Simon and Schuster, 2009), 110.

16. See M. Vartan Malcolm, *The Armenians in America* (Boston: The Pilgrim Press, 1919), 83–126.

17. See *In re* Halladjian, 174 F. 834 (C.C.D. Mass. 1909).

18. United States v. Thind, 261 U.S. 204, 214 (1923).

19. See *Black's Law Dictionary*, 6th ed., s.v. "Dicta."

20. Correspondence from Commissioner of Naturalization Raymond Crist to Secretary of Labor James Davis dated Aug. 2, 1923, in Records of the Immigration and Naturalization Service of the United States, RG 85, Box 1573, NAB.

21. See *Immigration Act of 1924*, 68th Cong., 1st Sess., *U.S. Statutes at Large* 43 (1924): §§ 13(c), 28(c).

22. See Shaw and Shaw, *History of the Ottoman Empire*.

23. See Earlene Craver, "On the Boundary of White: The *Cartozian* Naturalization Case and the Armenians, 1923–1925," *Journal of American Ethnic History* 28 (2009): 56; Phillip Lothyan, "A Question of Citizenship," *Prologue: Quarterly of the National Archives* 21 (1989): 272.

24. "The Status of Armenians," *Washington Post*, Aug. 1, 1925.

25. See Correspondence from Commissioner of Naturalization Richard Campbell to the Secretary of Labor dated March 22, 1913 and Correspondence from M. Vartan Malcolm to Commissioner of Naturalization Raymond Crist dated Jan. 8, 1924, in Box 1573, Records of the Immigration and Naturalization Service of the United States, RG 85, NAB.

26. Correspondence from M. Vartan Malcolm to Commissioner of Naturalization Raymond Crist dated Jan. 8, 1924, in Box 1573, Records of the Immigration and Naturalization Service of the United States, RG 85, NAB.

27. Because expert witnesses Paul Rohrbach, Roland Dixon, James Barton, and Franz Boas testified by deposition and their depositions were introduced into the trial as evidence, textual references to the transcript may alternatively or collectively refer to the transcript of evidence of the two-day bench trial held on May 8–9, 1924, in Portland, Oregon, and to the transcript of expert depositions held between April 5–9, 1924. The notes identify whether one or both transcripts serve as documentation of referenced content.

28. See *Halladjian*, 174 F. 834.

29. John Tehranian, *Whitewashed: America's Middle Eastern Minority* (New York: New York University Press, 2009), 51–54.

30. See Lothyan, "A Question of Citizenship," 14. Likewise, Earlene Craver primarily focuses on direct evidence of assimilability in her article discussing the archival records in the case. See Craver, "On the Boundary of White," 56.

31. Ian Haney López, *White by Law: The Legal Construction of Race* (New York: New York University Press, 1996), 4–5.

32. See Ariela Gross, *What Blood Won't Tell: A History of Race on Trial in America* (Cambridge: Harvard University Press, 2008), 235; Matthew Frye Jacobson, *Whiteness of a Different Color: European Immigrants and the Alchemy of Race* (Cambridge: Harvard University Press, 1998), 240.

33. Beyza Tekin, *Representations and Othering in Discourse: The Construction of Turkey in the EU Context* (Amsterdam: John Benjamins, 2010), 28.

34. *Richard II*, *The Oxford Shakespeare: The Complete Works*, 2nd ed., ed. John Jowett, William Montgomery, Gary Taylor, and Stanley Wells (Oxford: Clarendon, 2005), 4.1.83–86.

35. *Halladjian*, 174 F. at 841.

36. Tekin, *Representations and Othering in Discourse*, 56; see also Bey, *The Evil of the East*.

37. Asiatic Exclusion League, *Proceedings of the Asiatic Exclusion League* (Nov. 1909), at 6, in Asiatic Exclusion League, *Proceedings of the Asiatic Exclusion League*.

38. Stoddard, *The Rising Tide of Color*, 57–62.

39. See, e.g., Susan Brewer, *Why America Fights: Patriotism and War Propaganda from the Philippines to Iraq* (New York: Oxford University Press, 2009), 46–86.

40. United States v. Thind, 261 U.S. 204, 214 (1923). Although John Tehranian argues that in the history of the racial eligibility cases only "occasionally, and by the slimmest of margins, [were] Middle Easterners . . . considered white," this conclusion considers only the published judicial opinions in the cases and is debatable even with regard to those. See Tehranian, *Whitewashed*, 49. There is ample evidence that Middle Easterners were more frequently classified as "free white persons" for purposes of naturalization consistent with the Bureau of Naturalization's official policy of not opposing the naturalization of Arabs and other petitioners from the Middle East. See, e.g., "When 'White' Is Not White," *The State* (Columbia, SC), Oct. 20, 1909 (reporting that a number of Turks employed in Indiana factories had been naturalized); "'Free Whites' From Turkey," *Washington Post*, Nov. 8, 1909 (reporting that Judge Arthur Brown of the United States District Court for the District of Rhode Island admitted Jacob Thompson, a "subject of the Sultan of Turkey and a native of Armenia," to citizenship over the government's objection, stating that "it has been the practice of this court for many years to recognize Armenians and Turks as coming within the designation of free white persons, and the court will continue so to consider them until a court of higher authority decides otherwise"); Correspondence from the Acting Secretary of the Department of Commerce and Labor to Messrs. O'Brien et al. dated Nov. 15, 1909, in Box 1573, File 19783/43, Records of the Immigration and Naturalization Service of the United States, RG 85, NAB (reporting that "the records of the Department show but three cases in which courts have held Syrians are not white persons" and attaching a table of the cases); *In re* Najour, 174 F. 735 (C.C.N.D. Ga. 1909) (holding that a Syrian "from Mt. Lebanon, near Beirut" was a "free white person"); Correspondence from Secretary of the Department of Commerce and Labor Charles Nagel to Secretary of State Philander Knox dated Dec. 7, 1909, in Box 1573, File 19783/43, Records of the Immigration and Naturalization Service of the United States, RG 85, NAB (writing that "neither the Department [of Commerce and Labor] nor the Division of Naturalization has requested that appeals be taken in any of the cases" in which Syrian petitioners had been held to be "free white persons"); *Halladjian*, 174 F. at 845 (noting previous naturalizations of

Armenians "as well as Syrians and Turks," who had all been "freely natu-raliz[ed] in this court until now"); *In re* Mudarri, 176 F. 465 (C.D. Mass. 1910) (holding that a Syrian "born in Damascus" was a "free white person"); *In re* Ellis, 179 F. 1002 (D. Or. 1910) (holding that a Syrian who was "a native of the province of Palestine" and "a Turkish subject" was a "free white person") (cited with approval in Ozawa v. United States, 260 U.S. 178, 197 (1922)); Dow v. United States, 226 F. 145 (4th Cir. 1915) (holding that a Syrian was a "free white person" and that "a large number of Syrians have been naturalized without question," and reversing *Ex parte* Dow, 211 F. 486 (E.D.S.C. 1914) and *In re* Dow, 213 F. 355 (E.D.S.C. 1914) (on rehearing)), *In re* Sallak, No. 14876 (N.D. Ill. June 27, 1924), in Significant Civil and Criminal Case Files, 1899–1925, District of Oregon (Portland), Records of U.S. Attorneys and Marshals, RG 118, NAPAR (holding that a petitioner "born in Palestine" was a "free white person"); *In re* S—, 1 I. & N Dec. 174 (B.I.A. 1941) (holding that a native and citizen of Iraq, whose parents were "full-blooded Arabians" and whose ancestors "came from Turkish stock" was a "free white person"); U.S. Department of Justice, Immigration and Naturalization Service, "The Eligibility of Arabs to Naturalization," *Monthly Review* 1 (1943): 12–16 (concluding that persons of "the Arabian race" were "free white persons"); U.S. Department of Justice, Immigration and Naturalization Service, "Summaries of Recent Court Decisions," *Monthly Review* 1 (1944): 12 (reporting a ruling of the United States District Court for the Western District of Pennsylvania that "an Arab born in Beit Hanina, Palestine" was a "free white person"); *In re* Shaikhaly, No. 119332 (S.D. Cal. Dec. 20, 1944), in Folder 119332, Contested Naturalizations, Southern District of California, Central Division (Los Angeles), RG 21, NAPR (LN) (holding that "a native and citizen of Palestine . . . of the Arabian race," was a "free white person"); *In re* K—, 2 I. & N. Dec. 253 (B.I.A. 1945) (holding that a native and citizen of Afghanistan, "of the Afghan race," was a "white person"). Even Lothrop Stoddard, who concluded that people from the Near and Middle East had an "instinctive Asiatic feeling," wrote that the Persians and Ottoman Turks were "largely white" in contrast to other groups in the region. Stoddard, *The Rising Tide of Color*, 54–55.

41. Cartozian Trial Transcript at 17–18.

42. See, e.g., Leslie Davis, *The Slaughterhouse Province: An American Diplomat's Report on the Armenian Genocide, 1915–1917* (New Rochelle, NY: Aristide Caratzas, 1989).

43. Cartozian Trial Transcript at 60–61, 126–27; *Richard II*, *The Oxford Shakespeare: The Complete Works*, 2nd ed., ed. John Jowett, William Montgomery, Gary Taylor, and Stanley Wells (Oxford: Clarendon, 2005), 4.1.83–86.

44. Robert Ferguson, "Becoming American: High Treason and Low Invective in the Republic of Laws," in *The Rhetoric of Law*, ed. Austin Sarat and Thomas Kearns (Ann Arbor: University of Michigan Press 1994), 103.

45. Vahakn Dadrian, "The Armenian Genocide: An Interpretation," in *America and the Armenian Genocide of 1915*, ed. Jay Winter (Cambridge: Cambridge University Press, 2003), 52.

46. See Cathie Carmichael, *Genocide before the Holocaust* (New Haven: Yale University Press, 2009), 3.

47. See ibid., 3, 10; see also Jones, *Genocide*, 149.

48. See Cartozian Trial Transcript at 138, 141; see also Craver, "On the Boundary of White," 56.

49. *Immigration Act of 1917*, 64th Cong, 2nd Sess., *U.S. Statutes at Large* 39 (1917): § 3.

50. Johnson v. Tertzag, 2 F.2d 40, 41 (1st Cir. 1924).

51. See Cartozian Trial Transcript at 8.

52. See ibid., 3–4.

53. *Black's Law Dictionary*, 6th ed., s.v. "Judicial notice"; see also Bryan Garner, *A Dictionary of Modern Legal Usage*, 2nd ed. (Oxford: Oxford Univ. Press, 1995), s.v. "Judicial notice; judicial cognizance."

54. See Cartozian Trial Transcript at 8.

55. United States v. Cartozian, 6 F.2d 919, 922 (D. Or. 1925); see also Cartozian Trial Transcript at 1–5.

56. The works cited include Johann Friedrich Blumenbach's *On the Natural Variety of Mankind*; Friedrich Braun's "The Aboriginal Population of Europe and the Origin of the Teutonic People"; Daniel Brinton's *Races and Peoples: Lectures of the Science of Ethnography*; Roland Dixon's *The Racial History of Man*; Wynfrid Duckworth's *Studies from the Anthropological Laboratory*; Louis Figuier's *Les Races Humaines*; Madison Grant's *The Passing of the Great Race*; Alfred Haddon's *The Races of Man and Their Distribution*; Jean Baptiste Julien d'Omalius d'Halloy's *Des Races Humaines ou Eléments d'Ethnographie*; Johann Heinrich Hübschmann's *Armenische Studien*; Paul Kretschmer's *Der Nationale Name der Armenier Haik*; Felix von Luschan's *The Early Inhabitants of Western Asia*; Henry Lynch's *Armenia: Travels and Studies*; Jacques de Morgan's *The History of the Armenian People: From the Remotest*

Times to Present Day; William Ripley's *Races of Europe*; Otto Schrader's *Prehistoric Antiquities of the Aryan Peoples: A Manual of Comparative Philology and the Earliest Culture*; and Giuseppe Sergi's *Man, His Origin, Antiquity, Variety and Geographical Distribution*. See Transcript of the Depositions of Dr. Paul Rohrbach, Roland Dixon, Dr. James Barton, and Dr. Franz Boas at 5, United States v. Cartozian, No. E-8668 (D. Or. Apr. 5,8–9, and 11, 1924), in Significant Civil and Criminal Case Files, 1899–1925, District of Oregon (Portland), Records of U.S. Attorneys and Marshals, RG 118, NAPAR (Cartozian Deposition Transcript); Cartozian Trial Transcript at 101, 128–29.

57. In the same chapter of *The Geography* that the defense cites, Strabo reports that the Armenians descended from Jason and Medea, a reference to the epic myth by which Jason, after being raised by a centaur, led the Greek Argonauts on a quest for the Golden Fleece, which was guarded by a dragon that never slept. See Strabo, *The Geography of Strabo*, trans. H. C. Hamilton and W. Falconer (London: G. Bell, 1903), 269. Strabo also writes that the ancient origin of Armenia derives from Armenus of Armenium, who accompanied Jason in his expedition into Armenia, and that the Jasonia serve as proof of Jason's expedition. See ibid., 272; cf. *The Reader's Encyclopedia: An Encyclopedia of World Literature and the Arts*, ed. William Rose Benét (New York: T. Y. Crowell, 1948), 45, 555, 707. In addition to the mythic origins of the Armenians, Strabo notes that Armenia was originally a small country enlarged by the conquest of surrounding areas, consolidating under one language a variety of heterogeneous peoples. See Strabo, *The Geography*, 269, 273–74.

58. See Malcolm, *The Armenians in America*, 49.

59. See Mardiros Ananikian, "Armenian Mythology," in *The Mythology of All Races*, ed. Canon John Arnott MacCulloch (Boston: Marshall Jones, 1925), 7:7–8. According to Ananikian, the Armenians conquered the Urartians and reduced many to serfdom, imposing on them the Armenian name, language, religion, and civilization, such that "it is very natural that such a relation should culminate in a certain amount of fusion between the two races." Ibid.

60. Lee Baker, "The Cult of Franz Boas and His 'Conspiracy' to Destroy the White Race," *Proceedings of the American Philosophical Society* 154, no. 1 (2010): 8–9; see Franz Boas, "Eugenics," *Scientific Monthly* 3, no. 5 (1916): 472 (concluding that a real anthropologist "believes that different types of man may reach the same civilization").

61. See Cartozian Deposition Transcript at 36; Cartozian Trial Transcript at 103.

62. Cartozian Deposition Transcript at 35.

63. Ibid., 82; Cartozian Trial Transcript at 103.

64. Cartozian Trial Transcript at 17, 52.

65. See Tehranian, *Whitewashed*, 51–54; Salah Hassan, "Arabs, Race and the Post–September 11 National Security State," *Middle East Report* 224 (2002): 16–21.

66. *Halladjian*, 174 F. at 841. Renaissance cartographers also located the Garden of Eden and other sacred sites of biblical literature in or near Armenia, see Balakian, *The Burning Tigris*, 29–30, and the Caucasian racial classification long centered around hypotheses about the location of Mount Ararat and the subsequent spread of Noah's progeny, see Michael Keevak, *Becoming Yellow: A Short History of Racial Thinking* (Princeton: Princeton University Press, 2011), 74, 80.

67. Walt Whitman, *Leaves of Grass*, ed. Harold Blodgett and Sculley Bradley (New York: New York University Press, 1965), 146.

68. Koolakian, *Struggle for Justice*, 23.

69. See Balakian, *The Burning Tigris*, 75, 291.

70. Herbert Hoover, *The Memoirs of Herbert Hoover: Years of Adventure 1874–1920* (New York: MacMillan, 1951), 385. This powerful identification intensified in the 1890s, when the Hamidian massacres were widely published in American headlines and had a profound impact on the American public, even prompting debate about military intervention in the region before the turn of the century. See Balakian, *The Burning Tigris*, xix, 4, 10–11, 66–67, 207, 282–85, 345; "Another Armenian Holocaust," *New York Times*, Sept. 10, 1895.

71. See Henry Morgenthau, *Ambassador Morgenthau's Story* (Garden City, NY: Doubleday, 1918), 301–25.

72. Ibid., 305, 322.

73. Balakian, *The Burning Tigris*, 314–17.

74. See Cartozian Trial Transcript at 19, 56–57.

75. Ibid., 101–104.

76. Ibid., 138.

77. See Cartozian Deposition Transcript at 46.

78. Cartozian Trial Transcript at 153–54.

79. Ibid., 155.

80. Ibid., 18.

81. See, e.g., Cartozian Trial Transcript at 68, 130–31.

82. Cartozian Trial Transcript at 14.

83. Herbert Lee, "Armenia as the Measure of Our Civilization," *The New Armenia* 8 (1921): 67–69.

84. See Cartozian Trial Transcript at 11–12, 20–21, 38–40, 42, 44–46, 56, 62, 81, 84, 89, 98, 114, 117, 166. See also Defendant's Exhibit listing "names, addresses, occupations, the maiden name of those that are married, citizenship, membership and affiliation with native American fraternal, educational, religious, and social institutions, of 339 persons of Armenian parentage, now residing in all parts of the United States, and who are engaged in business and in some professions," United States v. Cartozian, No. E-8668 (D. Or.), in Significant Civil and Criminal Case Files, 1899–1925, District of Oregon (Portland), Records of U.S. Attorneys and Marshals, RG 118, NAPAR (Cartozian Tabulation Exhibit).

85. Cartozian Deposition Transcript at 12–13.

86. Ibid., 54–55. The defense's reliance on Armenian Christianity as evidence of whiteness follows a theme among racial eligibility cases during the early twentieth century of associating whiteness with Christianity. See, e.g., *Thind*, 261 U.S. at 213 (using the biblical allusion *bone of their bone and flesh of their flesh* to describe those European immigrants whom the First Congress intended by the phrase *white person*); *Halladjian*, 174 F. at 841 (noting that "by reason of their Christianity, [Armenians] generally ranged themselves against the Persian fire-worshipers, and against the Mohammedans, both Saracens and Turks," that when the Armenians were conquered by the Saracens in the seventh century they recovered their independence in the ninth century under princes who they claimed "were of the lineage of David," and that when the Armenians were finally conquered in Armenia by the Turks their refugees set up an independent state in Cilicia "streaming the ensign of the Christian cross against black pagans, Turks, and Saracens"); *Ellis*, 179 F. at 1003 (noting that a Syrian applicant was "reared a Catholic, and is still of that faith"); *In re* Dow, 213 F. 355, 364 (E.D.S.C. 1914), *rev'd*, 226 F. 145 (4th Cir. 1915) (writing that the modern inhabitant of the Lebanon District of Syria in which a Syrian applicant was born was not the location either of the Old Testament or of "the labors of Christ"); *In re* Hassan, 48 F. Supp. 843, 845 (E.D. Mich. 1942) (canceling the naturalization certificate of an Arab applicant based on the conclusion that Arabs were "part of the Mohammedan world and that a wide gulf separates their culture from that of the predominately Christian peoples of Europe"). Of

course, the association of whiteness and Christianity also has a long history in Western imperialism. See, e.g., Jacobson, *Whiteness of a Different Color*, 212; Rubin Weston, *Racism in U.S. Imperialism: The Influence of Racial Assumptions on American Foreign Policy, 1893–1946* (Columbia: University of South Carolina Press, 1972), 39; Robert Williams, *The American Indian in Western Legal Thought: The Discourses of Conquest* (New York: Oxford University Press, 1990), 14–15, 21, 46–47.

87. See Cartozian Deposition Transcript at 36, 77, 88.

88. Cartozian Trial Transcript at 67.

89. See generally, e.g., Edward Queen II, Stephen Prothero, and Gardiner Shattuck Jr., *Encyclopedia of American Religious History*, 3rd ed. (New York: Facts on File, 2009): 1:52–53.

90. See Kenneth Burke, *A Grammar of Motives*, Calif. ed. (Berkeley: University of California Press, 1969), 35–38.

91. Cartozian Trial Transcript at 17, 52.

92. See, e.g., Cartozian Trial Transcript at 9–15, 19–24, 26–29, 47–50, 56–95, 64–66, 99, 104–27, 136; Cartozian Deposition Transcript at 5–11, 36–37, 52–55, 90–93. In its presentation of assimilability evidence, the defense went to extraordinary lengths to establish that Armenians had been freely admitted to numerous "whites only" fraternal organizations such as the Freemasons, the Benevolent and Protective Order of Elks, the Independent Order of Foresters, the Fraternal Order of Eagles, the Modern Woodmen of America, the Loyal Order of Moose, the Independent Order of Odd Fellows, and the Knights of Pythias. See Cartozian Trial Transcript at a–d, 104; see also Craver, "On the Boundary of White," 56. The defense not only offered evidence that Armenians were members of these fraternal organizations, but presented testimony from organizational officers of the Freemasons, the Benevolent and Protective Order of Elks, the Loyal Order of the Moose, the Independent Order of Odd Fellows, and the Knights of Pythias regarding racial eligibility for membership in their groups, even introducing the constitution and statutes of the Benevolent and Protective Order of Elks into evidence. See Cartozian Trial Transcript at 39–40. The Deputy Grand Master of the Independent Order of Odd Fellows, for example, testified that the Odd Fellows admitted Armenians but excluded Chinese, Japanese, and Hindus from membership on racial grounds. Ibid., 36–38. The defense also elicited testimony from the deputy grand master that the racial classification of Syrians for purposes of Odd Fellows membership had been "adjudicated" within the organization and that they had

been classified as "white." Ibid. The admission of evidence regarding fraternal membership practices and private adjudications of whiteness within these organizations raises particularly interesting questions about the relationship between private dispute resolution and public law in the case.

93. See Cartozian Tabulation Exhibit.

94. See ibid.; Cartozian Trial Transcript at 23.

95. Cartozian Trial Transcript at 96.

96. Ibid., 96–97.

97. Cartozian Deposition Transcript at 82–83.

98. Cartozian Trial Transcript at 64, 68.

99. See Cartozian Deposition Transcript at 93.

100. See Richard Hovannisian, "The Armenian Question, 1878–1923," in *A Crime of Silence: The Armenian Genocide*, ed. Gérard Libaridian (London: Zed, 1985), 28.

101. See generally *In re* Thind, 268 F. 683 (D. Or. 1920), *rev'd*, 261 U.S. 204 (1923).

102. *Ellis*, 179 F. at 1002–03.

103. See *Thind*, 268 F. at 684.

104. *Cartozian*, 6 F.2d at 920.

105. See *Oxford English Dictionary*, 2nd ed., s.v. "Aloof."

106. See *Hamlet, The Oxford Shakespeare: The Complete Works*, 2nd ed., eds. John Jowett, William Montgomery, Gary Taylor, and Stanley Wells (Oxford: Clarendon Press, 2005): 5.2.193.

107. *Cartozian*, 6 F.2d at 920.

108. See, e.g., Gualtieri, "Becoming 'White,'" 41 (discussing the Ottoman *millet* system in the context of the racial eligibility cases involving Syrian applicants).

109. Cartozian Deposition Transcript at 35.

110. Ibid., 101–104.

111. Cartozian Trial Transcript at 153–54.

112. Ibid., 18.

113. Ibid., 138.

114. *Cartozian*, 6 F.2d at 920. Judge Wolverton's use of the word *spontaneously* in this passage appeals to the notion of "racial instincts," again responding to *Thind* in which the Supreme Court concluded that the racial difference of high caste Hindus was such that "the great body of our people instinctively recognize it." *Thind*, 261 U.S. at 210–11. The Supreme Court's opinion in *Plessy v. Ferguson* (1896) had similarly claimed that "legislation

is powerless to eradicate racial instinct, or to abolish distinctions based upon physical differences." Plessy v. Ferguson, 163 U.S. 537, 551 (1896). Although a theory of racial instincts is also suggested by the defense's theory of the case, Wolverton's claim that Armenians "spontaneously" intermingled with other "whites" is more explicit than any suggestion of racial instincts made during the trial.

115. See Cartozian Deposition Transcript at 66.

116. Cartozian Trial Transcript at 155.

117. *Cartozian*, 6 F.2d at 920 (emphasis added).

118. Ibid.

119. Ibid., 921.

120. See Craver, "On the Boundary of White," 56.

121. See Keevak, *Becoming Yellow*, 4, 75–76; see also Sam Keen, *Faces of the Enemy: Reflections of the Hostile Imagination* (San Francisco: Harper, 1986), 26 ("The old image of Genghis Khan and the Mongol hordes still haunts us and is retooled and pressed into service when needed.").

122. Lee, "Armenia as the Measure," 67–69.

123. Ananikian, "Armenian Mythology," 3.

124. Lee, "Armenia as the Measure," 67–69.

125. See, e.g., Benedict Anderson, *Imagined Communities: Reflections on the Origin and Spread of Nationalism*, rev. ed. (New York: Verso, 2006), 4; Jean Elshtain, "Sovereignty, Identity, Sacrifice," in *Reimagining the Nation*, ed. Marjorie Ringrose and Adam Lerner (Buckingham, UK: Open University Press, 1993), 159–75; Rebecca Herzig, "In the Name of Science: Suffering, Sacrifice, and the Formation of American Roentgenology," *American Quarterly* 53, no. 4 (2001): 563–89; Adam Lerner, "The Nineteenth-Century Monument and the Embodiment of National Time," in *Reimagining the Nation*, ed. Marjorie Ringrose and Adam Lerner (Buckingham, UK: Open University Press, 1993), 176–96; Michael Rowlands, "Memory, Sacrifice and the Nation," *New Formations* 30, no. 4 (1996): 8–17.

126. Nikki Shepardson, *Burning Zeal: The Rhetoric of Martyrdom and the Protestant Community in Reformation France, 1520–1570* (Bethlehem, PA: Lehigh University Press, 2007), 23, 118; see also Donald Riddle, *The Martyrs: A Study in Social Control* (Chicago: University of Chicago Press, 1931).

127. Shepardson, *Burning Zeal*, 112–19.

128. Ibid., 149.

129. See, e.g., Louis Fenech, "Martyrdom and the Sikh Tradition," *Journal of the American Oriental Society* 117, no. 4 (1997): 623–42.

130. Reprinted in Kushwant Singh and Satindra Singh, *Ghadar 1915: India's First Armed Revolution* (New Delhi: R & K, 1966), 20–21.

131. Philip Schrag, *A Well-Founded Fear: The Congressional Battle to Save Political Asylum in America* (New York: Routledge, 2000), 28–29.

CHAPTER 4. WORLD WAR II ALLIANCES IN ASIA AND
THE END OF RACIAL ELIGIBILITY FOR NATURALIZATION

1. See *Immigration Act of 1917*, 64th Cong, 2nd Sess., *U.S. Statutes at Large* 39 (1917): 874; *Immigration Act of 1924*, 68th Cong., 1st Sess., *U.S. Statutes at Large* 43 (1924): 153.

2. See, e.g., Arra Avakian, *The Armenians in America* (Minneapolis: Lerner, 1977), 45–46.

3. See United States v. Ali, 20 F.2d 998 (E.D. Mich. 1927); United States v. Javier, 22 F.2d 879 (D.C. Cir. 1927); United States v. Gokhale, 26 F.2d 360 (2d Cir. 1928).

4. See *In re* Fisher, 21 F.2d 1007 (N.D. Calif. 1927) and *In re* Cruz, 23 F. Supp. 774 (E.D.N.Y. 1938).

5. See *In re* Din, 27 F.2d 568 (N.D. Calif. 1928).

6. See *In re* I—, 1 I. & N. Dec. 627 (B.I.A. 1943) (finding without discussion that a native and citizen of Canada was "a person of the white race"); *In re* P—, 2 I. & N. Dec. 84 (B.I.A. 1944) (same); *In re* M—, 2 I. & N. Dec. 196 (B.I.A. 1944) (finding without discussion that a native and citizen of Mexico was "a person of the white race"); *In re* C—, 2 I. & N. Dec. 220 (B.I.A. 1944) (same); *In re* K—, 2 I. & N. Dec. 411 (B.I.A. 1945) (finding without discussion that a native and citizen of Hungary was "a person of the white race"); *In re* T—, 2 I. & N. Dec. 614 (B.I.A. 1946) (finding without discussion that a native and citizen of Italy was "a person of the white race"); *In re* B—, 2 I. & N. Dec. 492 (B.I.A. 1947) (finding without discussion that a native and citizen of Portugal was "a person of the white race").

7. Ian Haney López, *White by Law: The Legal Construction of Race* (New York: New York University Press, 1996), 33.

8. *Nationality Act of 1940*, 76th Cong., 3rd Sess., *U.S. Statutes at Large* 54 (1940): 1137; *Filipino and Indian Naturalization Act of 1946*, 79th Cong., 2nd Sess., *U.S. Statutes at Large* 60 (1946): 416.

9. See *Second War Powers Act of 1942*, 77th Cong., 2nd Sess., *U.S. Statutes at Large* 56 (1942): 182; Charles Gordon, "The Racial Barrier to

American Citizenship," *University of Pennsylvania Law Review* 93 (1945): 248; Petition for Writ of Certiorari to the United States Circuit Court of Appeals for the Ninth Circuit and Brief in Support Thereof at 42–48, Samras v. United States, No. 130 (U.S. Sup. Ct. May 14, 1942).

10. *Chinese Exclusion Repeal Act of 1943,* 78th Cong., 1st Sess., *U.S. Statutes at Large* 57 (1943): 600; *Chinese Exclusion Repeal Act of 1943,* 78th Cong., 1st Sess., *Congressional Record* 89 (Oct. 20, 1943): 8572–605; Department of Justice, Immigration and Naturalization Service, "Proposed Repeal of the Chinese Exclusion Acts," *Monthly Review* 1 (August 1943): 14; Gordon, "The Racial Barrier to American Citizenship," 237.

11. *Ex parte Mohriez,* 54 F. Supp. 941, 943 (D. Mass. 1944); see *In re* Shaikhaly, No. 119332 (S.D. Cal. Dec. 20, 1944), in Folder 119332, Contested Naturalizations, Southern District of California, Central Division (Los Angeles), RG 21, NAPR (LN).

12. Gordon, "The Racial Barrier to American Citizenship," 251–58.

13. *Filipino and Indian Naturalization Act of 1946,* 79th Cong., 2nd Sess., *U.S. Statutes at Large* 60 (1946): 416; Gordon, "The Racial Barrier to American Citizenship," 248–50.

14. Hirabayashi v. United States, 320 U.S. 81, 110–11 (1943) (Murphy, concurring).

15. See Brown v. Board of Education, 347 U.S. 483 (1954).

16. *Chinese Exclusion Repeal Act of 1943,* HR 314, 78th Cong., 1st Sess., *Congressional Record* 89 (Oct. 20, 1943): 8596, 8602.

17. Gordon, "The Racial Barrier to American Citizenship," 253.

18. See, e.g., Carol Anderson, *Eyes Off the Prize: The United Nations and the African American Struggle for Human Rights, 1944–1955* (Cambridge: Cambridge University Press, 2003); Thomas Borstelmann, *The Cold War and the Color Line: American Race Relations in the Global Arena* (Cambridge: Harvard University Press, 2003); Mary Dudziak, *Cold War Civil Rights: Race and the Image of American Democracy* (Princeton: Princeton University Press, 2000); Gerald Horne, *Black and Red: W. E. B. DuBois and the African American Response to the Cold War* (Albany: State University of New York Press, 1986); Brenda Gayle Plummer, *Rising Wind: Black Americans and U.S. Foreign Affairs, 1935–1960* (Chapel Hill: University of North Carolina Press, 1996); Jonathan Rosenberg, *How Far the Promised Land? World Affairs and the American Civil Rights Movement from the First World War to Vietnam* (Princeton: Princeton University Press, 2006.

19. Brief of Attorney General at 48, *In re* Yamashita, No. 202 (Wash. Sup. Ct. 1902).

20. See Petition for Writ of Certiorari to the United States Circuit Court of Appeals for the Ninth Circuit and Brief in Support Thereof at 21, Samras v. United States, No. 130 (U.S. Sup. Ct. June 8, 1942) (arguing that limiting naturalization to certain races "was and is unconstitutional because it is so manifestly and grossly irrational, illogical, arbitrary and capricious upon its face because of its discriminatory classification solely because of race or color as to constitute a violation of the due process of law clause of the Fifth Amendment to the Constitution of the United States" and noting that no constitutional objection to racial eligibility for naturalization had been urged in "any . . . case thus far"). Samras filed his petition for certiorari in the United States Supreme Court one day late, and as a result his petition was dismissed as untimely.

21. *Prelude to War*, DVD, directed by Frank Capra (New York: GoodTimes Home Video, 2000). Another film in the series, *War Comes to America*, cites the proclamation in the Declaration of Independence that "all men are created equal" as a guiding ideal of the war. *War Comes to America*, DVD, directed by Frank Capra (New York: GoodTimes Home Video, 2000).

22. See, e.g., Sean Brawley, *The White Peril: Foreign Relations and Asian Immigration to Australasia and North America 1919–78* (Sydney: University of New South Wales Press, 1995), 84–89.

23. Ibid., 85–86.

24. See ibid., 87.

25. Savel Zimand, "Color Issue Breeds Unrest in the East," *New York Times*, Oct. 26, 1924.

26. Raymond Buell, "America's Course Toward Japan: A Momentous Decision," *New York Times*, Dec. 23, 1934.

27. Dudziak, *Cold War Civil Rights*, 250.

28. See *Immigration Act of 1924*, 68th Cong., 1st Sess., *U.S. Statutes at Large* 43 (1924): 153.

29. John Dower, *War Without Mercy: Race and Power in the Pacific War* (New York: Pantheon, 1986), 4–11; see also Pearl Buck, "The Race Barrier 'That Must Be Destroyed,'" *New York Times*, May 31, 1942 ("Although we may not be willing to know it, it is possible that we are already embarked upon the bitterest and the longest of human wars, the war between the East and the West, and this means the war between the white man and his world and the colored man and his world.").

30. *Filipino and Indian Naturalization Act of 1946*, 79th Cong., 2nd Sess., *Congressional Record* 91 (Oct. 10, 1945), 9541.

31. Dower, *War Without Mercy*, 5.

32. Pearl Buck, *American Unity and Asia* (New York: John Day, 1942), 29.

33. Quoted in Department of Justice, Immigration and Naturalization Service, "Proposed Repeal of the Chinese Exclusion Acts," *Monthly Review* 1 (1943): 14.

34. Dower, *War Without Mercy*, 6–7.

35. *Chinese Exclusion Repeal Act of 1943*, 78th Cong., 1st Sess., *Congressional Record* 89 (Oct. 20, 1943), 8579, 9995.

36. See Department of Justice, "Proposed Repeal of the Chinese Exclusion Acts," 13–14.

37. *Chinese Exclusion Repeal Act of 1943*, 78th Cong., 1st Sess., *Congressional Record* 89 (Oct. 20, 1943), 8573, 8579, 8581, 8597, 8600.

38. Ibid., 8580–81, 8583, 8591, 8597.

39. Ibid., 8580.

40. Ibid., 8573–98.

41. Ibid., 8594.

42. Ibid., 8574.

43. Ibid., 8591.

44. Ibid., 8597.

45. Ibid., 8573.

46. Ibid., 8579.

47. Ibid., 8576.

48. Ibid., 8582.

49. Ibid., 8577.

50. Ibid., 9996.

51. Ibid., 8590.

52. Ibid., 8586.

53. Ibid., 9990.

54. Ibid., 8576.

55. Ibid., 8589.

56. Ibid., 8600–8601.

57. Ibid., 8579.

58. Cf. Jeremy Engels, *Enemyship: Democracy and Counter-Revolution in the Early Republic* (East Lansing: Michigan State University Press, 2010).

59. Fred Riggs, *Pressures on Congress: A Study of the Repeal of Chinese Exclusion* (New York: King's Crown, 1950), 35.

60. Quoted in Ronald Takaki, *Strangers From a Different Shore: A History of Asian Americans*, rev. ed. (New York: Little, Brown, 1998), 370, 373.

61. "China Symbolizes War Aims, Wallace Asserts," *Los Angeles Times*, Oct. 11, 1943.

62. Capra, *Prelude to War*.

63. *Mission to Moscow*, DVD, directed by Michael Curtiz (1943; Burbank, CA: Warner Home Video, 2009).

64. *The Purple Heart*, DVD, directed by Lewis Milestone (1944; Beverly Hills: Twentieth Century Fox Home Entertainment, 2007).

65. Conclusions of the Court and Order Granting Petition for Naturalization, *In re* Shaikhaly, No. 119332 (S.D. Cal. Dec. 20, 1944), in Folder 119332, Contested Naturalizations, Southern District of California, Central Division (Los Angeles), RG 21, NAPR (LN).

66. *In re* Hassan, 48 F. Supp. 843, 845 (E.D. Mich. 1942).

67. U.S. Department of Justice, Immigration and Naturalization Service, "The Eligibility of Arabs to Naturalization," *Monthly Review* 1 (1943): 16; cf. *In re* S—, 1 I. & N Dec. 174 (1941) (holding that a native and citizen of Iraq whose parents were "full-blooded Arabians," whose ancestors "came from Turkish Stock," and who stated that he was "of Arabian blood" was a "white person" within the meaning of the Nationality Act of 1940).

68. Gordon, "The Racial Barrier to American Citizenship," 246.

69. *Ex parte* Mohriez, 54 F. Supp. 941, 942 (D. Mass. 1944) (citations omitted).

70. Bonham v. Bouiss, 161 F.2d 678, 678 (9th Cir. 1947) (also noting that the couple "cohabited and although appellee's moral character is not in issue the record shows that in Japan she also openly engaged in immoral practices with various other men").

71. See *In re* B—, 3 I. & N. Dec. 729 (1949); *In re* N—, A-7483378 (56247/95) C.O. May 16, 1950 (cited in *In re* S—, 4 I. & N. Dec. 104, 106 (1950)); U.S. Department of Justice, Immigration and Naturalization Service, "Summaries of Recent Court Decisions," *Monthly Review* 1 (1944): 44 (reporting a ruling that a Polynesian born on the Society Islands was neither a "free white person" nor a descendant of a race "indigenous to the Western Hemisphere" for purposes of naturalization); see also Memorandum Regarding Racial Eligibility for Naturalization of Maoris, L. Paul Winings to Commissioner Ugo Carusi, April 27, 1945, in File 56013/383, Box 1596, Records of the Immigration and Naturalization Service of the United States, RG 85, NAB (reporting the opinion of the General Counsel of the

Immigration and Naturalization Service that Maoris were not racially eligible for naturalization).

72. *In re* B—, 3 I. & N. Dec. 304, 306 (1948).

73. See *Nye-Lea Act,* 74th Cong., 1st Sess., *U.S. Statutes at Large* 49 (1935): 397.

74. *Filipino and Indian Naturalization Act of 1946,* 79th Cong., 2nd Sess., *U.S. Statutes at Large* 60 (1946): 416.

75. New York Congressman Emanuel Celler speaking about wartime legislation to extend eligibility for citizenship to Asian Indians, quoted in Takaki, *Strangers from a Different Shore,* 368.

76. Quoted by Ohio congressman Edward McCowen, *Filipino and Indian Naturalization Act of 1946,* 79th Cong., 2nd Sess., *Congressional Record* 91 (1945), 9524.

77. Ibid., 9527.

78. Quoted by New York congressman Samuel Dickstein, *Filipino and Indian Naturalization Act of 1946,* 79th Cong., 2nd Sess., *Congressional Record* 91 (1945), 9524.

79. Ibid., 9531.

80. *Filipino and Indian Naturalization Act of 1946,* 79th Cong., 2nd Sess., *Congressional Record* 91 (1945), 9521, 9523, 9542.

81. Ibid., 9538.

82. Ibid., 9521.

83. Ibid., 9523.

84. Ibid., 9530.

85. W. H. Auden, "September 1, 1939," *Poets.org,* http://www.poets. org/poetsorg/poem/september-1-1939 (accessed Nov. 12, 2014). This line of Auden's poem is later alluded to in Lyndon Johnson's famous "Daisy Girl" campaign commercial during the 1964 presidential campaign in relation to the nuclear threat. See Lyndon Johnson Presidential Campaign, *Daisy Girl* (1964), television advertisement; from YouTube, *DAISY: LBJ Campaign Commercial (1964),* video, https://www.youtube.com/watch?v=oYcgw0x-fAZ0 (accessed Nov. 12, 2014).

86. *Filipino and Indian Naturalization Act of 1946,* 79th Cong. 2nd Sess., *Congressional Record* 91, 9527.

87. Ibid., 9528.

88. Ibid.

89. The Tatars of the Golden Horde were notorious enemies of European Russians until Ivan the Terrible conquered the Volga Tatars north and

west of the Caspian Sea in the sixteenth century. Although the Volga Tatars shared a close relationship with Russia as its largest ethnic and religious minority through the early twentieth century, the Russian Orthodox Church and many Russian and Soviet elites viewed them with suspicion and closely monitored protonationalist, pan-Islamic, and pan-Turkic elements among them, eventually leading to the execution or exile of Tatar leaders after they formed their own nation following the Bolshevik Revolution. See Galina Yemelianova, "Volga Tatars, Russians and the Russian State at the Turn of the Nineteenth Century: Relationships and Perceptions," *The Slavonic and East European Review* 77 (1999): 449–53, 458–61, 471–77. According to Galina Yemelianova, during the early twentieth century Russian and Tatar peasants held "rigid stereotypes of each other, most of which were negative and mutually insulting," accumulated in collective memory and perpetuated through national folklore, proverbs, and songs. Ibid., 453.

90. Madison Grant, *The Passing of the Great Race; or, the Racial Basis of European History* (1916; repr., London: Forgotten Books, 2012), 129; Theodore Lothrop Stoddard, *The Rising Tide of Color Against White World Supremacy* (New York: Charles Scribner's Sons, 1921), 57.

91. Arthur Koestler, *Darkness at Noon*, trans. Daphne Hardy (New York: Scribner, 1941), 59, 61.

92. See, e.g., Volodymyr Prytula, "Ukraine: A Bittersweet Homecoming for Crimea's Tatars," *Radio Free Europe/Radio Liberty*, Jan. 20, 2012, http://www.rferl.org/content/article/1078529.html (accessed Jan. 20, 2012).

93. Harold Lamb, *Suleiman the Magnificent: Sultan of the East* (Garden City, NY: Doubleday, 1951), 341.

94. Michael Keevak, *Becoming Yellow: A Short History of Racial Thinking* (Princeton: Princeton University Press, 2011), 70–76.

95. See, e.g., Robert Service, *Lenin: A Political Life,* Vol. 1: *The Strengths of Contradiction* (London: Macmillan, 1985), 11–13.

96. "Ghengis Khan Horde Remnant Gets a Home in a Valley in Paraguay," *New York Times*, Sept. 8, 1950.

97. See *Smith Act*, 76th Cong, 3d Sess., *U.S. Statutes at Large* 54 (1940): 670; Dennis v. United States, 341 U.S. 494 (1951); see also, e.g., Marjorie Garber and Rebecca Walkowitz, eds., *Secret Agents: The Rosenberg Case, McCarthyism and Fifties America* (New York: Routledge, 2013); Peter Steinberg, *The Great "Red Menace": United States Prosecution of American Communists, 1947–1952* (Westport, CT: Greenwood Press, 1984).

98. *Displaced Persons Act of 1948*, 80th Cong., 2nd Sess., *U.S. Statutes at Large* 62 (1948): 1009.

99. President Harry Truman, "Special Message to the Congress on Aid for Refugees and Displaced Persons," March 24, 1952, *The American Presidency Project*, http://www.presidency.ucsb.edu/ws/index.php?pid=14435&st=displaced+persons+act&st1#axzz1jTaZnYId (accessed Jan. 14, 2012).

100. *Mohriez*, 54 F. Supp. at 942.

101. Only the first letters of the last names of the immigrants were disclosed in BIA opinions.

102. In seventeenth century England, Tatars were frequently equated with the ancient Scythians, infamous for their barbarism and savagery, and Tatars were described as an extraordinarily barbarous, vile, and savage people, as reflected in Giles Fletcher the Elder's statement that they were "the most vile and barbarous Nation of all the World." Fletcher argued that the Russian Tatars were the lost ten tribes of Israel, who God had "cast . . . down from the highest Heaven, to the lowest Center of dishonour, even ad Tartaros" because of their idolatry in the ancient kingdom of Israel. See Richard Cogley. "'The Most Vile and Barbarous Nation of all the World': Giles Fletcher the Elder's *The Tartars Or, Ten Tribes* (ca. 1610)," *Renaissance Quarterly* 58 (2005): 783–84, 796–99, 807.

103. *S—*, 4 I. & N. Dec. at 104.

104. *S—*, 4 I. & N. Dec. at 105 and 105 n. 2 (citing the "Treatise of Ayaz Ishaki-Idelli, found in the record.").

105. Ibid., 106 n. 3.

106. Ibid., 107.

107. Ibid.

108. Cf. Susan Brewer, *Why America Fights: Patriotism and War Propaganda from the Philippines to Iraq* (New York: Oxford University Press, 2009), 47, 61, 85. During World War II, Frank Capra's film *The Nazis Strike* compared Adolf Hitler to the "barbarian hordes" led by Genghis Khan that arose "out of the wilds of Mongolia" to conquer most of the world in the thirteenth century. According to the film, Hitler viewed the area of Eastern Europe and Russia that coincided with the old empire of Genghis Khan as central to his plan of conquest. *The Nazis Strike*, DVD, directed by Frank Capra (New York: GoodTimes Home Video, 2000).

109. President Harry Truman, "Special Message to the Congress on Aid for Refugees and Displaced Persons," March 24, 1952, *The American Presidency Project*, http://www.presidency.ucsb.edu/ws/index.

php?pid=14435&st=displaced+persons+act&st1#axzz1jTaZnYId (accessed Jan. 14, 2012).

110. *S—*, 4 I. & N. Dec. at 104–05 and 105 n. 2.

111. *In re* R—, 4 I. & N. Dec. 275, 275–76 (B.I.A. 1951).

112. Ibid., 276.

113. The BIA lists among these other ethnic groups of Russia "Great Russians, Belorussians (White Russians), Ukrainians, Tartars, Ossetians, Nogaystys, Armenians, Georgians, Bashkirs, Kirgiz–Kazkas, and Dagestans, to mention a few." Ibid., 278 n. 9.

114. Ibid., 276.

115. Ibid., 286.

116. Ibid., 282.

117. Ibid., 284–85 (citing the *Dictionary of Races and Peoples, Encyclopedia Americana, Encyclopedia Britannica, New International Encyclopedia*, John Hammerton and Harry Barnes's *Illustrated World History*, Carlton Hays and Parker Moon's *Ancient and Medieval History*, Jacob Schapiro's *Modern and Contemporary European History*, and Louis Segal's *Concise History of Russia*).

118. *R—*, 4 I. & N. Dec. at 283.

119. *S—*, 4 I. & N. Dec. at 105 (emphasis added) and *R—*, 4 I. & N. Dec. at 284–85 (emphasis added in both).

120. Gordon, "The Racial Barrier to American Citizenship," 246.

121. Ibid., 246–51 254, 257.

122. See generally, e.g., Sean Brawley, *The White Peril: Foreign Relations and Asian Immigration to Australasia and North America 1919–78* (Sydney: University of New South Wales Press, 1995); David Dutton, *One of Us?: A Century of Australian Citizenship* (Sydney: University of New South Wales Press, 2002); Andrew Markus, *Fear and Hatred: Purifying Australia and California 1850–1901* (Sydney: Hale and Iremonger, 1979); Charles Price, *The Great White Walls Are Built: Restrictive Immigration to North America and Australasia 1836–1888* (Canberra: Australian National University Press, 1974); Patricia Roy, *A White Man's Province: British Columbia Politicians and Chinese and Japanese Immigrants, 1858–1914* (Vancouver: University of British Columbia Press, 1989); W. Peter Ward, *White Canada: Popular Attitudes and Public Policy Toward Orientals in British Columbia* (Montreal: McGill-Queen's University Press, 1978); Myra Willard, *History of the White Australia Policy to 1920* (London: Cass, 1967).

123. See Milton Konvitz, *The Alien and the Asiatic in American Law* (Ithaca: Cornell University Press, 1946), viii, 80–81.

124. Department of Justice, Immigration and Naturalization Service, "The Eligibility of Arabs to Naturalization," *Monthly Review* 1 (1943): 16.

125. *Immigration and Nationality Act of 1952*, 82nd Cong., 2nd Sess., *U.S. Statutes at Large* 66 (1952): 169.

126. See, e.g., *Judd Bill for Equality in Naturalization and Immigration*, 81st Cong., 1st Sess., *Congressional Record* 95 (1949), 1676–83; *Immigration and Nationality Act of 1952*, 82nd Cong., 2nd Sess., *U.S. Statutes at Large* 98, 4433–35.

127. *Judd Bill for Equality in Naturalization and Immigration*, 81st Cong., 1st Sess., *Congressional Record* 95 (1949), 1676.

128. Ibid., 1684.

129. Ibid., 1680.

130. *Immigration and Nationality Act of 1952*, 82nd Cong., 2nd Sess., *U.S. Statutes at Large.*

131. Carl Becker, *The Declaration of Independence: A Study in the History of Political Ideas* (New York: Vintage, 1922), 207.

132. Ibid., 205–206 (emphasis in original).

133. Thomas Jefferson, *Autobiography* (1821), in Thomas Jefferson, *Writings*, ed. Merrill Peterson (New York: Literary Classics of the U.S., 1984), 70–71.

134. Cf. William Smith, "The Rhetoric of the Declaration of Independence," *College English* 26 (1965): 309.

135. Scott v. Sandford, 60 U.S. 393, 403–07, 415–20 (1857).

136. Brief of Attorney General at 48 (citations omitted), *In re* Yamashita, No. 202 (Wash. Sup. Ct. 1902).

CONCLUSION

1. Simone Weil, "The *Iliad*, or the Poem of Force," *Chicago Review* 18 (1965): 6.

2. Ibid., 23–28.

3. Ibid.

4. Kenneth Burke, "The Rhetoric of Hitler's 'Battle,'" in *The Philosophy of Literary Form: Studies in Symbolic Action*, 3rd ed. (Berkeley: University of California Press, 1971), 192–97, 202–204, 209.

5. Ibid., 205–206, 219–20.

6. Ibid., 219.

7. Jeremy Engels, *Enemyship: Democracy and Counter-Revolution in the Early Republic* (East Lansing: Michigan State University Press, 2010), 215.

8. Kenneth Burke, *A Rhetoric of Motives*, Calif. ed. (Berkeley: University of California Press, 1969), 25.

9. Jeffrey Cohen, *Hybridity, Identity and Monstrosity in Medieval Britain: On Difficult Middles* (New York: Palgrave Macmillan, 2006), 12.

10. Matthew Frye Jacobson, *Whiteness of a Different Color: European Immigrants and the Alchemy of Race* (Cambridge: Harvard University Press, 1998), 203–22.

11. See Murray Edelman, *Constructing the Political Spectacle* (Chicago: University of Chicago Press, 1988), 81.

12. See *In re* Singh, 246 F. 496, 498–500 (E.D. Pa. 1917).

13. See Brief Submitted by the Appellant at 126–27, United States v. Balsara, No. 186 (2d Cir. 1909–1910).

14. See *In re* Rodriguez, 81 F. 337, 337, 349 (W.D. Tex. 1897); cf. *In re* M—, 2 I. & N. Dec. 196 (B.I.A. 1944).

15. See *Naturalization Act of 1918*, 65th Cong., 2nd Sess., *U.S. Statutes at Large* 40 (1918): 542; *Indian Citizenship Act of 1919*, 66th Cong., 1st Sess., *U.S. Statutes at Large* 41 (1919): 350; *Indian Citizenship Act of 1924*, 68th Cong., 2nd Sess., *U.S. Statutes at Large* 43 (1924): 253; *Nye-Lea Act*, 74th Cong., 1st Sess., *U.S. Statutes at Large* 49 (1935): 397; see also Kevin Brunyeel, "Challenging American Boundaries: Indigenous People and the 'Gift' of American Citizenship," *Studies in American Political Development* 18 (2004): 31 n. 5; Jeanette Wolfley, "Jim Crow, Indian Style: The Disenfranchisement of Native Americans," *American Indian Law Review* 16 (1991): 179–80.

16. See United States v. Thind, 261 U.S. 204 (1923); United States v. Pandit, No. G-111-T (S.D. Cal. Jan. 9, 1925); United States v. Pandit, 15 F.2d 285 (9th Cir. 1926), *cert. denied*, 273 U.S. 759 (1927).

17. See United States v. Cartozian, 6 F.2d 919 (D. Or. 1925).

18. See *Nationality Act of 1940*, 76th Cong., 3rd Sess. *U.S. Statutes at Large* 54 (1940): 1137.

19. See *Chinese Exclusion Repeal Act of 1943*, 78th Cong., 1st Sess., *U.S. Statutes at Large* 57 (1943): 600.

20. See *Second War Powers Act of 1942*, 77th Cong., 2nd Sess., *U.S. Statutes at Large* 56 (1942): 182.

21. See *Filipino and Indian Naturalization Act of 1946*, 79th Cong., 2nd Sess., *U.S. Statutes at Large* 60 (1946): 416; *In re* S—, 4 I. & N. Dec. 104 (B.I.A. 1950); *In re* R—, 4 I. & N. Dec. 275, 276, 280, 286 (B.I.A. 1951).

22. Åshlid Næss, *Prototypical Transitivity* (Amsterdam: John Benjamins, 2007), 30.

23. Ibid., 33, 36, 38, 42.

24. Ibid., 38.

25. Robert Ivie, "Images of Savagery in American Justifications for War," *Communication Monographs* 47 (1980): 279, 290–91.

26. Ibid., 283–87, 291.

27. Cf. Ioannis Evrigenis, *Fear of Enemies and Collective Action* (Cambridge: Cambridge University Press, 2008), 1–2, 5; see also Neal Wood, "Sallust's Theorem: A Comment on 'Fear' in Western Political Thought," *History of Political Thought* 16, no. 2 (1995): 174–89.

28. Derek Heater, *A Brief History of Citizenship* (New York: New York Univ. Press, 2004), 6–11.

29. Tyrtaeus of Sparta, "Courage," The Sparta Pages, http://uts.cc. utexas.edu/~sparta/topics/articles/academic/poetry.htm#tyrtaeus (accessed July 18, 2015).

30. Heater, *A Brief History of Citizenship*, 10.

31. See generally Charles Gordon, "The Racial Barrier to American Citizenship," *University of Pennsylvania Law Review* 93 (1945): 248; Michael LeMay and Elliott Barkan, eds., *U.S. Immigration and Naturalization Laws and Issues: A Documentary History* (Westport, CT: Greenwood, 1999), 116–18, 121–22.

32. Norman Trenholme, *The Right of Sanctuary in England: A Study in Institutional History* (Columbia: University of Missouri, 1903), 2–3.

33. See, e.g., ibid., 1–10.

34. Marilyn Baseler, *"Asylum for Mankind": America 1607–1800* (Ithaca: Cornell University Press, 1998), 2–7.

35. Thomas Paine, *Common Sense*, in *The Life and Major Writings of Thomas Paine*, ed. Philip Foner (New York: Citadel Press, 1945), 31.

36. Thomas Aleinkoff, David Martin, Hiroshi Motomura, and Maryellen Fullerton, *Immigration and Citizenship: Process and Policy*, 6th ed. (St. Paul: Thomson West, 2008), 828, 847–48.

37. Philip Schrag, *A Well-Founded Fear: The Congressional Battle to Save Political Asylum in America* (New York: Routledge, 2000), 28–29.

38. See Christopher Einolf, *The Mercy Factory: Refugees and the American Asylum System* (Chicago: Ivan R. Dee, 2001), 3–10; Schrag, *A Well-Founded Fear*, 28–29.

39. Hannah Arendt, *The Origins of Totalitarianism*, new ed. with additional prefaces (New York: Harcourt Brace, 1973), 280–81.

40. Chae Chan Ping v. United States, 130 U.S. 581, 595–96, 606–607 (1889).

41. Sumi Cho and Gil Gott, "The Racial Sovereign," in *Sovereignty, Emergency, Legality*, ed. Austin Sarat (Cambridge: Cambridge University Press, 2010), 189–91.

42. Ibid., 212–13.

43. Carl Schmitt, *Dictatorship: From the Origin of the Modern Concept of Sovereignty to Proletarian Class Struggle*, trans. Michael Hoelzl and Graham Ward (Cambridge: Polity Press, 2014), 13; Gopal Balakrishnan, *The Enemy: An Intellectual Portrait of Carl Schmitt* (New York: Verso, 2000), 45.

44. Schmitt, *Dictatorship*, 13; Giorgio Agamben, *States of Exception*, trans. Kevin Attell (Chicago: University of Chicago Press, 2005), 4.

45. Agamben, *States of Exception*, 4.

46. Ibid., 2.

47. Austin Sarat, "Introduction: Toward New Conceptions of the Relationship of Law and Sovereignty under Conditions of Emergency," in *Sovereignty, Emergency, Legality*, ed. Austin Sarat (Cambridge: Cambridge University Press, 2010), 212–13.

48. Achille Mbembe, "Necropolitics," trans. Libby Meintjes, *Public Culture* 15, no. 1 (2003): 18, 23–24.

49. See Margaret Kohn and Keally McBride, "Colonialism and the State of Exception," in *Political Theories of Decolonization: Postcolonialism and the Problem of Foundations*, ed. Margaret Kohn and Keally McBride (Oxford: Oxford University Press, 2011).

50. Cho and Gott, "The Racial Sovereign," 212–13.

51. Anthony Anghie, *Imperialism, Sovereignty, and the Making of International Law* (Cambridge: Cambridge University Press, 2004), 102.

52. Ibid., 101–102, 105.

53. Derrick Bell Jr., "*Brown v. Board of Education* and the Interest-Convergence Dilemma," *Harvard Law Review* 93 (1980): 523–24.

54. Evrigenis, *Fear of Enemies and Collective Action*, 5.

55. Bell, "*Brown v. Board of Education*," 523–24; cf. Mary Dudziak, "*Brown* as a Cold War Case," *Journal of American History* 91 (2004): 38.

56. Derrick Bell Jr., "The Role of Fortuity in Racial Policy-Making: Blacks as Fortuitous Beneficiaries of Racial Policies," in *The Derrick Bell Reader*, ed. Richard Delgado and Jean Stefanic (New York: New York University Press, 2005), 40–41.

57. See Philip Muehlenbeck, "Preface," in *Race, Ethnicity, and the Cold War*, ed. Philip Muehlenbeck, vii (Nashville: Vanderbilt University Press, 2012); see also, e.g., Carol Anderson, *Eyes Off the Prize: The United Nations and the African American Struggle for Human Rights, 1944–1955* (Cambridge: Cambridge University Press, 2003); Thomas Borstelmann, *The Cold War and the Color Line: American Race Relations in the Global Arena* (Cambridge: Harvard University Press, 2003); Mary Dudziak, *Cold War Civil Rights: Race and the Image of American Democracy* (Princeton: Princeton University Press, 2000); Gerald Horne, *Black and Red: W.E.B. DuBois and the African American Response to the Cold War* (Albany: State University of New York Press, 1986); Brenda Plummer, *Rising Wind: Black Americans and U.S. Foreign Affairs, 1935–1960* (Chapel Hill: University of North Carolina Press, 1996); Jonathan Rosenberg, *How Far the Promised Land? World Affairs and the American Civil Rights Movement from the First World War to Vietnam* (Princeton: Princeton University Press, 2006.

58. Dudziak, *Cold War Civil Rights*, 250; see also Dudziak, "*Brown* as a Cold War Case."

59. Dudziak, *Cold War Civil Rights*, 67–76, 221–26.

60. See Anderson, *Eyes Off the Prize*; Horne, *Black and Red*.

61. Dudziak, *Cold War Civil Rights*, 250.

62. Michael Krenn, "Token Diplomacy: The United States, Race, and the Cold War," in *Race, Ethnicity, and the Cold War*, 22; Dudziak, *Cold War Civil Rights*, 236.

63. Dudziak, *Cold War Civil Rights*, 252.

64. David Kertzer, *Ritual, Politics, and Power* (New Haven: Yale University Press, 1988), 67–69.

65. Cho and Gott, "The Racial Sovereign," 212–13.

66. See Debra Bassett, "Toward a Nonracial Sovereign," in *Sovereignty, Emergency, Legality*, ed. Austin Sarat (Cambridge: Cambridge University Press, 2010), 234–25.

67. Omi and Winant, *Racial Formation in the United States*, 82; cf. Howard Winant, *Racial Conditions: Politics, Theory, Comparisons* (Minneapolis: University of Minnesota Press, 1994), 112.

68. See Anghie, *Imperialism*, 101–102, 105; Margaret and Keally, "Colonialism and the State of Exception."

69. Cheryl Harris, "Whiteness as Property," *Harvard Law Review* 106 (1993): 1707–14; see also Elise Boddie, "Racial Territoriality," *UCLA Law Review* 58 (2010): 401, 406.

70. *Chae Chan Ping*, 130 U.S. at 595–96, 606–607.

71. Michael Omi and Howard Winant, "Racial Formation," in *Race Critical Theories: Text and Context*, ed. Philomena Essed and David Theo Goldberg (Oxford: Blackwell, 2002), 123.

72. Gerald Wetlaufer, "Rhetoric and Its Denial in Legal Discourse," *Virginia Law Review* 76 (1990): 1591.

73. Roberto Unger, "The Critical Legal Studies Movement," *Harvard Law Review* 96 (1983): 584; see also Peter Gabel and Paul Harris, "Building Power and Breaking Images: Critical Legal Theory and the Practice of Law," *New York University Review of Law and Social Change* 11 (1982): 376.

74. See Kimberlé Crenshaw, Neil Gotanda, Gary Peller, and Kendall Thomas, eds. *Critical Race Theory: The Key Writings That Formed the Movement* (New York: The New Press, 1995), xiii; Richard Delgado, "Liberal McCarthyism and the Origins of Critical Race Theory," *Iowa Law Review* 94 (2009): 1505–45.

75. Raymie McKerrow, "Critical Rhetoric: Theory and Praxis," *Communication Monographs* 56 (1989): 104.

76. James Boyd White, *Heracles' Bow: Essays on the Rhetoric and Poetics of the Law* (Madison: University of Wisconsin Press, 1985), 33.

BIBLIOGRAPHY

Adam, Thomas. *Germany and the Americas: Culture, Politics, and History.* Santa Barbara, CA: ABC-CLIO, 2005.

Agamben, Giorgio. *States of Exception.* Translated by Kevin Attell. Chicago: University of Chicago Press, 2005.

Aleinkoff, Thomas, David Martin, Hiroshi Motomura, and Maryellen Fullerton. *Immigration and Citizenship: Process and Policy*, 6th ed. St. Paul: Thomson West, 2008.

Ananikian, Mardiros. "Armenian Mythology." In *The Mythology of All Races*, Vol. 7, edited by Canon John Arnott MacCulloch, 1–19. Boston: Marshall Jones, 1925.

Ancheta, Angelo. *Scientific Evidence and Equal Protection of the Law.* New Brunswick: Rutgers University Press, 2006.

Anderson, Benedict. *Imagined Communities: Reflections on the Origin and Spread of Nationalism.* Rev. ed. New York: Verso, 2006.

Anderson, Carol. *Eyes Off the Prize: The United Nations and the African American Struggle for Human Rights, 1944–1955.* Cambridge: Cambridge University Press, 2003.

Anghie, Anthony. *Imperialism, Sovereignty, and the Making of International Law.* Cambridge: Cambridge University Press, 2004.

Angus, Henry. "The Legal Status in British Columbia of Residents of Oriental Race and Their Descendants." In *The Legal Status of Aliens in Pacific Countries: An International Survey of Law and Practice Concerning Immigration, Naturalization, and Deportation of Aliens and Their Legal Rights and Disabilities*, edited by Norman MacKenzie, 77–87. London: Oxford University Press, 1937.

Arendt, Hannah. *The Origins of Totalitarianism.* New ed. with additional prefaces. New York: Harcourt Brace, 1973.

———. *Essays in Understanding 1930–1954.* New York: Schocken Books, 1994.

Aristotle. *Rhetoric.* Translated by W. Rhys Roberts. In *The Rhetoric and Poetics of Aristotle.* New York: Modern Library, 1984.

Asiatic Exclusion League. *Proceedings of the Asiatic Exclusion League, 1907–1913.* New York: Arno Press, 1977.

Avakian, Arra. *The Armenians in America.* Minneapolis: Lerner, 1977.

Baker, Lee. "The Cult of Franz Boas and His 'Conspiracy' to Destroy the White Race." *Proceedings of the American Philosophical Society* 154, no. 1 (2010): 8–18.

Balakian, Peter. *The Burning Tigris: The Armenian Genocide and America's Response.* New York: HarperCollins, 2003.

―――. "Raphael Lemkin, Cultural Destruction, and the Armenian Genocide." *Holocaust and Genocide Studies* 27, no. 1 (2013): 57–89.

Balakrishnan, Gopal. *The Enemy: An Intellectual Portrait of Carl Schmitt.* New York: Verso, 2000.

Baseler, Marilyn. *"Asylum for Mankind": America 1607–1800.* Ithaca: Cornell University Press, 1998.

Bassett, Debra. "Toward a Nonracial Sovereign." In *Sovereignty, Emergency, Legality,* edited by Austin Sarat, 228–39. Cambridge: Cambridge University Press, 2010.

Becker, Carl. *The Declaration of Independence: A Study in the History of Political Ideas.* New York: Vintage, 1922.

Benét, William, ed. *The Reader's Encyclopedia: An Encyclopedia of World Literature and the Arts.* New York: T. Y. Crowell, 1948.

Bell, Derrick Jr. "*Brown v. Board of Education* and the Interest-Convergence Dilemma." *Harvard Law Review* 93 (1980): 518–33.

―――. "The Role of Fortuity in Racial Policy-Making: Blacks as Fortuitous Beneficiaries of Racial Policies." In *The Derrick Bell Reader,* edited by Richard Delgado and Jean Stefanic, 40–41. New York: New York University Press, 2005.

Bell, Robert, Matthew McGlone, and Marko Dragojevic. "Bacteria as Bullies: Effects of Linguistic Agency Assignment in Health Message." *Journal of Health Communication* 19, no. 3 (2013): 340–58.

―――. "Vicious Viruses and Vigilant Vaccines: Effects of Linguistic Agency Assignment in Health Policy Advocacy." *Journal of Health Communication* 19, no. 10 (2014): 1178–93.

Bey, Kesnin. *The Evil of the East; or, Truths about Turkey.* London: Vizetelley, 1888.

Bhabha, Homi. *The Location of Culture.* New York: Routledge, 1994.

Bickel, Alexander, and Henry Wellington. "Legislative Purpose and the Judicial Process: The *Lincoln Mills* Case." *Harvard Law Review* 71 (1957): 1–39.

Biesecker, Barbara. "Of Historicity, Rhetoric: The Archive as Scene of Invention." *Rhetoric & Public Affairs* 9, no. 1 (2006): 124–31.

Bloxham, Donald, and Fatma Göçek. "The Armenian Genocide." In *The Historiography of Genocide*, edited by Dan Stone, 344–72. New York: Palgrave Macmillan, 2008.

Blumenbach, Johann Friedrich. *The Anthropological Treatises of Johann Friedrich Blumenbach*. Translated and edited by Thomas Bendyshe. London: Longman, Green, Longman, Roberts & Green, 1865.

Boas, Franz. "Eugenics." *Scientific Monthly* 3, no. 5 (1916): 471–78.

Bobelian, Michael. *Children of Armenia: A Forgotten Genocide and the Century-Long Struggle for Justice*. New York: Simon and Schuster, 2009.

Boddie, Elise. "Racial Territoriality." *UCLA Law Review* 58 (2010): 401–63.

Borstelmann, Thomas. *The Cold War and the Color Line: American Race Relations in the Global Arena*. Cambridge: Harvard University Press, 2003.

Braman, Donald. "Of Race and Immutability." *UCLA Law Review* 46 (1999): 1375–1463.

Brawley, Sean. *The White Peril: Foreign Relations and Asian Immigration to Australasia and North America 1919–78*. Sydney: University of New South Wales Press, 1995.

Brewer, Susan. *Why America Fights: Patriotism and War Propaganda from the Philippines to Iraq*. New York: Oxford University Press, 2009.

Brown, Giles. "The Hindu Conspiracy, 1914–1917." *Pacific Historical Review* 17 (1948): 299–310.

Brunyeel, Kevin. "Challenging American Boundaries: Indigenous People and the 'Gift' of American Citizenship." *Studies in American Political Development* 18 (2004): 30–43.

Buck, Pearl. *American Unity and Asia*. New York: John Day, 1942.

Buell, Raymond. "Some Legal Aspects of the Japanese Question." *The American Journal of International Law* 17 (1923): 29–49.

Burke, Kenneth. *A Grammar of Motives*. Calif. ed. Berkeley: University of California Press, 1969.

———. *A Rhetoric of Motives*. Calif. ed. Berkeley: University of California Press, 1969.

———. "The Rhetoric of Hitler's 'Battle.'" In *The Philosophy of Literary Form: Studies in Symbolic Action*. 3rd ed. Berkeley: University of California Press, 1971.

———. *Dramatism and Development.* Barre, MA: Clark University Press, 1972.

Cairns, David. *Advocacy and the Making of the Adversarial Criminal Trial 1800–1865.* Oxford: Clarendon Press, 1998.

Canetti, Elias. *Crowds and Power.* New York: Viking 1962.

Carmichael, Cathie. *Genocide before the Holocaust.* New Haven: Yale University Press, 2009.

Chase, Ray, and S. G. Pandit. *An Examination of the Opinion of the Supreme Court of the United States Deciding Against the Eligibility of Hindus for Citizenship.* Los Angeles: S. G. Pandit, 1926.

Chin, Gabriel. "Twenty Years on Trial: Takuji Yamashita's Struggle for Citizenship." In *Race on Trial: Law and Justice in American History,* edited by Annette Gordon-Reed, 103–17. Oxford: Oxford University Press, 2002.

Cho, Sumi, and Gil Gott. "The Racial Sovereign." In *Sovereignty, Emergency, Legality,* edited by Austin Sarat, 182–227. Cambridge: Cambridge University Press, 2010.

Chvany, C. V. "Foregrounding, 'Transitivity,' Saliency in Sequential and Nonsequential Prose." *Essays in Poetics,* 10, no. 2 (1985): 1–26.

Clark, Tom, and Brian Galligan. "'Aboriginal Native' and the Institutional Construction of the Australian Citizen 1901–48." *Australian Historical Studies* 26 (1995): 523–43.

Clarke, John. *Oriental Enlightenment: The Encounter between Asian and Western Thought.* London: Routledge, 1997.

Code, Lorraine. *Rhetorical Spaces: Essays on Gendered Locations.* New York: Routledge, 1995.

Cogley, Richard. "'The Most Vile and Barbarous Nation of all the World': Giles Fletcher the Elder's *The Tartars Or, Ten Tribes* (ca. 1610)." *Renaissance Quarterly* 58 (2005): 796–99.

Cohen, Jeffrey. *Hybridity, Identity, and Monstrosity in Medieval Britain: On Difficult Middles.* New York: Palgrave Macmillan, 2006.

Condit, Celeste. "The Functions of Epideictic: The Boston Massacre Orations as Exemplar." *Communication Quarterly* 33 (1985): 290–91.

Cottrell, Catherine. "Different Emotional Reactions to Different Groups: A Sociofunctional Threat-Based Approach to 'Prejudice.'" *Journal of Personality and Social Psychology* 88 (2005): 770–89.

Cover, Robert. "*Nomos* and Narrative." In *Narrative, Violence, and the Law: The Essays of Robert Cover*, edited by Martha Minow, Michael Ryan, and Austin Sarat. Ann Arbor: University of Michigan Press, 1995.

Craver, Earlene. "On the Boundary of White: The *Cartozian* Naturalization Case and the Armenians, 1923–1925." *Journal of American Ethnic History* 28 (2009): 30–56.

Crenshaw, Kimberlé, Neil Gotanda, Gary Peller, and Kendall Thomas, eds. *Critical Race Theory: The Key Writings That Formed the Movement.* New York: The New Press, 1995.

Dadrian, Vahakn. "The Naim-Andonian Documents on the World War I Destruction of Ottoman Armenians: The Anatomy of a Genocide." *International Journal of Middle East Studies* 18 (1986): 311–60.

———. "The Turkish Military Tribunal's Prosecution of the Authors of the Armenian Genocide: Four Major Court-Martial Series." *Holocaust and Genocide Studies* 11 (1997): 28–59.

———. "The Armenian Genocide: An Interpretation." In *America and the Armenian Genocide of 1915*, edited by Jay Winter, 52–100. Cambridge: Cambridge University Press, 2003.

Dahl, Robert. "Decision-Making in a Democracy: The Supreme Court as a National Policy-Maker." *Journal of Public Law* 6 (1957): 279–95.

Daniels, Roger, and Harry Kitano. *American Racism: Exploration of the Nature of Prejudice.* Englewood Cliffs, NJ: Prentice-Hall, 1970.

Darian-Smith, Eve. "Postcolonialism: A Brief Introduction." *Social and Legal Studies* 5 (1996): 291–99.

Das, Mary. "True Status of Hindus Regarding American Citizenship." *Modern Review* 41 (1927): 461–65.

Das, Taraknath. "India and the League of Nations." *Modern Review* 35 (1924): 163–67.

———. "What Is at the Back of Anti-Asianism of the Anglo-Saxon World?" *Modern Review* 35 (1924): 262–68.

———. "Stateless Persons in the U.S.A." *Calcutta Review* 16 (1925): 40–46.

———. "American Naturalization Law Is Against the Chinese, Japanese and Hindustanees." *Modern Review* 39 (1926): 349–50.

———. *Foreign Policy in the Far East.* New York: Longmans, Green, 1936.

———. "People of India and U.S. Citizenship." *India Today* (1941): 3–4.

Davis, Leslie. *The Slaughterhouse Province: An American Diplomat's Report on the Armenian Genocide, 1915–1917.* New Rochelle, NY: Aristide D. Caratzas, 1989.

Delgado, Richard. "Liberal McCarthyism and the Origins of Critical Race Theory." *Iowa Law Review* 94 (2009): 1505–45.

———, and Jean Stefanic, eds. *Critical Race Theory: The Cutting Edge.* Philadelphia: Temple University Press, 2000.

Deol, Gurdev. *The Role of the Ghadar Party in the National Movement.* Delhi: Sterling, 1969.

Dignan, Don. "The Hindu Conspiracy in Anglo-American Relations during World War I." *Pacific Historical Review* 40 (1971): 57–76.

Doniger, Wendy. *The Hindus: An Alternative History.* New York: Penguin, 2009.

Dooner, Pierton. *Last Days of the Republic.* San Francisco: Alta, 1880.

Douglas, J. Allen. "The 'Priceless Possession' of Citizenship: Race, Nation and Naturalization in American Law, 1880–1930." *Duquesne Law Review* 43 (2005): 416–17.

Dower, John. *War Without Mercy: Race and Power in the Pacific War.* New York: Pantheon, 1986.

Dubois, Abbé. *Letters on the State of Christianity in India; in Which the Conversion of the Hindoos Is Considered as Impracticable.* 1823. Reprint, New Delhi: Asian Educational Services, 1995.

Dudziak, Mary. *Cold War Civil Rights: Race and the Image of American Democracy.* Princeton: Princeton University Press, 2000.

———. "*Brown* as a Cold War Case." *Journal of American History* 91 (2004): 32–42.

Dutton, David. *One of Us?: A Century of Australian Citizenship.* Sydney: University of New South Wales Press, 2002.

Edelman, Murray. *Constructing the Political Spectacle.* Chicago: University of Chicago Press, 1988.

Einolf, Christopher. *The Mercy Factory: Refugees and the American Asylum System.* Chicago: Ivan R. Dee, 2001.

Eisenhart, Christopher. "Reporting Waco: The Constitutive Work of Bureaucratic Style." In *Rhetoric in Detail: Discourse Analyses of Rhetorical Talk and Text,* edited by Barbara Johnstone and Christopher Eisenhart, 57–79. Philadelphia: John Benjamins, 2008.

Elshtain, Jean. "Sovereignty, Identity, Sacrifice." In *Reimagining the Nation,* edited by Marjorie Ringrose and Adam Lerner, 159–75. Buckingham, UK: Open University Press, 1993.

Endlich, Gustav. *A Commentary on the Interpretation of Statutes: Founded on the Treatise of Sir Peter Benson Maxwell.* Jersey City: Frederick D. Linn, 1888.

Engels, Jeremy. *Enemyship: Democracy and Counter-Revolution in the Early Republic.* East Lansing: Michigan State University Press, 2010.

Evrigenis, Ioannis. *Fear of Enemies and Collective Action.* Cambridge: Cambridge University Press, 2008.

Fenech, Louis. "Martyrdom and the Sikh Tradition." *Journal of the American Oriental Society* 117, no. 4 (1997): 623–42.

Ferguson, Robert. "Becoming American: High Treason and Low Invective in the Republic of Laws." In *The Rhetoric of Law,* edited by Austin Sarat and Thomas Kearns, 103–34. Ann Arbor: University of Michigan Press 1994.

Fiske, Susan. "What We Know Now About Bias and Intergroup Conflict, the Problem of the Century." *Current Directions in Psychological Science* 2 (2002): 123–28.

Foner, Philip. *History of the Labor Movement in the United States: Postwar Struggles, 1918–1920.* New York: International Publishers, 1987.

Ford, Nancy. *Americans All! Foreign-Born Soldiers in World War I.* College Station: Texas A & M University Press, 2001.

Frank, Jerome. "What Courts Do in Fact, Part One." *Illinois Law Review* 26 (1932): 645–66.

———. "What Courts Do in Fact, Part Two." *Illinois Law Review* 26 (1932): 761–84.

Fuller, Lon. *The Morality of Law.* Revised ed. New Haven: Yale University Press, 1969.

Gabel, Peter, and Paul Harris. "Building Power and Breaking Images: Critical Legal Theory and the Practice of Law." *New York University Review of Law and Social Change* 11 (1982): 369.

Garber, Marjorie, and Rebecca Walkowitz, eds. *Secret Agents: The Rosenberg Case, McCarthyism, and Fifties America.* New York: Routledge, 2013.

Garner, Bryan. *A Dictionary of Modern Legal Usage.* 2nd ed. Oxford: Oxford University Press, 1995.

Garver, Eugene, and Philip Keith, eds. "Focus on James Boyd White." *Rhetoric Society Quarterly* 21, no. 3 (1991).

Garza, Amanda de la. *Doctorji: The Life, Teachings, and Legacy of Dr. Bhagat Singh Thind.* Malibu, CA: David Singh Thind, 2010.

Gerstle, Gary. *American Crucible: Race and Nation in the Twentieth Century.* Princeton: Princeton University Press, 2001.

Gilliam, Edward. "The African Problem," *North American Review* 139 (1884): 417–30.

Giuliani, Allessandro. "The Influence of Rhetoric on the Law of Evidence and Pleading." *The Juridical Review*, new ser., 7 (1962): 216–51.

Gordon, Charles. "The Racial Barrier to American Citizenship." *University of Pennsylvania Law Review* 93 (1945): 237–58.

Gossett, Thomas. *Race: The History of an Idea in America.* New ed. Oxford: Oxford University Press, 1997.

Gould, Harold. *Sikhs, Swamis, Students, and Spies: The India Lobby in the United States, 1900–1946.* Thousand Oaks, CA: SAGE, 2006.

Grant, Charles. *Observations on the State of Society Among the Asiatic Subjects of Great-Britain, Particularly with Respect to Morals; and on the Means of Improving It.* East-India House, 1797.

Grant, Madison. *The Passing of the Great Race; or, the Racial Basis of European History.* 1916. Reprint, London: Forgotten Books, 2012.

Griffis, William. "Are the Japanese Mongolian?" *North American Review* 197 (1913): 721–60.

Gross, Ariela. *What Blood Won't Tell: A History of Race on Trial in America.* Cambridge: Harvard University Press, 2008.

Gualtieri, Sarah. "Becoming 'White': Race, Religion and the Foundations of Syrian/Lebanese Ethnicity in the United States." *Journal of American Ethnic History* 20, no. 4 (2001): 29–58.

Gustainis, J. Justin. "Crime as Rhetoric: The Trial of the Catonsville Nine." In *Popular Trials: Rhetoric, Mass Media, and the Law*, edited by Robert Hariman, 164–78. Tuscaloosa: University of Alabama Press, 1990.

Gutiérrez-Jones, Carl. *Critical Race Narratives: A Study of Race, Rhetoric, and Injury.* New York: New York University Press, 2001.

Halliday, Michael. *Halliday's Introduction to Functional Grammar*, 4th ed., revised by Christian Matthiessen. London: Routledge, 2013.

Hanifin, Patrick. "To Dwell on the Earth in Unity: *Rice, Arakaki*, and the Growth of Citizenship and Voting Rights in Hawai'i." *Hawaii Bar Journal* 5 (2002): 15–44.

Harris, Cheryl. "Whiteness as Property." *Harvard Law Review* 106 (1993): 1707–91.

Hart, Henry Jr. "Foreward: The Time Chart of the Justices." *Harvard Law Review* 73 (1959): 84–127.

Hasian, Marouf Jr. *Legal Memories and Amnesias in America's Rhetorical Culture.* Boulder: Westview, 2000.

Hassan, Salah. "Arabs, Race and the Post–September 11 National Security State." *Middle East Report* 224 (2002): 16–21.

Heater, Derek. *A Brief History of Citizenship*. New York: New York University Press, 2004.

Hedges, Chris. *War Is a Force That Gives Us Meaning*. New York: Anchor, 2002.

Herzig, Rebecca. "In the Name of Science: Suffering, Sacrifice, and the Formation of American Roentgenology." *American Quarterly* 53, no. 4 (2001): 563–89.

Hess, Gary. "The Forgotten Asian Americans: The East Indian Community in the United States." In *The History and Immigration of Asian Americans*, edited by Franklin Ng, 106–26. New York: Garland, 1998.

———. "The 'Hindu' in America: Immigration and Naturalization Policies and India, 1917–1946." *Pacific Historical Review* 38 (1969): 59–79.

Hoglund, Arthur. *Finnish Immigrants in America 1880–1920*. Madison: University of Wisconsin Press, 1960.

Hohmann, Hanns. "The Dynamics of Stasis: Classical Rhetorical Theory and Modern Legal Argumentation." *The American Journal of Jurisprudence* 34 (1989): 171–97.

Hoover, Herbert. *The Memoirs of Herbert Hoover: Years of Adventure 1874–1920*. New York: MacMillan, 1951.

Hoover, Karl. "The Hindu Conspiracy in California, 1913–1918." *German Studies Review* 8 (1985): 258–59.

Hopper, Paul, and Sandra Thompson. "Transitivity in Grammar and Discourse." *Language* 56, no. 2 (1980): 251–99.

Horne, Gerald. *Black and Red: W. E. B. DuBois and the African American Response to the Cold War*. Albany: State University of New York Press, 1986.

———. "Race from Power: U.S. Foreign Policy and the General Crisis of White Supremacy." In *Window on Freedom: Race, Civil Rights, and Foreign Affairs 1945–1988*, edited by Brenda Gayle Plummer, 45–66. Chapel Hill: University of North Carolina Press, 2003.

Hovannisian, Richard. "Confronting the Armenian Genocide." In *Pioneers of Genocide Studies,* edited by Samuel Totten and Steven Leonard Jacobs, 27–46. New Brunswick, NJ: Transaction, 2002.

Huttenback, Robert. *Racism and Empire: White Settlers and Colored Immigrants in the British Self-Governing Colonies 1830–1910*. Ithaca: Cornell University Press, 1976.

Isaacs, Harold. *Scratches on Our Minds: American Views of China and India.* 1958. Reprint, Armonk, NY: M. E. Sharpe, 1980.

Ivie, Robert. "Images of Savagery in American Justifications for War." *Communication Monographs* 47 (1980): 279–94.

Jackson, Jay. "Realistic Group Conflict Theory: A Review and Evaluation of the Theoretical and Empirical Literature." *Psychological Record* 43 (1993): 395–415.

Jacobs, James, and Leslie Hayes. "Aliens in the U.S. Armed Forces: A Historico-Legal Analysis." *Armed Forces and Society* 7, no. 2 (1981): 187–208.

Jacobson, Matthew Frye. *Whiteness of a Different Color: European Immigrants and the Alchemy of Race.* Cambridge: Harvard University Press, 1998.

Japtok, Martin. "'The Gospel of Whiteness': Whiteness in African American Literature." *American Studies* 49 (2004): 483–98.

Jasinski, James. *Sourcebook on Rhetoric: Key Concepts in Contemporary Rhetorical Studies.* Thousand Oaks, CA: SAGE, 2001.

Jefferson, Thomas. *Autobiography* (1821). In Thomas Jefferson, *Writings*, edited by Merrill Peterson. New York: Literary Classics of the U.S., 1984.

Jenks, Kevin. "Before the 'Yellow Peril.'" *Social Contract* 6, no. 4 (1996).

Jones, Adam. *Genocide: A Comprehensive Introduction.* 2nd ed. New York: Routledge, 2011.

Kaiwar, Vasant. "The Aryan Model of History and the Oriental Renaissance." In *Antinomies of Modernity: Essays on Race, Orient, Nation*, edited by Vasant Kaiwar and Sucheta Mazumdar, 13–61. Durham: Duke University Press, 2003.

Kang, Laura. *Compositional Subjects: Enfiguring Asian/American Women.* Durham: Duke University Press, 2002.

Keen, Sam. *Faces of the Enemy: Reflections of the Hostile Imagination.* San Francisco: Harper, 1986.

Keevak, Michael. *Becoming Yellow: A Short History of Racial Thinking.* Princeton: Princeton University Press, 2011.

Kertzer, David. *Ritual, Politics, and Power.* New Haven: Yale University Press, 1988.

King, Desmond. *Making Americans: Immigration, Race, and the Origins of the Diverse Democracy.* Cambridge: Harvard University Press, 2000.

Kipling, Rudyard. "The White Man's Burden." *McClure's Magazine* 12, no. 4 (February 1899): 4.

Klinger, Geoffrey. Review of *Rhetorical Knowledge in Legal Practice and Critical Legal Theory*, by Francis Mootz III. *Argumentation and Advocacy* 44 (2008): 160–64.

Kohn, Margaret, and Keally McBride. "Colonialism and the State of Exception." In *Political Theories of Decolonization: Postcolonialism and the Problem of Foundations*, by Margaret Kohn and Keally McBride, 77–97. Oxford: Oxford University Press, 2011.

Koestler, Arthur. *Darkness at Noon*. Translated by Daphne Hardy. New York: Scribners, 1941.

Konvitz, Milton. *The Alien and the Asiatic in American Law*. Ithaca: Cornell University Press, 1946.

Koolakian, Robert. *Struggle for Justice: A Story of the American Committee for the Independence of Armenia, 1915–1920*. Dearborn: Armenian Research Center, University of Michigan–Dearborn, 2008.

Krenn, Michael. "Token Diplomacy: The United States, Race, and the Cold War." In *Race, Ethnicity, and the Cold War*, edited by Philip Muehlenbeck, 3–32. Nashville: Vanderbilt University Press, 2012.

Kuo, Joyce. "Excluded, Segregated, and Forgotten: A Historical View of the Discrimination of Chinese Americans in Public Schools." *Asian American Law Journal* 5 (1998): 181–212.

Lacy, Michael, and Kent Ono, eds. *Critical Rhetorics of Race*. New York: New York University Press, 2011.

Lamb, Harold. *Suleiman the Magnificent: Sultan of the East*. Garden City, NY: Doubleday, 1951.

Lapp, Randolph. *Blacks in Gold Rush California*. New Haven: Yale University Press, 1977.

Laski, Harold. *Studies in the Problem of Sovereignty*. New Haven: Yale University Press, 1917.

Lee, Herbert. "Armenia as the Measure of Our Civilization." *The New Armenia* 8 (1921): 67–69.

Lefebvre, Henri. *The Production of Space*. Translated by Donald Nicholson-Smith. 1991. Reprint, Oxford: Blackwell, 1995.

LeMay, Michael, and Elliott Barkan, eds. *U.S. Immigration and Naturalization Laws and Issues: A Documentary History*. Westport, CT: Greenwood, 1999.

Lerner, Adam. "The Nineteenth-Century Monument and the Embodiment of National Time." In *Reimagining the Nation*, edited by Marjorie

Ringrose and Adam Lerner, 176–96. Buckingham, UK: Open University Press, 1993.

LeShan, Lawrence. *The Psychology of War: Comprehending Its Mystique and Its Madness*. Chicago: The Noble Press, 1992.

Levinson, Sanford. "The Rhetoric of the Judicial Opinion." In *Law's Stories: Narrative and Rhetoric in the Law*, edited by Peter Brooks and Paul Gewirtz, 187–205. New Haven: Yale University Press, 1996.

Lloyd, Anthony. *My War Gone By, I Miss It So*. New York: Atlantic Monthly, 1999.

López, Ian Haney. *White by Law: The Legal Construction of Race*. New York: New York University Press, 1996.

Lorelle. "The Battle of the Wabash: A Letter from the Invisible Police." *Californian* 2, no. 10 (1880): 364–76.

Lorenzen, David. "Imperialism and the Historiography of Ancient India." In *India: History and Thought, Essays in Honor of A. L. Basham*, edited by S. N. Mukherjee, 84–102. Calcutta: Subarnarekha, 1982.

Lothyan, Phillip. "A Question of Citizenship." *Prologue: Quarterly of the National Archives* 21 (1989): 267–73.

Lucaites, John. "Between Rhetoric and 'The Law': Power, Legitimacy, and Social Change." Review of *A Guide to Critical Legal Studies*, by Mark Kelman, *Interpreting Law and Literature: A Hermeneutic Reader*, edited by Sanford Levinson and Steven Mailloux, and *The Critical Legal Studies Movement*, by Roberto Unger. *Quarterly Journal of Speech* 76 (1990): 435–49.

Lyman, Stanford. "The Race Question and Liberalism: Casuistries in American Constitutional Law." *International Journal of Politics, Culture, and Society* 5 (1991): 183–247.

Lyons, Scott. "Rhetorical Sovereignty: What Do American Indians Want from Writing?" *CCC* 51, no. 3 (2000): 447–68.

MacMillan, Margaret. *Paris 1919: Six Months That Changed the World*. New York: Random House, 2002.

Malcolm, M. Vartan. *The Armenians in America*. Boston: The Pilgrim Press, 1919.

Malcolm, Roy. "American Citizenship and the Japanese." *Annals of the American Academy of Political and Social Science* 93 (1921): 77–81.

Markus, Andrew. *Australian Race Relations 1788–1993*. St. Leonards, Aus.: Allen and Unwin, 1994.

———. *Fear and Hatred: Purifying Australia and California 1850–1901.* Sydney: Hale and Iremonger, 1979.

Mayo, Jessica. "Court-Mandated Story Time: The Victim Narrative in U.S. Asylum Law." *Washington University Law Review* 89 (2012): 1485–1522.

Mazumdar, Sucheta. "Racist Responses to Racism: The Aryan Myth and South Asians in the United States." *South Asia Bulletin* 9 (1989): 47–55.

Mbembe, Achille. "Necropolitics." Translated by Libby Meintjes. *Public Culture* 15, no. 1 (2003): 11–4.

McDorman, Todd. Review of *Troubling Confessions: Speaking Guilt in Law and Literature,* by Peter Brooks. *Argumentation and Advocacy* 38 (2002): 189–92.

McGlone, Matthew, Robert Bell, Sarah Zaitchik, and Joseph McGlynn III. "Don't Let the Flu Catch You: Agency Assignment in Printed Educational Materials about the H1N1 Influenza Virus." *Journal of Health Communication* 18, no. 6 (2012): 740–56.

McGovney, Dudley. "Race Discrimination in Naturalization." *Iowa Law Bulletin* 8 (1923): 129–61.

———. "Naturalization of the Mixed-Blood—A Dictum." *California Law Review* 22 (1934): 377–91.

McKerrow, Raymie. "Critical Rhetoric: Theory and Praxis." *Communication Monographs* 56 (1989): 91–111.

Menchaca, Martha. *Naturalizing Mexican Immigrants: A Texas History.* Austin: University of Texas Press, 2011.

Molina, Natalia. "'In a Race All Their Own': The Quest to Make Mexicans Ineligible for U.S. Citizenship." *Pacific Historical Review* 79 (2010): 167–201.

Morgenthau, Henry. *Ambassador Morgenthau's Story.* Garden City, NY: Doubleday, 1918.

Morris, Charles. "Archival Queer." *Rhetoric & Public Affairs* 9, no. 1 (2006): 145–51.

———. "The Archival Turn in Rhetorical Studies; Or, the Archive's Rhetorical (Re)turn." *Rhetoric & Public Affairs* 9, no. 1 (2006): 1113–15.

Mountford, Roxanne. "On Gender and Rhetorical Space." *Rhetoric Society Quarterly* 31, no. 1 (2001): 41–71.

Muehlenbeck, Philip. "Preface." In *Race, Ethnicity, and the Cold War,* edited by Philip Muehlenbeck, vii–viii. Nashville: Vanderbilt University Press, 2012.

Murphy, Gretchen. "How the Irish Became Japanese: Winnifred Eaton's Racial Reconstructions in a Transnational Context." *American Literature* 79 (2007): 29–56.

Muzumdar, Haridas. *America's Contributions to India's Freedom.* Allahabad: Central Book Depot, 1962.

Næss, Åshlid. *Prototypical Transitivity.* Amsterdam: John Benjamins, 2007.

Naidis, Mark. "Propaganda of the *Gadar* Party." *Pacific Historical Review* 20 (1951): 251–60.

Nakayama, Thomas, and Robert Krizek. "Whiteness: A Strategic Rhetoric." *Quarterly Journal of Speech* 81 (1995): 291–309.

National Reform Association. *The World's Moral Problems: Addresses at the Third World's Christian Citizenship Conference.* Pittsburgh: Murdoch-Kerr Press, 1920.

Ngai, Mae. *Impossible Subjects: Illegal Aliens and the Making of Modern America.* Princeton: Princeton University Press, 2004.

Nowlan, Philip. *Armageddon 2419 A.D.* 1928. Reprint, Project Gutenberg, 2010. http://www.gutenberg.org/files/32530/32530-h/32530-h.htm.

———. *The Airlords of Han.* 1929. Reprint, Project Gutenberg, 2010. http://www.gutenberg.org/files/25438/25438-h/25438-h.htm.

Nugent, Walter. *Habits of Empire: A History of American Expansionism.* 2008. Reprint, New York: Vintage, 2009.

Okoomian, Janice. "Becoming White: Contested History, Armenian American Women, and Racialized Bodies." *MELUS* 27 (2002): 213–37.

Omi, Michael, and Howard Winant. *Racial Formation in the United States from the 1960s to the 1980s.* 2nd ed. New York: Routledge, 1994.

———. "Racial Formation." In *Race Critical Theories: Text and Context,* edited by Philomena Essed and David Theo Goldberg, 123–45. Oxford: Blackwell, 2002.

O'Rourke, Sean. "The Rhetoric of Law." Review of *Metaphor and Reason in Judicial Opinions,* by Haig Bosmajian, *Political Literacy: Rhetoric, Ideology, and the Possibility of Justice,* by Frederic Gale, and *The Rhetoric of Law,* edited by Austin Sarat and Thomas Kearns. *Rhetoric Review* 14 (1995): 213–20.

———. "The Rhetoric of Legal Scholarship." Review of *The Law of the Other: The Mixed Jury and Changing Conceptions of Citizenship, Law and Knowledge,* by Marianne Constable, and *Reinterpreting Property,* by Margaret Radin. *Rhetoric Society Quarterly* 26 (1996): 119–23.

Paine, Thomas. *Common Sense.* In *The Life and Major Writings of Thomas Paine,* edited by Philip Foner. New York: Citadel Press, 1945.

Park, John. *Elusive Citizenship: Immigration, Asian Americans, and the Paradox of Civil Rights.* New York: New York University Press, 2004.

Parker, Kunal. "Citizenship and Immigration Law, 1800–1924." In *The Cambridge History of Law in America,* edited by Michael Grossberg and Christopher Tomlins, 194–95. Cambridge: Cambridge University Press, 2008.

Patterson, Orlando. *Freedom, Vol. I: Freedom in the Making of Western Culture.* New York: Basic Books, 1991.

Patton, Laurie. "Cosmic Men and Fluid Exchanges: Myths of *Ārya, Varṇa,* and *Jāti* in the Hindu Tradition." In *Religion and the Creation of Race and Ethnicity: An Introduction,* edited by Craig Prentiss, 181–96. New York: New York University Press, 2003.

Perelman, Chaïm, and Lucie Olbrechts-Tyteca. *The New Rhetoric: A Treatise on Argumentation.* Translated by John Wilkinson and Purcell Weaver. Notre Dame: University of Notre Dame Press, 1969.

Petersen, William, Michael Novak, and Philip Gleason. *Concepts of Ethnicity.* Cambridge: Harvard University Press, 1980.

Plummer, Brenda. *Rising Wind: Black Americans and U.S. Foreign Affairs, 1935–1960.* Chapel Hill: University of North Carolina Press, 1996.

Predergast, Catherine. "Race: The Absent Presence in Composition Studies." *CCC* 50, no. 1 (1998): 36–53.

———. "Review of *Brown v. Board of Education: A Civil Rights Milestone and Its Troubled Legacy,*" by James Patterson. *Rhetoric Review* 53 (2001): 170–73.

Price, Charles. *The Great White Walls Are Built: Restrictive Immigration to North America and Australasia 1836–1888.* Canberra: Australian National University Press, 1974.

Puri, Harish. *Ghadar Movement: Ideology, Organisation & Strategy.* Amritsar: Guru Nanak Dev University, 1983.

Queen, Edward, II, Stephen Prothero, and Gardiner Shattuck Jr. *Encyclopedia of American Religious History.* 3rd ed. 2 vols. New York: Facts on File, 2009.

Reed, Elizabeth. *Hinduism in Europe and America.* New York: G. P. Putnam's Sons, 1914.

Renan, Ernest. "What Is a Nation?" In *Nation and Narration,* edited by Homi Bhabha, 8–22. New York: Routledge: 1990.

Riddle, Donald. *The Martyrs: A Study in Social Control.* Chicago: University of Chicago Press, 1931.

Riggs, Fred. *Pressures on Congress: A Study of the Repeal of Chinese Exclusion.* New York: King's Crown, 1950.

Ritivoi, Andreea. "Talking the (Political) Talk: Cold War Refugees and Their Political Legitimation through Style." In *Rhetoric in Detail: Discourse Analyses of Rhetorical Talk and Text,* edited by Barbara Johnstone and Christopher Eisenhart, 33–56. Philadelphia: John Benjamins, 2008.

Roberts-Miller, Patricia. "John Quincy Adams's *Amistad* Argument: The Problem of Outrage; Or, the Constrains of Decorum." *Rhetoric Society Quarterly* 32, no. 2 (2002): 5–25.

Roediger, David. *Working toward Whiteness: How America's Immigrants Became White: The Strange Journey from Ellis Island to the Suburbs.* New York: Basic Books, 2005.

Rosenberg, Jonathan. *How Far the Promised Land? World Affairs and the American Civil Rights Movement from the First World War to Vietnam.* Princeton: Princeton University Press, 2006.

Rowlands, Michael. "Memory, Sacrifice and the Nation." *New Formations* 30, no. 4 (1996): 8–17.

Roy, Patricia. *A White Man's Province: British Columbia Politicians and Chinese and Japanese Immigrants, 1858–1914.* Vancouver: University of British Columbia Press, 1989.

Rundquist, Paul. "A Uniform Rule: The Congress and the Courts in American Naturalization, 1865–1952." PhD diss., University of Chicago, 1975.

Said, Edward. *Orientalism.* 25th Anniversary ed. New York: Vintage, 1994.

Salyer, Lucy. "Baptism by Fire: Race, Military Service, and U.S. Citizenship Policy, 1918–1935." *Journal of American History* 91 (2004): 847–76.

Sarat, Austin. "Introduction: Toward New Conceptions of the Relationship of Law and Sovereignty under Conditions of Emergency." In *Sovereignty, Emergency, Legality,* edited by Austin Sarat, 1–15. Cambridge: Cambridge University Press, 2010.

Sareen, Tilak, ed. *Selected Documents on the Ghadr Party.* New Delhi: Mounto, 1994.

Schmitt, Carl. *Dictatorship: From the Origin of the Modern Concept of Sovereignty to Proletarian Class Struggle.* Translated by Michael Hoelzl and Graham Ward. Cambridge: Polity Press, 2014.

Schoeck, Richard. "Rhetoric and Law in Sixteenth-Century England." *Studies in Philology* 50 (1953): 110–27.

Schrag, Philip. *A Well-Founded Fear: The Congressional Battle to Save Political Asylum in America*. New York: Routledge, 2000.

Seed, David. "Constructing America's Enemies: The Invasions of the USA." *The Yearbook of English Studies* 37, no. 2 (2007): 64–84.

Service, Robert. *Lenin: A Political Life*, Vol. 1: *The Strengths of Contradiction*. London: Macmillan, 1985.

Shah, Nyan. *Stranger Intimacy: Contesting Race, Sexuality, and the Law in the North American West*. Berkeley: University of California Press, 2011.

Shakespeare, William. *Hamlet*. In *The Oxford Shakespeare: The Complete Works*. 2nd ed. Edited by John Jowett, William Montgomery, Gary Taylor, and Stanley Wells. Oxford: Clarendon Press, 2005.

———. *Richard II*. In *The Oxford Shakespeare: The Complete Works*. 2nd ed. Edited by John Jowett, William Montgomery, Gary Taylor, and Stanley Wells. Oxford: Clarendon, 2005.

Shapiro, Barbara. "Classical Rhetoric and the English Law of Evidence." In *Rhetoric and Law in Early Modern Europe*, edited by Victoria Kahn and Lorna Hutson, 54–72. New Haven: Yale University Press, 2001.

Shaw, Stanford, and Ezel Shaw. *History of the Ottoman Empire and Modern Turkey*. 2 vols. New York: Cambridge University Press, 1976–77.

Shepardson, Nikki. *Burning Zeal: The Rhetoric of Martyrdom and the Protestant Community in Reformation France, 1520–1570*. Bethlehem, PA: Lehigh University Press, 2007.

Sherif, Muzafer, and Carolyn Sherif. "Research on Intergroup Relations." In *The Social Psychology of Intergroup Relations*, edited by William Austin and Stephen Worchel, 7–32. Monterey, CA: Brooks/Cole, 1979.

Sherif, Muzafer, O. J. Harvey, B. Jack White, William Hood, and Carolyn Sherif. *The Robbers Cave Experiment: Intergroup Conflict and Cooperation*. 1961. Reprint, Middletown, CT: Wesleyan University Press, 1988.

Sheth, Falguni. *Toward a Political Philosophy of Race*. Albany: State University of New York Press, 2009.

Shuman, Amy, and Carol Bohmer. "Representing Trauma: Political Asylum Narrative." *Journal of American Folklore* 117 (2004): 394–414.

Shwab, Raymond. *The Oriental Renaissance: Europe's Rediscovery of India and the East, 1680–1880*. Translated by Gene Patterson-Black and Victor Reinking. New York: Columbia University Press, 1984.

Singh, Kushwant, and Satindra Singh. *Ghadar 1915: India's First Armed Revolution.* New Delhi: R & K, 1966.

Singh, Pardaman. *Ethnological Epitome of the Hindustanees of the Pacific Coast.* Stockton, CA: The Pacific Coast Khalsa Diwan Society, 1936.

Slate, Nico. *Colored Cosmopolitanism: The Shared Struggle for Freedom in the United States and India.* Cambridge: Harvard University Press, 2012.

Sloane, Thomas, ed. *Encyclopedia of Rhetoric.* New York: Oxford University Press, 2001.

Smith, Darrell. *The Bureau of Naturalization: Its History, Activities, and Organization.* Baltimore: Johns Hopkins Press, 1926.

Smith, Rogers. *Civic Ideals: Conflicting Visions of Citizenship in U.S. History.* New Haven: Yale University Press, 1997.

———. "Review of White by Law: The Legal Construction of Race, by Ian F. Haney López." *The American Journal of Legal History* 42 (1998): 65–68.

Smith, William. "The Rhetoric of the Declaration of Independence." *College English* 26 (1965): 306–309.

Snow, Jennifer. "The Civilization of White Men: The Race of the Hindu in *United States v. Bhagat Singh Thind.*" In *Race, Nation, and Religion in the Americas*, edited by Henry Goldschmidt and Elizabeth McAlister, 259–80. New York: Oxford University Press, 2004.

Song, Min. "Pahkar Singh's Argument with Asian America: Color and the Structure of Race Formation." In *A Part, Yet Apart: South Asians in Asian America*, edited by Lavina Dhingra Shankar and Rajini Srikanath, 79–102. Philadelphia: Temple University Press, 1998.

Steinberg, Peter. *The Great "Red Menace": United States Prosecution of American Communists, 1947–1952.* Westport, CT: Greenwood Press, 1984.

Strabo. *The Geography of Strabo.* Translated by H. C. Hamilton and W. Falconer. London: G. Bell, 1903.

Stoddard, Theodore Lothrop. *The Rising Tide of Color against White World Supremacy.* New York: Charles Scribner's Sons, 1921.

Stoler, Ann. "Colonial Archives and the Arts of Governance." *Archival Science* 2 (2002): 87–109.

Stratman, James. "Legal Rhetoric." In *Encyclopedia of Rhetoric and Composition: Communication from Ancient Times to the Information Age*, edited by Theresa Enos. New York: Routledge, 2010.

Streets, Heather. *Martial Races: The Military, Race and Masculinity in British Imperial Culture, 1857–1914*. Manchester, UK: Manchester University Press, 2004.

Suleri, Sara. *The Rhetoric of English India*. Chicago: University of Chicago Press, 1992.

Sumner, William. *Folkways: A Study of the Sociological Importance of Usages, Manners, Customs, Mores, and Morals*. New York: Ginn, 1906.

Takaki, Ronald. *Strangers from a Different Shore: A History of Asian Americans*. Revised ed. New York: Little, Brown, 1998.

Tchen, John. *New York Before Chinatown: Orientalism and the Shaping of American Culture, 1776–1882*. Baltimore: Johns Hopkins University Press, 1999.

Tehranian, John. *Whitewashed: America's Middle Eastern Minority*. New York: New York University Press, 2009.

Tekin, Beyza. *Representations and Othering in Discourse: The Construction of Turkey in the EU Context*. Amsterdam: John Benjamins, 2010.

Thapar, Romila. "Imagined Religious Communities? Ancient History and the Modern Search for a Hindu Identity." *Modern Asian Studies* 23, no. 2 (1989): 209–31.

Thompson, David. "Equitable Estoppel of the Government." *Columbia Law Review* 79 (1979): 551–71.

Tindale, Christopher. *Reason's Dark Champions: Constructive Strategies of Sophistic Argument*. Columbia: University of South Carolina Press, 2010.

Trautmann, Thomas. *Aryans and British India*. Berkeley: University of California Press, 1997.

Trenholme, Norman. *The Right of Sanctuary in England: A Study in Institutional History*. Columbia: University of Missouri, 1903.

Trelles, Oscar, and James Bailey, eds. *Immigration and Nationality Acts: Legislative Histories and Related Documents, 1950–1978*. Buffalo: W. S. Hein, 1977.

Unger, Roberto. "The Critical Legal Studies Movement." *Harvard Law Review* 96 (1983): 561–675.

U.S. Department of Justice, Immigration and Naturalization Service. "The Eligibility of Arabs to Naturalization." *Monthly Review* 1 (1943): 12–16.

———. "Proposed Repeal of the Chinese Exclusion Acts." *Monthly Review* 1 (1943): 13–19.

———. "Summaries of Recent Court Decisions." *Monthly Review* 1 (1943): 11–12.

U.S. Senate Committee on Immigration. *Hearings on S.J. Res. 128, Providing for the Ratification and Confirmation of Naturalization of Certain Persons of the Hindu Race.* 69th Cong., 2nd Sess. Washington, DC: GPO, 1926.

Valdes, Francisco, Jerome Culp, and Angela Harris. "Battles Waged, Won, and Lost: Critical Race Theory at the Turn of the Millennium." Introduction to *Crossroads, Directions, and a New Critical Race Theory,* edited by Francisco Valdes, Jerome Culp, and Angela Harris, 1–6. Philadelphia, Temple University Press, 2002.

Vugt, Mark van, David de Cremer, and Dirk Janssen. "Gender Differences in Cooperation and Competition: The Male Warrior Hypothesis." *Psychological Science* 18 (2007): 19–23.

Walker, Jeffrey. *Rhetoric and Poetics in Antiquity.* Oxford: Oxford University Press, 2000.

Ward, W. Peter. *White Canada: Popular Attitudes and Public Policy toward Orientals in British Columbia.* Montreal: McGill-Queen's University Press, 1978.

Weil, Simone. "The *Iliad,* or the Poem of Force." *Chicago Review* 18 (1965): 5–30.

Weiner, Mark. *Americans without Law: The Racial Boundaries of Citizenship.* New York: New York University Press, 2006.

Wells, H. G. *The Outline of History: Being a Plain History of Life and Mankind.* 2 Vols. New York: Macmillan, 1920.

Weston, Rubin. *Racism in U.S. Imperialism: The Influence of Racial Assumptions on American Foreign Policy, 1893–1946.* Columbia: University of South Carolina Press, 1972.

Wetlaufer, Gerald. "Rhetoric and Its Denial in Legal Discourse." *Virginia Law Review* 76 (1990): 1545–97.

White, G. Edward. "The Evolution of Reasoned Elaboration: Jurisprudential Criticism and Social Change." *Virginia Law Review* 59 (1973): 279–302.

White, James Boyd. *Heracles' Bow: Essays on the Rhetoric and Poetics of the Law.* Madison: University of Wisconsin Press, 1985.

———. "'Our Meanings Can Never Be the Same': Reflections on Language and Law." *Rhetoric Society Quarterly* 21, no. 3 (1991): 68–77.

Whitman, Walt. *Leaves of Grass*. Edited by Harold Blodgett and Sculley Bradley. New York: New York University Press, 1965.

Whitney, Abwell. *Almond-Eyed: A Story of the Day.* San Francisco: A. L. Bancroft, 1878.

Wiethoff, William. "Critical Perspectives on Perelman's Philosophy of Legal Argument." *Journal of the American Forensic Association* 22 (1985): 88–95.

Wigmore, John. "American Naturalization and the Japanese." *American Law Review* 28 (1894): 818–27.

Willard, Myra. *History of the White Australia Policy to 1920*. London: Cass, 1967.

Williams, Robert. *The American Indian in Western Legal Thought: The Discourses of Conquest*. New York: Oxford University Press, 1990.

Williams, S. Wells. *The Middle Kingdom: A Survey of the Geography, Government, Literature, Social Life, Arts, and History of the Chinese Empire and Its Inhabitants*. Rev. ed. Vol. 1. London: W. H. Allen, 1883.

Winant, Howard. *Racial Conditions: Politics, Theory, Comparisons*. Minneapolis: University of Minnesota Press, 1994.

Wolfley, Jeanette. "Jim Crow, Indian Style: The Disenfranchisement of Native Americans." *American Indian Law Review* 16 (1991): 167–202.

Woltor, Robert. *Truthful History of the Taking of Oregon and California in the Year A.D. 1899*. San Francisco: A. L. Bancroft, 1882.

Wong, Edlie. *Racial Reconstruction: Black Inclusion, Chinese Exclusion, and the Fictions of Citizenship*. New York: New York University Press, 2015.

Wood, Neal. "Sallust's Theorem: A Comment on 'Fear' in Western Political Thought." *History of Political Thought* 16, no. 2 (1995): 174–89.

Wu, William. *The Yellow Peril: Chinese Americans in American Fiction, 1850–1940*. Hamden, CT: Archon, 1982.

Yemelianova, Galina. "Volga Tatars, Russians, and the Russian State at the Turn of the Nineteenth Century: Relationships and Perceptions." *The Slavonic and East European Review* 77 (1999): 448–84.

Yuki, Masaki, and Kunihiro Yokota. "The Primal Warrior: Outgroup Threat Priming Enhances Intergroup Discrimination in Men But Not Women." *Journal of Experimental Social Psychology* 45 (2009): 271–74.

Zarefsky, David. "Reflections on Making the Case." In *Making the Case: Advocacy and Judgment in Public Argument*, edited by Kathryn Olson, Michael Pfau, Benjamin Ponder, and Kirt Wilson. East Lansing: Michigan State University Press, 2012.

JUDICIAL OPINIONS

In re Alverto, 198 F. 688 (E.D. Pa. 1912).

In re Balsara, 171 F. 294 (C.C.S.D.N.Y. 1909).

Bessho v. United States, 178 F. 245 (4th Cir. 1910).

Bonham v. Bouiss, 161 F.2d 678 (9th Cir. 1947).

Brown v. Board of Education, 347 U.S. 483 (1954).

In re Burton, 1 Ala. 111 (1900).

In re Camille, 6 F. 256 (C.C.D. Or. 1880).

Caminetti v. United States, 242 U.S. 470 (1917).

Chae Chan Ping v. United States, 130 U.S. 581 (1889).

In re Chang, 24 P. 156 (Cal. 1890).

In re Charr, 273 Fed. 207 (W.D. Mo. 1921).

In re Cruz, 23 F. Supp. 774 (E.D.N.Y. 1938).

Dennis v. United States, 341 U.S. 494 (1951).

In re Din, 27 F.2d 568 (N.D. Calif. 1928).

Ex parte Dow, 211 F. 486 (E.D.S.C. 1914).

In re Dow, 213 F. 355 (E.D.S.C. 1914).

Dow v. United States, 226 F. 145 (4th Cir. 1915).

Elk v. Wilkins, 112 U.S. 94 (1884).

In re Ellis, 179 F. 1002 (D. Or. 1910).

In re Fisher, 21 F.2d 1007 (N.D. Calif. 1927).

Gokhale v. United States, 278 U.S. 662 (1928).

In re Halladjian, 174 F. 834 (C.C.D. Mass. 1909).

In re Hassan, 48 F. Supp. 843 (E.D. Mich. 1942).

Hauge v. United States, 276 F. 111 (9th Cir. 1921).

Hirabayashi v. United States, 320 U.S. 81 (1943).

Kane v. McCarthy, 63 N.C. 299 (N.C. 1869).

In re Knight, 171 F. 299 (E.D.N.Y. 1909).

In re Kumagai, 163 Fed. 922 (W.D. Wash. 1908).

Luria v. United States, 231 U.S. 9 (1913).

In re MacFarlane, 11 Haw. 166 (Haw. 1897).

Mendez v. Westminster School District, 64 F. Supp. 544 (C.D. Cal. 1946).

In re Minook, 2 Ala. 200 (1904).

Ex parte Mohriez, 54 F. Supp. 941 (D. Mass. 1944).

In re Mozumdar, 207 F. 115 (E.D. Wash. 1913).

Mozumdar v. United States, 299 F. 240 (9th Cir. 1924).

In re Mudarri, 176 F. 465 (C.C.D. Mass. 1910).

In re Najour, 174 F. 735 (C.C.N.D. Ga. 1909).

In re Nian, 21 P. 993 (Utah 1889).

Ozawa v. United States, 260 U.S. 178 (1922).

People v. Hall, 4 Cal. 399 (Cal. 1854).

Plessy v. Ferguson, 163 U.S. 537 (1896).

In re Po, 7 Misc. 471 (City Ct. N.Y. 1894).

In re Rallos, 241 F. 686 (E.D.N.Y. 1917).

In re Rodriguez, 81 F. 337 (W.D. Tex. 1897).

In re Saito, 62 F. 126 (C.C.D. Mass. 1894).

In re Sallak, No. 14876 (N.D. Ill. June 27, 1924).

Samras v. United States, 125 F.2d 879 (9th Cir. 1942).

Sato v. Hall, 217 P. 520 (Cal. 1923).

Scott v. Sandford, 60 U.S. 393 (1856).

Ex parte Shahid, 205 F. 812 (E.D.S.C. 1913).

In re Shaikhaly, No. 119332 (S.D. Cal. Dec. 20, 1944).

In re Singh, 246 F. 496 (E.D. Pa. 1917).

In re Singh, 257 F. 209 (S.D. Cal. 1919).

In re Thind, 268 F. 683 (D. Or. 1920).

United States v. Ali, 7 F.2d 728 (E.D. Mich. 1925).

United States v. Ali, 20 F.2d 998 (E.D. Mich. 1927).

United States v. Balsara, 180 F. 694 (2d Cir. 1910).

United States v. Cartozian, 6 F.2d 919 (D. Or. 1925).

United States v. Ching Tai Sai, 1 U.S. Dist. Ct. Haw. 118 (1901).

United States v. Dolla, 177 F. 101 (5th Cir. 1910).

United States v. Gokhale, 26 F.2d 360 (2d Cir. 1928).

United States v. Javier, 22 F.2d 879 (D.C. Cir. 1927).

United States v. Kamm, 247 F. 968 (E.D. Wash. 1918).

United States v. Khan, 1 F.2d 1006 (W.D. Penn. 1924).

United States v. Mozumdar, 296 F. 173 (S.D. Cal. 1923).

United States v. Pandit, No. G-111-T (S.D. Cal. Jan. 9, 1925).

United States v. Pandit, 15 F.2d 285 (9th Cir. 1926).

United States v. Pandit, 273 U.S. 759 (1927).

United States v. Thind, 261 U.S. 204 (1923).
United States v. Wong Kim Ark, 169 U.S. 649 (1897).
In re Yamashita, 10 P. 482 (Wash. 1902).
In re Young, 195 F. 645 (W.D. Wash. 1912).
In re Young, 198 F. 715 (W.D. Wash. 1912).
In re Yup, 1 F. Cas. 223 (C.C.D. Cal. 1878).

BOARD OF IMMIGRATION APPEALS OPINIONS

In re B—, 2 I. & N. Dec. 492 (B.I.A. 1947).
In re B—, 3 I. & N. Dec. 304 (B.I.A. 1948).
In re C—, 2 I. & N. Dec. 220 (B.I.A. 1944).
In re I—, 1 I. & N. Dec. 627 (B.I.A. 1943).
In re J— W— F—, 6 I. & N. Dec. 200 (B.I.A. 1954).
In re K—, 2 I & N. Dec. 253 (B.I.A. 1945).
In re K—, 2 I. & N. Dec. 411 (B.I.A. 1945).
In re M—, 2 I. & N. Dec. 196 (B.I.A. 1944).
In re N—, A-7483378 (56247/95) C.O. May 16, 1950.
In re P—, 2 I. & N. Dec. 84 (B.I.A. 1944).
In re R—, 4 I & N. Dec. 275 (B.I.A. 1951).
In re S—, 1 I & N Dec. 174 (B.I.A. 1941).
In re S—, 4 I & N. Dec. 104 (B.I.A. 1950).
In re T—, 2 I. & N. Dec. 614 (B.I.A. 1946).

ARCHIVES CONSULTED

National Archives Building, Washington, DC. Records of the Immigration
    and Naturalization Service of the United States. Record Group 85.
National Archives and Records Administration Pacific Alaska Region, Seattle,
    WA. Significant Civil and Criminal Case Files, 1899–1925. District
    of Oregon (Portland). Records of U.S. Attorneys and Marshals.
    Record Group 118.
———. Civil, Criminal and Admiralty Case Files, 1911–1922. Southern
    District of California, Central Division (Los Angeles). Records of
    the District Courts of the United States. Record Group 21.

National Archives and Records Administration Pacific Region, Laguna Niguel, CA. Contested Naturalizations. Southern District of California, Central Division (Los Angeles). Records of the District Courts of the United States. Record Group 21.

————. Equity Case Files. Southern District of California, Central Division (Los Angeles). Records of the District Courts of the United States. Record Group 21.

National Archives and Records Administration Pacific Region, San Bruno, CA. Records of the U.S. Courts of Appeals. Record Group 276.

Oriental and India Office Collections. British Library, London.

South Asians in North America Collection. University of California at Berkeley Library, Berkeley, CA.

INDEX

Adams, John Quincy, 64–65, 98
Afghans, xi, xvii, 22, 27, 92, 116,
    141, 144, 146, 169n8
African Americans, xvi, 6, 21–22,
    121, 186n96. *See also* "aliens of
    African nativity"; blacks; slavery
    "persons of African descent," ix,
    xi, 16–17, 46, 158, 168n7,
    186n96
Agamben, Giorgio, 160–61
Ainus, 35
Alaska, 8–9, 180n36
Algerians, 26, 29–31
"aliens of African nativity," ix, xi, 16,
    158
"all men are created equal," 119–20,
    126–27, 130, 137, 148–49,
    151–52, 229n21. *See also*
    Declaration of Independence:
    proclamation of equality
Alpine subdivision of the Caucasian
    race, 72, 100, 108, 112
American Indian veterans, xxiii, 8,
    156
American Indians
    Chinese and, 2–3, 6, 14–15
    genocide and, 15, 151
    naturalization, xxiii, 4, 6–8, 43,
        156
    as (not) "free white persons," 6,
        21–22
    as (not) "white," 2, 21–22
    sovereignty of, 7
    terminology for, 14
American Revolution, 150–51. *See
    also* Revolutionary War

annexation treaties, 4–6, 8–9, 158,
    180n36
Arabs, xi, xvii, xxiv, 25, 27, 74,
    189n122, 219n40. *See
    also* Asiatic Barred Zone;
    Palestinians; *specific cases*
Arendt, Hannah, xxviii, 86–87, 159
Armenian Genocide, 89, 96–97,
    102–3, 111
    literature on, 102–3
    perpetrators of, prosecuted in
        Turkish war crimes tribunals,
        215n7
    terminology for and characteriza-
        tions of, 89–90
Armenian Genocide denial, 89–90,
    102
Armenian Genocide survivors and
    refugee crisis, 90–92, 97, 104.
    See also Armenian statelessness;
    Cartozian; *Halladjian*; World
    War I: statelessness following
Armenian history, x, 114, 221n57,
    221n59, 223n86
Armenian martyrdom and shared suf-
    fering, 112–14
Armenian Massacres of 1894–1896,
    89, 95
Armenian statelessness, 97, 99, 104,
    113–14. *See also* Armenian
    Genocide survivors and refugee
    crisis
Armenians, x, xxiv, 216n13. *See also*
    Armenian Genocide; *Cartozian*;
    Halladjian; World War I: state-
    lessness following

269